2's complement pp 91-92

Programming & Interfacing the 6502, With Experiments

by
Marvin L. De Jong

D1707114

Howard W. Sams & Co., Inc.
4300 WEST 62ND ST. INDIANAPOLIS, INDIANA 46268 USA

FIRST EDITION
FIRST PRINTING—1980

James V. Santiawo, Ham Festival, March '93

International Standard Book Number: 0-672-21651-5
Library of Congress Catalog Card Number: 79-67130

Printed in the United States of America.

Preface

It is interesting that most of us have a completely different feeling toward learning something that involves a physical skill than the feeling we have when we approach an intellectual challenge. I have observed people trying to learn to water ski, for example, enduring failure after failure before finally coming up out of the water to experience the exhilaration of a successful first run. The entire process seems to provoke very little frustration or aggravation. On the other hand, the world is full of books that purport to make learning something easy, and most of us are easily frustrated and angered when we cannot understand something involving our intellects the very first time we try. Perhaps we are too vain, but I think the real problem is our unrealistic attitude toward learning.

All of this leads up to my hope that you will not give up easily if you want to learn to program the 6502. Be patient with yourself, and try to see if you can enjoy the process as much as the product. Although I have made a serious attempt to explain concepts so that newcomers to the field of 6502 assembly language programming can easily understand them, no one can subtract from the efforts (and enjoyment) required of the student. This is not a novel. It is a challenge to you, the reader, to see if you can acquire a new and exciting skill.

Moreover, I would like to emphasize the importance of obtaining "hands-on" experience. Current theories of learning emphasize the importance of concrete experiences before the ability to think abstractly is acquired. This is the principal reason for including experiments in the book. The experiments, or demonstrations, as many might more properly be called, are intended to give you the practice and concrete experiences required for the challenge of writing your own microcomputer programs, a task that requires abstract thinking.

MARVIN L. DE JONG

This book is dedicated to technology that is compatible with nature.

Acknowledgments

I give my editor in the Blacksburg group special thanks for making many excellent suggestions that led to a much improved manuscript. I am very appreciative of the interest and aid I received from both Rockwell International and Synertek. Their marketing and engineering staffs were always prompt and friendly when I had questions or needed documentation.

I thank my wife, Donna, for typing the manuscript, and my son, Jeff, and my daughters, Jane and Mary, for their interest in the project.

Finally, I would like to thank my dog and my cat. Their complete and obvious lack of concern gave me a perspective I needed for writing this book.

Contents

CHAPTER 9

CHAPTER 10

CHAPTER 11

CHAPTER 12

CHAPTER 13

PART I

Programming the 6502

CHAPTER 1

Introduction to
Microcomputers

OBJECTIVES

At the completion of this chapter you should be able to:

- Identify the major components of a microcomputer and describe their function. These include the microprocessor, R/W memory, ROM, peripheral interface adapters, keyboard, display, and monitor.
- Understand the READ and WRITE operations.
- Describe the function of registers in the microprocessor, in particular the accumulator.
- Define addressing and decoding.
- Understand the concept of memory space, memory blocks, and pages.
- Examine and modify the contents of a memory location using the keyboard and display.

INTRODUCTION

The power and versatility of microcomputers become evident when one makes a list of some of the applications in which they are currently being used.

- Traffic Controllers • Music Synthesizers • Solar Panel Orientation Controllers • Cash Registers • Chess Challengers • Scientific Instruments • Automobile Ignition Systems • Video Games • Industrial Controllers • Biomedical Instruments • Computer Assisted Instruction Devices • Speech Recognizers • Office Machines • On-Line Data Processors • Word Processing Systems • Video Tape Recorders • Process Controllers • RTTY and Morse Code to ASCII Converters • Surveying Instruments • Indoor Environmental Controllers • Home Security Systems

The preceding list is just a beginning. It appears that there will be an almost endless variety of applications. Programming and interfacing a microcomputer are creative, challenging, and rewarding endeavors. This book is intended to make you a part of these exciting developments by combining your study of the subject with active "hands-on" experience.

The specific microprocessor chosen for study in this book is the 6502. It was first manufactured by MOS Technology, Inc., Valley Forge Corporate Center, 950 Rittenhouse Road, Norristown, PA 19401. MOS Technology is now owned by Commodore Business Machines, Inc., 3330 Scott Boulevard, Santa Clara, CA 95050. The 6502 microprocessor is also manufactured by Rockwell International, Microelectronic Devices Division, P.O. Box 3669, Anaheim, CA 92803, and it is manufactured by Synertek® Systems Corporation, 150 South Wolfe Road, Sunnyvale, CA 94086. The 6502 is currently the most widely manufactured microprocessor,[1] and several other companies will soon be added to the list of those that manufacture the 6502.

Although the contents of this book are applicable to any 6502-based microcomputer system, particular emphasis is placed on three of the most popular microcomputer systems. These are the KIM-1 manufactured by MOS Technology for Commodore Business Machines, the SYM-1 manufactured by Synertek Systems Corporation, and the AIM 65 manufactured by Rockwell International. Photographs of these systems are shown in Figs. 1-1, 1-2, and 1-3. These three systems were chosen because of their popularity and the fact that their edge connectors are compatible. Thus, the experiments we describe may be performed on any of these three systems.

Other small computers that use the 6502 microprocessor and that you may wish to use as a laboratory tool in connection with this book include the PET, Apple II, JOLT, Puzzle, OSI Challenger, and others. Some firms that handle mail orders and that specialize in 6502 products are:

The Computerist, Inc.
P.O. Box 3
South Chelmsford, MA 01824

Micro Technology Unlimited
Box 4596
Manchester, NH 03108

[1]Libes, Sol, "BYTE News," *BYTE*, *4*, February 1979, p. 64.

Fig. 1-1. AIM 65 Microcomputer.

Johnson Computer
P.O. Box 523
Medina, OH 44256

RNB Enterprises, Inc.
2967 West Fairmount Avenue
Phoenix, AZ 85017

Seawell Marketing, Inc.
P.O. Box 17006
Seattle, WA 98107

WHAT IS A MICROCOMPUTER?

We will define a microcomputer as any computer system that uses one of the popular microprocessors as its principal processing unit. Popular microprocessors include the 6502, 8080A, 8085, 6800, Z80, and the 1802. These microprocessors are typically 40-pin integrated-circuit chips mounted in a dual-in-line package (DIP).

The terms microprocessor and microcomputer are frequently used interchangeably. We will take *microprocessor* to mean one of

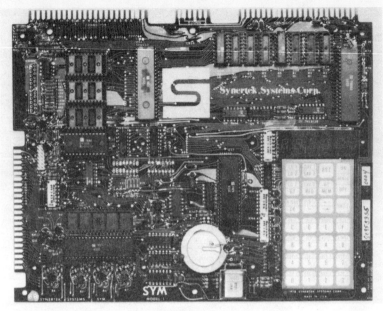

Fig. 1-2. SYM-1 Microcomputer

the integrated circuits mentioned above, while a *microcomputer* is a system of components including as a minimum:

- A microprocessor such as the 6502.
- A clock circuit (1-MHz crystal in the case of the KIM-1)
- Semiconductor Read/Write (R/W) memory, sometimes called RAM which is an acronym for Random Access Memory
- Decoding circuitry
- Input/Output ports based on the 6520, 6522, 6530, 6532, or other interface integrated circuits.

The components of a microcomputer system are connected by three sets of wires or printed-circuit conductors called *buses*. These are:

- The control bus—variable number of lines
- The bidirectional data bus—eight lines designated D7-D0
- The address bus—16 lines designated A15-A0.

Each of the conductors in a bus is called a *line*. Fig. 1-4 is a block diagram of the KIM-1 system that illustrates some of the components and connections mentioned previously. In addition to these components, the diagram shows that the KIM-1 also has a keypad and a display. Most prototyping systems (microcomputers designed to

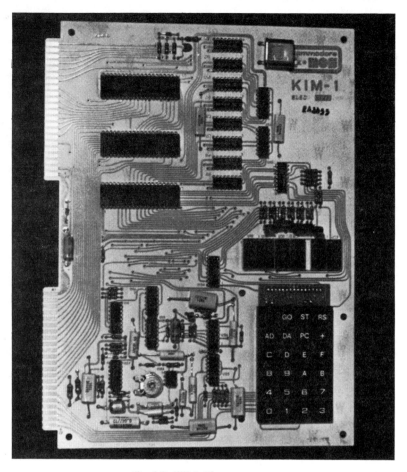

Fig. 1-3. KIM-1 Microcomputer.

test and develop new programs and designs) such as the AIM 65, SYM-1, and KIM-1 have keyboards and displays for interfacing with human beings.

Other features that may be included in a microcomputer include cassette tape interface, ASCII keyboard interface, teletypewriter interface, CRT or oscilloscope output, line printer, floppy-disc memory, multichannel A/D and D/A converters, arithmetic logic units, high-level language (BASIC, FORTRAN, PASCAL, etc.) interpreters in ROM, speech-input circuits, etc. It is ironic that sometimes the microprocessor is one of the cheapest ($10.00-$15.00) components in the system. The fact that $15.00 integrated circuits are surrounded by several thousand dollars worth of peripheral

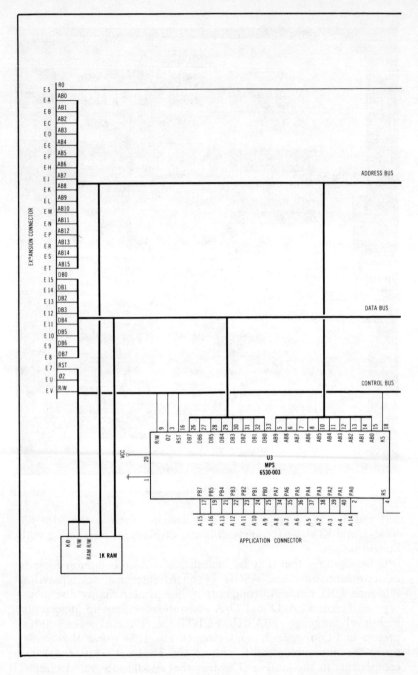

Fig. 1-4. Block diagram

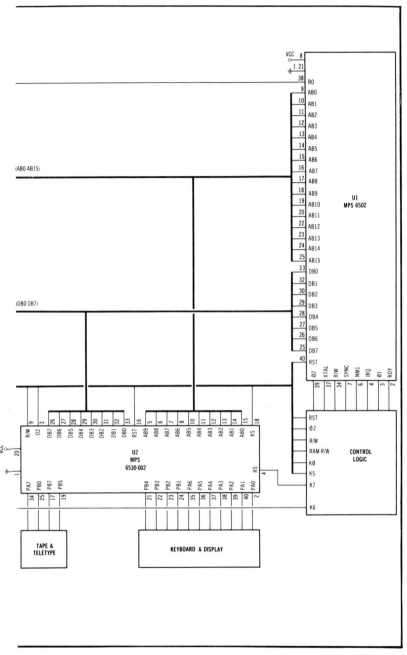

Courtesy Commodore Business Machines, Inc.

of KIM-1 Microcomputer.

equipment is a tribute to the power and versatility of the microprocessor.

Some of the components in the microcomputer will be discussed at this point because an understanding of their basic functions is essential for learning how to program a microcomputer.

THE 6502 MICROPROCESSOR

Sixteen pins on the 6502 are dedicated to *addressing;* that is, they control the two possible logic levels on each of the 16 lines that form the address bus. Refer to Fig. 1-4 to identify pin numbers. The logic levels are called "zero" and "one" although electrically they are voltage levels. The address pins on the 6502, AB15, AB14, AB13, . . . , AB0 in Fig. 1-4, determine a 16-bit binary number called the *address* of a memory location (defined in the next section). The address *names* and *orders* memory locations.

Since there are 2^{16} unique 16-bit binary numbers, the 6502 is capable of addressing 65,536 memory locations. The 16-bit address is frequently divided into two bytes, a high-order byte or address high (ADH), and a low-order byte or address low (ADL). In turn, each of these bytes may be represented by two hexadecimal digits, 0-9 and A-F. The entire address is represented by four hexadecimal digits. In this book, all hexadecimal numbers will have a "$" prefix. Thus, $A9F4 is an example of an address. Readers who are unfamiliar with binary and hexadecimal numbers are urged to study Appendix A first.

Eight pins on the 6502 are connected to the data bus of the microcomputer. Refer again to Fig. 1-4 for details. The READ/WRITE or R/W pin on the 6502 is connected to a line of the control bus called the R/W line. Introducing these pins allows us to define two important operations of the microprocessor.

A *READ* operation (the R/W line is at logic one) causes eight bits of information (usually called data) to be transferred over the data bus, from the memory location specified by the address on the address bus to an 8-bit register in the microprocessor.

A *WRITE* operation (the R/W line is at logic zero) causes eight bits of information to be transferred from an 8-bit register in the microprocessor to a memory location specified by the address on the address bus. The words "load" and "store" are sometimes used synonymously with the words "read" and "write," respectively.

Because data are moved in one direction by a read or load operation and in the other direction by a write or store operation, the data bus is said to be *bidirectional.* Furthermore, since data are transferred as 8-bit binary numbers, that is, one byte at a time, the 6502 is called an 8-bit microprocessor.

A *register* is an 8-bit storage location in the microprocessor. It is used to store data upon which the microprocessor is to operate. The contents of a register may also control the operation of the microprocessor itself. The most commonly used register as far as the programmer is concerned is the *accumulator*. Other registers in the 6502 include the *index registers, X* and *Y;* the *processor status register, P;* the *stack pointer, SP;* and a pair of registers called the *program counter high, PCH,* and the *program counter low, PCL.* The X and Y registers are used like the accumulator, but in addition they may serve another purpose to be discussed in Chapter 8. The program counter will be described in Chapter 2, the status register in Chapter 6, and the stack pointer in Chapter 9.

Memory

There are four kinds of memory locations:

- RAM—RAM is an acronym for Random Access Memory. It is more precise to call it Read/Write or R/W memory.
- ROM—ROM is an acronym for Read Only Memory.
- Input/Output Ports—These include the so-called *data direction registers* (DDR) that determine whether a port will be used to input data or output data. See Chapter 3.
- Interval Timers—One or more bytes of data stored at these locations determine the length of a time interval. See Chapter 10.

An R/W memory location consists of eight ordered bistable semiconductor devices, each capable of storing one bit of a binary number. Many such devices are located on a single integrated-circuit chip. For example, the R/W memory chips on the KIM-1 have 1024_{10} such devices on each chip. The 2114 R/W memory integrated circuits on the AIM 65 and SYM-1 have 4096_{10} such devices. Each memory location stores one byte of data. The data bits are ordered D7, D6, D5, . . . , D0, from the most-significant bit to the least-significant bit. One state of the bistable memory device corresponds to the bit being zero, while the other state corresponds to a bit being one. The byte of data stored at any location may be displayed in hexadecimal using the microcomputer output.

The microcomputer can read the data at an R/W location and it can write data to an R/W location. Data in an R/W location is lost when power to the microcomputer is removed. In contrast, data at an ROM location is permanent, but the microprocessor can only read the contents of an ROM location: it cannot write to that location. The purpose of having ROM locations is to store frequently used programs and data that the user does not want to be altered, either because of power failure or for other reasons.

In 6502-based systems the Input/Output ports are separate integrated circuits usually called interface adapters. Examples include the 6530 and the 6532. These chips not only contain the I/O ports and corresponding DDR, but may have additional R/W or ROM locations as well as interval timers. Chapters 3 and 10 will cover these topics in more detail.

Addressing and Decoding

The *address* of a memory location is a 16-bit number which names and orders the location in memory space. Each R/W location, ROM location, I/O port, DDR, and interval timer has a 16-bit address. The *address space* of a microprocessor is the total of all memory locations which the microprocessor is capable of addressing. As pointed out above, the 6502 has 65,536 possible locations in its address space.

The microcomputer keyboard can be used to enter an address in hexadecimal. The address is then displayed by the microcomputer display output. Usually the byte of data stored at that location appears in the two hexadecimal display digits on the right of the address display.

The microprocessor performs all of the addressing operations in small systems. (Larger systems may use DMA, an acronym for Direct Memory Access, where peripheral devices control the address bus.) The process of activating a particular memory location when the microprocessor places its address on the address bus is called *decoding*. Frequently, much of the decoding is accomplished on the memory chips. The R/W memory chips on the KIM-1, AIM 65, and SYM-1 decode the lowest 10 address lines, A9-A0. Lines A15-A10 are decoded by other integrated circuits. Lines A15-A12 are not decoded at all on the KIM-1. Address decoding will be considered in more detail in Chapter 11.

Address Space

It is convenient to divide the address space into *blocks*. The smallest block size is called a *page* and consists of 256_{10} memory locations. Table 1-1 shows how the address space is divided into pages. It is seen from the diagram that the high-order address byte (ADH) is the page number, while the ADL byte gives the memory location within a page.

The next larger block size after a page is a unit of 1024_{10} locations which is usually referred to as *1K of memory*. Recall that $2^{10} = 1024_{10}$. This means that 10 address bits uniquely specify each location in a 1K block. This leaves six address bits, A15-A10, to "name" a 1K block. Six address bits can name 2^6 or 64_{10} blocks; thus there are 64 1K blocks of memory in the address space, and bits A15-A10 determine the number of the block. (It might be added that memory

Table 1-1. Dividing Address Space Into Pages

Address High ADH	Address Low ADL	Address
(Binary)		(Hexadecimal)
00000000	00000000	$0000
00000000	00000001	$0001
•	•	•
•	•	• PAGE ZERO
•	•	•
•	•	•
00000000	11111111	$00FF
00000001	00000000	$0100
00000001	00000001	$0101
•	•	•
•	•	• PAGE ONE
•	•	•
•	•	•
00000001	11111111	$01FF
•	•	•
•	•	•
•	•	•
•	•	•
•	•	•
11111111	00000000	$FF00
11111111	00000001	$FF01
•	•	•
•	•	• PAGE 255$_{10}$
•	•	•
•	•	•
11111111	11111111	$FFFF

is usually sold in K units. For example, 4K, 8K, 16K and sometimes 32K bytes of memory are on a single printed-circuit board.)

The largest block size that will be discussed in this context is the 8K block consisting of 8×1024 locations. Each 8K block has 8192_{10} locations. Since $8192 = 2^{13}$, the remaining address bits A15-A13 are used to "name" each 8K block. Table 1-2 shows how the address

Table 1-2. Dividing Address Space Into 8K Blocks

A15	A14	A13	Block Name	Hexadecimal Addresses
0	0	0	8K0	$0000-$1FFF
0	0	1	8K1	$2000-$3FFF
0	1	0	8K2	$4000-$5FFF
0	1	1	8K3	$6000-$7FFF
1	0	0	8K4	$8000-$9FFF
1	0	1	8K5	$A000-$BFFF
1	1	0	8K6	$C000-$DFFF
1	1	1	8K7	$E000-$FFFF

space is divided into 8K blocks. The 8K blocks are named and ordered by a block name, such as 8K0 for the lowest 8K block and 8K7 for the highest 8K block.

The KIM-1 microcomputer uses only the 8K0 block of address space, and not all of the 8K0 block is filled. An off-the-shelf KIM-1, AIM 65, or SYM-1 comes with 1K R/W memory located in the lowest four pages of the address space; that is, hex addresses $0000 to $03FF. The KIM-1 has eight pages of ROM which contain its monitor program. A memory map of this system is given in Fig. 1-5. Memory maps of the AIM 65 and SYM-1 are given in Figs. 1-6

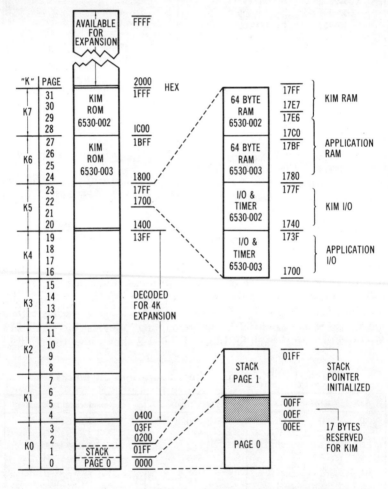

Courtesy Commodore Business Machines, Inc.

Fig. 1-5. KIM-1 memory map.

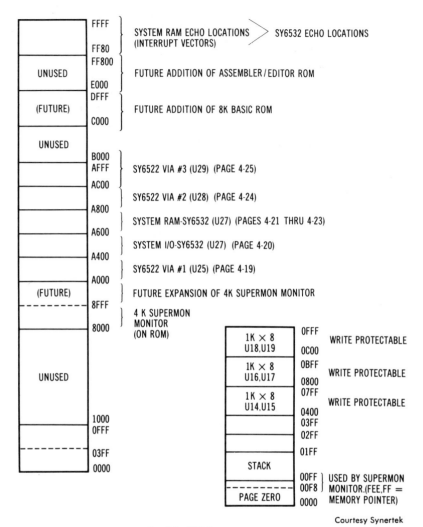

Fig. 1-6. SYM-1 memory map.

Courtesy Synertek

and 1-7. You can see that these two systems have more ROM space for their more elaborate monitor programs.

Monitor

The monitor is a program stored in ROM. The computer begins to execute this program when power is supplied and/or when a *reset* button on the microcomputer is pressed. The monitors of the KIM-1, SYM-1, and AIM 65 differ widely in their capabilities, but they have in common the following features:

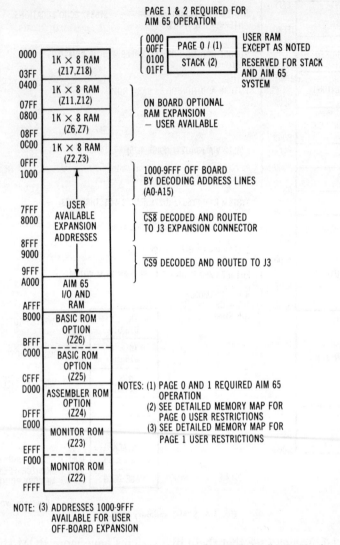

NOTE: (3) ADDRESSES 1000-9FFF
AVAILABLE FOR USER
OFF-BOARD EXPANSION

Courtesy Rockwell International

Fig. 1-7. AIM 65 memory map.

- They allow the user to address any location with the keyboard, and to display the address and the contents of that location.
- They allow the user to modify the contents of any R/W memory location with data that is input from the keyboard.
- They allow the user to transfer control of the microprocessor from the monitor to the user's program.

- They allow the user to interface the microcomputer with a cassette tape recorder for the purpose of storing programs.

You may wish to compare and contrast the remaining features of the monitors using the manufacturers' literature before deciding on a purchase. For the purposes of this book, it is the preceding features that are important.

INTRODUCTION TO THE EXPERIMENTS

The experiments in this chapter are designed to acquaint you with some of the concepts that were introduced. You will also become familiar with your microcomputer. Before starting the experiments consult your user's guide to make the necessary power connections. Also read the sections in that manual that describe how to display and modify the contents of any memory location. The three microcomputer systems require different keystrokes to accomplish this operation, and there is not sufficient space here to warrant including the instructions for each of the different microcomputers.

EXPERIMENT NO. 1

Step 1

Apply power to your microcomputer and press the RESET button. The display should light. If it does not, check your connections with the instructions in your user's manual.

Step 2

Examine the contents of the location whose address is $0000. You will have to press the "0" key at least four times, once for each of the hexadecimal digits that represent the address of this location. What data are found in this location?

Step 3

Enter the hexadecimal number $55 in location with address $0000.

Step 4

Now examine and modify the contents of $03FF; that is, load $33 into the location whose address is $03FF.

Step 5

Return and examine the contents of $0000. What do you find there?

(You should find that the number $55 is still there.)

Step 6

Remove the power supply connections to your microcomputer or turn the power off. Turn it back on again, then examine the contents of locations $0000 and $03FF. What do you find?

(You will not find $55 in $0000 or $33 in $03FF because removing power to an R/W memory location destroys the contents of that location.)

EXPERIMENT NO. 2

Step 1

Using the memory map for your microcomputer (see Figs. 1-5, 1-6, and 1-7), identify an ROM location.

($1800 is an ROM location in the KIM-1, $8030 is an ROM location in the SYM-1, and $F947 is an ROM location in the AIM 65.)

Step 2

Examine the locations given above for your microcomputer. What byte of data do you find there?

(You should find a $A9 in the location mentioned.)

Step 3

Remove power, then examine the ROM location again. What do you observe?

(You should observe that the data are unchanged by a loss of power.)

Step 4

Using the same ROM location, attempt to modify the data at that address by writing a $FF to it. What do you observe?

(You should not be able to modify the contents of any ROM location.)

EXPERIMENT NO. 3

Step 1

Examine the contents of location $13FF. What is the byte of data found at this location?

Step 2

Modify the contents of $13FF; that is, load some hexadecimal number such as $99 into this location. What do you observe?

(You should observe that you are unable to load any data into this location because it contains no memory device. Off-the-shelf KIM-1s, AIM 65s, and SYM-1s have no memory devices at this location.)

CHAPTER 2

Writing and Executing Simple Programs Using Data Transfer Instructions

OBJECTIVES

At the completion of this chapter you should be able to:

- Understand the terms: instruction, op code, mnemonic, program, assemble, load, execute, program counter, labels, and symbols.
- Use the following addressing modes: immediate, absolute, zero page, and implied.
- Use these instructions: LDA, STA, LDX, STX, LDY, STY, TAX, TAY, TXA, TYA, and BRK. See Table 2-1 for a summary.
- Write, assemble, load, and execute short programs using the data transfer instructions and the BRK instruction.
- Use the single-step mode for executing a program.

INTRODUCTION

You are urged to learn as many of the 6502 instructions as possible. Although you will find that you can begin to write programs with only a few instructions, fast and efficient programs for complex tasks require a thorough understanding of the entire 6502 instruction set and the various addressing modes. Some instructions and ad-

Table 2-1. Summary of Instructions and Op Codes Introduced in Chapter 2

Instruction	Description	Addressing Mode			
		Immediate	Absolute	Zero-Page	Implied
LDA	Load Accumulator with Memory	A9	AD	A5	
STA	Store Accumulator in Memory		8D	85	
LDX	Load X Register with Memory	A2	AE	A6	
STX	Store X Register in Memory		8E	86	
LDY	Load Y Register with Memory	A0	AC	A4	
STY	Store Y Register in Memory		8C	84	
TAX	Transfer Accumulator to X Register				AA
TXA	Transfer X Register to Accumulator				8A
TYA	Transfer Y Register to Accumulator				98
TAY	Transfer Accumulator to Y Register				A8
BRK	Force Interrupt				00

dressing modes are more efficient than others. More efficient programs generally run faster and take fewer memory locations for storage of the program. It is the program that controls all of the activity of a microcomputer.

Before describing instructions in detail, it might be worthwhile to give the reader an overview of the 6502 instruction capabilities. In other words, what can the 6502 do? A listing of the 6502 instructions by categories, with simple descriptions of each one, is given in Table 2-2. A cursory examination of this table indicates that the 6502 can transfer information from a memory location to an internal register and vice versa; it can do simple arithmetic operations; it can perform a variety of logical operations; it can test for certain conditions and branch to another part of the program depending on the outcome of the test (the branch and test instructions); the 6502 can shift the contents of memory locations and registers; and it can perform a variety of other operations, including doing nothing (the NOP instruction). The reader is not expected to fully comprehend the instruction set at this time. The purpose of this book is to provide an in-depth understanding of the instructions as we progress through the various chapters that explain and illustrate the instructions with a variety of programs.

MICROCOMPUTER INSTRUCTIONS

The basic elements of microcomputer programs are the instructions. A microcomputer *instruction* is a set of one, two, or three

Table 2-2. 6502 Instructions by Categories

Data Transfer Instructions

LDA	Load Accumulator with Memory	**STA**	Store Accumulator in Memory
LDX	Load X Register with Memory	**STX**	Store X Register in Memory
LDY	Load Y Register with Memory	**STY**	Store Y Register in Memory
TAX	Transfer Accumulator to X Register	**TXA**	Transfer X Register to Accumulator
TAY	Transfer Accumulator to Y Register	**TYA**	Transfer Y Register to Accumulator

Arithmetic Operation Instructions

ADC	Add Memory to Accumulator with Carry	**SBC**	Subtract Memory from Accumulator with Borrow

Logical Operation Instructions

AND	AND Memory with Accumulator	**ORA**	OR Memory with Accumulator
EOR	EXCLUSIVE-OR Memory with Accumulator		

Shift and Modify Instructions

DEC	Decrement Memory by One	**INC**	Increment Memory by One
DEX	Decrement X Register by One	**INX**	Increment X Register by One
DEY	Decrement Y Register by One	**INY**	Increment Y Register by One
ASL	Shift Left One Bit	**LSR**	Shift Right One Bit
ROL	Rotate Left One Bit	**ROR**	Rotate Right One Bit

Test Instructions

CMP	Compare Memory and Accumulator	**CPX**	Compare Memory and X Register
		CPY	Compare Memory and Y Register
BIT	Test Bits in Memory with Accumulator		

Branch Instructions

BCC	Branch on Carry Clear	**BCS**	Branch on Carry Set
BEQ	Branch on Result Zero	**BNE**	Branch on Result Not Zero
BMI	Branch on Result Minus	**BPL**	Branch on Result Plus
BVC	Branch on Overflow Clear	**BVS**	Branch on Overflow Set

Modify Processor Status Register Instructions

CLC	Clear Carry Flag	**SEC**	Set Carry Flag
CLD	Clear Decimal Mode	**SED**	Set Decimal Mode
CLI	Clear Interrupt Flag	**SEI**	Set Interrupt Flag
CLV	Clear Overflow Flag		

Jump Instructions

JMP	Jump to New Location	**RTS**	Return from Subroutine
JSR	Jump to Subroutine	**RTI**	Return from Interrupt Routine
BRK	Jump to Interrupt Routine		

Stack Operation Instructions

PHA	Push Accumulator on Stack	**PLA**	Pull Accumulator from Stack
PHP	Push P Register on Stack	**PLP**	Pull P Register from Stack
TXS	Transfer X Register to Stack Pointer	**TSX**	Transfer Stack Pointer to X Register

Do Nothing Instruction

NOP	No Operation

bytes which, when read into the microprocessor in the correct sequence, causes it to carry out a specific operation. Three simple examples are:

- *Load* a byte of data from the memory location with the address ADH-ADL into the accumulator.
- *Store* the contents of the accumulator in a memory location whose address is ADH-ADL.
- *Add* the byte of data stored at the memory location whose address is ADH-ADL to the byte of data in the accumulator.

The *first* byte of an instruction determines the specific operation to be carried out by the computer. In the three previous examples, the *second* byte specifies the low-order byte of the address (ADL) and the *third* byte specifies the high-order byte of the address (ADH) of the location where the microprocessor is to find the data.

The particular instructions to which the 6502 responds are called its *instruction set*. The 6502 instruction set is summarized in Table 2-3. This particular form of the instruction set is used extensively. The 6502 is capable of carrying out 56 different operations, some of which may be done in as many as eight different ways called *addressing modes*.

Since the first byte of an instruction determines the nature of the operation as well as the addressing mode, it is these 8-bit numbers that the user must know in order to program the microprocessor. Because 8-bit numbers are difficult to remember and recognize, one seldom sees the binary representation of instructions. Instead, they are most often represented in a hexadecimal format. The hexadecimal equivalent of the first byte of an instruction will be called the *operation code* or *op code*. Furthermore, as an aid in programming, each instruction is given a *mnemonic* which is an abbreviated name suggestive of the operation to be performed. Two other descriptions of instructions are commonly used. One is the *logical expression* and the other is an *English language description*. The four ways of describing an instruction are illustrated in Example 1 for three different instructions.

Example 1: Illustration of Four Ways of Describing an Instruction

Mnemonic	Logical Expression	Op Code	Description
LDA	$M \rightarrow A$	AD	*Load* the accumulator, A, with a byte from memory, M.
STA	$A \rightarrow M$	8D	*Store* the contents of the accumulator, A, in memory, M.
ADC	$A + M + C \rightarrow A$	6D	*Add* the byte in memory to the contents of the accumulator. Add the carry; result into A.

Table 2-3. 6502 Instruction Set Summary

MNEMONIC	OPERATION	IMMEDIATE OP N #	ABSOLUTE OP N #	ZERO PAGE OP N #	ACCUM. OP N #	IMPLIED OP N #	(IND,X) OP N #	(IND),Y OP N #	Z.PAGE,X OP N #	ABS.X OP N #	ABS.Y OP N #	RELATIVE OP N #	INDIRECT OP N #	Z.PAGE,Y OP N #	N Z C I D V
ADC	A + M + C → A [1]	69 2 2	6D 4 3	65 3 2			61 6 2	71 5 2	75 4 2	7D 4 3	79 4 3				√ √ √ — — √
AND	A ∧ M → A [1]	29 2 2	2D 4 3	25 3 2			21 6 2	31 5 2	35 4 2	3D 4 3	39 4 3				√ √ — — — —
ASL	C ←□←□←0		0E 6 3	06 5 2	0A 2 1				16 6 2	1E 7 3					√ √ √ — — —
BCC	BRANCH ON C=0 [2]											90 2 2			— — — — — —
BCS	BRANCH ON C=1 [2]											B0 2 2			— — — — — —
BEQ	BRANCH ON Z=1 [2]											F0 2 2			— — — — — —
BIT	A ∧ M		2C 4 3	24 3 2											M_7 √ — — — M_6
BMI	BRANCH ON N=1 [2]											30 2 2			— — — — — —
BNE	BRANCH ON Z=0 [2]											D0 2 2			— — — — — —
BPL	BRANCH ON N=0 [2]											10 2 2			— — — — — —
BRK	BREAK					00 7 1									— — — 1 — —
BVC	BRANCH ON V=0 [2]											50 2 2			— — — — — —
BVS	BRANCH ON V=1 [2]											70 2 2			— — — — — —
CLC	0 → C					18 2 1									— — 0 — — —
CLD	0 → D					D8 2 1									— — — — 0 —
CLI	0 → I					58 2 1									— — — 0 — —
CLV	0 → V					B8 2 1									— — — — — 0
CMP	A − M [1]	C9 2 2	CD 4 3	C5 3 2			C1 6 2	D1 5 2	D5 4 2	DD 4 3	D9 4 3				√ √ √ — — —
CPX	X − M	E0 2 2	EC 4 3	E4 3 2											√ √ √ — — —
CPY	Y − M	C0 2 2	CC 4 3	C4 3 2											√ √ √ — — —
DEC	M − 1 → M		CE 6 3	C6 5 2					D6 6 2	DE 7 3					√ √ — — — —
DEX	X − 1 → X					CA 2 1									√ √ — — — —
DEY	Y − 1 → Y					88 2 1									√ √ — — — —
EOR	A ⊻ M → A [1]	49 2 2	4D 4 3	45 3 2			41 6 2	51 5 2	55 4 2	5D 4 3	59 4 3				√ √ — — — —
INC	M + 1 → M		EE 6 3	E6 5 2					F6 6 2	FE 7 3					√ √ — — — —
INX	X + 1 → X					E8 2 1									√ √ — — — —
INY	Y + 1 → Y					C8 2 1									√ √ — — — —
JMP	JUMP TO NEW LOCATION		4C 3 3										6C 5 3		— — — — — —
JSR	JUMP SUBROUTINE		20 6 3												— — — — — —
LDA	M → A [1]	A9 2 2	AD 4 3	A5 3 2			A1 6 2	B1 5 2	B5 4 2	BD 4 3	B9 4 3				√ √ — — — —

CONDITION CODES

MNEMONIC	OPERATION	IMMEDIATE OP N #	ABSOLUTE OP N #	ZERO PAGE OP N #	ACCUM OP N #	IMPLIED OP N #	(IND,X) OP N #	(IND),Y OP N #	Z.PAGE,X OP N #	ABS,X OP N #	ABS,Y OP N #	RELATIVE OP N #	INDIRECT OP N #	Z.PAGE,Y OP N #	COND CODES N Z C I D V
LDX	M → X[1]	A2 2 2	AE 4 3	A6 3 2							BE 4 3			B6 4 2	✓ ✓ — — — —
LDY	M → Y[1]	A0 2 2	AC 4 3	A4 3 2					BC 4 2	BC 4 3					✓ ✓ — — — —
LSR	0→☐→C		4E 6 3	46 5 2	4A 2 1				56 6 2	5E 7 3					0 ✓ ✓ — — —
NOP	NO OPERATION					EA 2 1									— — — — — —
ORA	A ∨ M → A	09 2 2	0D 4 3	05 3 2			01 6 2	11 5 2	15 4 2	1D 4 3	19 4 3				✓ ✓ — — — —
PHA	A → Ms S-1 → S					48 3 1									— — — — — —
PHP	P → Ms S-1 → S					08 3 1									— — — — — —
PLA	S+1 → S Ms → A					68 4 1									✓ ✓ — — — —
PLP	S+1 → S Ms → P					28 4 1									(RESTORED)
ROL	☐←☐←C		2E 6 3	26 5 2	2A 2 1				36 6 2	3E 7 3					✓ ✓ ✓ — — —
ROR	C→☐→☐		6E 6 3	66 5 2	6A 2 1				76 6 2	7E 7 3					✓ ✓ ✓ — — —
RTI	RETURN FROM INTERRUPT					40 6 1									(RESTORED)
RTS	RETURN FROM SUBROUTINE					60 6 1									— — — — — —
SBC	A − M − C̄ → A [1]	E9 2 2	ED 4 3	E5 3 2			E1 6 2	F1 5 2	F5 4 2	FD 4 3	F9 4 3				✓ ✓ ✓ — — ✓ [3]
SEC	1 → C					38 2 1									— — 1 — — —
SED	1 → D					F8 2 1									— — — — 1 —
SEI	1 → I					78 2 1									— — — 1 — —
STA	A → M		8D 4 3	85 3 2			81 6 2	91 6 2	95 4 2	9D 5 3	99 5 3				— — — — — —
STX	X → M		8E 4 3	86 3 2										96 4 2	— — — — — —
STY	Y → M		8C 4 3	84 3 2					94 4 2						— — — — — —
TAX	A → X					AA 2 1									✓ ✓ — — — —
TAY	A → Y					A8 2 1									✓ ✓ — — — —
TSX	S → X					BA 2 1									✓ ✓ — — — —
TXA	X → A					8A 2 1									✓ ✓ — — — —
TXS	X → S					9A 2 1									— — — — — —
TYA	Y → A					98 2 1									✓ ✓ — — — —

[1] ADD 1 TO "N" IF PAGE BOUNDARY IS CROSSED
[2] ADD 1 TO "N" IF BRANCH OCCURS TO SAME PAGE
    ADD 2 TO "N" IF BRANCH OCCURS TO DIFFERENT PAGE
[3] CARRY NOT = BORROW

X	INDEX X
Y	INDEX Y
A	ACCUMULATOR
M	MEMORY PER EFFECTIVE ADDRESS
Ms	MEMORY PER STACK POINTER

+	ADD
−	SUBTRACT
∧	AND
∨	OR
⊻	EXCLUSIVE OR
→	MODIFIED

— NOT MODIFIED
M_7 MEMORY BIT 7
M_6 MEMORY BIT 6
N NO. CYCLES
NO. BYTES

PROCESSOR STATUS REG. "P"

7							0
N	V	—	B	D	I	Z	C

CARRY   1 = TRUE
ZERO   1 = RESULT ZERO
IRQ DISABLE 1 = DISABLE
DECIMAL MODE 1 = TRUE
BRK COMMAND
OVERFLOW 1 = TRUE
NEGATIVE 1 = NEG.

Courtesy Synertek

ADDRESSING MODES

Study the instruction set summary in Table 2-3. The first column gives the instruction mnemonic, the second gives the logical expression, and the remaining 13 columns list the op codes for the various addressing modes. In addition to the op code, the 13 columns list the number of clock cycles, N, that each instruction requires for execution. The cycle time of the 6502 is typically 1 microsecond, so the total length of time required to execute an instruction is N microseconds. The number of bytes (#) in each instruction is also given.

The names of the various addressing modes are found at the heading of each column, for example IMMEDIATE, ABSOLUTE, ZERO-PAGE, etc. Addressing modes are one of the more confusing concepts for the beginner, and only a simplified explanation is given at this point. Very briefly, the addressing mode is related to *where* and *how* the microprocessor locates the data upon which it operates.

Suppose we are dealing with the LDA instruction which is "load a byte of data from memory into the accumulator." Where does the microprocessor get the byte upon which it is to operate?

- In the ABSOLUTE mode, the second and third bytes of the instruction specify the *address* of the memory location where the data is located. Assume the data is in location $1703. Then the complete LDA instruction is specified by the three hexadecimal numbers, AD 03 17.
- In the ZERO-PAGE mode, the second byte of the instruction specifies the *low-order byte of the address in page zero* (first 256 addresses) where the data is located. Suppose the data is in location $003F. Then the complete LDA instruction is specified by the two hexadecimal numbers, A5 3F.
- In the IMMEDIATE mode, the second byte of the instruction *is the data*. Assume we want to load the accumulator with the value $7F. The complete LDA instruction is specified by the two hexadecimal numbers, A9 7F.

Each addressing mode requires a *unique* op code, even though the same instruction is involved. This can be seen from the preceding explanation where the LDA instruction had op codes of $AD, $A5, and $A9, depending on the addressing mode. Refer to Table 2-3 and notice that the LDA instruction had a total of eight op codes, one for each of its eight addressing modes.

When, in the process of executing a program, the microprocessor reads the op code, it decodes or interprets that unique bit pattern to determine the nature of the instruction *and* the addressing mode.

The meaning of the remaining bytes of the instruction are also determined at the same time. If it reads an op code of $AD, it knows that there will be two more bytes in the instruction, and that they will be the ADL and ADH of the location of the data to be loaded into the accumulator. You can more fully understand the instruction decoding process carried out by the 6502 if you study Butterfield's[1] op-code chart (Chart 2-1). Sometimes this format is more useful than the standard chart shown in Table 2-3.

Not all instructions have the same set of addressing modes. For example, the TAX instruction does not have any of the addressing modes described above for the LDA instruction. The TAX instruction, when executed by the microprocessor, *transfers* the contents of the *accumulator* to the *X register*. These registers are internal to the 6502, hence they have no address. The op code contains all the necessary information for the instruction to be executed, since no addressing information is required. This addressing mode is called *implied addressing,* since the instruction itself implies both the source and destination of the data. All instructions using the implied addressing mode are single byte instructions. Other addressing modes will be covered in subsequent chapters.

THE MICROCOMPUTER PROGRAM

A microcomputer *program* is an ordered set of instructions designed to accomplish an objective. Some examples of program objectives are:

- Multiply two 8-bit numbers.
- Measure the time interval between successive logic-zero to logic-one transitions at an input port.
- Convert serial data on a telephone line to a printed output on a teletypewriter.
- With appropriate sensors in the left-turn lanes and side streets, control a traffic light to optimize the flow of traffic through a busy intersection.
- Produce a digital representation of an analog voltage level using an analog-to-digital converter, display the result using bcd-to-seven-segment display decoders, and up-date the result every five seconds.
- Execute commands and instructions in FORTRAN. Such a program is called an interpreter.

Clearly, the objectives of some programs are very simple and can be accomplished with a few instructions, while others require long

---

[1]Butterfield, Jim, "6502 Op-Codes," *6502 User Notes,* No. 13 1979, p. 6.

Chart 2-1. 6502 Op Codes Arranged in Logical Order

Op Code Ends in -2, -6, or -E

	IMM 2	ZPAG 2	Z,X 2	Z,Y 2	ABS 3	A,X 3	A,Y 3
ASL		06	16		0E	1E	
ROL		26	36		2E	3E	
LSR		46	56		4E	5E	
ROR		66	76		6E	7E	
STX		86		96	8E		
LDX	A2	A6		B6	AE		BE
DEC		C6	D6		CE	DE	
INC		E6	F6		EE	FE	

Misc. -0, -4, -C

	IMM 2	ZPAG 2	Z,X 2	ABS 3	A,X 3
BIT		24		2C	
STY		84	94	8C	
LDY	A0	A4	B4	AC	BC
CPY	C0	C4		CC	
CPX	E0	E4		EC	

Op Code Ends in -1, -5, -9, or -D

	IMM 2	ZPAG 2	Z,X 2	(I,X) 2	(I),Y 2	ABS 3	A,X 3	A,Y 3
ORA	09	05	15	01	11	0D	1D	19
AND	29	25	35	21	31	2D	3D	39
EOR	49	45	55	41	51	4D	5D	59
ADC	69	65	75	61	71	6D	7D	79
STA		85	95	81	91	8D	9D	99
LDA	A9	A5	B5	A1	B1	AD	BD	B9
CMP	C9	C5	D5	C1	D1	CD	DD	D9
SBC	E9	E5	F5	E1	F1	ED	FD	F9

Branches -0

	ZPAG 2		A,X 3
BPL	10	BMI	30
BVC	50	BVS	70
BCC	90	BCS	B0
BNE	D0	BEQ	F0

Jumps

	ABS 3	(IND)
JSR	20	
JMP	4C	6C

Single-Byte Op Codes -0, -8, -A

	0-	1-	2-	3-	4-	5-	6-	7-	8-	9-	A-	B-	C-	D-	E-	F-
-0	BRK				RTI		RTS									
-8	PHP	CLC	PLP	SEC	PHA	CLI	PLA	SEI	DEY	TYA	TAY	CLV	INY	CLD	INX	SED
-A	ASL-A		ROL-A		LSR-A		ROR-A		TXA	TXS	TAX	TSX	DEX		NOP	

sophisticated programs. The first example above can be implemented with 10 to 15 instructions using about 30 bytes of memory, while the last objective may require more than 8K bytes of memory for the program.

The instructions are stored in memory and are *ordered* by their addresses. In the 6502, there is a pair of registers known as the *program counter*. They insure that the instructions are performed in the proper sequence. The program counter contains the address of the next byte of the program to be read. After each byte of a program has been read from memory, the program counter is incremented by one to point to the memory address at which the computer will find the next program byte. Exceptions to this occur only in the case of subroutines and interrupts. These topics will be covered in Chapter 9.

A SIMPLE PROGRAM

An illustration will help at this point. Suppose the object of a program is to transfer the contents of the location whose address is $0300 to the memory location whose address is $02FF. A program to accomplish this is shown in Example 2. The program requires six bytes of memory, its starting address is $0200, and it requires only two instructions. The LDA instruction is contained in the first three bytes of the program, and the STA instruction is contained in the last three bytes.

Example 2: A Simple Data Transfer Program

Location	Contents	Comments
0200	AD	Fetch the contents of the location whose
0201	00	address is $0300 and place them in the accumulator.
0202	03	
0203	8D	Store the contents of the accumulator in the
0204	FF	memory location whose address is $02FF.
0205	02	

If the program counter in the 6502 is initialized to $0200, the starting address of the program, then the 6502 will execute the program. As far as the 6502 is concerned, the actual location of the program or its starting point makes no difference. However, it is absolutely necessary that each byte of an instruction, and the instructions themselves, be in the proper order.

The activity on the address and data buses of the microcomputer during the execution of the program in Example 2 may be described by referring once again to Example 2 and also Figs. 2-1 and 2-2. Assume that the microprocessor system clock is running at 1 megahertz, or each clock cycle takes 1 microsecond. (Detailed timing considerations will be discussed in Chapter 12.)

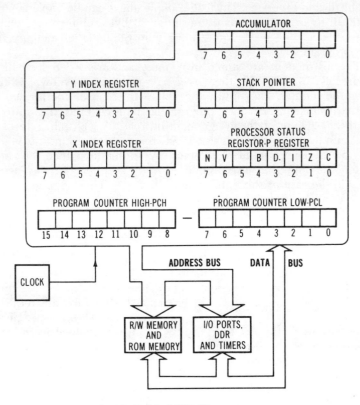

Fig. 2-1. Model of 6502 Microprocessor.

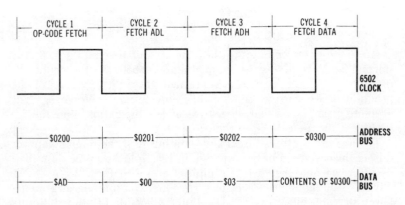

Fig. 2-2. Activity on Address Bus and Data Bus by clock cycles during LDA instruction.

- During the first clock cycle, the contents of the program counter (PCH-PCL = $0200) are placed on the address bus, and the 6502 reads the op code on the data bus. The program counter is incremented to $0201.
- During the second clock cycle, the contents of the program counter, now $0201, are placed on the address bus, the ADL ($00) is fetched from location $0201 and appears on the data bus, the op code is interpreted by the microprocessor, and the program counter is incremented.
- During the third clock cycle, the contents of the program counter ($0202) appear on the address bus and the ADH ($03) is fetched from location $0202. The program counter is incremented again.
- During the fourth clock cycle, the ADH-ADL = $0300 appears on the address bus. The byte of data in location $0300 is placed on the data bus, and is clocked into the 6502 at the conclusion of this cycle.
- During the fifth clock cycle, the contents of the program counter, now $0203, are placed on the address bus, the next op code ($8D) is read from location $0203, the program counter is incremented, and the previous instruction is implemented in the microprocessor. This last step means the byte of data read during the fourth clock cycle is moved into the accumulator.
- During the sixth clock cycle, $0204 appears on the address bus to fetch the ADL ($FF) of the destination location. The op code fetched during the fifth cycle is interpreted, and the program counter is incremented again.
- During the seventh clock cycle, $0205 appears on the address bus to fetch the ADH ($02) of the destination location. The program counter is incremented.
- During the eighth clock cycle, the ADH-ADL = $02FF is on the address bus, the microprocessor places the contents of the accumulator on the data bus, and the control lines clock the data into location $02FF.

This completes the program of Example 2, amounting to eight clock cycles or 8 microseconds. Note from Table 2-3 that both the LDA and STA instructions require four cycles in the absolute addressing mode, which checks with our analysis above. To find the time necessary for an instruction to be executed, multiply the number of clock cycles, N, from Table 2-3 by the clock period (as we multiplied 8 clock cycles times 1 microsecond to obtain 8 microseconds in this example). The length of a program is the sum of the time intervals required for each of the instructions.

WRITING A PROGRAM

As a matter of fact, programs are not written in the form illustrated in Example 2. The procedure for writing a program is outlined as follows:

- Have the objective clearly in mind and, if necessary, flowchart the steps required to achieve the objective.
- Write an *assembly language* version of the program using *labels* for addresses, *mnemonics* for instructions, and *symbols* for addresses of memory locations that store data.
- Translate the program into hexadecimal *machine language*.

These ideas will be illustrated shortly. For the moment we will concentrate on the assembly language program which will be arranged in four columns.

- The address of the first byte of any instruction may have a name called a *label*. Labels are found in the first column.
- The second column contains the instruction *mnemonic*.
- The third column is the *operand*. It is empty if a single byte instruction is involved. It may be a byte of *data* if the immediate addressing mode is used. It may be a *symbol* for a location where a byte of data is found. It may be a *label*, symbolizing a program address.
- The fourth column contains *comments* that interpret or clarify the instruction.

To illustrate, consider the program in Example 2 whose object was the transfer of a byte of data from location $0300 to location $02FF. Let address $0300 be represented by the *symbol* LOC1, and let address $02FF be represented by the symbol LOC2. The choice of symbols is up to the programmer. Assume that the starting address of the program is represented by the *label* START. Then the assembly language version of this program is shown in Example 3. The third column is called the *operand* column because it is either the data to be operated upon, or it is the location of the data to be used in an operation.

(Do not be overly concerned if you cannot comprehend all of these facts at once. It will require several examples and perhaps a re-reading before you begin to feel comfortable with these new concepts.)

Example 3: Assembly Language Data Transfer Program

Label	Mnemonic	Operand	Comments
START	LDA	LOC1	Load the data at LOC1 into A.
	STA	LOC2	Store the contents of A at LOC2.

Step three in writing a program consists of translating the labels, mnemonics, and symbols into their hexadecimal equivalents. This translation is called a *machine language* program because it is in the form used to load it into the microprocessor. The machine language version is usually placed directly to the left of the assembly language version. The completed program with which we have been working is given in Example 4.

Some microcomputers have programs that convert mnemonics entered on keyboards to machine language. Such programs are called *assemblers*. Some assemblers have extensive error detection techniques programmed into them, and they will handle symbol tables, labels, and branch calculations. Others, like the one in the AIM 65 monitor, simply convert mnemonics to op codes and enter the program into memory.

Example 4: Completed Data Transfer Program Using Absolute Addressing

Location	Instruction	Label	Mnemonic	Operand	Comments
0200	AD 00 03	START	LDA	LOC1	Load the contents of $0300 into A.
0203	8D FF 02		STA	LOC2	Store the contents of A at $02FF.

Shortly we will describe several programs that perform data transfers, using several of the addressing modes previously mentioned. Before that, we note that the instructions, op codes, and addressing modes of all of the instructions introduced in this chapter are itemized in Table 2-1. Also, refer again to the form of the program in Example 4, which is the form of all of the programs in this book. While the form of programs varies from book to book, no confusion is likely to occur with the form we have adopted. You may think that the address skips two locations, from $0200 to $0203. Actually, location $0200 stores the $AD, location $0201 stores the $00, and location $0202 stores the $02. The entire instruction is on a single line. The label refers to the first byte of the instruction, and the remaining bytes of the instruction must be stored at immediately subsequent locations in memory. In the examples that follow, the headings used to identify the columns in Example 4 will be omitted. However, the columns in subsequent examples will contain the corresponding information.

The program given in Example 5 illustrates the LDA instruction in the *immediate* addressing mode. The assembly language version will contain the byte of data whenever immediate addressing is used, and in Example 5 observe that the data byte "$00" appears in the first instruction. After the program has executed, both locations $0300 and $0301 will contain $00.

Object: Store $00 in locations $0300 and $0301.

0208	A9 00	START	LDA $00	Load A (immediate) with $00.
020A	8D 00 03		STA MEM1	Store the contents of A in location $0300.
020D	8D 01 03		STA MEM2	Store the contents of A in location $0301.

In Example 6 the immediate addressing mode is used for the LDA instruction, while the zero-page addressing mode is used for the STA instruction. The advantage of using page zero of memory for storing data is that zero-page addressing requires only two instruction bytes in the program, compared to the three bytes required in the absolute addressing mode, and zero-page addressing requires one less clock cycle than absolute addressing.

Example 6: Data Transfer Program Using Zero-Page Addressing Mode

Object: Store $FF in locations $0000 and $003F.

0212	A9 FF	ORIGIN	LDA $FF	Load A with $FF (immediate mode).
0214	85 00		STA LOZ1	Store A in zero-page location $0000.
0216	85 3F		STA LOZ2	Store A in $003F (zero-page mode).

Example 7 illustrates a data transfer using the X register, and Example 8 illustrates a data transfer using the Y register. The LDX instruction uses the zero-page addressing mode, while the LDY instruction uses the immediate addressing mode. In long programs with many symbols, the program is usually preceded by a symbol table in which the symbols are related to the addresses they symbolize. Although the length of the programs in Examples 7 and 8 does not warrant a symbol table, we have included them to illustrate the point.

Example 7: Data Transfer Program Using the X Register

Object: Transfer the contents of location $0000 to location $03FF without using the accumulator.

$0000 = LOZ				
$03FF = MEM				
021A	A6 00	START	LDX LOZ	Load the X register with the contents of location $0000.
021C	8E FF 03		STX MEM	Store X in $03FF.

Example 8: Data Transfer Program Using the Y Register

Object: Load locations $0000 to $0002 with $7F without using the X register or the accumulator.

$0000 = HERE				
$0001 = THERE				
$0002 = LOCT				
0221	A0 7F	BEGIN	LDY $7F	Load the Y register with $7F.
0223	84 00		STY HERE	Store Y in $0000.
0225	84 01		STY THERE	Store Y in $0001.
0227	84 02		STY LOCT	Store Y in $0002.

PROGRAM NAME _____   PAGE _____ OF _____

PROGRAMMER _____   DATE _____

ADDRESS	INSTRUCTION B1	B2	B3	LABEL	MNEMONIC	OPERAND	COMMENTS

Fig. 2-3. Sample programming form.

A programming form is of considerable help in writing programs. One possible form is shown in Fig. 2-3.

LOADING AND EXECUTING A PROGRAM

Once a program has been written in assembly language and translated into machine language, it is ready to be loaded into the microcomputer. This means that, beginning with the starting address of the program, the program bytes are stored in successive locations in memory. In the case of the KIM-1, AIM 65, and SYM-1 this is accomplished with the keyboard and the display. All microcomputers with monitors will have some means of loading and executing a program.

To execute the program, the program counter must be initialized to be identical to the address of the first byte in the program. In the SYM-1, KIM-1, and AIM 65, the monitors have the ability to initialize the program counter to the correct value. Consult your user's manual for the proper initialization procedure.

THE BRK INSTRUCTION

Since the 6502 does not have a HALT instruction, another technique is used to end the demonstration programs that we will use. The last instruction in the program will be a single-byte instruction called BRK. BRK has an op code of $00. Its effect is described as follows:

- Upon reading and decoding the BRK instruction, the microprocessor reads a location symbolized by IRQL to get the low-order byte for the program counter and the next location, IRQH, to get the high-order byte for the program counter.

- The program continues execution with these new values in the program counter, that is, at the instruction whose address is PCH-PCL.

In the KIM-1, the addresses for IRQL and IRQH are $17FE and $17FF, respectively. In these locations you must load $00 and $1C, respectively. The address $1C00 is an address in the KIM-1 monitor. Therefore, upon reading and executing the BRK instruction, the KIM-1 will continue its execution *in the monitor*. This prevents the microcomputer from wandering off to perform "nonsense" instructions that are generated as patterns of binary digits when the power is applied to the computer. The SYM-1 and AIM 65 operate in a similar way except that IRQL and IRQH are preloaded by the RESET button, and the user need not load these locations himself. Example 9 illustrates how our first program, the one given in Example 4, is modified to include the BRK instruction.

Example 9: Data Transfer Program Illustrating the BRK Instruction

Object: Transfer the contents of location $0300 to location $02FF. End the program with a BRK instruction.

```
$02FF = LOC2
$0300 = LOC1
$17FE = IRQL; KIM-1 users load with $00.
$17FF = IRQH; KIM-1 users load with $1C.
0200   AD 00 03    START    LDA LOC1
0203   8D FF 02             STA LOC2
0206   00                   BRK         Break to the monitor.
```

The reason for using a BRK instruction as opposed to a jump to the monitor instruction is that all of the important registers in the 6502 are saved when the BRK to the monitor instruction is used. The AIM 65, SYM-1, and KIM-1 all give the user the ability to examine these registers after a BRK instruction. Each system has a

Table 2-4. Addresses of Locations Where the Monitor Stores 6502 Registers

Register Name	Symbol	Monitor Storage Locations		
		KIM-1	AIM 65	SYM-1
Program Counter Low	PCL	$00EF	$A425	$A659
Program Counter High	PCH	$00F0	$A426	$A65A
Accumulator	A	$00F3	$A421	$A65D
X Register	X	$00F5	$A422	$A65E
Y Register	Y	$00F4	$A423	$A65F
Processor Status	P	$00F1	$A420	$A65C
Stack Pointer	SP	$00F2	$A424	$A65B

different means of displaying the registers, so the user is referred to the respective system manual for details. Table 2-4 lists the addresses of the locations where these registers are saved.

THE SINGLE-STEP MODE

The monitors and control circuitry of the KIM-1, SYM-1, and the AIM 65 microcomputer systems allow the user to execute a program one instruction at a time. This feature is very useful in debugging programs, because the user can examine the effect of each instruction as it is executed. The user may also examine the contents of each of the 6502 registers after an instruction has been executed, because in the single-step mode, the monitor stores the registers in the locations shown in Table 2-4. Each of the three systems mentioned has a somewhat different technique of implementing the single-step mode; the user is referred to the appropriate system manual for details.

INTRODUCTION TO THE EXPERIMENTS

The purpose of the experiments in this chapter is to teach you to load and execute simple programs. You will also examine the contents of the locations which are modified by the data transfer instructions, and you will be asked to write simple programs. KIM-1 users should refer again to the Single-Step Mode section to set up the IRQH and IRQL locations before they begin.

EXPERIMENT NO. 1

Step 1

Load the program of Example 4 into memory. For convenience we list the program.

```
0200   AD 00 03    START   LDA LOC1
0203   8D FF 02             STA LOC2
0206   00                   BRK
```

Step 2

Put $00 in location $02FF. Refer to your user manuals if you do not remember how to examine and modify the contents of a location.

Step 3

Put $33 in location $0300.

Step 4

Initialize the program counter to $0200 using your manual instructions, then execute the program.

Step 5

After the program has been executed, the display will light. Now examine the contents of locations $02FF and $0300. What do you observe in each location?

(We observed a $33 in both locations $02FF and $0300, indicating that the program had transferred the contents of location $0300 to location $02FF. Recall that location $02FF contained $00 before the program was executed.)

EXPERIMENT NO. 2

Step 1

Load the program given in Example 5. A listing is given below for convenience.

```
0208   A9 00      START   LDA $00
020A   8D 00 03           STA MEM1
020D   8D 01 03           STA MEM2
0210   00                 BRK
```

Step 2

Put any nonzero value in locations $0300 and $0301.

Step 3

Run the program, then examine the contents of locations $0300 and $0301. What data are there?

(If the program was entered correctly you should find $00 in both locations.)

Step 4

Change the second byte of the program to $7F, then rerun the program. What do you observe in locations $0300 and $0301?

(Since the first instruction is an LDA in the immediate mode, $7F is first transferred to the accumulator and then loaded into locations $0300 and $0301.)

EXPERIMENT NO. 3

Step 1

Load the program given in Example 6. A listing is provided here.

```
0212   A9 FF    ORIGIN    LDA $FF
0214   85 00              STA LOZ1
0216   85 3F              STA LOZ2
0218   00                 BRK
```

Step 2

Execute the program and examine locations $0000 and $003F. What data are stored in these locations?

(You should find $FF in both of these zero-page locations.)

Step 3

Change the byte at $0213 to $00. Run the program again. Predict what data you will find at locations $0000 and $003F.

(You should find $00 in these locations.)

EXPERIMENT NO. 4

Step 1

Put $FF in location $0000.

Step 2

Load the program listed in Example 7. Omit the BRK command at location $021F. Put anything at location $021F except $00. Run the program, then describe what happens. A listing is as follows.

```
021A   A6 00    START    LDX LOZ
021C   8E FF 03           STX MEM
021F   00                 BRK
```

(We observed on the KIM-1 and AIM 65 that the display remained dark, and we could not tell when or if the program executed properly.)

Step 3

Press the RESET key. Examine location $03FF. Did the program work?

(We found that the program had worked.)

Step 4

Insert the BRK instruction at location $021F and run the program again.

EXPERIMENT NO. 5

Step 1

Load the program in Example 8. A listing is provided. Execute the program.

```
0221   A0 7F    BEGIN    LDY $7F
0223   84 00             STY HERE
0225   84 01             STY THERE
0227   84 02             STY LOCT
0229   00               BRK
```

Step 2

Examine locations $0000 to $0002. What do you find there?

(If the program works you should find $7F in all three locations.)

Step 3

Single-step through the program to make sure you understand the single-step mode of your microcomputer.

EXPERIMENT NO. 6

Step 1

Write a program to load the accumulator with the contents of location $0000, the X register with the contents of location $0200, and the Y register with the contents of location $0300. Locate your program from location $022A upward. End your program with a BRK instruction.

(Your program should look something like this:

```
022A   A5 00    START    LDA MEMZ
022C   AE 00 02          LDX LOC
022F   AC 00 03          LDY STG
0232   00               BRK)
```

Step 2

Load location $0000 with $11, location $0200 with $22, and location $0300 with $33.

Step 3

Execute the program, and then examine the registers using the monitor program in your microcomputer. Refer to Table 2-4 for the addresses of the locations where the registers are stored.

Step 4

Use your monitor to modify the accumulator, X register, and Y register locations so that they are all loaded with $00.

Step 5

Start the program again using the single-step mode. Examine the contents of each register after each step in the program. You should observe that each register changes after the instruction in which it is modified is executed. Experience gained in "following a register" through a program will be useful in debugging programs.

EXPERIMENT NO. 7

Step 1

Write a program to load the accumulator with $00, and then transfer this information to both the X register and Y register.

(Your program should look like this:

```
0233    LDA  $00
        TAX
        TAY
        BRK
```

You can fill in the remaining addresses and op codes. Run the program and examine the registers to see if your program works.)

CHAPTER 3

Simple Input/Output Techniques

OBJECTIVES

At the completion of this chapter you should be able to:

- Understand the operation of memory mapped I/O ports.
- Use a data direction register to program an I/O port to either input or output data.
- Use the INC, DEC, JMP, INX, INY, DEX, and DEY instructions. See Table 3-1 for a summary.
- Write programs with loops.

INTRODUCTION

The input/output operations of a microcomputer are fundamental to any useful application. Some examples of the function of an input port in a microcomputer system are:

- A key depression produces a voltage level on an input pin corresponding to a binary zero. Software then inputs this voltage, determines which key on a hexadecimal keyboard has been pressed, and converts the key value to its hexadecimal equivalent.
- If the temperature exceeds a given value, a thermostat produces a voltage level on an input pin corresponding to a binary one. A program reads the input pin to test the temperature.

Two examples of the function of an output port are the following.

Table 3-1. Summary of Instructions and Op Codes Introduced in Chapter 3

Instruction	Description	Addressing Mode			
		Absolute	Zero-Page	Implied	Indirect
INC	Increment Memory by One	EE	E6		
DEC	Decrement Memory by One	CE	C6		
INX	Increment X Register by One			E8	
DEX	Decrement X Register by One			CA	
INY	Increment Y Register by One			C8	
DEY	Decrement Y Register by One			88	
JMP	Jump to New Location	4C			6C

- Light the appropriate segments in a seven-segment LED display to indicate a hexadecimal digit.
- Turn a heating element off if a thermostat indicates a temperature above a given value.

The task of connecting electronic or mechanical devices to the I/O ports of a microcomputer is often called *interfacing*, although this term also refers to the process of interconnecting the various components of a microcomputer. Clearly, interfacing requires some experience with electronics, and the interested reader is referred to books in the Blacksburg Continuing Education Series, especially the *NCR Basic Electronics Course* and *Logic and Memory Experiments* (two volumes) published by Howard W. Sams & Co., Inc., Indianapolis, IN 46268. Programming a microcomputer, including the I/O operations, requires little, if any, background in electronics, but any programmer would find such a background extremely useful.

INPUT/OUTPUT PORTS

The purpose of an input port is to provide information for the computer from the outside world. This is usually accomplished by an external device, a photocell for example, controlling the voltage level at one to eight pins on an integrated circuit. Typically a voltage of near 5 volts corresponds to a binary one, while a voltage of near zero volts corresponds to a binary zero. This integrated circuit is connected to the data bus and the address bus of the microcomputer. When the address of the input port is placed on the address bus by the 6502, then the input port integrated circuit controls the logic levels on the data bus, and the 6502 *READS* the binary number represented by the voltage levels at the input port. These integrated circuits are sometimes called "interface adapters."

This mode of operation, in which input ports act like any other memory device in the sense that they supply data to the 6502 only when they are addressed, is called *memory mapped input.* As far as the 6502 is concerned, an input port is simply another location in memory, and it might just as well be a ROM or R/W memory location because the microprocessor does not know the difference.

The purpose of an output port is to provide information from the microcomputer to the outside world. An integrated circuit is connected to the data bus and the address bus, like the case of the input port. This integrated circuit has one to eight pins that may be connected to external devices, a relay for example. The 6502 *WRITES* data to an output port by placing the address of the output port integrated circuit on the address bus, while simultaneously placing the byte of data intended for the output port on the data bus. This data byte is usually stored in the integrated circuit that acts as the output port, and it determines the voltage levels on the output pins of this integrated circuit. A binary zero produces a voltage level near 0 volts, while a binary one produces a voltage level near 5 volts, perhaps with enough current capability to close a relay for example.

This mode of operation, in which output ports act like R/W memory devices in the sense that a byte of data can be written to them only when they are addressed by the 6502, is called *memory mapped output.* Again, the 6502 does not know whether it is writing data to an R/W location or an output port; only the programmer knows this.

To summarize, an *input/output port* is a *location in memory* that can be used to transfer data either from the microprocessor to an external device or from an external device to the microprocessor. All the data transfer instructions described in Chapter 2 and all the instructions you will learn in this and subsequent chapters may be used either to read the data at an input port or to write data to an output port. For example, an LDA INPUT instruction might be used to read an input port where INPUT is a symbol for the address of the port. A STA OUTPUT instruction might be used to write data to an output port, where OUTPUT is a symbol for the address of the port. Examples of I/O external devices include:

- Keypads and keyboards
- Transistors that drive LEDs, relays, speakers, or other electromechanical devices
- Integrated circuits, a 7490 decade counter for example
- Mechanical switches
- Phototransistors or photoresistors
- Hexadecimal displays.

The 6502 uses memory mapped I/O exclusively as compared to the 8080A which uses a special mode called accumulator I/O in addition to memory mapped I/O. To reiterate, corresponding to each I/O port is a set of pins, terminals, or connectors on the microcomputer where the data are made available. The data are actually voltage levels or current levels at a series of pins. A voltage of 5 volts corresponds to an I/O port data bit being a one, and a voltage of 0 volts corresponds to an I/O port data bit being a zero. The two possible voltage levels are referred to in a variety of ways in computer literature. These include +5 V or 0 V, high or low, V_{cc} or Gnd, H or L, and logic one or logic zero. We prefer using the logic one and logic zero description of voltage levels at an I/O port. Finally, an I/O port normally consists of eight bits with their corresponding pins, in other words one byte of data, but only one, two, three, or even five bits may be used for interfacing purposes. For a more extensive discussion of input/output port interfacing, see Chapters 11, 12, and 13.

I/O PORTS AND DATA DIRECTION REGISTERS

Input/output ports are implemented with integrated circuits connected to the 6502 by the address bus, data bus, and control bus. Refer to Fig. 3-1 for a number of details. In 6502 systems such as the AIM 65, SYM-1, and KIM-1, the integrated circuits used for I/O ports are so-called *family* chips such as the 6520, 6522, 6530,

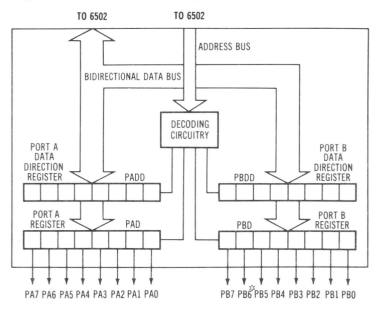

Fig. 3-1. Block diagram of 6530 and 6522 I/O Ports. *See text.

and 6532 which not only perform I/O functions but also have interval timers, R/W, or ROM locations on the chips. Although these various chips differ considerably in their capabilities, they have in common the ability to implement two I/O ports, each of which may be programmed as either an input port or an output port. In fact, each of the pins of a port may be either an input pin or an output pin, independent of the other pins in the same port.

Corresponding to each pin or bit of an I/O port, is a bit in a data direction register (DDR) which is also a location in memory. These registers are located on the same integrated circuits that contain the I/O ports. See Fig. 3-1 for a simplified model of the I/O port and DDR structure of the 6530 and the 6522 interface adapters. The bit value in the DDR determines whether the corresponding I/O bit will be an input bit or an output bit. A bit value of zero in the DDR makes the corresponding port bit an input bit, whereas a bit value of one in the DDR makes the corresponding port bit an output bit. A data direction register also consists of eight bits or one byte, and the microprocessor can read or write to a DDR just as if it were a regular R/W memory location.

Not all integrated circuits used as input ports or output ports are programmable, that is, may be programmed to be either an input port or an output port. In Part II of this book we will illustrate how to interface other integrated circuits that are designed to be either input ports or output ports, but not both. Most 6502 family interface adapter chips are programmable, but in some cases other integrated circuits make less expensive I/O ports.

I/O PORT SYMBOLS

On the KIM-1, SYM-1, and AIM 65 microcomputers, the I/O ports are accessed at an edge connector called the *applications connector*. In the remainder of this book, the two I/O ports which are accessed at this 22/44 pin connector will be called Port A and Port B. Refer again to Fig. 3-1. The pin connections for the two I/O ports are identical in the three microcomputers: KIM-1, SYM-1, and AIM 65. See Table 3-2 for pin identification. The individual pins of Port A will be referred to as PA7, PA6, . . . , PA0, while those of Port B will be PB7-PB0. PB6 is not available for the user on either the KIM-1 or the SYM-1 microcomputers. The address of Port A will be symbolized by PAD, an acronym for Port A Data, and the address of Port B will be symbolized by PBD. In the SYM-1 and AIM 65 literature, these ports are named ORA and ORB, but no confusion is likely to occur. The corresponding data direction registers will be symbolized by PADD, an acronym for Port A Data Direction, and PBDD. The data direction registers are called DDRA

**Table 3-2. Port A and Port B Pin Assignments
on the Applications Connector**

Port A = PAD	Pin	Port B = PBD	Pin
PA7	8	PB7	15
PA6	7	PB6*	17
PA5	6	PB5	16
PA4	5	PB4	13
PA3	2	PB3	12
PA2	3	PB2	11
PA1	4	PB1	10
PA0	14	PB0	9

*PB6 is not available on KIM-1 or SYM-1, but is available on AIM 65.

and DDRB in SYM-1 and AIM 65 literature. A summary of the locations in memory of the ports and their DDR are given in Table 3-3.

Let us illustrate some of the points mentioned. If a $FF is stored in PADD. then all the bits in the DDR are ones, and all eight pins of PAD are output pins, making it an 8-bit output port. If $00 is stored in PADD, then all eight pins are input pins and PAD is an 8-bit input port. If $83 is stored in PADD, then pins PA7, PA1, and PA0 are output pins, while PA6-PA2 are input pins. A system *reset* pulse clears the DDR (sets all bits to zero) and all the pins are input pins. The system may be reset by pressing the RESET button or key, or by a power-up condition. The task of the programmer is to know which pins are supposed to act as outputs and, after reset, to initialize the DDR by programming these registers accordingly.

Table 3-3. I/O Port and Data Direction Register Addresses

	KIM-1	SYM-1	AIM 65
Port A = PAD	$1700	$A001	$A001
DDRA = PADD	$1701	$A003	$A003
PORT B = PBD	$1702	$A000	$A000
DDRB = PBDD	$1703	$A002	$A002

INPUT/OUTPUT PROGRAMMING

In this section we list some programs that relate to the ideas mentioned above. Note that the program comments take on a different character than in the previous chapter. The comments do not always *describe* the instruction, but rather they may suggest the purpose or reason for the instruction. It will be assumed that you have become familiar with the instructions so no further descriptions are necessary. You should study the programs carefully to see how some simple I/O operations are performed.

Example 1: Program to Make Port A an Output Port

Object: Make Port A an output port and set pins PA7, PA6, and PA0 at logic one. The diagram illustrates the desired configuration.

	PA7	PA6	PA5	PA4	PA3	PA2	PA1	PA0	
PADD	1	1	1	1	1	1	1	1	= $FF
DATA	1	1	0	0	0	0	0	1	= $C1

0200	A9 FF	START	LDA $FF	Set the DDR for Port A so that
0202	8D 01 17		STA PADD	all the pins are outputs.
0205	A9 C1		LDA $C1	Set pins PA7, PA6, and PA0
0207	8D 00 17		STA PAD	to logic one, others at logic zero.
020A	00		BRK	

Example 2: Program to Make Port B an Input Port

Object: Make Port B an input port and read the port, storing its contents in location $0000.

0200	A9 00	START	LDA $00	Initialize Port B to be an
0202	8D 03 17		STA PBDD	input port by clearing DDR.
0205	AD 02 17		LDA PBD	Read the port.
0208	85 00		STA LOZ	Store port data in LOZ.
020A	00		BRK	

Example 3: Program to Read Port B and Store its Contents in Port A

Object: Read Port B and load its contents into Port A which will be an output port.

0200	A9 FF	START	LDA $FF	Initialize Port A to be
0202	8D 01 17		STA PADD	an output port.
0205	AD 02 17		LDA PBD	Get data from Port B.
0208	8D 00 17		STA PAD	Transfer to Port A.
020B	00		BRK	

Example 4: Program to Illustrate a Loop

Object: Continuously read Port B and store its contents into Port A.

0200	A9 FF	START	LDA $FF	
0202	8D 01 17		STA PADD	
0205	AD 02 17	HERE	LDA PBD	Get data from Port B.
0208	8D 00 17		STA PAD	Store it in Port A.
020B	4C 05 02		JMP HERE	Reset program counter to $0205.

Note that in Example 1 the KIM-1 addresses for Port A and the Port A DDR were used. SYM-1 users and AIM 65 users must change these addresses to conform with Table 3-3. The program in this example is not of any particular use other than as a demonstration of how to set up the Port A data direction register so that Port A is an output port. In that connection, it is very important because setting up the data direction registers for the I/O ports is one of the first initialization steps in any program. You will see the first two instructions in the program of Example 1 in many subsequent programs in this book.

The first two instructions in Example 2 may be omitted if the system monitor loads a $00 into the DDR, or if it leaves the DDR unaltered after a system RESET. Unless you know the state of the

DDRs, it is good practice to initialize the DDR with your program. The next two instructions in Example 2 might be part of a larger program to read a keyboard connected to Port B, and to store the keyboard data in a zero-page location. It is a bit unfortunate that both the KIM-1 and the SYM-1 use PB6 for other purposes and, consequently, it is not available to the user. Thus, Port B is really a 7-bit port.

The program in Example 3 simply reads Port B and writes it to Port A. This kind of program might be used in a keyboard-video monitor input/output system. If Port B represents the keyboard, and Port A is the output to the video monitor, then whenever a key is read, the character would appear on the screen so the operator can see what has been typed. Note that PBDD was not initialized to $00 in Example 3, as it was assumed that the system RESET or the monitor cleared this register.

The program in Example 4 is essentially the same as the program in Example 3, except that the JMP instruction causes the program to continuously read Port B and output the result to Port A. Although this program has no particular use at this point, it does illustrate a program loop and the JMP instruction, which we now describe.

JMP INSTRUCTION

The JMP instruction used in Example 4 has the effect of resetting the program counter to the value labeled HERE. The program will repeat the LDA PBD, STA PAD, and JMP HERE instructions, continuously and forever, unless the RESET key is depressed or power is removed. A program or a portion of a program which repeats itself one or more times is called a *loop*. The three instructions just mentioned form a loop in the program of Example 4. The JMP instruction may be used to reset the program counter to any 16-bit number. Note that in the absolute addressing mode, as used in Example 4, the low-order byte of the program counter (PCL) is the second byte of the JMP instruction while the high-order byte of the program counter (PCH) is the third byte.

The JMP instruction has one other addressing mode called *indirect*. In this mode, the second and third bytes of the instruction form an address ADH-ADL whose contents contain PCL, while PCH is found at ADH-ADL + 1. The indirect JMP instruction is illustrated with the modification of Example 4 shown in Example 5.

In Example 5, THERE = $0003 and in this location should be stored the ADL of HERE. That is, in location $0003 put $05, the address low of HERE. In $0004 put $02, the address high of HERE. The indirect addressing mode is indicated by putting parentheses around the operand portion of the instruction. Any available location

Example 5: Program to Illustrate JMP Instruction in Its Indirect Addressing Mode

Object: Continuously read Port B and store its contents in Port A.

$0003 = THERE; Load with $05, the ADL of HERE.
$0004; Load with $02, the ADH of HERE.
$A000 = PBD; AIM 65 or SYM-1 address.
$A001 = PAD; AIM 65 or SYM-1 address.
$A002 = PBDD; Port B DDR, AIM 65 or SYM-1 address.
$A003 = PADD; Port A DDR, AIM 65 or SYM-1 address.

0200	A9 FF	START	LDA $FF	
0202	8D 03 A0		STA PADD	
0205	AD 00 A0	HERE	LDA PBD	
0208	8D 01 A0		STA PAD	
020B	6C 03 00		JMP (THERE)	Indirect JMP instruction. See Text.

may be used to store the new value of the program counter in the indirect mode. Refer again to Table 3-1 for a description and the op codes of the JMP instruction. To summarize:

- In the *absolute* mode, the second and third bytes of the JMP instruction are the new values of the PCL and PCH, respectively.
- In the *indirect* mode, the second and third bytes of the JMP instruction are the ADL and the ADH of a location which *contains* the new PCL. PCH is in (ADH,ADL + 1).

INC AND DEC INSTRUCTIONS

The I/O techniques learned so far will be used to illustrate two other instructions, INC and DEC, described in Table 3-1. The logical expressions for the INC and DEC instructions are $M + 1 \rightarrow M$, and $M - 1 \rightarrow M$, respectively. Simply stated, the INC instruction *increments* the contents of a memory location by one, whereas the DEC instruction *decrements* the contents of a memory location by one. In the zero-page addressing mode, the second byte of either instruction is the page-zero ADL of the memory location to be modified. In the absolute mode, the second and third bytes are the ADL and the ADH of the location to be modified.

As an example of the application of these instructions, suppose that a logic zero at PA0 turns a device (a heater, for example) on, while a logic one turns the same device off. Suppose further that PA0 has been programmed to be an output pin by loading $01 in PADD, and that PA0 is currently in the logic-one state. Then the instruction DEC PAD turns the device on and the instruction INC PAD will turn it off. Remember that the "address," PAD, corresponds to an output port, and not a ROM or R/W memory location.

Some programs which will demonstrate the use of the INC and DEC instructions follow.

Example 6: Program to Demonstrate the INC Instruction

Object: Apply successive increments to Port A which is programmed to be an output port.

0200	A9 FF		START	LDA $FF	Initialize Port A to be
0202	8D 01 17			STA PADD	an output port.
0205	8D 00 17			STA PAD	Begin with $FF in Port A.
0208	EE 00 17		HERE	INC PAD	Increment Port A.
020B	4C 08 02			JMP HERE	Loop to continuously increment.

Example 7: Program to Toggle an Output Pin ON and OFF

Object: Toggle (switch on and off) pin PA0. Start with PA0 at logic one.

0200	A9 01		START	LDA $01	Make PA0 an output pin by loading
0202	8D 01 17			STA PADD	one in bit zero of the DDR.
0205	8D 00 17			STA PAD	Initialize PA0 to logic one.
0208	CE 00 17			DEC PAD	Decrement PAD.
020B	EE 00 17			INC PAD	Increment PAD.
020E	00			BRK	

If the Port A pins are used to light LEDs (see the experiments at the end of this chapter), then the program in Example 6 will demonstrate successively all *binary* numbers from *zero to 255* on the LEDs. Other instructions may be used to accomplish the same effect, but the INC or DEC instructions are very efficient ways to increment or decrement a memory location. The program in Example 6 produces a 6-microsecond negative-going one-shot pulse at pin PA0 of Port A. A pulse such as this might be used to trigger an oscilloscope or start a counter. A series of pulses may be produced by replacing the BRK instruction with a JMP HERE instruction where HERE = $0208.

INX, INY, DEX, AND DEY INSTRUCTIONS

There are four instructions that increment or decrement the X and Y index registers. They are introduced here because of their similarity to the INC and DEC instructions. Their mnemonics, descriptions, and op codes are given in Table 3-1. These instructions use the implied addressing mode. For example, when the INX instruction is used, it is *implied* that the data to be operated upon (incremented in this case) are in the 8-bit X register. No other information about the location of the data is necessary, and, there-

Example 8: Program to Demonstrate the INX Instruction

Object: Successively decrement the X index register. Store the result in output Port A.

0200	A2 FF		START	LDX $FF	Initialize index register to $FF.
0202	8E 01 17			STX PADD	Make Port A an output port.
0205	8E 00 17		BACK	STX PAD	Output the X register to Port A.
0208	CA			DEX	Decrement the X register.
0209	4C 05 02			JMP BACK	Loop to successively decrement.

fore, in the implied mode, only single-byte instructions are necessary. The program in Example 8 on the preceding page illustrates one of these instructions.

INTRODUCTION TO THE EXPERIMENTS

The experiments in this and subsequent chapters will make extensive use of the I/O Ports on the KIM-1, SYM-1, and AIM 65. However, it should be noted that most of these experiments may be simulated using R/W memory locations rather than the I/O Ports if you do not want either to breadboard or to purchase the I/O circuit described below. We recommend the use of the I/O circuit, involving switches and output LEDs, because the experiments and demonstrations become much more vivid and realistic with the use of this circuit.

The I/O interface circuit is shown in Fig. 3-2. Note that Port B, symbolized by PBD in the examples, is controlled by eight switches. This port will be used as an *input* port, and the switches PB7-PB0 determine the number that the computer reads with an LDA PBD instruction. There are several important points to note in connection with the Port B input switches.

- *Do not* try to use Port B as an output port by writing $FF in its data direction register, PBDD. The switches connected to Port B are tied to ground in the logic-zero position, the position indicated in Fig. 3-2. Damage to the integrated circuits on the microcomputer boards may occur if you make Port B an output port with the switches in the logic-zero position. It is also good practice to leave the switches in the logic-one position when they are not being used.
- The PB0 and PB1 switches are electronically "debounced." Several experiments require debounced switches.
- The PB0 switch may also be used to produce a nonmaskable interrupt ($\overline{\text{NMI}}$) signal. See Chapter 9 for details regarding interrupts. An external connection between the $\overline{\text{NMI}}$ pin in Fig. 3-2 and the $\overline{\text{NMI}}$ connection on the expansion connector will be required.
- The PB7 pin on the microcomputer can be connected either to *switch* PB7 or to the $\overline{\text{IRQ}}$ pin. This option is provided because the KIM-1 timers use pin PB7 to operate the timers in the interrupt mode. See Chapter 10 for details. Again, an external connection is required.
- Neither the KIM-1 or the SYM-1 makes pin PB6 available to the user. If you have one of these systems you may wish to spot glue the PB6 switch in the logic-one position.

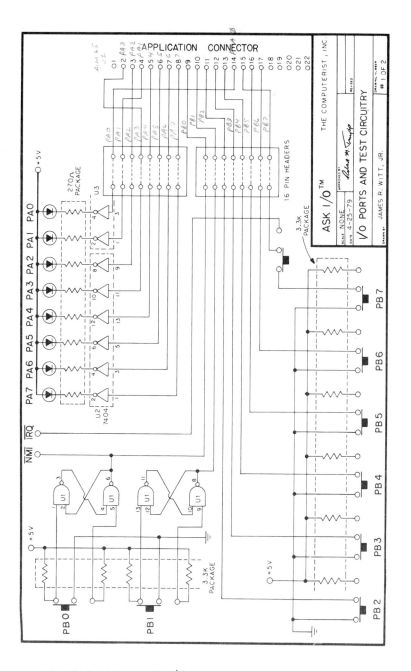

Fig. 3-2. Circuit diagram for I/O board used in experiments in this book.

Port A is used as an *output* port, and the logic levels on the Port A pins are indicated by the status of the Port A LEDs. If the logic level is one, the corresponding LED will be lit. In order for Port A, symbolized by PAD in the examples, to operate the LEDs, it *must* be configured as an output port by writing $FF to the Port A data direction register, symbolized by PADD in the examples and experiments.

If you have some electronics experience, then you may wish to breadboard the circuit in Fig. 3-2. A ribbon cable from the application connector pins given in Fig. 3-2 to a DIP connector (the entire cable assembly is called a DIP JUMPER) that plugs into a Proto-board or Superstrip will work nicely. The integrated circuits, switches, resistors, and LEDs may be mounted on the Protoboard or Superstrip.

If you do not have electronics experience, or if you want to buy an assembled version of the I/O board, then the experiments can be performed with the ASK I/O™ board, manufactured and sold by: The Computerist, Inc., P.O. Box 3, S. Chelmsford, MA 01824 (ASK I/O is a trademark of The Computerist, Inc.). The ASK I/O board connects directly to the application connector of the AIM 65, SYM-1, or KIM-1. The 16-pin headers shown in Fig. 3-2 allow the ports to be used to operate other devices such as relays. The additional circuitry will also be made available by the The Computerist, Inc.

In the experiments that follow, KIM-1, AIM 65, and SYM-1 users should employ the addresses for PAD, PADD, PBD, and PBDD given in Table 3-3. Note that with the I/O board connected to the applications connector, all the LEDs will light when the micro-computer system is RESET. The reason for this is that a RESET makes all the pins inputs, and as inputs they act like logic-one volt-age levels for the LED TTL drivers. This is an important considera-tion for "power-up" procedures, but is of little concern here.

EXPERIMENT NO. 1

Step 1

Load the program in Example 1.

```
0200   A9 FF        START   LDA $FF      Set the DDR for Port A so that
0202   8D 01 17             STA PADD     all the pins are outputs.
0205   A9 C1                LDA $C1      Set pins PA7, PA6, and PA0
0207   8D 00 17             STA PAD      to logic one, others to logic zero.
020A   00                   BRK
```

Step 2

Execute the program and observe the effect on the LEDs. Which LEDs on the I/O board glow?

(The PA7, PA6, and PA0 LEDs should glow.)

Step 3

Change the program byte at $0206 to $55 and run the program again. Which LEDs glow?

(The PA6, PA4, PA2, and PA0 LEDs should glow.)

Step 4

Experiment with various values for the program byte at $0206. What would you need at this location to turn all of the LEDs off?

(A $00 in location $0206 would turn the LEDs off.)

EXPERIMENT NO. 2

Step 1

Load the program in Example 2.

```
0200  A9 00     START   LDA $00     Initialize Port B to be an
0202  8D 03 17          STA PBDD    input port by clearing DDR.
0205  AD 02 17          LDA PBD     Read the port.
0208  85 00             STA LOZ     Store port data in LOZ.
020A  00                BRK
```

Step 2

Set the input switches at Port B to logic one. Execute the program.

Step 3

Examine the contents of location $0000. Does it reflect values of the switch settings? Remember that you may not have control over PB6.

Step 4

Experiment with different switch settings, checking location $0000 after each run of the program to confirm your switch settings.

EXPERIMENT NO. 3

Step 1

Load the program in Example 3.

```
0200  A9 FF        START    LDA $FF      Initialize Port A to be
0202  8D 01 17               STA PADD     an output port.
0205  AD 02 17               LDA PBD      Get data from Port B.
0208  8D 00 17               STA PAD      Transfer to Port A.
020B  00                     BRK
```

Step 2

Set the switches on the I/O board to any desired value. Execute the program.

Step 3

Campare the LEDs with the switch settings.

EXPERIMENT NO. 4

Step 1

Load and execute the program in Example 4.

```
0200  A9 FF        START    LDA $FF
0202  8D 01 17               STA PADD
0205  AD 02 17     HERE      LDA PBD      Get data from Port B.
0208  8D 00 17               STA PAD      Store it in Port A.
020B  4C 05 02               JMP HERE     Reset program counter to $0205.
```

Step 2

Vary the settings of the input switches at Port B while the program is running. Explain your results.

(The LEDs will follow the switch settings because the program is in a loop that inputs the switch settings and outputs them to the LEDs.)

EXPERIMENT NO. 5

Step 1

Load and execute the program in Example 6. Describe what you observe.

```
0200  A9 FF        START    LDA $FF      Initialize Port A to be
0202  8D 01 17               STA PADD     an output port.
0205  8D 00 17               STA PAD      Begin with $FF in Port A.
0208  EE 00 17     HERE      INC PAD      Increment Port A.
020B  4C 08 02               JMP HERE     Loop to continuously increment.
```

(All the LEDs appear to glow. The reason is that they are being turned on and off so rapidly that the eye does not perceive them switching.)

Step 2

Starting with the first instruction, single-step through the program, paying close attention to the LEDs on the I/O board and the instructions as they are executed. Note how the loop works by observing the program counter. Explain your observations.

(When the program is single stepped the user can observe that the Port A LEDs are actually "counting" in binary. The reason is that the binary number in Port A is continually being incremented by the INC instruction.)

EXPERIMENT NO. 6

Step 1

Load the program in Example 7, replacing the BRK statement by a JMP HERE instruction, namely 4C 08 02. A listing follows:

```
0200   A9 01      START   LDA $01      Make PA0 an output pin by
0202   8D 01 17           STA PADD     loading a one in bit zero of its DDR.
0205   8D 00 17           STA PAD      Initialize PA0 to logic one.
0208   CE 00 17   HERE    DEC PAD      Decrement PAD.
020B   EE 00 17           INC PAD      Increment PAD.
020E   4C 08 02           JMP HERE
```

Step 2

Execute the program and describe what you observe. Why does this happen? Would you expect to observe this behavior based upon your understanding of the program? Can you observe any changes at the PA0 LED as the program is executing? Why not?

(All the LEDs appear to glow continuously, but the PA0 LED is actually being toggled. The eye cannot perceive its off state whose duration is only six microseconds.)

Step 3

Can you suggest a method that could be used to observe the behavior at PA0? There are several that may be used.

(The single-step mode is probably the easiest to implement. Place the program in the single-step mode and again run the program.)

Step 4

Is it possible to observe any change at the PA0 LED in the single-step mode? When do the changes take place? Is this reasonable?

EXPERIMENT NO. 7

Step 1

Load and execute the program in Example 8.

```
0200   A2 FF      START   LDX  $FF      Initialize the X register to $FF.
0202   8E 01 17           STX  PADD     Make Port A an output port.
0205   8E 00 17   BACK    STX  PAD      X into Port A.
0208   CA                 DEX           Decrement X.
0209   4C 05 02           JMP  BACK
```

Step 2

Describe and explain the effect you expect to observe on the Port A LEDs? Do you observe this effect?

Step 3

Single step this program and compare its effect on the Port A LEDs with the results of the program in Example 6.

(The program of Example 6 starts counting from $00 and goes up. This program counts backward. The counting can only be observed in the single-step mode.)

EXPERIMENT NO. 8

Step 1

Write a program to toggle pin PA0. Use the Y register and the DEY instruction. Initialize PA0 to logic one before the toggle operation starts. Put the toggle operation in a loop.

Step 2

Load, execute, and single step your program to test your success. (One possible answer is the following program.)

```
0200   A0 01      START   LDY  $01      Initialize PA0 to be output
0202   8C 01 17           STY  PADD     pin.
0205   8C 00 17           STY  PAD      Set PA0 to logic one.
0208   88         THERE   DEY           Decrement the Y register.
0209   4C 08 02           JMP  THERE    Loop to continuously decrement.
```

CHAPTER 4

Logical Operations

OBJECTIVES

At the completion of this chapter you should be able to:

- Understand and use the AND, ORA, and EOR instructions. See Table 4-1 for a summary.
- Understand the concept of masking.
- Perform complementation with the EOR instruction.
- Be able to set individual bits in a memory location to either binary one or binary zero.

INTRODUCTION

Because he works with logic circuits and is familiar with digital techniques, the experienced logic-circuit designer will immediately recognize the importance of the logical operations. He is aware that logical operations are involved in such diverse designs as digital bathroom scales and cruise missiles. However, the beginner frequently wonders how the logical instructions will be used. We can only promise that the answers will become obvious as we proceed. Once the skills with the fundamentals are obtained, then potential applications begin to appear.

One historical note: The logical operations originate in an area of mathematics called Boolean algebra. George Boole was a 19th century mathematician who could not possibly have anticipated the widespread use of his work in symbolic logic. The moral should be obvious.

Table 4-1. Summary of Instructions and Op Codes Introduced in Chapter 4

Instruction	Description	Addressing Mode		
		Immediate	Absolute	Zero-Page
AND	AND Memory with Accumulator	29	2D	25
ORA	OR Memory with Accumulator	09	0D	05
EOR	EXCLUSIVE-OR Memory with Accumulator	49	4D	45

LOGICAL OPERATIONS

There are four logical operations that we will use. To describe them, let A and B stand for 1-bit binary numbers. The four logical operations are:

- The AND operation, symbolized by $A \cdot B$.* $A \cdot B$ is read "A *and* B."
- The OR operation, symbolized by $A+B$.* $A+B$ is read "A *or* B."
- The *Exclusive* OR (EOR) operation, symbolized by $A \oplus B$.* $A \oplus B$ is read "A e-or B" or "A x-or B."
- The *COMPLEMENT* (or inversion) operation, symbolized by $\overline{A}$. That is, the complement of A is $\overline{A}$. $\overline{A}$ is read "not A."

Table 4-2 summarizes the operations with truth tables, and it gives all the possible combinations of the operations for 1-bit numbers. Fig. 4-1 gives the logic design symbols for each operation. The Exclusive-OR function in Fig. 4-1 is not a special gate because it can be implemented with ANDs and ORs; that is, $A \oplus B = (\overline{A} \cdot B) + (A \cdot \overline{B})$.

A and B need not be 1-bit binary numbers. An 8-bit microcomputer operates on eight bits simultaneously. Any 8-bit logical opera-

Table 4-2. Summary of Logical Operations

AND			OR			EOR			Complement	
A	B	$A \cdot B$	A	B	$A+B$	A	B	$A \oplus B$	A	$\overline{A}$
1	1	1	1	1	1	1	1	0	1	0
1	0	0	1	0	1	1	0	1	0	1
0	1	0	0	1	1	0	1	1		
0	0	0	0	0	0	0	0	0		
$1 \cdot 1 = 1$			$1 + 1 = 1$			$1 \oplus 1 = 0$			$\overline{1} = 0$	
$1 \cdot 0 = 0$			$1 + 0 = 1$			$1 \oplus 0 = 1$			$\overline{0} = 1$	
$0 \cdot 1 = 0$			$0 + 1 = 1$			$0 \oplus 1 = 1$				
$0 \cdot 0 = 0$			$0 + 0 = 0$			$0 \oplus 0 = 0$				

*The symbols $\wedge$, $\vee$, and $\underline{\vee}$ frequently replace $\cdot$, $+$, and $\oplus$, respectively. The dot ($\cdot$) is sometimes understood; that is, $AB = A \cdot B$.

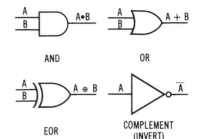

Fig. 4-1. Logic symbols for the AND,
OR, EOR, and COMPLEMENT operations.

tion can be performed by doing the single-bit operation on corresponding bits. If the eight bits of A are represented by A7, A6, A5, . . . , A0, the eight bits of B by B7, B6, B5 . . . , B0, and if the answer to $A \cdot B$ is C, then the operation $A \cdot B = C$ is realized by

$$A7 \cdot B7 = C7$$
$$A6 \cdot B6 = C6$$
$$A5 \cdot B5 = C5$$
$$\cdot \quad \cdot \quad \cdot$$
$$\cdot \quad \cdot \quad \cdot$$
$$\cdot \quad \cdot \quad \cdot$$
$$A0 \cdot B0 = C0$$

Table 4-3 gives 8-bit examples for all four operations. It also suggests that the work is easier to do if the operation is arranged so that the binary numbers are placed one under the other. Table 4-3 also expresses the numbers and the results of the operations in hexadecimal. It is worthwhile to familiarize yourself with the operations and results in hexadecimal since this is the form that will be used in programs. The experiments at the end of this chapter will provide additional practice. The operations may be summarized as follows:

- The result of an AND is one only if both bits are one.
- The result of an OR is zero only if both bits are zero.
- The result of an EOR is zero if the bits are alike; otherwise it is one.
- The complement of a one is zero and vice versa.

Table 4-3. Examples of 8-Bit Logical Operations ✗

AND	OR	EOR
· A = 1100 1100 = $CC B = 1010 1010 = $AA	+ A = 1100 1100 = $CC B = 1010 1010 = $AA	⊕ A = 1100 1100 = $CC B = 1010 1010 = $AA
C = 1000 1000 = $88	C = 1110 1110 = $EE **Complement** A = 1100 1100 = $CC $\overline{A}$ = 0011 0011 = $33	C = 0110 0110 = $66

✗ THM $\quad C = A \cdot B, \ D = A + B \Rightarrow C \leq A \ \& \ C \leq B \ \& \ D \geq A \ \& \ D \geq B$
FURTHERMORE, $C = A$ OR $D = A$ IFF $A = B$.

69

The preceding four statements are easy to remember, and with them truth tables such as the ones in Table 4-2 can be constructed.

Before turning to the 6502 logical instructions, we note that the instruction set does not include a COMPLEMENT operation. To produce the complement of an 8-bit number, the Exclusive OR operation (EOR) is performed with the number to be complemented and an 8-bit binary number having a one in every bit; that is, $FF. See Example 1. The result

$$A \oplus \$FF = \overline{A},$$

illustrated in Example 1, is general. It will be used to produce the complement of a number.

Example 1: Complementing an 8-Bit Number Using Exlusive OR Operation

Let A = 1100 1100 = $CC. Then

$$\oplus \quad \begin{array}{l} A = 1100\ 1100 = \$CC \\ 1111\ 1111 = \$FF \end{array}$$

$$A \oplus \$FF = 0011\ 0011 = \$33$$

and

$$A = 1100\ 1100 = \$CC$$

$$\overline{A} = 0011\ 0011 = \$33$$

showing that in this case A $\oplus$ $FF = $\overline{A}$.

AND, ORA, AND EOR INSTRUCTIONS

- The *AND* instruction forms the logical AND operation with a byte of data from memory and the contents of the accumulator. The result is stored in the accumulator. Symbolically $A \cdot M \to A$.
- The *ORA* instruction forms the logical OR operation with a byte of data from memory and the contents of the accumulator. The result is stored in the accumulator. Symbolically $A+M \to A$.
- The *EOR* instruction forms the Exclusive OR operation with a byte of data from memory and the contents of the accumulator. The result is stored in the accumulator. Symbolically $A \oplus M \to A$.

A variety of addressing modes are available for these instructions, including immediate, absolute, and zero-page. These modes were described in Chapter 2; you may want to review that material before proceeding to study the programs.

PROGRAMS TO DEMONSTRATE ORA, AND, AND EOR INSTRUCTIONS

In Examples 2, 3, and 4 we list programs that will demonstrate each of the three instructions, ORA, AND, and EOR. The two numbers to be used in the operations are stored at addresses $0000 and $0001. The result of the logical operation is stored in Port A so you can see the result on the Port A LEDs. It would be equally suitable to store the result in location $0003, which could then be examined after executing the program to find the result of the operation. These three programs will be used in the experiments to see what happens when specific binary numbers are ANDed, ORed, EORed, and complemented.

Example 2: Program to Demonstrate the ORA Instruction

Object: Find R+S and output the result to Port A.

```
$0000 = R
$0001 = S
$A001 = PAD
$A003 = PADD
0200   A9 FF      START    LDA   $FF      Set up Port A to be
0202   8D 03 A0            STA   PADD     an output port.
0205   A5 00               LDA   R        Get the first number.
0207   05 01               ORA   S        OR it with the second number.
0209   8D 01 A0            STA   PAD      Output the result to Port A.
020C   00                  BRK            Finish.
```

Example 3: Program to Demonstrate the AND Instruction

Object: Find R·S and output the result to Port A.

```
$0000 = R
$0001 = S
$1700 = PAD
$1701 = PADD
0200   A9 FF      START    LDA   $FF
0202   8D 01 17            STA   PADD
0205   A5 00               LDA   R        Get the first number.
0207   25 01               AND   S        AND it with the second number,
0209   8D 00 17            STA   PAD      then output the result to Port A.
020C   00                  BRK            Finish.
```

Example 4: Program to Demonstrate the EOR Instruction

Object: Find R ⊕ S and output the result to Port A.

```
$0000 = R
$0001 = S
$1700 = PAD
$1701 = PADD
0200   A9 FF      START    LDA   $FF
0202   8D 01 17            STA   PADD
0205   A5 00               LDA   R        Get the first number.
0207   45 01               EOR   S        EOR it with the second number.
0209   8D 00 17            STA   PAD      Output the result to Port A.
020C   00                  BRK            Finish.
```

USING ORA, AND, AND EOR INSTRUCTIONS TO CONTROL BIT VALUES

The logical operation instructions are frequently used to change specific bits in a memory location. These techniques are used quite frequently in programs. To illustrate, suppose that we wish to change PA0 (bit zero of Port A) to be an output pin, leaving all the other pins of Port A unaffected as far as their input/output status is concerned. Recall from Chapter 3 that the I/O status of a pin is determined by the corresponding bit value in the DDR. If PADD is the Port A DDR, then our task is to set bit zero of PADD to one, leaving the others unaffected. This may be accomplished by ORing PADD with 0000 0001 = $01. Note that $0 + X = X$ where X is any bit value. Thus, ORing with a zero *leaves* the corresponding bit unchanged. On the other hand $1 + X = 1$ where X is any bit value. Thus, ORing a bit with a one *insures* that a one will appear in that bit. Example 5 illustrates how bit six of a number may be set to a binary one using the OR operation. In the experiments we will use a program to demonstrate these ideas.

Example 5: Setting a Bit to a Binary One with the OR Operation

Given the 8-bit binary number 1001 1010 = $9A, modify it to have a one in bit six, but leave the other bits unchanged.

Solution: This may be accomplished by ORing the given number with the binary number 0100 0000 = $40, since

$$
\begin{array}{r}
1001\ 1010 = \$9A \\
+\ 0100\ 0000 = \$40 \\
\hline
=\ 1101\ 1010 = \$DA
\end{array}
$$

How can you set bit seven to binary one? Bit five? Bit four?

The AND operation is used to clear a bit to binary zero. Suppose we wish to clear bit seven to zero in the binary number 1100 1010 = $CA. This is accomplished by ANDing the given number with a number having a zero in the specified bit and binary ones in all the other bits. For the case under consideration the appropriate number is 0111 1111 = $7F. See Example 6 for details. Further practice in clearing bits will be given in the experiments.

Example 6: Clearing a Bit to Zero with the AND Operation

Show that bit seven in $CA may be cleared (set equal to zero) without affecting the other bit values by ANDing with $7F.

Solution:

$$
\begin{array}{r}
1100\ 1010 = \$CA \\
0111\ 1111 = \$7F \\
\hline
=\ 0100\ 1010 = \$4A
\end{array}
$$

How would you clear bit six? Bit five? Bit four?

The process of clearing one or more bits of a given number, leaving the other bits unchanged, is called *masking*. The cleared bits are said to be *masked*. For example, to *mask* the low-order nibble of an 8-bit number, it is ANDed with $F0 = 1111 0000. Masking the high-order nibble requires an AND operation with $0F = 0000 1111.

How would you mask the odd numbered bits of an 8-bit binary number?

To change a bit to its complement, that is, change a binary zero to a binary one and vice versa, perform an Exclusive-OR operation with ones in the bit positions to be changed. Given the number 1100 0101 = $C5, the lowest four bits can be changed to have opposite bit values by forming an Exclusive-OR with 0000 1111 = $0F. Try this, using the truth table in Table 4-2. The program in Example 4 will be used to demonstrate this in the experiments at the end of this chapter.

OTHER USES OF LOGICAL OPERATIONS

As another example of how the logical operation instructions might be used, suppose that a microcomputer is operating a business security system consisting of:

- A smoke detector that produces a logic one on PB7 (pin seven of Port B) if it detects smoke.
- A touch sensitive detector on the safe produces a logic zero on PB2 if the safe is touched.
- A switch connected to PB5 to disable the security system during opening hours.

The programs listed in Examples 7 through 9 illustrate how the Port B pins might be tested to check the detectors and control the system. Note that these programs are illustrative examples. A microprocessor based security system would have a much more complex program, including as segments some of the programs illustrated here.

Several of the ideas mentioned in the previous section are illustrated with the programs in Examples 7 and 8. For example, in the fourth instruction in the program in Example 7 the concept of masking is used to mask all of the bits of Port B except bit seven, since that is the one connected to the smoke detector. In the program in Example 8, the EOR $FF instruction complements the touch sensitive detector bit (and all the other bits) to produce a logic one when PB2 is at logic zero. Next, all the other bits except

Example 7: Program to Test the Logic Level of Bit Seven of an Input Port

Object: Make PA7 (pin seven of Port A) logic one if the smoke detector is on, otherwise output a logic zero to PA7.

0220	A9 FF	BEGIN	LDA	$FF	Load the Port A data direction
0222	8D 03 A0		STA	PADD	register to make Port A an output port.
0225	AD 00 A0	HERE	LDA	PBD	Read Port B, then AND the contents
0228	29 80		AND	$80	of Port B with $80 to mask all except
022A	8D 01 A0		STA	PAD	bit seven. Output result to Port A.
022D	4C 25 02		JMP	HERE	Loop to read Port B continuously.

Example 8: Program to Test the Logic Level of Bit Two of an Input Port

Object: Continue the program above, but also make PA2 equal to logic one if the safe is touched; that is, if PB2 is at logic zero.

0220	A9 FF	BEGIN	LDA	$FF	
0222	8D 03 A0		STA	PADD	
0225	AD 00 A0	HERE	LDA	PBD	
0228	29 80		AND	$80	Mask bits zero through six.
022A	8D 01 A0		STA	PAD	Output smoke detector level to Port A.
022D	AD 00 A0		LDA	PBD	Read Port B again, then complement its
0230	49 FF		EOR	$FF	contents by an Exclusive-OR with $FF.
0232	29 04		AND	$04	Mask all bits except bit two.
0234	0D 01 A0		ORA	PAD	OR the safe bit with the existing
0237	8D 01 A0		STA	PAD	contents of Port A. Result into Port A.
023A	4C 25 02		JMP	HERE	Loop to read the smoke detector and the safe inputs continuously.

bit two are masked by the AND $04 instruction, isolating the logic value of bit two, the touch sensitive detector input. If this bit is a one, then the next ORA PAD will set bit two of PAD to logic one without affecting the other bits. In other words, a bit has been set using an ORA instruction as described in the previous section. The STA PAD instruction outputs both the smoke detector information and the touch sensitive detector information to Port A. All of this logic is placed in a loop by the JMP HERE instruction.

Before proceeding, you are urged to study the programs until you understand each step. It is educational to "follow the accumulator." To illustrate, consider the program in Example 8, and assume that PB7 is at logic one (the smoke detector is on) and PB2 is at logic zero (the safe has been touched). The program should cause both PA7 and PA2 of Port A to be at logic one. Starting at HERE in the program, list the contents of the accumulator after the completion of each instruction, as shown in Table 4-4.

The program in Example 9 continues with the same theme. We would like the security system to be able to be disabled, for example

Table 4-4. Trace of the Accumulator Through the Program of Example 8

Step	Label	Accumulator	Comments
1	HERE	1XXX X0XX	PB7 is at logic one, PB2 is at logic zero. X = don't care.
2		1000 0000	Result of the AND with 1000 0000 = $80.
3		1000 0000	Result into Port A, turning PA7 on.
4		1XXX X0XX	PBD into the accumulator again.
5		0XXX X1XX	Result of EOR with $FF. All the bits are complemented.
6		0000 0100	Result of AND with $04.
7		1000 0100	Result of ORA with PAD containing 1000 0000.
8		1000 0100	Result into Port A, turning PA7 and PA2 on.
9		XXXX XXXX	Program jumps to HERE to read Port B again.

if the alarms have already sounded or something in the system is being repaired. Recall from our specifications that PB5 (pin five of Port B) is used to implement this function. A logic zero on PB5 disables the security system, and a logic one enables it. The interesting feature of this program is the use of the indirect jump instruction. Refer to the program and note that as long as PB5 is at logic zero, the JMP instruction will restart the program at $0200 because the contents of locations $0000 and $0001 are $00 and $02, respectively. But if PB5 is at logic one, then $20 is stored at the location whose address is $0000, and the program will jump to BEGIN. There may be more efficient ways of accomplishing our objective, but our purpose of illustrating several instructions has been achieved.

There are several other bit tests that are important in many applications. For example, in an event counter we may wish to test whether an input port bit received a negative pulse, that is, a logic one to logic-zero to logic-one transition. Or we may be interested in whether or not an input bit has changed its state. Programs such as this make use of branch instructions, and illustrations will be postponed until Chapter 6.

Example 9: Using an Indirect Jump Instruction to Control the Security System

Object: Read PB5 to see if the system should be disabled. A logic zero on PB5 disables it, and a logic one enables it.

$0000 = LOZ; contains the ADL for the indirect jump instruction.

$0001 = HIZ; contains the ADH for the indirect jump instruction.

0200	A9 00	ORIGIN	LDA	$00	Store $00 in Port A to start all
0202	8D 01 A0		STA	PAD	the outputs at logic zero.
0205	A9 FF		LDA	$FF	Initialize Port A to be an output
0207	8D 03 A0		STA	PADD	port by putting $FF into its DDR.
020A	A9 02		LDA	$02	Initialize indirect JMP by putting
020C	85 01		STA	HIZ	PCH of $02 in location $0001.
020E	AD 00 A0	HERE	LDA	PBD	Read Port B to get PB5 value.
0211	29 10		AND	$20	Mask all but bit five.
0213	85 00		STA	LOZ	Result into $0000 which will contain
0215	6C 00 00		JMP	(LOZ)	PCL for indirect JMP.
.			.		(Dotted locations are "don't care"
.			.		values.)
.			.		
0220	AD 00 A0		LDA	PBD	Check smoke detector.
0223	29 80		AND	$80	Mask bits zero through six.
0225	8D 01 A0		STA	PAD	Result into Port A.
0228	AD 00 A0		LDA	PBD	Now get result from the safe.
022B	49 FF		EOR	$FF	Complement it.
022D	29 04		AND	$04	Mask all bits except bit two.
022F	0D 01 A0		ORA	PAD	OR the safe bit with the existing
0232	8D 01 A0		STA	PAD	contents of Port A, then output the result.
0235	4C 0E 02		JMP	HERE	

INTRODUCTION TO THE EXPERIMENTS

Most of these experiments make use of the ASK I/O board. If you do not want to use this board, then store the results of the operations in any available memory location, to be examined when the program is finished. KIM-1 users should *always* begin the experiments by loading locations $17FE and $17FF with numbers $00 and $1C, respectively. Also, always make sure the single-step mode is not being used, unless you are specifically requested to use it.

EXPERIMENT NO. 1

Step 1

Load the program described in Example 2.

```
0200   A9 FF      START    LDA  $FF      Set up Port A to be
0202   8D 03 A0            STA  PADD     an output port.
0205   A5 00               LDA  R        Get the first number.
0207   05 01               ORA  S        OR it with the second number.
0209   8D 01 A0            STA  PAD      Output the result to Port A.
020C   00                  BRK           Finish.
```

Step 2

The numbers to be ORed are put into locations $0000 and $0001. We will use the program to learn some facts about the OR operation. For each pair of numbers given below, write the result obtained from ORing them. Express the result in hexadecimal.

$00 + $F0 = _____ $00 + $55 = _____
$00 + $0F = _____ $00 + $FF = _____

What do you conclude is the result of ORing any number with $00?

$FF + $34 = _____ $FF + $C5 = _____

What do you conclude is the result of ORing any number with $FF.

$7F + $80 = _____ $33 + $CC = _____
$A1 + $5E = _____ $EE + $11 = _____

The last four problems involve ORing a number with its complement. What do you conclude is the result of ORing a number with its complement?

EXPERIMENT NO. 2

Step 1

In this experiment we will experiment with setting bits to binary one. Load the following program. Leave the blank byte unchanged until STEP 2.

```
0200   A9 FF        START    LDA  $FF
0202   8D 01 17               STA  PADD
0205   A9 00                  LDA  $00
0207   8D 00 17               STA  PAD    Initialize Port A to $00.
020A   A9 __                  LDA  __     Load A with a byte.
020C   0D 00 17               ORA  PAD    OR it with Port A's contents.
020F   00                     BRK         Finish.
```

Step 2

Put a number in the blank byte, location $020B, that will set bit zero of Port A to logic one. Run the program to test your answer. What numbers must be loaded into the blank byte at location $020B to set the following bits to logic one? Fill in the following blanks with the correct hexadecimal numbers.

Bit Number	Byte	Bit Number	Byte	Bit Numbers	Byte
1	_____	4	_____	3, 1	_____
2	_____	6	_____	7, 0	_____
3	_____	7	_____	6, 3	_____

EXPERIMENT NO. 3

Step 1

Load the program described in Example 3. The numbers to be ANDed are put in locations $0000 and $0001. The result of the AND operation appears at Port A.

```
0200   A9 FF        START    LDA  $FF
0202   8D 01 17               STA  PADD
0205   A5 00                  LDA  R       Get the first number.
0207   25 01                  AND  S       AND it with the second number,
0209   8D 00 17               STA  PAD      then output the result to Port A.
020C   00                     BRK          Finish.
```

Step 2

For each pair of numbers given below, write the result obtained by ANDing them.

$$\$00 \cdot \$FF = \text{_____} \qquad \$00 \cdot \$37 = \text{_____}$$
$$\$00 \cdot \$7F = \text{_____} \qquad \$00 \cdot \$00 = \text{_____}$$

What do you conclude is the result of ANDing a number with $00?

$FF · $11 = _____ $FF · $5C = _____

What do you conclude is the result of ANDing a number with $FF?

$0F · $88 = _____ $F0 · $88 = _____

Can you describe the effect of an AND operation with $0F? $F0?

EXPERIMENT NO. 4

Step 1

Load this program. The blank byte will be filled in STEP 2.

```
0200   A9 FF      START    LDA  $FF
0202   8D 03 A0            STA  PADD
0205   8D 01 A0            STA  PAD     Set all the bits of Port A to logic
0208   A9 __               LDA  __      one.
020A   2D 01 A0            AND  PAD      AND with Contents of Port A.
020D   8D 01 A0            STA  PAD
0210   00                  BRK
```

Step 2

What number must you load in the blank byte, location $0209, to clear the following bits to logic zero? Fill in the blanks with hexadecimal numbers.

Bit Number	Byte	Bit Number	Byte	Bit Numbers	Byte
0	_____	5	_____	7,6,5,4	_____
1	_____	6	_____	3,2,1,0	_____
2	_____	7	_____	7,5,3,1	_____

Either find your answers using hand calculations and test your logic with the program, or use the program to find the answer.

EXPERIMENT NO. 5

Step 1

Load the program described in Example 4. The numbers to be EORed are stored in locations $0000 and $0001. The result is stored in Port A.

```
0200   A9 FF      START    LDA  $FF
0202   8D 01 17            STA  PADD
0205   A5 00               LDA  R      Get the first number.
0207   45 01               EOR  S      EOR it with the second number.
0209   8D 00 17            STA  PAD    Output the result to Port A.
020C   00                  BRK        Finish.
```

Step 2

Proceeding as in the previous experiments, use the program to find the following answers in hexadecimal.

$$\text{\$FF} \oplus \text{\$00} = \rule{2cm}{0.4pt} \qquad \text{\$FF} \oplus \text{\$C8} = \rule{2cm}{0.4pt}$$
$$\text{\$FF} \oplus \text{\$55} = \rule{2cm}{0.4pt} \qquad \text{\$FF} \oplus \text{\$81} = \rule{2cm}{0.4pt}$$

Compare your answers with the complements of the numbers $00, $55, $C8, and $81. What do you conclude is the result of EORing a number with $FF?

$$\text{\$C3} \oplus \text{\$3C} = \rule{2cm}{0.4pt} \qquad \text{\$A5} \oplus \text{\$5A} = \rule{2cm}{0.4pt}$$
$$\text{\$44} \oplus \text{\$BB} = \rule{2cm}{0.4pt} \qquad \text{\$82} \oplus \text{\$7D} = \rule{2cm}{0.4pt}$$

The numbers to be EORed in the last four problems are complements of each other. What do you conclude is the result of EORing a number with its complement?

$$\text{\$01} \oplus \text{\$0F} = \rule{2cm}{0.4pt} \qquad \text{\$80} \oplus \text{\$0F} = \rule{2cm}{0.4pt}$$
$$\text{\$02} \oplus \text{\$0F} = \rule{2cm}{0.4pt} \qquad \text{\$40} \oplus \text{\$0F} = \rule{2cm}{0.4pt}$$

From this last result, explain how you can change the bit value of a particular bit; that is, how can you complement any specific bit or group of bits (up to eight bits).

EXPERIMENT NO. 6

Step 1

The program listed below toggles PA0 (pin zero of Port A) using the EOR instruction. It illustrates how a specific bit, bit zero in this case, may be switched in its logic value. Load the following program.

```
0200  A9 FF     BEGIN   LDA $FF      Initialize the Port A
0202  8D 01 17          STA PADD     DDR.
0205  8D 00 17          STA PAD      Initialize all LEDs to glow.
0208  A9 01     HERE    LDA $01      Bit zero in A set to one.
020A  4D 00 17          EOR PAD      EOR with contents of PAD.
020D  8D 00 17          STA PAD      Result into PAD.
0210  4C 08 02          JMP HERE     Loop to toggle PA0.
```

Step 2

Execute the program. What do you observe? What can you do to see PA0 toggle?

Step 3

Single step the program if you want to see the PA0 LED toggle. At the same time, prepare a table similar to the one in Table 4-4, tracing the contents of the accumulator. At what instruction does the PA0 LED change its state? What effect does the EOR PAD instruction have on the other bits of PAD?

You have obtained a good deal of practice with the logical operations if you have completed the previous experiments. You may wish to experiment with the programs in Examples 7 through 9, the security system program. These programs were written so the ASK I/O board switches simulate the smoke detector, touch sensitive detector, and system-disable inputs, while the Port A LEDs simulate the output conditions. You might also try to write programs to prove these Boolean Algebra Theorems: $A \oplus B = (\overline{A} \cdot B) + (A \cdot \overline{B})$, $\overline{A+B} = \overline{A} \cdot \overline{B}$, and $\overline{A \cdot B} = \overline{A} + \overline{B}$.

CHAPTER 5

Arithmetic Operations

OBJECTIVES

At the completion of this chapter you should be able to:

- Understand some of the functions of the processor status register.
- Use the ADC, SBC, CLC, SEC, CLD, and SED instructions to add and subtract binary or decimal numbers. See Table 5-1 for a summary of these instructions.
- Do multibyte addition and subtraction.
- Understand and use twos complement arithmetic.
- Do elementary signed number arithmetic.

INTRODUCTION

Probably the least surprising fact about a microprocessor is that it performs some arithmetic operations. In this age of electronic calculators, one of the most surprising facts to the beginner is that microprocessors do not have multiply and divide instructions. In Chapter 7 we will see that short programs can be written to perform these operations; for the present, however, we will concentrate on addition and subtraction. In this chapter, "+" will mean "add." No confusion with the "OR" operation described in the previous chapter is likely to occur because the intended operation will be clear from its context.

6502 PROCESSOR STATUS REGISTER

Several of the 6502 internal registers have already been mentioned. A complete model of the 6502 register structure is shown

Table 5-1. Summary of Instructions and Op Codes
Introduced in Chapter 5

Instruction	Description	Addressing Mode			
		Immediate	Absolute	Zero-Page	Implied
ADC	Add Memory to Accumulator with Carry	69	6D	65	
SBC	Subtract Memory from Accumulator with Borrow	E9	ED	E5	
CLC	Clear the Carry Flag				18
SEC	Set the Carry Flag				38
CLD	Clear the Decimal Mode Flag				D8
SED	Set the Decimal Mode Flag				F8

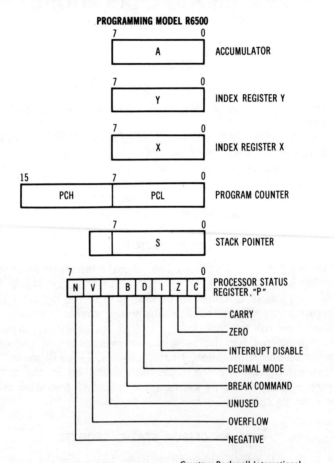

PROGRAMMING MODEL R6500

Courtesy Rockwell International

Fig. 5-1. Model of 6502 internal register structure.

in Fig. 5-1. The register of the greatest interest in the next few chapters will be the *processor status register,* symbolized by P.

Each bit of the P register is called a *status bit,* and each bit has its own identity, independent of the other status bits in the register. The status bits are frequently called *condition codes* or *flags* because they act as signals for certain conditions. We make the following definitions:

- If the carry flag is *set,* then there is a *one* in bit zero, the carry bit, of the P register.
- If the carry flag is *clear,* then there is a *zero* in bit zero, the carry bit, of the P register.

Similar definitions apply to other bits (or flags) of the P register. The carry idea is related to addition, as a recollection of elementary arithmetic will suggest. That it is also related to subtraction will become clear in the subsequent discussion.

FLAG MODIFICATION INSTRUCTIONS

Refer again to Table 5-1 for a summary of the CLC, SEC, CLD, and SED instructions. These single-byte instructions use *implied* addressing because their only effect is to change flags in the P register. No address is needed after the op code since the processor knows the P register is an internal register. Table 5-2 gives some additional information about the flag modification instructions. The circumstances under which these instructions are used will become apparent from the examples and programs. More details connected with the P register will be given in Chapter 6.

Table 5-2. Descriptions of CLC, SEC, CLD, and SED Instructions

Mnemonic	OP Code	Operation	Logical Description
CLC	18	Clear the Carry Flag	
SEC	38	Set the Carry Flag	
CLD	D8	Clear the Decimal Mode Flag	
SED	F8	Set the Decimal Mode Flag	

ADC INSTRUCTION

The truth table in Table 5-3 summarizes the binary addition operation for single-bit numbers. The sum of two single-bit numbers produces a result, R, and a carry, C. C is zero unless two binary ones were added. The carry, C, must be added to the next most significant bit in multibit operations such as the 8-bit operations performed by the 6502. Refer to Fig. 5-2 for a pictorial representation of an 8-bit addition that demonstrates the "carry" concept. Observe that the carry from the seventh bit is what appears in the carry flag. If there is a carry, then the carry flag in the processor status register is set to one. If there is no carry, then the C flag in the P register is cleared. The ADC (add with carry) instruction is described as follows.

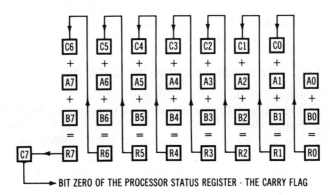

BIT ZERO OF THE PROCESSOR STATUS REGISTER - THE CARRY FLAG

Fig. 5-2. Diagram of an 8-bit binary addition, $A+B=R$ with Carry.

- The ADC instruction *adds* the contents of a memory location, the contents of the accumulator, and the carry flag. The result is stored in the accumulator. The carry flag is added as a one or as a zero.
- Symbolically the ADC instruction is written $A + M + C \rightarrow A$, where A and M contain 8-bit numbers but C is a 1-bit number.
- If the result of the addition operation exceeds $\$FF = 255_{10}$, then the carry flag is set; otherwise it is cleared.

In the examples that follow, the status of the carry flag *after* the operation is indicated to the right of the result. Example 1 illustrates how two binary numbers are added. A program to add these same two numbers is given in Example 2.

In Example 2, the carry flag was cleared prior to the ADC instruction because the state of the carry flag is generally unknown. It is always good practice to clear this flag before doing additions.

Table 5-3. Truth Table for Binary Addition (R is Result, C is Carry)

A	B	R	C	A + B = R
0	0	0	0	0 + 0 = 0 [C] = 0
0	1	1	0	0 + 1 = 1 [C] = 0
1	0	1	0	1 + 0 = 1 [C] = 0
1	1	0	1	1 + 1 = 0 [C] = 1

Example 1: Adding Two Binary Numbers with a Cleared Carry Flag

Add $85 and $21. Carry flag is clear.

Solution:
$$\begin{array}{rll} \$85 = & 1000\ 0101 & A \\ +\ \$21 = & 0010\ 0001 & M \\ +\ 0 = & 0 & C \\ \hline \$A6 = & 1010\ 0110 & A\ [C] = 0 \end{array}$$

Example 2: Program to Add Two Binary Numbers

Object: Add the two binary numbers represented by $85 and $21.

0200	D8	START	CLD		Clear the decimal flag to do the addition
0201	18		CLC		in the binary mode. Clear carry flag.
0202	A9 85		LDA	$85	Put $85 into the accumulator.
0204	69 21		ADC	$21	Add $21.
0206	85 00		STA	MEM	Store the result in MEM = $0000.
0208	00		BRK		Finish.

The result of the addition is stored in location $0000. It can be examined to see if the correct answer, $A6, was obtained. Example 3 is another illustration of a binary addition. It introduces a new complication. Observe that the answer to Example 3 should be $153, not $53. In this example, the carry flag indicated that the answer exceeded or *overflowed* the range of numbers that can be represented by eight bits. More than one byte is necessary to represent the answer. All is not lost, however, because the carry bit can be obtained and stored in a second byte. The program in Example 4 illustrates this. It is a simple modification of the program in Example 2. The numbers added are those from Example 3.

Example 3: Adding Two Binary Numbers that Cause an Overflow

Add $93 and $C0. Carry flag is clear.

Solution:
$$\begin{array}{rll} \$93 = & 1001\ 0011 & A \\ +\ \$C0 = & 1100\ 0000 & M \\ +\ 0 = & 0 & C \\ \hline \$53 & 0101\ 0011 & A\ [C] = 1 \end{array}$$

In Example 4 observe that the complete answer is now contained in two bytes, located at addresses $0000 and $0001 that contain the least-significant byte of the sum and the most-significant byte of the sum, respectively. That is, location $0000 should contain $53 and

Example 4: Program to Add Two Binary Numbers and Save the Carry Bit

Object: Add $93 to $C0 and save any carry from this sum in location $0001.

0200	D8	START	CLD		Clear the decimal flag.
0201	18		CLC		Clear the carry flag.
0202	A9 93		LDA	$93	Put $93 into A.
0204	69 C0		ADC	$C0	Add $C0.
0206	85 00		STA	SUMLO	Store the result in SUMLO = $0000.
0208	A9 00		LDA	$00	Put $00 into A.
020A	69 00		ADC	$00	Add $00 and the carry from the previous
020C	85 01		STA	SUMHI	addition. Store in SUMHI = $0001.
020E	00		BRK		Finish.

location $0001 should contain $01, giving $0153 as the correct answer. The program in Example 4 hints at our next problem, adding numbers that cannot be represented by a single byte.

MULTIBYTE ADDITION

In the event that the numbers to be added require more than one byte to represent them, or if the answer cannot be represented with a single byte, then so-called "multibyte arithmetic" is required. If two bytes are used to represent a number, we call this *double-precision* arithmetic. If three bytes are used to represent each number in an arithmetic operation, then we speak of *triple-precision* arithmetic. In Example 5, we illustrate a double-precision addition by adding $1234 to $05D2. The low-order bytes of the two numbers to be added are $34 and $D2, while the high-order bytes are $12 and $05. The low-order bytes are added first. Any carry from this addition is added to the sum of the high-order bytes. The program in Example 6 illustrates how double-precision arithmetic is done on the microcomputer. Again, it is absolutely essential that the double-precision addition be carried out in the order low-order byte first, high-order byte second, because any carry from the first addition must be included in the second.

Example 5: Adding Two-Byte Numbers

Solution: Add $1234 and $05D2. Carry flag is clear.

+	$12 = 0001 0010	A	+	$34 = 0011 0100	A
+	$05 = 0000 0101	M		$D2 = 1101 0010	M
	1 1	C (from $34 + $D2)		0 0	C
	$18 = 0001 1000	A [C] = 0		$06 = 0000 0110	A [C] = 1

Thus, $1234 + $05D2 = $1806.

Example 6: Program to Add Two Two-Byte Numbers

Object: Perform a double-precision addition using the memory assignments given here; that is, the numbers to be added are stored in these locations:

$0301 = HI1; high-order byte of number one
$0300 = LO1; low-order byte of number one

```
                $0303 = HI2; high-order byte of number two
                $0302 = LO2; low-order byte of number two
                $0305 = SHI; high-order byte of the sum
                $0304 = SLO; low-order byte of the sum
0200  D8        START   CLD         Clear decimal mode.
0201  18                CLC         Clear carry flag.
0202  AD 00 03          LDA LO1     Get low-order byte of Number 1.
0205  6D 02 03          ADC LO2     Add low-order byte of Number 2.
0208  8D 04 03          STA SLO     Result into low-order byte of sum.
020B  AD 01 03          LDA HI1     Get high-order byte of Number 1.
020E  6D 03 03          ADC HI2     Add high-order byte of Number 2 and carry,
0211  8D 05 03          STA SHI     if any, from previous sum. Result
0214  00                BRK         into high-order byte of sum. Finish.
```

DECIMAL ADDITION

The 6502 is also capable of adding decimal (base-ten) numbers. This is a useful feature because there are instances in which input and output data are decimal numbers. The most obvious situation is when human beings must input data to the microcomputer or read the output of the microcomputer. However, there are less obvious situations, such as when a decade counter is interfaced to a microcomputer, providing data in a binary-coded-decimal (bcd) representation, which must then be operated upon with decimal arithmetic instructions. Other interfacing problems also require decimal operations, since numerous instruments output data in the bcd form.

In the decimal mode, each digit is represented by four bits. The conversion scheme is shown in Table 5-4. Since each decimal digit requires four bits, a single byte of data represents two decimal digits; that is, a two-digit number. Thus, the numbers 0 to 99 are represented by a single byte in memory. If we were to add 48 to 43 and output the result to Port A, then since $48 + 43 = 91$, the answer appearing at Port A would be 1001 0001 because the bcd representation of nine is 1001 and the bcd representation of one is 0001. Refer to Table 5-4 to convert other numbers. If 48 were in some memory location, its binary representation would be 0100 1000, while 43 would be 0100 0011.

If the microcomputer is going to add two decimal numbers to obtain a decimal sum, then the decimal mode flag must be set with the SED instruction before the addition is carried out. In the decimal mode, the carry flag is set if the sum exceeds 99; otherwise it is cleared. The carry bit can be saved in exactly the same way illustrated in Example 4, and double-precision decimal arithmetic is accomplished in exactly the same way that we illustrated in Example 6, except that the decimal mode flag must be set.

A program to illustrate the decimal mode by adding 43 to 48 is shown in Example 7. Note that it is exactly like the program in

Table 5-4. Binary Representation (BCD) of Decimal Digits

Decimal Digit	Binary Code (BCD)
0	0000
1	0001
2	0010
3	0011
4	0100
5	0101
6	0110
7	0111
8	1000
9	1001

Example 2, except the decimal mode flag is set by the first instruction. Of course, other numbers can be added with the same program, provided the locations in the program that contain the numbers to be added are changed. The curious reader is sure to try some hexadecimal numbers like $CD + $3F in the decimal mode, just to see what happens.

Example 7: Program to Add Two Decimal Numbers

Object: Add the decimal numbers 43 and 48.

```
0200   F8        START   SED           Set the decimal mode flag.
0201   18                CLC           Clear the carry flag.
0202   A9 43             LDA  43       Put 43 into A.
0204   69 48             ADC  48       Add 48.
0206   85 00             STA  SUM      Result into SUM = $0000.
0208   00                BRK           Finish.
```

To summarize the use of the carry flag:

- The carry flag should be cleared with a CLC instruction prior to doing a sum, unless the state of the carry flag is known.
- The carry flag will be set if the result of a binary sum exceeds $FF = 255$; otherwise it will be cleared.
- The carry flag will be set if the result of a decimal sum exceeds 99; otherwise it will be cleared.
- The carry flag can be used to implement double-precision sums, either in the binary mode or the decimal mode, in the event that the numbers to be added or the sum cannot be represented by a single byte.

TWOS-COMPLEMENT ARITHMETIC

Microprocessors and other integrated circuits that handle digital information neither subtract nor recognize plus and minus signs. To understand how subtraction is performed and signed numbers

are handled, an understanding of *twos-complement* arithme
necessary. The purpose of this section is to provide the backg
information for subtraction and signed-number arithmetic, topics
that are covered in the next several sections. The ideas presented
here will also be useful in Chapter 6 when relative addressing and
branching are introduced.

Recall from elementary arithmetic that three numbers are involved
in subtraction: the *minuend,* the *subtrahend,* and the *difference.*
The *subtrahend,* s, is subtracted from the *minuend,* m, to form the
difference, d. We can express this in this way,

$$m - s = d \qquad (1)$$

Although most of us do not subtract using the technique that follows, it is possible to subtract by *adding* the *negative* of the subtrahend. This can be expressed as follows,

$$m - s = m + (-s) = d \qquad (2)$$

For example, $8 - 5 = 8 + (-5) = 3$.

On the computer, subtraction *is* performed with this technique,
namely adding the "negative" of the subtrahend to the minuend.

What is the negative of a binary number? For that matter, what
is the negative of any number? Mathematicians *define* the negative
of a number as that number which when added to the number, gives
zero. For example $5 + (-5) = 0$, so (-5) is the negative of $+5$. To
summarize, a *negative* number, $(-m)$ has the property that

$$m + (-m) = 0 \qquad (3)$$

In dealing with binary numbers in a computer, there is no way
of indicating a "$-$" sign to inform the computer that the number
is a negative number. However, it is possible to discover a relationship between binary numbers that is identical to Equation 3, and
that can be used to define the "negative" of a binary number. We
now prove this.

Suppose M is an 8-bit binary number. You can easily verify with
a few examples that

$$M + \overline{M} = \$FF \qquad (4)$$

For example, if $M = 1100\ 0101 = \$C5$, then $\overline{M} = 0011\ 1010 = \$3A$,
and $M + \overline{M} = 1111\ 1111 = \$FF$. This works every time. Since add-
ing one to $\$FF$ gives $\$00$ (with a one in the carry flag), we can also
state that

$$M + (\overline{M} + 1) = 0 \qquad (5)$$

This last equation fits the definition of a negative number perfectly,
and it requires no minus sign. Note that Equation 5 has exactly the

same form as Equation 3. In words, our conclusion is, the "negative" of an 8-bit binary number is found by complementing the number and adding one.

If M is an 8-bit binary number, then its "negative" is $(\overline{M} + 1)$. The number $(\overline{M} + 1)$ is not called the "negative" of M in computer language. Rather, it is called the *twos-complement* of M. But remember, it has all the properties of a negative number, and, therefore, it can be used in subtraction operations.

Recall that to subtract a number we may add the negative of the number. To *subtract* an 8-bit binary number M from another 8-bit binary number A, we can *add* the twos-complement of M, namely $(\overline{M} + 1)$. In symbols,

$$A - M = A + (\overline{M} + 1) \qquad (6)$$

Direct subtraction in a microprocessor, as the left-hand side of Equation 6 indicates, is difficult to implement. On the other hand, complementation of M followed by adding one, as the right-hand side of Equation 6 indicates, is relatively simple. Microprocessors implement subtraction by performing the right-hand side of Equation 6; that is, the computer reads the data from memory, complements it, adds it to the accumulator, then adds one to get the final result. Example 8 will help to illustrate these ideas.

Carefully study Example 8. Note that the addition operation is

Example 8: Subtraction by Twos-Complement Addition

Subtract $33 from $83 using twos-complement arithmetic.

Solution: Step 1—Complement $33.
$33 = 0011\ 0011,$ so $\overline{\$33} = 1100\ 1100 = \$CC$
Step 2—Add 1 to $\overline{\$33}$.
$\$CC + 1 = \$CD$
Step 3—Add $CD to $83.

$$
\begin{array}{rll}
  & \$83 = 1000\ 0011 & A \\
+ & \$CD = 1100\ 1101 & \overline{M} + 1 \\
\hline
  & \$50 = 0101\ 0000 & A\ [C] = 1
\end{array}
$$

identical to all the previous examples in this chapter. A sharp observer would also see that Step 2 in Example 8 would not be necessary *if* the carry flag had been set prior to the entire subtraction process. That is, to add $\overline{M} + 1$ we could *set* the carry flag and then simply add $\overline{M}$. Since the microprocessor already uses the carry flag to perform the addition operation, it is convenient to use it to form the twos-complement. If the carry flag, C, is set, then $(\overline{M} + C)$ is the twos-complement of M. Then our subtraction problem, $A - M$, may be expressed as

$$A - M = A + (\overline{M} + C) \qquad (7)$$

Study Equation 7 carefully. If C is set, as it should be if the subtraction operation is to work, then $\overline{C}$ is zero. But if $\overline{C}$ is zero, then Equation 7 could just as well be written as follows,

$$A - M - \overline{C} = A + (\overline{M} + C) \qquad (8)$$

Refer to the instruction set summary and observe that Equation 8 is the equivalent of the SBC instruction. We have arrived. If C is set, then Equation 8 gives $A - M$. If C is cleared, then Equation 8 gives $A - M$ with a one *borrowed* from it.

The SBC instruction may now be summarized as follows:

- The SBC instruction subtracts the contents of a memory location from the contents of the accumulator. The complement of the carry flag, $\overline{C}$, is also subtracted from the accumulator. The result is stored in the accumulator.
- Symbolically the SBC instruction is written $A - M - \overline{C} \rightarrow A$.
- If the result of the subtraction is less than zero in either the decimal mode or the binary mode, then the carry flag is *cleared*.

In a subtraction operation the carry flag serves the purpose of indicating a *borrow*. It may be helpful to think of the *complement* of the carry flag as a *borrow* flag.

Another example will help to illustrate these ideas. In Example 9 we subtract $62 from $AF, and in Example 10 we give a program to perform the same subtraction. In the program note that the carry flag is *set*. If we think of $\overline{C}$ as the borrow flag, then the borrow flag was cleared prior to the subtraction operation.

Example 9: Demonstration of Carry Flag in Twos-Complement Subtraction

Subtract $62 from $AF. Carry flag is set.

Solution: Step 1—Complement $62.

$62 = 0110\ 0010$, so $\overline{\$62} = 1001\ 1101 = \$9D$

Step 2—Add $9D to $AF with carry.

$AF = 1010\ 1111	A
$9D = 1001\ 1101	M
1	C
$4D = 0100\ 1101	A [C] = 1

Example 10: Program to Subtract Two Numbers

Object: Subtract $62 from $AF using the binary mode.

0200	D8	START	CLD	Clear the decimal mode flag.
0201	38		SEC	Set the carry (or clear the borrow) flag.
0202	A9 AF		LDA $AF	Minuend into A.
0204	E9 62		SBC $62	Subtract subtrahend.
0206	85 00		STA DIFF	Difference into DIFF = $0000.
0208	00		BRK	Finish.

Our last example in this section is a program to perform a double-precision, decimal mode subtraction. This program is given in Example 11. Compare this program to the double-precision, binary mode addition program given in Example 6. In Example 11 we set the decimal mode flag and we set the carry flag before doing the subtraction, while in Example 6 we cleared the decimal mode flag and cleared the carry flag before doing the addition. Both programs are easily extended to handle three or more bytes.

Example 11: Program to Subtract Two Two-Byte Numbers in the Decimal Mode

Object: Perform a double-precision subtraction in the decimal mode using the following memory assignments.

$0300 = LOM; low-order byte of the minuend
$0301 = HIM; high-order byte of the minuend
$0302 = LOS; low-order byte of the subtrahend
$0303 = HIS; high-order byte of the subtrahend
$0304 = LOD; low-order byte of the difference
$0305 = HID; high-order byte of the difference

0200	F8		START	SED		Set the decimal mode flag.
0201	38			SEC		Set the carry (clear the borrow) flag.
0202	AD	00 03		LDA	LOM	Low-order byte of the minuend into A.
0205	ED	02 03		SBC	LOS	Subtract subtrahend, low-order byte.
0208	8D	04 03		STA	LOD	Result into low-order byte of difference.
020B	AD	01 03		LDA	HIM	Get high-order byte of the minuend.
020E	ED	03 03		SBC	HIS	Minus the subtrahend and borrow, if any.
0211	8D	05 03		STA	HID	Result into difference, high-order byte.
0214	00			BRK		Finish.

SIGNED NUMBER ARITHMETIC

In the previous section we showed that the 8-bit number $(\overline{M} + 1)$ may be regarded as the "negative" of the 8-bit number M. The number $(\overline{M} + 1)$, called the twos-complement of M, has all the mathematical properties of negative numbers. For example, you know that in decimal arithmetic $+0 = -0 = 0$; that is, zero is neither minus nor plus. Is this true in the twos-complement arithmetic of binary numbers? Note that the complement of $00 is $FF, and $FF + 1 = $00, so the twos-complement (negative) of zero is zero as in the case of decimal numbers.

These and other facts have led the computer industry to adopt the following conventions for 8-bit *signed* binary numbers:

- 8-bit binary numbers represent the decimal integers from −128 to +127. Refer to Table 5-5 to observe the pattern of integers, binary numbers, and hexadecimal numbers.
- Bit seven is called the "*sign bit.*" A one in bit seven indicates a negative number. A zero in bit seven indicates a positive number. Refer again to Table 5-5 to observe this pattern.

With regard to signed hexadecimal representations,

Table 5-5. Twos Complement Representations of Numbers from −128 to +127

Number	Twos Complement	Hexadecimal
+127	0111 1111	$7F
•	•	•
•	•	•
•	•	•
+5	0000 0101	$05
+4	0000 0100	$04
+3	0000 0011	$03
+2	0000 0010	$02
+1	0000 0001	$01
0	0000 0000	$00
−1	1111 1111	$FF
−2	1111 1110	$FE
−3	1111 1101	$FD
−4	1111 1100	$FC
−5	1111 1011	$FB
•	•	•
•	•	•
•	•	•
−128	1000 0000	$80

- The numbers $00 to $7F represent the non-negative integers from zero to 127.
- The numbers $80 to $FF represent the negative integers from −128 to −1.

Table 5-6 gives the decimal integers corresponding to any hexadecimal number between $00 and $FF.

To handle numbers greater than +127 and less than −128, two or more bytes are used, but bit seven in the most significant byte remains as the sign bit. Thus, a 16-bit signed number could have values between +32767 and −32768.

Refer again to the P register model in Fig. 5-1. When *any* operation produces a one in bit seven, then the N flag of the P register is set. Thus, when an *add* or *subtract* operation sets the N flag, a negative result is indicated. On the other hand, if an add or subtract operation clears the N flag, a positive result is indicated. An *N* symbolizes negative. You will learn that the N flag has uses other than indicating the signs of binary numbers.

SIGNED ARITHMETIC AND OVERFLOW STATUS BIT

We begin with some examples of signed arithmetic. As in the case of ordinary addition and subtraction, the carry flag should be cleared before an addition and it should be set before a subtraction.

Table 5-6. Hexadecimal Equivalents of Signed Decimal Integers

Most Significant Hex Digit	Least Significant Hex Digit															
	0	**1**	**2**	**3**	**4**	**5**	**6**	**7**	**8**	**9**	**A**	**B**	**C**	**D**	**E**	**F**
0	0	1	2	3	4	5	6	7	8	9	10	11	12	13	14	15
1	16	17	18	19	20	21	22	23	24	25	26	27	28	29	30	31
2	32	33	34	35	36	37	38	39	40	41	42	43	44	45	46	47
3	48	49	50	51	52	53	54	55	56	57	58	59	60	61	62	63
4	64	65	66	67	68	69	70	71	72	73	74	75	76	77	78	79
5	80	81	82	83	84	85	86	87	88	89	90	91	92	93	94	95
6	96	97	98	99	100	101	102	103	104	105	106	107	108	109	110	111
7	112	113	114	115	116	117	118	119	120	121	122	123	124	125	126	127
8	−128	−127	−126	−125	−124	−123	−122	−121	−120	−119	−118	−117	−116	−115	−114	−113
9	−112	−111	−110	−109	−108	−107	−106	−105	−104	−103	−102	−101	−100	−99	−98	−97
A	−96	−95	−94	−93	−92	−91	−90	−89	−88	−87	−86	−85	−84	−83	−82	−81
B	−80	−79	−78	−77	−76	−75	−74	−73	−72	−71	−70	−69	−68	−67	−66	−65
C	−64	−63	−62	−61	−60	−59	−58	−57	−56	−55	−54	−53	−52	−51	−50	−49
D	−48	−47	−46	−45	−44	−43	−42	−41	−40	−39	−38	−37	−36	−35	−34	−33
E	−32	−31	−30	−29	−28	−27	−26	−25	−24	−23	−22	−21	−20	−19	−18	−17
F	−16	−15	−14	−13	−12	−11	−10	−9	−8	−7	−6	−5	−4	−3	−2	−1

Example 12: Adding Two Signed Numbers

Add +12 and −7. Carry flag is cleared.

Solution:
$$+ \quad +12 = 0000\ 1100 = \$0C \quad A$$
$$+ \quad -7 = 1111\ 1001 = \$F9 \quad M$$
$$ \quad 0 \qquad\qquad 0 \qquad 0 \quad C$$
$$\overline{+5 = 0000\ 0101 = \$05 \quad A\ [C] = 1}$$

Example 13: Subtracting Two Signed Numbers

Subtract −7 from −12. Carry flag is set. Recall that subtraction is implemented by adding the complement of the number and the carry flag.

Solution:
$$+ \quad -12 = 1111\ 0100 = \$F4 \quad A$$
$$+ \quad +6 = 0000\ 0110 = \$06 \quad \overline{M}$$
$$ \quad 1 \qquad\qquad 1 \qquad 1 \quad C$$
$$\overline{-5 = 1111\ 1011 = \$FB \quad A\ [C] = 0}$$

Refer to Table 5-6 to study these examples. You can obtain the hexadecimal representations of the signed integers from this table, and you can convert the hexadecimal numbers to binary numbers. In Example 13 the logic one in bit seven of the result indicates that the answer is negative in twos-complement form. To put the answer in a representation which is more easily recognized, form the twos-complement of the answer and use bit seven to inform the user that the answer is negative. The complement of 1111 1011 is 0000 0100. Adding one to form the twos-complement gives 0000 0101 = 5. The N flag was a logic one so the answer is −5. The N flag can be tested, as you will see later, to determine if the middle horizontal segment in a seven-segment digit should be lit, indicating a minus sign.

The carry bit has no meaning when *signed* (seven data bits, plus a sign bit) operations are performed. Remember that signed operations use values in the range of −128 to +127. Thus, when +127 and +127 are added, the result is 254 or 1111 1110. If we consider this result to be a signed number, it turns out to be negative (bit seven = logic one). This is incorrect. The entire 8-bit number represents the result, and the sign bit must be ignored. In this case, an *overflow* condition exists since the sum "overflowed" into the sign bit, giving an erroneous result. When the addition of two signed numbers exceeds +127, 0111 1111, the overflow status bit, V, is set to a logic one. Remember, the V flag is present as bit six in the P register.

Overflow may also occur when the sum of two negative numbers is less than −128. The microprocessor also recognizes this situation and sets the overflow flag. Overflow may occur when a negative number is subtracted from a positive number giving an answer greater than +127, or when a positive number is subtracted from a negative number giving an answer less than −128. The overflow flag will be set if any of these overflow conditions occurs; otherwise it will be cleared. Overflow cannot occur when a positive number is added to a negative number, a positive number is subtracted from another positive number, or when a negative number is subtracted from another negative number.

To the programmer using signed arithmetic, the overflow flag has the same meaning as the carry flag in ordinary arithmetic. The programmer who is not using signed arithmetic may ignore the overflow flag and the sign in bit seven. Finally, the overflow flag may be cleared with the CLV instruction, op code B8.

Since the overflow flag does not directly enter a sum or difference like the carry flag does, signed arithmetic programs require *branch instructions* to inform the user of an overflow or to correct for the result. Branch instructions will be introduced in Chapter 6.

EXPERIMENT NO. 1

Step 1

Load and execute the program in Example 2. What answer is found at the address $0000?

0200	D8	START	CLD		Clear the decimal flag.
0201	18		CLC		Clear the carry flag.
0202	A9 85		LDA	$85	$85 into A.
0204	69 21		ADC	$21	Add $21.
0206	85 00		STA	MEM	Sum into location $0000.
0208	00		BRK		

(After the program has run you should find $A6 in location $0000.)

Step 2

What answer would you get if the carry flag had not been cleared before the program was executed? Try this by exchanging the CLC instruction for an SEC instruction in the preceding listing.

Step 3

Use the program to add the following numbers:

$7F + $80 = _____ $33 + $CC = _____
$A1 + $5E = _____ $EE + $11 = _____

These four problems involve adding a number to its complement. What do you conclude is the result of adding a number to its complement if the carry flag is cleared? If the carry flag is set?

Step 4

How could you modify the program to add two numbers located at addresses $0001 and $0002?

(Change the immediate addressing modes of the LDA and ADC instructions to their zero-page modes. Reference location $0001 with the LDA instruction and reference location $0002 with the ADC instruction.)

EXPERIMENT NO. 2

Step 1

Load the program in Example 6.

Object: Perform a double-precision addition using the memory assignments given here; that is, the numbers to be added are stored in these locations:

$0301 = HI1; high-order byte of number one
$0300 = LO1; low-order byte of number one
$0303 = HI2; high-order byte of number two
$0302 = LO2; low-order byte of number two
$0305 = SHI; high-order byte of the sum
$0304 = SLO; low-order byte of the sum

0200	D8		START	CLD		Clear decimal mode.
0201	18			CLC		Clear carry flag.
0202	AD	00 03		LDA	LO1	Get low-order byte of Number 1.
0205	6D	02 03		ADC	LO2	Add low-order byte of Number 2.
0208	8D	04 03		STA	SLO	Result into low-order byte of sum.
020B	AD	01 03		LDA	HI1	Get high-order byte of Number 1.
020E	6D	03 03		ADC	HI2	Add high-order byte of Number 2 and carry,
0211	8D	05 03		STA	SHI	if any, from previous sum. Result
0214	00			BRK		into high-order byte of sum. Finish.

Step 2

Use this program to add $1234 to $05D2. Where should these numbers be stored? Where will the answer be? What is it?

Step 3

Single step the program while it is adding the numbers in step 2, noting the contents of the processor status register after each instruction. What is the status of the carry flag after the CLC instruction? After the first ADC instruction? After the second ADC instruction? Note that the carry flag is bit zero of the P register. If the carry flag is clear, then the number in the P register is even. If the carry flag is set, then the number in the P register is odd.

EXPERIMENT NO. 3

Step 1

Load the following program. It is intended to add the contents of location $0000 to the contents of $0001. The result is loaded into Port A, an output port, so the answer can be observed on the Port A LEDs on the I/O board. We use the PA7 (bit seven of Port A) LED as the sign of the result in the sense that + = OFF, − = ON.

0200	A9 FF	ORIGIN	LDA $FF	Put $FF in the Port A DDR.
0202	8D 01 17		STA PADD	
0205	D8		CLD	Clear decimal mode flag.
0206	18	AGN	CLC	Clear carry flag.
0207	A5 00		LDA LOZ1	Get addend from LOZ1.
0209	25 00		ADC LOZ2	Add contents of LOZ2.
020B	8D 00 17		STA PAD	Result into Port A.
020E	4C 06 02		JMP AGN	Loop to add again.

Load the program using the op codes. Do not use an assembler.

Step 2

Put $22 in location $0000. Enter $20 in location $0001. Run the program. What do you expect to observe on the Port A LEDs?

(You should observe a $42 = 0100 0010. Do you get this answer?)

Step 3

There is a bug in the program since it does not give the correct answer. We obtained a $20 at Port A, which is clearly not the sum of $22 and $20. Start the program over and use the single-step mode. Examine the contents of the accumulator after each instruction is executed. Compare this to what you know should be in the accumulator. Where is the bug? Correct the program.

(Instruction ADC has an op code of $65, not $25.)

Step 4

Add the following numbers by changing the contents of locations $0000 and $0001. The numbers are in base ten, and must be converted to hexadecimal. Negative numbers must be converted to their twos-complement representation using Table 5-6. In each case try to indicate the state of the Port A LEDs before doing the problem. Remember, the PA7 LED is the sign indicator. Write down the sum and the status of the overflow bit, bit six of the P register.

$$6 + 2 = \underline{\hspace{1cm}}\ \underline{\hspace{1cm}} \qquad\qquad 120 + 8 = \underline{\hspace{1cm}}\ \underline{\hspace{1cm}}$$

$$6 + (-2) = \underline{\hspace{1cm}}\ \underline{\hspace{1cm}} \qquad -120 + (-8) = \underline{\hspace{1cm}}\ \underline{\hspace{1cm}}$$

$$6 + (-8) = \underline{\hspace{1cm}}\ \underline{\hspace{1cm}} \qquad -120 + (-9) = \underline{\hspace{1cm}}\ \underline{\hspace{1cm}}$$

Remember that negative answers are in twos-complement form. Use Table 5-6 to convert back to a decimal number before filling in the blank.

EXPERIMENT NO. 4

Step 1

Write a program to do signed binary subtraction. The program in Experiment No. 3 is a good starting point. Then repeat the problems in Step 4 of Experiment 3, assuming they are subtraction problems instead of addition problems. Be sure to write down the status of the overflow bit after each operation. Use the PA7 LED to indicate the sign of the result.

EXPERIMENT NO. 5

Step 1

Try writing a program to do signed arithmetic in the decimal mode.

CHAPTER 6

Branches and Loops

OBJECTIVES

At the completion of this chapter you should be able to:

- Use the branch instructions BCC, BCS, BEQ, BNE, BMI, BPL, BVS, and BVC. See Table 6-1 for a summary.
- Understand and use the compare instructions CMP, CPX, and CPY.
- Use the BIT test instruction.
- Write programs that test for pulses and logic transitions at input ports.

INTRODUCTION

The ability of the microprocessor to "make decisions" based on external or internal conditions makes it the powerful tool that it is. Although each decision is admittedly simple (for example, if the logic level on an input pin is one, change an output pin to logic zero; otherwise leave it unchanged), a set of decisions can be used to monitor or control complex operations. This chapter deals with the decision making instructions. We will begin by describing all of the instructions given in Table 6-1 in the order *branch instructions, comparison instructions,* and the *bit test instruction.* Then we will describe a number of programs that make use of these instructions.

BRANCH INSTRUCTIONS

The *branch* instructions *test* the values of specific bits in the *processor status register* (P register). If the value or *condition* tested

Table 6-1. Summary of Instructions Introduced in Chapter 6

Instruction	Description	Immediate	Absolute	Zero-Page	Relative
		Addressing Mode			
BCC	Branch on Carry Clear				90
BCS	Branch on Carry Set				B0
BEQ	Branch on Result Zero				F0
BNE	Branch on Result not Zero				D0
BMI	Branch on Negative Result				30
BPL	Branch on Non-Negative Result				10
BVS	Branch on Overflow Set				70
BVC	Branch on Overflow Clear				50
CMP	Compare Memory and Ac-cumulator	C9	CD	C5	
CPX	Compare Memory and X Reg-ister	E0	EC	E4	
CPY	Compare Memory and Y Reg-ister	C0	CC	C4	
BIT	Test Bits in Memory with Accumulator		2C	24	

is met, the program counter is altered, causing the program to jump to an instruction other than the one following the branch instruction. If the *condition* tested *is not met,* the program continues in sequence. The branch instructions are

- BCS—Branch on Carry Set: The branch occurs if the carry flag (bit zero of the P register) is set ($C = 1$).
- BCC—Branch on Carry Clear: The branch occurs if the carry flag is clear ($C = 0$).
- BEQ—Branch on Result Equal Zero: The branch occurs if the zero flag (bit one of the P register) is set ($Z = 1$).

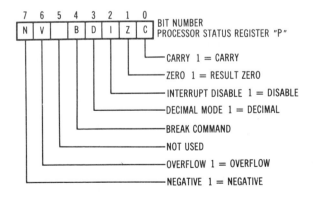

Fig. 6-1. Processor Status Register model.

- BNE—Branch on Result Not Equal Zero: The branch occurs if the zero flag is clear $(Z = 0)$.
- BMI—Branch on Minus: The branch occurs if the negative flag (bit seven of the P register) is set $(N = 1)$.
- BPL—Branch on Plus: The branch occurs if the negative flag is clear $(N = 0)$.
- BVS—Branch on Overflow Set: The branch occurs if the overflow flag (bit six of the P register) is set $(V = 1)$.
- BVC—Branch on Overflow Clear: The branch occurs if the overflow flag is clear $(V = 0)$.

The processor status register (P register) is illustrated in Fig. 6-1. Before describing the flow of a program during a branch, we review how some of the flags in the P register are set and cleared.

MODIFYING THE PROCESSOR STATUS REGISTER

The execution of some of the instructions in the 6502 instruction set may cause the contents of the processor status register to be modified. For example, in Chapter 5 we learned that the ADC instruction will result in the N flag being cleared if the sum has a zero in bit seven, and it will result in the C flag being set if the addition produces a carry. If the result of the ADC instruction were $00, then the Z flag would be set; otherwise it would be cleared.

These examples serve to illustrate the fact that the flags in the P register are set or cleared by the outcomes of various instructions. The instruction set summary in Table 2-3 indicates the *flags* or *condition codes* which each instruction modifies. Two examples will clarify this further. Refer to the Condition Code column of the instruction set summary in Table 2-3.

- How does the LDA instruction modify the P register? Referring to the instruction set summary, it is seen that the LDA instruction affects both the N flag and the Z flag. The checks ($\sqrt{}$) in the N and Z columns indicate this fact. If the byte transferred from memory to the accumulator has a one in bit seven, then the N flag will be set; otherwise it will be cleared. If the byte transferred is zero, then the Z flag will be set; otherwise it will be cleared.
- How does the DEC instruction modify the P register? The DEC instruction modifies the N and Z flags. If the DEC instruction produces a zero in a memory location, then the Z flag will be set; otherwise it will be cleared. If as a result of the DEC instruction a memory location has a one placed in bit seven, then the N flag will be set; otherwise it will be cleared.

It should be clear that during the course of a program the flags are constantly changing. Consequently, the programmer cannot test the effect of an LDA instruction on the Z flag with a BEQ instruction unless the BEQ instruction immediately follows the LDA instruction in the program, or he is absolutely sure that no intervening instructions affected the Z flag.

BRANCHING

Fig. 6-2 flowcharts the branch instruction sequence. Let us discuss it in terms of a particular example, say the "branch on plus" BPL instruction. In a program, the BPL instruction would be written:

```
0230    10 07    BPL OFFSET
0232    __ __    NEXT INSTRUCTION
```

where we have chosen an arbitrary location for the instruction. The BPL op code is $10, and we have also arbitrarily chosen a value of $07 for OFFSET. The second byte of the instruction, OFFSET, is

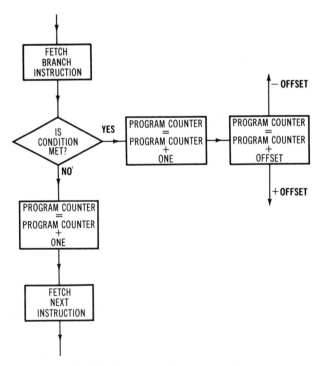

Fig. 6-2. Flowchart of Branch Instruction.

also referred to in Fig. 6-2. What happens when the program reaches the BPL instruction is described as follows.

- If the N flag is one, corresponding to a negative result, then the condition tested *is not met,* and program execution will continue with the NEXT INSTRUCTION in the program sequence.
- If the N flag is zero, corresponding to a positive result, then the condition tested *is met,* and program execution will continue at the instruction located at PROGRAM COUNTER + OFFSET.

Thus, if the N flag is one, the program will continue with the instruction located at $0232, but if the N flag is zero, the program will continue with the instruction located at $0232 + $07 = $0239.

There are three *important* points to be made at this time: refer both to the preceding example being discussed and Fig. 6-2.

- OFFSET is interpreted by the microprocessor as a twos-complement number. It therefore may be positive, zero, or negative. That is the reason the "OFFSET arrows" in Fig. 6-2 go both ways.
- The first reference to the program counter in Fig. 6-2 refers to the second byte of the branch instruction. In this example, this is $0231.
- Because the 6502 program counter is incremented *during* the time that it is reading the second byte of the branch instruction, the OFFSET will actually be added to the value of the program counter for the instruction *following* the branch instruction. In the example, this gives $0232 + $07 = $0239 as the new value of the program counter if the branch condition is met.

The offset is always *relative* to the location of the op code that follows the branch instruction. This use of the word "relative" is the reason that the addressing mode of the branch instructions is called *relative addressing.*

Example 1: Calculation of a Forward Branch

A branch instruction is stored in locations $AF25 and $AF26. The branch offset is $34. What is the location of the next instruction that will be executed by the microprocessor?

Solution: If the branch condition is not met, then the next instruction in the normal program sequence will be executed. It is located in memory immediately above the branch instruction, so its op code will be in location $AF27. If the branch condition is met, then the next instruction to be executed will be in $AF27 + $34 = $AF5B.

A simple rule to find small offsets in the forward direction is to count bytes 0, 1, 2, . . . in hexadecimal beginning with the location of the instruction following the branch instruction and ending with

A branch instruction is stored in locations $AF25 and $AF26. If the branch condition is met, it is desired that the program branch *backward* to an instruction whose op code is in $AF20. What offset should be used with the branch instruction?

Solution: The offset is relative to location $AF27. Therefore, OFFSET = $AF20 − $AF27 = −7 = $F9 in twos-complement notation. The twos-complement conversion may be facilitated with Table 5-6.

the location of the op code to be executed, if the branch condition is met. For backward branches, start counting 0, FF, FE, FD, . . . backward from the op code following the branch instruction to the op code to be executed, if the branch condition is met.

COMPARISON INSTRUCTIONS

The CMP, CPX, and CPY instructions are used to *compare* two numbers to see which, if either, is the larger. None of the 6502 registers other than the processor status register are changed, nor are any memory locations altered by the comparison instructions. Their only effect is to set or clear flags in the P register, based upon the result of the comparison operation. We describe the CMP instruction in detail.

- CMP—Compare the contents of the accumulator with the contents of a memory location: symbolically, A − M.
- If $A \geq M$, then C is set; otherwise it is cleared.
- If $A = M$, then Z is set; otherwise it is cleared.
- If the operation A − M leaves a one in bit seven of the result, then N is set; otherwise it is cleared.

Even though the operation is symbolized as a subtraction, the actual operation is "invisible," since no result, other than the changed flags, is observed.

The CPX and CPY instructions are identical to the CMP instruction in all respects, except that they compare the X and Y registers with the contents of a memory location. Replace the accumulator in

Example 3: Illustration of a CMP Operation

Assume $CF is in the accumulator, A, and $3E is in the memory location, M. What flags will be set by the CMP instruction?

Solution: Since $CF $\geq$ $3E, the C flag will be *set*. Since $CF $\neq$ $3E, the Z flag will be *cleared*. Since $CF − $3E = $81, the result of the subtraction has a one in bit seven, and the N flag will be *set*.

Example 4: Illustration of a CPX Operation

Assume the X register contains $80 and M contains $A0. What flags will be set by the CPX instruction?

Solution: Since $80 $<$ $A0, the C flag will be *cleared*. Since $80 $\neq$ $A0, the Z flag will be *cleared*. Since $80 − $A0 = $E0, the result of the subtraction has a one in bit seven; therefore, the N flag will be *set*.

the description of the CMP instruction with the X register, and you have a description of the CPX instruction. Likewise, the contents of the Y register may be compared to a memory location. Two comparison operations are illustrated in Examples 3 and 4.

BIT TEST INSTRUCTION

The BIT instruction is another test instruction that affects only the P register. It transfers bits seven and six of the memory location that it references to the corresponding bits in the P register. It also forms a logical AND between the contents of the accumulator, A, and the memory location, M, which it references. If the result of the AND operation is zero, then the Z flag is set; otherwise it is cleared. The logical description of the BIT instruction is $A \cdot M$, $M_7 \rightarrow N$, and $M_6 \rightarrow V$. As in the case of the comparison instructions, the result of ANDing the contents of the accumulator with the contents of a memory location $(A \cdot M)$ is "invisible." In fact, the AND operation caused by the BIT instruction serves only to set or clear the Z (zero) flag. The notation $M_7 \rightarrow N$ and $M_6 \rightarrow V$ means that bit seven of the memory location referenced by the BIT instruction is transferred to the N flag of the P register, and bit six of the same memory location is transferred to the V flag of the P register. Example 5 illustrates how a bit test works.

Example 5: Explanation of a BIT Test

If A contains $02 and M contains $43, how will the flags in the P register be changed by a BIT instruction that references M?

Solution: $A \cdot M = 02, so the result of the AND operation is not zero. The Z flag will be cleared. Since $43 = 0100\ 0011$, $M_7 = 0$ and $M_6 = 1$. Therefore, the N flag will be cleared and the V flag will be set.

The program examples that follow illustrate the use of the comparison and bit test instructions. Flowcharts are used to show some of the steps. The reader should study carefully the programs, program comments, and the flowcharts to become familiar with the instructions introduced in this chapter.

The first program example is given in Example 6. It detects negative pulses on pin PB0 (bit zero of Port B) and counts these pulses. A flowchart of the program, starting with the instruction labeled BACK, is shown in Fig. 6-3. Two branch instructions are used in this program; both of them are backward branches. Referring to the flowchart and the program, observe that the program will stay in the first loop as long as the voltage level at pin PB0 is at logic one. As soon as the logic level changes to zero, the program proceeds to the next loop. Thus, the first part of the program detects a logic-one to logic-zero transition. The program loops in the second loop as

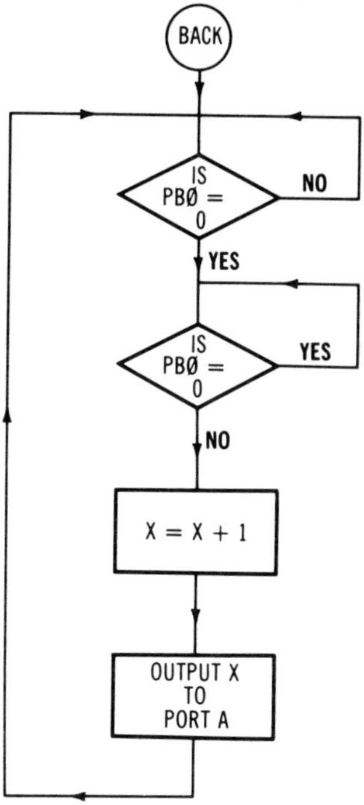

BACK

IS PBØ = 0 → NO

YES

IS PBØ = 0 → YES

NO

X = X + 1

OUTPUT X TO PORT A

Fig. 6-3. Flowchart for Example 6. Train of negative pulses will be counted and the answer stored in Port A.

long as the voltage level at pin PB0 is at logic zero. It emerges from the loop to increment X and store this new value of X in Port A after a complete negative pulse has occurred. It then jumps back to BACK to wait for the next negative pulse. The two mask operations (AND $01) were used to ensure that only bit zero of Port B entered the decision making process.

Example 6: Program to Detect and Count Negative Pulses

Object: Write a program to count negative pulses on pin PB0 of Port B. The pulses consist of transitions from logic one, to logic zero, and back to logic one. The X register will be used to count the pulses, and the result will be stored in Port A, an output port.

0200	A2 00	BEGIN	LDX	$00	Initialize X to zero.
0202	A9 FF		LDA	$FF	Set data direction register of Port A
0204	8D 03 A0		STA	PADD	so it is an output port.
0207	AD 00 A0	BACK	LDA	PBD	Read Port B.
020A	29 01		AND	$01	Mask all bits except PB0.
020C	D0 F9		BNE	BACK	Branch backwards $F9 = −7 bytes if
020E	AD 00 A0	LOOP	LDA	PBD	PB0 ≠ 0; otherwise read Port B.
0211	29 01		AND	$01	Mask all bits except PB0.
0213	F0 F9		BEQ	LOOP	If PB0 = 0, branch back to LOOP.
0215	E8		INX		Pulse detected, increment X.
0216	8E 01 A0		STX	PAD	Result into Port A.
0219	4C 07 02		JMP	BACK	Return to count more pulses.

For what can the program in Example 6 be used? Its application to event counting, for example, nuclear disintegrations, arrival of customers in a queue, or other events, and frequency counting should be obvious. A more elaborate procedure than the INX instruction and X register storage would be necessary to keep track of the number of pulses, but the most important ingredients are there. The ability of two loops in the program to detect logic level transitions could also be used in event timing. If a phototransistor or photoresistor circuit produced a negative transition at pin PB0 when the light was interrupted, then the first loop in the program in Example 6 could be used to hold the timer until the light was interrupted, the timing could begin at this transition, and the timing could end when the interruption ceased; or, both loops could be used to detect a negative pulse, after which timing would begin. Any application that involves detecting logic level transitions and carrying out some function as a result can use the ideas in this program.

A similar program, but one that makes use of pin PB7 of Port B, will illustrate some simplification in programming and several of the other instructions introduced in this chapter. This program is given in Example 7. It detects and counts positive pulses on pin seven of Port B, PB7. The BIT instruction is used to set or clear the N flag depending on the logic level on PB7. The BPL and BMI instructions produce the required branches. The program loops in the BACK loop until PB7 goes to logic one. It loops in the LOOP loop until PB7 goes back to logic zero when the positive pulse is complete. Then the pulse is counted by the INX instruction. Note also that the BPL and BMI instructions have nothing to do with arithmetic operations in this example.

Example 7: Program to Detect and Count Positive Pulses

Object: Count positive pulses at pin PB7 of Port B.

0300	A2 00	BEGIN	LDX $00	Initialize X to zero.
0302	A9 FF		LDA $FF	Set data direction register
0304	8D 03 A0		STA PADD	of Port A to output condition.
0307	2C 00 A0	BACK	BIT PBD	Test bit seven of Port B.
030A	10 FB		BPL BACK	If bit seven is zero, branch back.
030C	2C 00 A0	LOOP	BIT PBD	Test bit seven again.
030F	30 FB		BMI LOOP	If PB7 = 1, branch to LOOP.
0311	E8		INX	Count pulse.
0312	8E 01 A0		STX PAD	Result of count into Port A.
0315	4C 07 03		JMP BACK	Return to count pulses.

ASCII TO HEXADECIMAL CONVERSION

One of the most common ways of communicating with the microcomputer is by means of an ASCII-encoded keyboard. The ASCII is a binary code used to represent upper-case and lower-case alphabetic characters, numerals, punctuation marks, and other symbols and control codes. For example, when the "A" key on an ASCII keyboard is pressed, a 0100 0001 appears at its output, representing an upper case "A." If we assume that the keyboard output is another location in memory, as it would be in any memory mapped I/O system such as that on the 6502, then the hexadecimal value for "A," a $41, would appear in the memory location of the keyboard.

With this background, consider the following problem. Assume a key representing one of the 16 hexadecimal characters, 0–9 and A–F, is pressed. Its ASCII representation appears in a certain memory location. Convert the contents of this location into the binary (or hexadecimal) number it represents. Store it in the low-order nibble of another location. The program in Example 8 will do this. Refer to Table 6-2 for the ASCII representations of the hexadecimal characters. Refer also to Fig. 6-4 to see a flowchart of the program. Note that for numbers less than $0A, the numerical value may be obtained from the ASCII value by subtracting $30, while for ASCII numbers larger than $41 the numerical value may be obtained from the ASCII number by subtracting $37.

Most of the details of the program in Example 8 are illustrated by the flowchart in Fig. 6-4, but additional comments may be necessary. Observe that a CMP instruction was used. The only type of branch not explicitly covered in the flowchart is the BCS OVER. At that point in the program, the conversion for the hex numerals

Table 6-2. ASCII Representations of Hexadecimal Characters

Hexadecimal Character	ASCII Representation (Hexadecimal)	Numerical Value	
		(Binary)	(Hexadecimal)
0	30	0000 0000	$00
1	31	0000 0001	$01
2	32	0000 0010	$02
3	33	0000 0011	$03
4	34	0000 0100	$04
5	35	0000 0101	$05
6	36	0000 0110	$06
7	37	0000 0111	$07
8	38	0000 1000	$08
9	39	0000 1001	$09
A	41	0000 1010	$0A
B	42	0000 1011	$0B
C	43	0000 1100	$0C
D	44	0000 1101	$0D
E	45	0000 1110	$0E
F	46	0000 1111	$0F

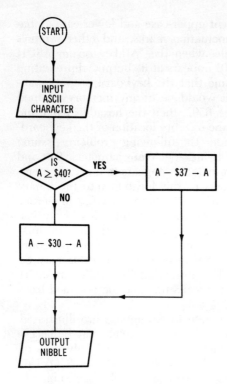

Fig. 6-4. Flowchart of program to convert Hex ASCII character to Hex Nibble.

zero through nine has been completed. If the program continued in sequence, the conversion for the numerals A–F would follow, ruining the previous result. Some means to jump around this conversion is necessary. A JMP OVER instruction could have been used where the BCS OVER instruction is. However, since the carry

Example 8: ASCII to Hexadecimal Conversion

Object: Change hex character represented in ASCII to hex number, and store this number in the low-order nibble of Port A. Read the ASCII character from $0300.

0230	D8		ORIGIN	CLD		Clear decimal mode.
0231	A9	FF		LDA	$FF	Make Port A an output port by
0233	8D	03 AO		STA	PADD	loading $FF into its DDR.
0236	AD	00 03		LDA	ASCI	Get ASCII from $0300.
0239	C9	40		CMP	$40	Compare it with $40. If it is
						larger, then it represents a numeral
023B	B0	05		BCS	ARND	A–F. Branch to subtract $37.
023D	38			SEC		Clear borrow flag.
023E	E9	30		SBC	$30	For numerals 1–9, subtract $30.
0240	B0	02		BCS	OVER	Jump to store result in PAD.
0242	E9	37	ARND	SBC	$37	
0244	8D	01 AO	OVER	STA	PAD	Result into Port A.
0247	00			BRK		

110

flag will be set after the subtraction, we used a BCS instead. The advantage of this is that the program may be *relocated* in memory with no changes in the program bytes. With a JMP instruction, the address following the JMP instruction would have to be changed to relocate the program. It is good programming practice to make programs relocatable whenever possible. Relocatable programs are easy for other programmers to add to their microcomputer systems because they can place the program in any available memory locations with no programming changes. Such programs are also easier to put on PROMs, programmable read-only memory chips.

USING BRANCH INSTRUCTIONS FOR TIME DELAYS

Another use of branch instructions is to form delay loops or timing loops. For example, in data logging applications it may be required that a specific interval elapse between the times at which the points are to be logged. A delay loop may be used to provide this interval. Consider the following set of instructions:

```
          LDX $10
LOOP      DEX
          BNE LOOP.
```

A flowchart of this loop is given in Fig. 6-5. Note that the program repeats the DEX and BNE instructions until X = 0; then it will proceed to the instruction following the BNE instruction.

To calculate the time required to execute the delay loop, we refer to the instruction set summary in Table 2-3 that lists the number of

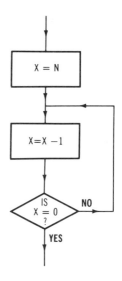

Fig. 6-5. Simple delay loop. N is number chosen by the programmer to determine time interval for delay.

clock cycles for each instruction. Our cycle account proceeds as follows:

- LDX instruction—2 cycles.
- DEX instruction—2 cycles each time, $10 times $= 32_{10}$ cycles.
- BNE instruction—3 cycles each time the branch is taken, $0F times $= 45_{10}$ cycles.
- BNE instruction—2 cycles when the branch is not taken, $01 times $= 2$ cycles.
- Total time of loop $= 2 + 32 + 45 + 2 = 81$ cycles.

For a clock cycle of one microsecond, the loop will take 81 microseconds. If NX is the number loaded into the X register, then the loop time in clock cycles is $(5NX + 1)$. Remember, NX must be converted to hexadecimal before using it in a program. If T is the required number of clock cycles, and if $(T - 1)$ is a multiple of five, then NX may be chosen to produce the *exact* interval that is desired. In all other cases, the time interval will be an approximation to the interval desired.

To create longer delays, delay loops may be nested. The program in Example 9 illustrates this technique. A flowchart is shown in Fig. 6-6. After each delay the number at Port A will be incremented so that the programmer may have a visible effect of the various delays if the Port A output pins operate LEDs. In this program, if NX is the number loaded into the X register and NY is the number loaded into the Y register, then the total delay time in the program in Example 9 is,

$$NX(5NY + 6) + 1$$

clock cycles. Note that if NY is 199_{10} then NX controls the number of one millisecond (approximately) intervals. The error, assuming the clock frequency is 1 megahertz, is $(NX + 1)$ microseconds. In Chapter 10, we will see that *interval timers* are much easier to use for delay loops and timing intervals.

Example 9: Nested Delay Loop Program

Object: Demonstrate the delay produced by a delay loop nested in another delay loop. After each delay increment Port A. Start with $FF in Port A.

0250	A9 FF	BEGIN	LDA $FF	Initialize Port A data direction
0252	8D 03 A0		STA PADD	register.
0255	8D 01 A0		STA PAD	
0258	A2 FF	BACK	LDX $FF	Set delay of X loop.
025A	A0 FF	LOOPX	LDY $FF	Set delay of Y loop.
025C	88	LOOPY	DEY	Decrement Y.
025D	D0 FD		BNE LOOPY	Branch back if Y $\neq$ 0.
025F	CA		DEX	Decrement X.
0260	D0 F8		BNE LOOPX	Branch back if X $\neq$ 0.
0262	EE 01 A0		INC PAD	Increment Port A.
0265	4C 58 02		JMP BACK	Repeat entire process.

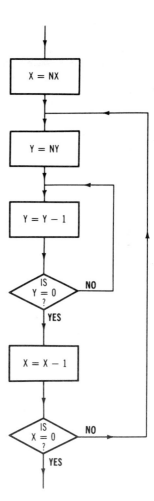

Fig. 6-6. Nested delay loop flowchart.

The last program to illustrate the instructions introduced in this chapter is a utility program to convert negative hexadecimal numbers into their twos-complement representations. A hexadecimal number is entered in Port B by means of the switches connected to the Port B pins. If the number is a negative number, PB7 is set to logic one; otherwise it is set to logic zero. The program converts negative numbers to their twos-complement representations, and outputs the result to the LEDs connected to the Port A outputs. Positive numbers will also be written to Port A. Bit six of Port B is masked because it has different values in the AIM 65, SYM-1, and KIM-1 microcomputers. You can refer to Table 5-6 to check your answers. The program is given in Example 10.

Object: Convert a negative number input at Port B to its twos-complement representation. Output the result to the Port A LEDs.

0270	A9 FF	START	LDA $FF	Set up data direction register
0272	8D 03 A0		STA PADD	for Port A.
0275	AD 00 A0	HERE	LDA PBD	Read Port B.
0278	29 BF		AND $BF	Mask bit six.
027A	10 05		BPL BRNCH	If positive, branch to output.
027C	49 FF		EOR $FF	Perform complement
027E	38		SEC	Set carry flag to add one to
027F	68 80		ADC $80	get twos-complement. Also add
0281	8D 01 A0	BRNCH	STA PAD	a one in bit seven. Result in PAD.
0284	4C 75 02		JMP HERE	Return to get other numbers.

INTRODUCTION TO THE EXPERIMENTS

The experiments make use of the I/O board introduced in a
previous chapter. All the experiments make use of the programs
previously listed in this chapter, and these were written in terms of
the SYM-1 and AIM 65 I/O port addresses. KIM-1 owners must
make the appropriate changes. The branch instructions are among
the most important for the potential user to understand. The programs and experiments should be studied carefully.

EXPERIMENT NO. 1

Step 1

Load the program in Example 6.

0200	A2 00	BEGIN	LDX $00	Initialize X to zero.
0202	A9 FF		LDA $FF	Set data direction register of Port A
0204	8D 03 A0		STA PADD	so it is an output port.
0207	AD 00 A0	BACK	LDA PBD	Read Port B.
020A	29 01		AND $01	Mask all bits except PB0.
020C	D0 F9		BNE BACK	Branch backwards $F9 = −7 bytes if
				PB0 ≠ 0; otherwise read Port B.
020E	AD 00 A0	LOOP	LDA PBD	Mask all bits except PB0.
0211	29 01		AND $01	Mask all bits except PB0.
0213	F0 F9		BEQ LOOP	If PB0 = 0, branch back to LOOP.
0215	E8		INX	Pulse detected, increment X.
0216	8E 01 A0		STX PAD	Result into Port A.
0219	4C 07 02		JMP BACK	Return to count more pulses.

Step 2

Place the PB0 switch in the logic-one position (up).

Step 3

Run the program. Toggle PB0 off and on. What do you observe?

(We observed that the PA0 LED lighted after one toggle.)

Step 4

Continue to toggle PB0. What do you observe?

[We observed that the LEDs at Port A count (in binary) the number of times PB0 was toggled from logic one to logic zero and back to logic one.]

Step 5

How would you modify the program to count positive pulses instead of negative pulses?

(Exchange the BNE and BEQ instructions to count positive pulses instead of negative pulses. Try this change and toggle PB0.)

Step 6

What is the shortest single pulse which the program will detect?

(If a negative pulse occurred after the first LDA PBD instruction, and if it were of such a duration that it returned to logic one before the completion of the same LDA instruction at the beginning of the second loop, then it would be missed. Thus, if it were shorter than the LDA, AND, and BNE instruction, then it might be missed. This amounts to nine clock cycles. If a clock cycle is 1 microsecond, then we may conservatively estimate the minimum detectable pulse width as 10 microseconds.)

EXPERIMENT NO. 2

Step 1

Load the program in Example 7.

0300	A2 00	BEGIN	LDX $00	Initialize X to zero.
0302	A9 FF		LDA $FF	Set data direction register
0304	8D 03 A0		STA PADD	of Port A to output condition.
0307	2C 00 A0	BACK	BIT PBD	Test bit seven of Port B.
030A	10 FB		BPL BACK	If bit seven is zero, branch back.
030C	2C 00 A0	LOOP	BIT PBD	Test bit seven again.
030F	30 FB		BMI LOOP	If PB7= 1, branch to LOOP.
0311	E8		INX	Count pulse.
0312	8E 01 A0		STX PAD	Result of count into Port A.
0315	4C 07 03		JMP BACK	Return to count pulses.

Step 2

Place the PB7 switch in the logic-zero position.

Step 3

Run the program. What do you expect to observe on the Port A LEDs if PB7 is switched to logic one?

(Offhand, one would expect to see a zero in Port A because the program should be in the second loop, waiting for a logic-one to logic-zero transition.)

Step 4

Switch PB7 to logic one. What do you observe at Port A?

[We observed a five (in binary) at Port A. You may not observe an identical result.]

Step 5

Switch PB7 back to logic zero, completing the positive pulse. What do you observe at Port A?

(We observed a six at Port A. You may not get the same answer. The explanation of these results lies in the fact that the switch on PB0 has been electronically "debounced." The PB7 switch is not debounced, and the mechanical bouncing of the switch produces several pulses when only one is intended. For some applications debouncing is not necessary, for others it is very important. Debouncing can also be done with a suitable delay loop in the program, but this will increase the minimum detectable pulse width. As a challenge you may want to experiment with delay loops in this experiment until you have solved the switch bounce problem.)

Step 6

Construct a flowchart for this program.

EXPERIMENT NO. 3

Step 1

Load the program in Example 8.

0230	D8	ORIGIN	CLD		Clear decimal mode.
0231	A9 FF		LDA	$FF	Make Port A an output port by
0233	8D 03 A0		STA	PADD	loading $FF into its DDR.
0236	AD 00 03		LDA	ASCI	Get ASCII from $0300.
0239	C9 40		CMP	$40	Compare it with $40. If it
023B	B0 05		BCS	ARND	is larger, then it represents a
023D	38		SEC		numeral A–F. Subtract $37.
023E	E9 37		SBC	$30	Otherwise, subtract $30.
0240	B0 02		BCS	OVER	Jump to output result.
0242	E9 37	ARND	SBC	$37	
0244	8D 01 A0	OVER	STA	PAD	Result into Port A.
0247	00		BRK		

Step 2

Put an ASCII representation ($30–$39 or $41–$46) for a hexa-decimal numeral (0–9 or A–F) in location $0300. (See Table 6-2.)

Step 3

Run the program. The corresponding hexadecimal number should appear at Port A in a binary representation. Try several numbers, some for hex numbers 0–9 and others for hex numerals A–F.

Step 4

What happens if you have an ASCII character other than one which represents 0–9 or A–F in location $0300? How could you "trap" this error or inform the user an input error has been made?

(You might start by comparing the number input by the keyboard with $30 and $46, because if it is outside this range then it is not an ASCII character for a hexadecimal numeral. This is a challenging problem; good luck with it.)

EXPERIMENT NO. 4

Step 1

Load and execute the program in Example 9.

0250	A9 FF	BEGIN	LDA	$FF	Initialize Port A data direction
0252	8D 03 A0		STA	PADD	register.
0255	8D 01 A0		STA	PAD	
0258	A2 FF	BACK	LDX	$FF	Set delay of X loop.
025A	A0 FF	LOOPX	LDY	$FF	Set delay of Y loop.
025C	88	LOOPY	DEY		Decrement Y.
025D	D0 FD		BNE	LOOPY	Branch back if Y ≠ 0.
025F	CA		DEX		Decrement X.
0260	D0 F8		BNE	LOOPX	Branch back if X ≠ 0.
0262	EE 01 A0		INC	PAD	Increment Port A.
0265	4C 58 02		JMP	BACK	Repeat entire process.

Step 2

What do you observe at Port A?

(We observed that the Port A LEDs count upward in binary. The delay loops allow enough time to see the counting take place.)

Step 3

Change the program byte at $0259 to $01. What do you observe?

(We observed that the low-order LEDs blinked too quickly to see them in their off state.)

Step 4

Change the program byte at $025B to $01. What do you observe?

(We observed that all the LEDs blinked too fast for the eye to perceive.)

Step 5

Experiment with different values in $0259 and $025B to vary the time of the loop. Calculate the delays first, then confirm them using the formulas in the text.

EXPERIMENT NO. 5

Step 1

Write a program that loops until any logic transition occurs at PB7. Output the transitions detected to Port A. The following program segment will serve as a hint.

```
START    LDY  PBD      Read Port B.
LOOP     TYA           Transfer Y to A.
         EOR  PBD
         BPL  LOOP
         INX
         STX  PAD
         JMP  START
```

Step 2

Be sure to include statements to initialize Port A to be an output port.

Step 3

Test your program using the PB7 input switch. How many transitions does it detect for one switch change?

EXPERIMENT NO. 6

Step 1

Using the program in Example 10, find the twos complement representations of the following decimal numbers. Enter the sign in bit seven of Port B, convert these numbers to binary, then run the program. Check your answers by hand computations. −1, −5, −10, −13, −28, −35, −47.

CHAPTER 7

Register-Shift Instructions

OBJECTIVES

At the completion of this chapter you should be able to:

- Understand and use the ASL, LSR, ROL, and ROR instructions. See Table 7-1 for a summary of these instructions.
- Multiply 4-bit and 8-bit numbers.
- Output the contents of the accumulator as two ASCII characters.
- Convert a two-digit base-ten number to its hexadecimal equivalent.
- Convert a two-digit hexadecimal number to its base-ten equivalent.

INTRODUCTION

With the addition of the register-shift instructions to the collection of instructions already learned, you can begin to write more complex programs. In fact, after these instructions are learned, you have the ability to use the great majority of instructions in the 6502 instruction set. The complexity of the programs in the latter part of this chapter will begin to reflect this. The need to have the ability to shift bits left or right in a memory location is less obvious than the need for arithmetic and logical operations. We can only promise that the value of these instructions will become obvious as we proceed.

Table 7-1. Summary of Instructions Introduced in Chapter 7

Instruction	Description	Addressing Mode		
		Absolute	Zero-Page	Accumulator
ASL	Shift Left One Bit	0E	06	0A
ROL	Rotate Left One Bit	2E	26	2A
LSR	Shift Right One Bit	4E	46	4A
ROR	Rotate Right One Bit	6E	66	6A

GETTING ACQUAINTED WITH REGISTER-SHIFT INSTRUCTIONS

The effect of the ASL, LSR, ROL, and ROR instructions is as easily demonstrated as it is explained. We shall define each instruction and then give a short program that will demonstrate the effect of each instruction, using the LEDs at Port A. Diagrams illustrating the effect of each instruction on the contents of the memory location upon which it operates are shown in Fig. 7-1. We begin with the definitions.

- ASL—Arithmetic Shift Left: Each bit in the memory location or register upon which this instruction operates is *shifted* to the *left*. That is, bit zero becomes bit one, bit one becomes bit two, . . . , bit six becomes bit seven, and *bit seven becomes the carry flag*. A zero is shifted into bit zero.
- LSR—Logical Shift Right: This instruction is similar to the ASL instruction, except the bits are *shifted right*. A zero is shifted into bit seven, and *bit zero is shifted into the carry flag*.
- ROL—Rotate One Bit Left: The contents of the memory location or register upon which this instruction operates are shifted to the left as in the ASL instruction, except that the carry flag is shifted into bit zero. Since bit seven is shifted into the carry flag, successive ROL instructions simply *rotate* the bits left. A succession of nine ROL instructions will leave the contents of the location and the carry flag unchanged.
- ROR—Rotate One Bit Right: The ROR instruction is exactly like the ROL instruction, except the bits are *rotated right*. Bit zero goes into the carry flag, and the carry flag is moved into bit seven.

These definitions should be studied in conjunction with Fig. 7-1.

A program to demonstrate each of these instructions using the single-step mode of the microcomputer is provided in Example 1. This program will demonstrate all four register-shift instructions by replacing the byte represented by a blank in Example 1 with the appropriate instruction, as follows:

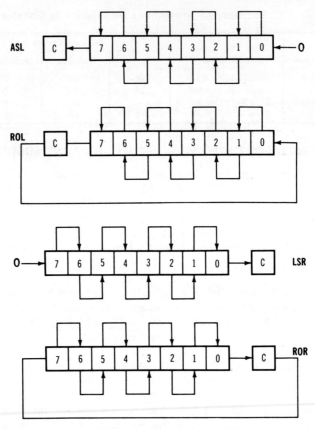

Fig. 7-1. Diagrams of Register-Shift Instructions.

- ASL—Op Code $0E
- LSR—Op Code $4E
- ROL—Op Code $2E
- ROR—Op Code $6E

Referring to the demonstration program in Example 1, assume that the ASL instruction is to be demonstrated, and that its op code has been entered as the byte at location $020D. The program reads the data at Port B. Suppose the Port B input switches are set to $01. Then, after execution of the STA PAD instruction, the PA0 LED will be lit. The ASL PAD instruction will cause a zero to be shifted into bit zero of Port A, while the one that was originally in bit zero is shifted into bit one, lighting the PA1 LED. The program repeatedly jumps to this ASL PAD instruction, causing the light to shift from PA0 to PA1, to PA2, . . . , and finally into the PA7 LED. The next time the ASL PAD instruction is executed, the logic one will be shifted into the carry flag, and all the LEDs will go out. Repeating this same demonstration with precisely the same conditions but using an ROL instruction will make the PA0 LED light again after nine ROL instructions. *Of course,* the program is to be executed in the *single-step* mode, or all of these events will happen too quickly for the eye to perceive. Changing the data that is input at Port B changes the effects observed, but not the basic ideas. Try rotating or shifting a $F in the high-order nibble to the low-order nibble.

Example 1: Register-Shift Instructions Demonstration Program

Object: Demonstrate the effect of the ASL, LSR, ROL, and ROR instructions on a memory location (Port A, an output port).

0200	A9 FF	START	LDA	$FF	Set up the Port A DDR by loading
0202	8D 01 17		STA	PADD	$FF into PADD.
0205	AD 02 17		LDA	PBD	Get some data from Port B.
0208	29 BF		AND	$BF	Mask bit six for the SYM-1 and KIM-1.
020A	8D 00 17		STA	PAD	Output the resulting number to Port A.
020D	___ 00 17	LOOP	___	PAD	Shift the contents of Port A, and put the
0210	4C 0D 02		JMP	LOOP	instruction in a loop for repeated shifts.

Before turning to some application programs that make use of the register-shift instructions, we note that a new addressing mode, called *accumulator addressing,* was introduced in Table 7-1. In this addressing mode, which only the register-shift instructions have, it is the contents of the accumulator that are shifted or rotated. The ASL, LSR, ROL, and ROR instructions are single-byte instructions when used in the accumulator addressing mode because no extra bytes to identify a memory location are necessary.

The ASL, LSR, ROL, and ROR instructions together with the INC and DEC instructions are collectively known as *read-modify-write* instructions. The reason for this name lies in the fact that the microprocessor must first *read* the contents of a memory location, *modify* it in accordance with the instruction, and then *write* the modified byte of data back to its original location.

A 4-BIT MULTIPLICATION PROGRAM

To illustrate an application for the ASL and LSR instructions, we will write a program to multiply two 4-bit numbers. To begin, note that the largest number represented by four bits is 15_{10}; consequently the largest product that is possible is $15 \cdot 15 = 225$, so the product will fit in one 8-bit memory location. To understand the program one must understand a typical binary multiplication problem, and one is illustrated in Example 2. Note the structural similarity between binary multiplication and your recollection (pre-electronic-calculator era) of elementary decimal multiplication.

Multiply $A by $9.

Solution: $A = 1010   Multiplicand 10_{10}
          $9 = 1001   Multiplier 9_{10}

          $5A   1010 ⎫ 90_{10}
                 0000 ⎪
                 0000 ⎬ Add to obtain product.
                 1010 ⎭

          $5A = 1011010   Product

The important point to recognize in the calculation of Example 2 is that the multiplicand appears in the sum for every *one* in the multiplier. With one exception, it is *shifted* to the left before it is added to obtain the product. For every zero in the multiplier, a zero is summed. The appearance of the *"left-shifted"* multiplicands, added to find the product, suggests a procedure for performing the multiplication with a computer program. The flowchart of Fig. 7-2 is our starting point. The 8-bit locations will be used for the 4-bit numbers, but they will have four leading zeros. The multiplicand will be symbolized by MCND, the multiplier by MLTP, and the product by PROD.

The multiplication program is listed in Example 3. The LSR MLTP instruction *shifts* the multiplier bit zero into the carry flag.

- If this sets the carry flag, then the multiplicand is added to the location containing the product.
- If this clears the carry flag, then nothing is added to the product.

Next, the multiplicand is shifted left. The next bit of the multiplier is tested by shifting the multiplier right, moving it into the carry

Example 3: A 4-Bit Multiplication Program

Object: Multiply two 4-bit numbers
$0000 = MCND; Multiplicand
$0001 = MLTP; Multiplier
$0003 = PROD; Product

0200	D8	START	CLD		Clear decimal mode.
0201	A9 00		LDA	$00	Clear location of product by
0203	85 03		STA	PROD	storing $00 in PROD.
0205	46 00	AGAN	LSR	MLTP	Shift multiplier right to test
0207	90 07		BCC	ARND	for zero or one in carry flag. If
0209	18		CLC		zero branch to shift multiplicand
020A	A5 01		LDA	MCND	left for next test. If one, add
020C	65 03		ADC	PROD	multiplicand to obtain product.
020E	85 03		STA	PROD	
0210	06 01	ARND	ASL	MCND	Shift multiplicand left for next sum.
0212	F0 04		BEQ	DONE	If multiplicand is zero, operation
0214	A5 00		LDA	MLTP	is finished. Same for multiplier.
0216	D0 ED		BNE	AGAN	Otherwise branch back to sum again.
0218	00	DONE	BRK		

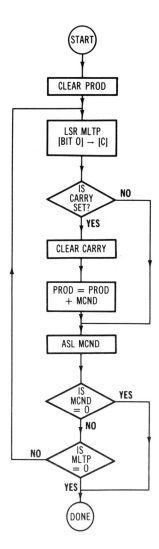

Fig. 7-2. Flowchart of 4-Bit Multiplication Program. MCND = Multiplicand, MLTP = Multiplier, and PROD = Product.

flag. The "left-shifted" multiplicand is added, if the carry flag is set; otherwise it is not added. The entire process is repeated until either the multiplicand or the multiplier have become zero by virtue of having had zeros shifted into successive bit positions.

The reader should study this program and the following 8-bit multiplication program for their use of the ASL and LSR instructions. These programs are not necessarily intended to provide you with ready-made multiplication routines.

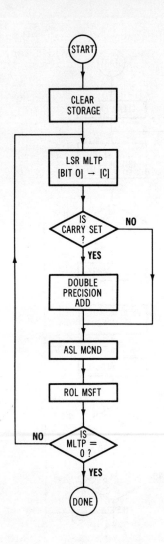

Fig. 7-3. Flowchart of 8-Bit Multiplication.
MCND = Multiplicand, MLTP = Multiplier,
MSFT = Left-Shifted Multiplicand.

AN 8-BIT MULTIPLICATION PROGRAM

The maximum product of two 8-bit numbers is $FF · $FF = $FE01; thus 16 bits are required for the answer. Recall that in our example of a 4-bit multiplication, the multiplicand was successively shifted left and added to form the final product. To shift an 8-bit multiplicand left requires that it be shifted into a new memory location. This is accomplished by the ASL MCND and ROL MSFT instructions in the flowchart of the 8-bit multiplication shown in Fig. 7-3. Note that an ASL operation shifts bit seven of the multiplicand (MCND) into the carry flag, and that an ROL takes the carry flag and moves it into bit zero of what we call MSFT for "multiplicand shifted." With these two instructions, the contents of one location may be successively shifted into another location. The product takes two locations (PRDLO and PRDHI), and a double-precision addition is required. Refer to Fig. 7-3 and Example 4 for further details.

One final note: In the flowcharts for the multiplication programs and in other flowcharts that follow, the bracket notation, "[ ]", will occasionally be used. In microcomputer literature the brackets are read "*contents of.*" That is, "[ALFA]" means "the *contents of* the memory location symbolized by "ALFA," or more simply, "the contents of ALFA." Thus, in the flowcharts "[Bit 0]" means "the contents of bit zero." The bracket notation will be used whenever it clarifies the actual events that are taking place.

Example 4: An 8-Bit Multiplication Program

Object: Multiply two 8-bit numbers.
$0000 = MCND; Multiplicand
$0001 = MSFT; Multiplicand is shifted into this location
$0002 = MLTP; Multiplier
$0003 = PRDLO; Low-order byte of the product
$0004 = PRDHI; High-order byte of the product

0200	D8	START	CLD	Clear decimal mode.
0201	A9 00		LDA $00	Clear storage locations for
0203	85 01		STA MSFT	MSFT, PRDLO, and PRDHI.
0205	85 03		STA PRDLO	
0207	85 04		STA PRDHI	
0209	46 02	AGAN	LSR MLTP	Shift multiplier right into carry
020B	90 0D		BCC ARND	flag to test for one or zero.
020D	18		CLC	Clear carry flag for addition.
020E	A5 00		LDA MCND	Get multiplicand.
0210	65 03		ADC PRDLO	Add to low-order byte of product.
0212	83 03		STA PRDLO	Store result.
0214	A5 01		LDA MSFT	Get shifted multiplicand.
0216	65 04		ADC PRDHI	Add to high-order byte of product.
0218	85 04		STA PRDHI	Store result.
021A	06 00		ASL MCND	Shift multiplicand and roll it
021C	26 01		ROL MSFT	into MSFT (multiplicand shifted).
021E	A5 02		LDA MLTP	If multiplier is not zero then the
0220	D0 E7		BNE AGAN	job is not finished: branch back again.
0222	00	DONE	BRK	Otherwise job is finished.

HEX TO ASCII

In Chapter 6, we listed a program to convert an ASCII character to a hexadecimal number. A related problem is the conversion of an 8-bit binary number represented by two hexadecimal numerals to their equivalent ASCII characters. To communicate with the user, the microcomputer usually has a means of displaying the contents of 8-bit memory locations and registers. The KIM-1 and SYM-1 use seven-segment LED displays, while the AIM 65 has 16-segment alphanumeric displays. The latter requires ASCII. Since displays, printers, and other output devices that represent hexadecimal numerals using ASCII characters are common, we take as a programming problem the conversion of the contents of the accumulator (or any memory location) to two hexadecimal numerals (0–9 and A–F) represented with ASCII. A simple description of this problem is "Two Hex Numerals to ASCII," or more simply "HEX to ASCII."

The contents of a memory location or register may be divided into a high-order nibble and a low-order nibble, each represented by one hex numeral. Refer to Table 6-2 for the ASCII representations of the hexadecimal numerals. To distinguish whether a nibble is to be represented by a hex numeral 0–9 rather than a hex numeral A–F, $A is subtracted from the nibble, and:

- If the result of the subtraction is non-negative, the carry flag is set; the value of the nibble must be represented by a numeral A–F.
- If the subtraction gives a negative result, the carry flag is clear; the nibble must be represented by a numeral 0–9.

The following were also used in the program to convert the contents of the accumulator to two ASCII characters:

- A nibble having a hex value $0–$9 is converted to ASCII by adding $30.
- A nibble having a hex value $A–$F is converted to ASCII by adding $37.

Since the program first subtracts $A from a nibble to test if it is a numeral 0–9 or A–F, the two points above are modified to add $30 + $A = $3A, and $37 + $A = $41, respectively. With this explanation, a study of the flowchart shown in Fig. 7-4 and the program comments should make the program understandable. In a typical case, writing an ASCII character to OUTPUT would cause it to appear on an output device like a crt or printer. The comments in the program are more detailed than usual because this is the most complex program presented thus far. Again, the program should be studied for its use of specific instructions. The purpose of this book is not to build a program library; it is to teach you how to program.

Example 5: Hex to ASCII Conversion Program

Object: Output the contents of a register or memory location as two ASCII characters representing two hexadecimal numerals. Assume the data to be converted is in DATA and the I/O location is OUTPUT.

$0000 = DATA
$03FF = OUTPUT

0350	A5 00	START	LDA	DATA	DATA contains the number to be converted to two ASCII characters.
0352	A8		TAY		Transfer A to Y for temporary storage of DATA.
0353	A2 FE		LDX	$FE	Initialize X to count characters.
0355	6A		ROR	A	High-order nibble must be output
0356	6A		ROR	A	first, so rotate accumulator
0357	6A		ROR	A	four bits to the right. High-order
0358	6A		ROR	A	nibble is now low-order nibble.
0359	29 0F	CHAR2	AND	$0F	Mask top nibble.
035B	38		SEC		Set carry for subtraction.
035C	E9 0A		SBC	$0A	Subtract $A to separate numerals
035E	B0 04		BCS	HERE	0–9 from A–F. Carry set means numerals A–F. Carry clear means numerals 0–9.
0360	69 3A		ADC	$3A	ASCII for numerals 0–9 obtained by adding $0A + $30 + Accumulator.
0362	B0 02		BCS	OVER	Jump over conversion of numerals A–F.
0364	69 40	HERE	ADC	$40	ASCII for numerals A–F obtained by adding $40 + Carry + Accumulator.
0366	8D FF 03	OVER	STA	OUTPUT	Output ASCII representation of nibble.
0369	E8		INX		Need to get another nibble?
036A	F0 04		BEQ	DONE	Not if X = 0.
036C	98		TYA		Transfer Y to A to put DATA back into accumulator.
036D	4C 59 03		JMP	CHAR2	Jump to output second character.
0370	00	DONE	BRK		

DECIMAL TO HEXADECIMAL

Suppose that a programmer enters two digits in a memory location, and he chooses to regard this two-digit number as a base-ten number. For purposes of illustration, suppose that the number is 59_{10}. The programmer must restrict his use of digits to the base-ten numerals 0–9.

Of course, the microcomputer will regard the number as an 8-bit binary number represented by two hex digits, which is not what the programmer intended. Therefore, before the "decimal value 59" can be used in subsequent operations, the program must convert it to a binary or hexadecimal number. (The only exception to this rule is in decimal addition and subtraction.)

Before providing the solution to the problem of converting a two-digit base-ten number into a hexadecimal number, consider some interesting properties of the ASL and LSR instructions, as shown by Examples 6 through 9.

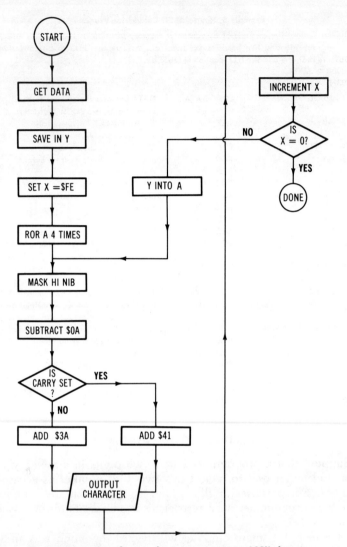

Fig. 7-4. Conversion of accumulator contents to two ASCII characters.

Example 6: Demonstration of the Effect of One ASL Instruction on a Number

What is $05 after one ASL instruction?

Solution: $05 = 0000\ 0101$, shifted once becomes $0000\ 1010 = \$A = 10_{10}$. Observe that one shift left is equivalent to multiplication by two.

Example 7: Demonstration of the Effect of Two ASL Instructions on a Number

What is $05 after two ASL instructions?

Solution: $05 = 0000\ 0101$, shifted twice becomes $0001\ 0100 = \$14 = 20_{10}$. Observe that two shifts left is equivalent to multiplication by four.

Example 8: Demonstration of the Effect of One LSR Instruction on a Number

What is $0C after one LSR instruction?

Solution: $12_{10} = \$0C = 0000\ 1100$, shifted right becomes $0000\ 0110 = \$06 = 6_{10}$. Observe that one shift right is equivalent to division by two.

Example 9: Demonstration of the Effect of Two LSR Instructions on a Number

What is $0C after two LSR instructions?

Solution: $12_{10} = \$0C = 0000\ 1100$, shifted twice is $0000\ 0011 = \$03 = 3_{10}$. Observe that two shifts right is equivalent to division by four.

From these examples we can conclude:

- A succession of ASL instructions is equivalent to multiplying by 2, 4, 8, 16, . . . , provided no significant bits are shifted out of the location.
- A succession of LSR instructions is equivalent to dividing by 2, 4, 8, 16, . . . , provided no significant bits are shifted out of the location.

Now return to the example of the 59, which the programmer intends to mean 59_{10} but which the computer supposes is 59_{16} or \$59. To convert 59_{10} to binary or hexadecimal we make use of the fact that

$$59_{10} = (5 \cdot 10_{10}) + (9 \cdot 1_{10}) = (5 \cdot \$A) + (9 \cdot \$1).$$

Clearly, we need only multiply the five by \$A and add it to nine in order to convert 59_{10} to hexadecimal. One problem remains. Recall that the low-order nibble is the one's place while the high-order nibble is the sixteen's place. The "5" is in the high-order nibble of the memory location, so the computer interprets it as being $(5 \cdot 16)$. We could convert this "5" in the sixteen's place to a five in the one's place by four shift-right (LSR) instructions, moving it from the high-order nibble to the low-order nibble, and then we could multiply it by \$A as outlined above.

There is a more efficient technique, however. We may leave the "5" in the sixteen's place and divide by 16 and multiply by \$A, using the following facts:

$$5 \cdot \$A = (5 \cdot \$A)\frac{16}{16} = (5 \cdot 16)\frac{\$A}{16} = (5 \cdot 16)\left(\frac{\$8 + \$2}{16}\right)$$

$$= (5 \cdot 16)\left(\frac{1}{2} + \frac{1}{8}\right) = \frac{(5 \cdot 16)}{2} + \frac{(5 \cdot 16)}{8}.$$

In other words, to multiply five times \$A, we may take the high-order nibble, $(5 \cdot 16)$, divide it by two, divide it by eight, and add these two results. This is what the equations above tell us.

The two rules regarding ASL and LSR instructions tell us that division by two is accomplished by one LSR instruction, and division by eight is accomplished by three LSR instructions. To divide the

$(5 \cdot 16)$ by two, the high-order nibble is shifted to the right by one LSR instruction. To divide the $(5 \cdot 16)$ by eight, the high-order nibble is shifted to the right by three LSR instructions. When these two results are added, we have converted 50_{10} to its binary or hexadecimal representation. Adding the nine in the one's place completes the conversion of 59_{10} to its hexadecimal representation. Other numbers are handled in the same way, and the program in Example 10 will convert any two-digit base-ten number to a hexadecimal number.

Example 10: Decimal to Hexadecimal Conversion Program

Object: Convert a two-digit base-ten number to hexadecimal. The base-ten number will be symbolized by DCML. The answer will be symbolized by HEX. TEMP will serve as a temporary storage location.

$0000 = DCML
$0001 = HEX
$0002 = TEMP

03A0	D8	BEGIN	CLD		Clear decimal mode.
03A1	A5 00		LDA	DCML	Get decimal number.
03A3	AA		TAX		Save A in X temporarily.
03A4	29 0F		AND	$0F	Mask high-order nibble.
03A6	85 01		STA	HEX	One's place in answer.
03A8	8A		TXA		Get A back again.
03A9	29 F0		AND	$F0	Mask low-order nibble.
03AB	4A		LSR	A	Divide by two (see text).
03AC	85 02		STA	TEMP	Store in temporary location.
03AE	4A		LSR	A	Total of three LSRs gives division
03AF	4A		LSR	A	by eight (see text).
03B0	18		CLC		Clear carry for addition.
03B1	65 02		ADC	TEMP	Add divide by two to divide by eight.
03B3	65 01		ADC	HEX	Add to answer.
03B5	85 01		STA	HEX	Result in answer location.
03B7	00	END	BRK		

HEXADECIMAL TO DECIMAL

In this section we consider the process of converting a hexadecimal number in one byte of memory to its bcd representation. Note that since $FF = 255_{10}$ and each byte of memory can represent only two decimal digits with bcd code, we will require two bytes of memory to represent the decimal equivalent of the hexadecimal number.

Let $PQ represent a hexadecimal number in the sense that P is the high-order nibble and Q is the low-order nibble. We intend to convert $PQ to its decimal equivalent. Note that P is in the 16's place while Q is in the one's place. That is,

$$\$PQ = (\$P \cdot 16_{10}) + (\$Q \cdot 1_{10})$$

This result suggests a means of converting $PQ to its decimal equivalent, namely, add 16_{10} to itself $P times using the decimal mode for addition, and add 1 to itself $Q times using the decimal mode. These two results are then added to give the final answer. Any carry from these sums will be added to another byte of memory, giving the complete two byte representation. The program is given in Example 11.

Suppose $PQ is in a location symbolized by PQ. We first mask $P, and transfer Q to the X register. X is then used as a counter to add one to the low-order byte of the decimal answer Q times. This addition is carried out in the decimal mode, and the result is stored in location DCMLO. There will be no carry from this addition. Next, $P is shifted into the low-order nibble of PQ with four LSR

Example 11: Hexadecimal to Decimal Conversion Program

Object: Convert a hexadecimal number in location PQ to a decimal number located in DCMLO and DCMHI. These two locations contain the least significant two digits and the most significant digit, respectively.

$0000 = PQ; Contains the hexadecimal number to be converted to decimal.
$0001 = DCMLO; Contains the two least-significant digits of the decimal answer.
$0002 = DCMHI; Contains the most-significant digit of the decimal answer.

0200	A9 00	ORIGIN	LDA	$00	Clear the locations that will
0202	85 01		STA	DCMLO	contain the decimal answer.
0204	85 02		STA	DCMHI	
0206	A5 00		LDA	PQ	Get the hexadecimal number.
0208	29 0F		AND	$0F	Mask $P, leaving $Q in A.
020A	F0 0C		BEQ	OVER	Branch to convert 16's place if one's place is zero.
020C	AA		TAX		Transfer $Q to X for counter.
020D	18		CLC		Make sure carry flag is clear.
020E	F8		SED		Set the decimal mode flag.
020F	A5 01	RPT1	LDA	DCMLO	Get DCMLO contents.
0211	69 01		ADC	01	Add one.
0213	85 01		STA	DCMLO	Result into DCMLO.
0215	CA		DEX		Decrement X until one has been
0216	D0 F7		BNE	RPT1	added $Q times.
0218	A5 00	OVER	LDA	PQ	Get the hexadecimal number again.
021A	4A		LSR	A	Shift it right four times to get
021B	4A		LSR	A	$P in the low-order nibble.
021C	4A		LSR	A	
021D	4A		LSR	A	
021E	F0 11		BEQ	FINISH	If 16's place is zero, end the conversion.
0220	AA		TAX		Transfer $P to X for counter.
0221	18		CLC		Clear carry flag in case LSRs set it.
0222	A5 01	RPT2	LDA	DCMLO	Get DCMLO contents.
0224	69 16		ADC	16	Add 16.
0226	85 01		STA	DCMLO	Result into DCMLO.
0228	A9 00		LDA	$00	Prepare to add carry, if any,
022A	65 02		ADC	DCMHI	to the contents of DCMHI.
022C	85 02		STA	DCMHI	Result into DCMHI.
022E	CA		DEX		Decrement X.
022F	D0 F1		BNE	RPT2	Repeat adding 16 until $P additions
0231	00	FINSH	BRK		have been completed. Finish.

133

instructions. It is then transferred to the X register for the purpose of counting $P additions of 16_{10} in the decimal mode. Up to two carries may result from these sums. so the carries are added to the contents of a location called DCMHI, which contains the high-order byte of the decimal representation of $PQ. This completes the conversion.

EXPERIMENT NO. 1

Step 1

Load the program in Example 1. Put an ASL instruction (op code $0E) in location $020D.

```
0200   A9 FF      START   LDA   $FF     Set up the Port A DDR by loading
0202   8D 01 17           STA   PADD    $FF into PADD.
0205   AD 02 17           LDA   PBD     Get some data from Port B.
0208   29 BF              AND   $BF     Mask bit six for the SYM-1 and KIM-1.
020A   8D 00 17           STA   PAD     Output the resulting number to Port A.
020D   __ 00 17   LOOP    __    PAD     Shift the contents of Port A, and
0210   4C 0D 02           JMP   LOOP    put the instruction in a loop for
                                        repeated shifts.
```

Step 2

Set the Port B switches to $01; that is, make PB0 logic one and all the other switches logic zero.

Step 3

Single-step the program, repeating the ASL PAD and JMP LOOP instructions at least eight times. Describe what you observe.

(We observed that after the STA PAD was executed the PA0 LED glowed. The ASL instruction shifted the logic one in PA0 to PA1, PA2, and so on, until the one was shifted out of PAD altogether.)

Step 4

Set the Port B switches to put a $05 in Port B. Run the program again (in the single-step mode) and describe what you observe.

(We observed that initially PA2 and PA0 light. Successive ASL instructions move each of these one bits to the left, until they are shifted out of Port A.)

EXPERIMENT NO. 2

Step 1

Change the ASL instruction to an ROL instruction (op code $2E) in the program in Experiment No. 1.

Step 2

Set the Port B switches to $01.

Step 3

Single-step the program, repeating the ROL PAD instruction at least nine times. What do you observe?

(You should observe that initially PA0 LED lights. After each execution of the ROL PAD instruction the glowing LED shifts left. After eight ROL instructions it disappears, but on the ninth ROL instruction the glowing LED appears at PA0 again.)

Step 4

Experiment with other settings of the Port B switches and the single-step mode.

EXPERIMENT NO. 3

Repeat Experiments 1 and 2 with LSR and ROR instructions, respectively. You may wish to set PB7 rather than PB0 to logic one, because the LSR and ROR instructions shift or rotate right. Also, experiment with other settings of the Port B switches. Describe and explain your results.

EXPERIMENT NO. 4

Step 1

Load the program in Example 7-3.

```
$0000 = MCND; Multiplicand
$0001 = MLTP; Multiplier
$0003 = PROD; Product
    0200   D8      START   CLD             Clear decimal mode.
    0201   A9 00           LDA $00         Clear location of product by
    0203   85 03           STA PROD        storing $00 in PROD.
    0205   46 00   AGAN    LSR MLTP        Shift multiplier right to test
    0207   90 07           BCC ARND        for zero or one in carry flag. If
    0209   18              CLC             zero branch to shift multiplicand
    020A   A5 01           LDA MCND        left for next test. If one, add
```

020C	65 03		ADC	PROD	multiplicand to obtain product.
020E	85 03		STA	PROD	
0210	06 01	ARND	ASL	MCND	Shift multiplicand left for next sum.
0212	F0 04		BEQ	DONE	If multiplicand is zero, operation
0214	A5 00		LDA	MLTP	is finished. Same for multiplier.
0216	D0 ED		BNE	AGAN	Otherwise branch back to sum again.
0218	00	DONE	BRK		

Step 2

Check the operation of the program by entering $02 in $0000 and $03 in $0001, execute the program, and check the answer in $0003. The answer should be $06.

Step 3

Now try some more difficult problems like $F · $A, $2 · $C, $9 · $E, and others. Check your results by hand calculations.

Step 4

Experiment with some 8-bit problems. Try $10 · $02, for example. What do you get for an answer? Try $10 · $20. What do you obtain for an answer?

(For the first answer we obtained $20 as expected. For the second answer we obtained $00 because the most significant byte is lost. The program does give the correct answer for the least significant byte.)

EXPERIMENT NO. 5

Repeat Experiment No. 4 using the 8-bit multiplication program instead of the 4-bit multiplication program. You should now be able to multiply two 8-bit numbers. In addition to the problems suggested in Experiment No. 4, try some more difficult ones such as $FF · $FE and $7C · $EA. Check your program by doing the calculations by hand.

EXPERIMENT NO. 6

Step 1

Load the program in Example 5.

```
$0000 = DATA
$03FF = OUTPUT
```

0350	A5 00	START	LDA	DATA	DATA contains the number to be converted to two ASCII characters.
0352	A8		TAY		Transfer A to Y for temporary storage of DATA

0353	A2 FE		LDX	$FE	Initialize X to count characters.
0355	6A		ROR	A	High-order nibble must be output
0356	6A		ROR	A	first, so rotate accumulator
0357	6A		ROR	A	four bits to the right. High-order
0358	6A		ROR	A	nibble is now low-order nibble.
0359	29 0F	CHAR2	AND	$0F	Mask top nibble.
035B	38		SEC		Set carry for subtraction.
035C	E9 0A		SBC	$0A	Subtract $A to separate numerals
035E	B0 04		BCS	HERE	0–9 from A–F. Carry set means
					numerals A–F. Carry clear means
					numerals 0–9.
0360	69 3A		ADC	$3A	ASCII for numerals 0–9 obtained by
					adding $0A + $30 + Accumulator.
0362	B0 02		BCS	OVER	Jump over conversion of numerals A–F.
0364	69 40	HERE	ADC	$40	ASCII for numerals A–F obtained by
					adding $40 + Carry + Accumulator.
0366	8D FF 03	OVER	STA	OUTPUT	Output ASCII representation of nibble.
0369	E8		INX		Need to get another nibble?
036A	F0 04		BEQ	DONE	Not if X = 0.
036C	98		TYA		Transfer Y to A to put DATA back
					into accumulator.
036D	4C 59 03		JMP	CHAR2	Jump to output second character.
0370	00	DONE	BRK		

Step 2

Put $C5 in location $0000. Run the program. What do you find in location $03FF after the program has been executed?

(The program first converts $C to its ASCII representation, which, if you refer to Table 6-2, is $43. Next the program converts $5 to its ASCII representation, which is $35. It is the ASCII representation of the second digit which you should find in $03FF, namely $35.)

Step 3

Put $5C in location $0000. Run the program and examine the contents of $03FF. What do you find there?

(You should find the ASCII representation of C, namely $43, in location $03FF.)

Step 4

Try some other numbers in location $0000 and make sure the program always gives the correct ASCII representation of the second digit.

EXPERIMENT NO. 7

Step 1

Load the program in Example 10.

```
$0000 = DCML
$0001 = HEX
$0002 = TEMP
```

03A0	D8		BEGIN	CLD		Clear decimal mode.
03A1	A5	00		LDA	DCML	Get decimal number.
03A3	AA			TAX		Save A in X temporarily.
03A4	29	0F		AND	$0F	Mask high-order nibble.
03A6	85	01		STA	HEX	One's place in answer.
03A8	8A			TXA		Get A back again.
03A9	29	F0		AND	$F0	Mask low-order nibble.
03AB	4A			LSR	A	Divide by two (see text).
03AC	85	02		STA	TEMP	Store in temporary location.
03AE	4A			LSR	A	Total of three LSRs gives division
03AF	4A			LSR	A	by eight (see text).
03B0	18			CLC		Clear carry for addition.
03B1	65	02		ADC	TEMP	Add divide by two to divide by eight.
03B3	65	01		ADC	HEX	Add to answer.
03B5	85	01		STA	HEX	Result in answer location.
03B7	00		END	BRK		

Step 2

Put a base-ten number like 59 in location $0000. Run the program. What number do you find in location $0001?

(You should find $3B in location $0001, since it is the hexadecimal equivalent of 59_{10}.)

Step 3

Try some other base-ten numbers to confirm that the program converts them to hexadecimal.

EXPERIMENT NO. 8

Here are a few additional programs and problems you might like to try.

- Convert a four-digit hexadecimal number to base ten.
- Input two ASCII representations of hexadecimal numbers and convert them to a hexadecimal number in the accumulator.
- Divide two 8-bit numbers. This is very challenging.
- Test the hexadecimal-to-decimal conversion program.
- Try constructing a flowchart for the hexadecimal-to-decimal conversion program.

CHAPTER 8

Indexed Addressing

OBJECTIVES

At the completion of this chapter you should be able to:

- Understand the function of an index.
- Use *absolute* and *zero-page indexed* addressing modes in computer programs. See Table 8-1 for a summary of the instructions that use this mode.
- Understand the concept of indirect addressing.
- Use the *indexed indirect* and *indirect indexed* addressinig modes in programs.

INTRODUCTION

So far, we have used, at various times, seven different addressing modes, including immediate, absolute, zero-page, accumulator, implied, relative, and, finally, the indirect jump.

In the immediate addressing mode, the data to be operated upon is included in the program as the byte following the op code. The absolute addressing mode uses two program bytes to specify the address of the location where the byte of data is to be found. Zero-page addressing is similar to the absolute addressing mode, except that only the low-order byte of the address of the data is given, it being understood that the high-order byte of the address is $00. The other addressing modes, accumulator, implied, and relative, will not be recapped here because they are not closely related to the topics of this chapter.

Table 8-1. Op Codes for Instructions Introduced in Chapter 8

Instructions	(IND,X)	(IND),Y	Z-PAGE,X	ABS,X	ABS,Y	Z-PAGE,Y
			Addressing Mode			
ADC	61	71	75	7D	79	
AND	21	31	35	3D	39	
ASL			16	1E		
CMP	C1	D1	D5	DD	D9	
DEC			D6	DE		
EOR	41	51	55	5D	59	
INC			F6	FE		
LDA	A1	B1	B5	BD	B9	
LDX					BE	B6
LDY			B4	BC		
LSR			56	5E		
ORA	01	11	15	1D	19	
ROL			36	3E		
ROR			76	7E		
SBC	E1	F1	F5	FD	F9	
STA	81	91	95	9D	99	
STX						96

Considering all the addressing modes learned so far, it can be seen from the 6502 instruction set summary in Table 2-3 that there are still six addressing modes to learn. The instructions, addressing modes, and the op codes used in this chapter are summarized in Table 8-1. These addressing modes have one feature in common, namely, the use of an *index*. As you shall see, the use of an index gives the microprocessor the ability to handle large amounts of data quickly, efficiently, and with a minimum amount of programming. The indirect addressing modes allow the microprocessor to fetch data from locations whose addresses have been *calculated*. The indirect addressing capability distinguishes the instruction set of the 6502 from the instruction sets of several other popular microprocessors.

To provide the motivation for learning about indexed addressing, consider the problem of writing the same number, say $FF, to all the locations on a single page of memory. This might be part of an R/W memory test, in which the same number is placed in all locations, and then all locations are read to see if that number is still present. (Good memory tests are more elaborate than this.) Without indexing, the 6502 program would have to be similar to the one in Example 1. Clearly such a program is extremely long, requiring more memory space for the program than for the page of memory to be tested. There has to be a better way, and the better way is accomplished with indexed addressing.

Example 1: Loading a Page of R/W Memory with a Number

Write a program to load $FF in all the memory locations in page three of memory.

```
Solution:   START    LDA $FF
                     STA $0300
                     STA $0301
                       .
                       .
                       .
                     STA $03FF
            END      BRK
```

ABSOLUTE INDEXED ADDRESSING

Before getting started, we note that the X and Y registers are central to the indexed addressing modes. In fact, these two registers are more properly called *index registers,* since *their contents will be the index* in all indexed addressing modes. No other registers may serve as an index. "X" will refer to the number in the X register and "Y" will refer to the number in the Y register.

To illustrate *absolute indexed addressing,* first consider the LDA instruction in the absolute addressing mode. In mnemonic form

LDA TABLE

means fetch the contents of the location symbolized by TABLE. Thus, TABLE is actually a 16-bit address consisting of an 8-bit address low (ADL) and an 8-bit address high (ADH). We may write:

TABLE = ADH-ADL.

The address, TABLE, may be *indexed* by the contents of register X in an addressing mode called "absolute indexed by X" or, more simply, "ABS,X." The mnemonic is written:

LDA TABLE,X.

This means that the LDA operation goes to an address that is the *sum* of the 16-bit address for TABLE (ADH-ADL) and the contents of the X register. The actual 16-bit address for TABLE is called the *base address,* and it is now symbolized as BAH-BAL for base-address high and base-address low. Thus,

TABLE,X = BAH-BAL + X.

The address BAH-BAL is called the *base* address of TABLE, and X is called the *index*. BAL and BAH are the second and third bytes, respectively, of any absolute indexed instruction. The data is obtained from location BAH-BAL + X.

In words, the microprocessor *adds* the contents of the X register to the BAL of TABLE, any carry from this addition is added to BAH, and the data is fetched from that location. Example 2 illustrates how this calculation proceeds.

Example 2: Illustration of Absolute Indexed Addressing Mode

In the program below, identify the address of the byte of data referenced by the LDA instruction.

```
0200    A2 2D       START    LDX $2D
0202    BD 00 03    END      LDA TABLE,X
```

Solution: BAL = $00 and BAH = $03, so the base address of TABLE is $0300. The X register contains $2D, so the byte of data is fetched from the location whose address is $0300 + $2D = $032D.

The addition of the contents of the X register to the BAL of the base address is accomplished within the 6502. It *does not involve* the *carry flag*, but it may involve a *carry* from the sum (X + BAL), to BAH. For example, if the base address is $23F5 and the X register contains $10, then the LDA TABLE,X instruction would fetch the contents of location $2405. In any case, where BAL is $00 no page boundary will be crossed because the maximum value of the X index is $FF, since the X register is an 8-bit register.

Of course, the LDA instruction is not the only instruction capable of being used in the ABS,X addressing mode. The arithmetic, logical, store, register-shift, compare, and several other instructions also have this absolute indexed addressing mode available. See Table 8-1 for details.

For most of these same instructions, the Y register may also be used as an index in an addressing mode called ABS,Y that functions in exactly the same way as the ABS,X addressing mode, except that the Y register is used as the index. Table 8-1 summarizes the new addressing modes introduced in this chapter.

ZERO-PAGE INDEXED ADDRESSING

The two zero-page indexed addressing modes, "Z-PAGE,X" and "Z-PAGE,Y" are similar to their ABS,X and ABS,Y counterparts. These instructions require only two bytes, the first being the op code from Table 8-1 and the second being the base address low (BAL); it is understood that BAH is $00, since page zero is being used. Another important difference between zero-page indexing and absolute indexing is that any carry from the addition of the BAL to the X register is discarded in zero-page indexing. This produces a "wrap-around" effect, since the high byte of the address will always be zero in this mode. For example, if the BAL is $F5, and the X register used for the index contains $10, then the location of the data to be operated upon in the Z-PAGE,X addressing mode is $0005, *not* $0105, which you would obtain from an addition of BAL to X with a carry going to BAH. See Example 3.

Example 3: Illustration of Zero-Page Indexed Addressing Mode

Identify the memory location referenced by the ADC instruction in the following program.

```
0200   A2 35    START    LDX $35
0202   A9 29             LDA $29
0204   75 20             ADC TABZ,X
```

Solution: The ADC instruction uses Z-PAGE,X addressing (see Table 8-1). The base address of TABZ is $0020. Adding the X index gives $0020 + $35 = $0055 as the location to be referenced.

To illustrate how indexing is used in programs, we will look at a variety of programs. To begin, refer to the problem posed in Example 1 in which we wish to address sequentially the 256 locations in a given page of memory. The program in that example would have required at least 256 3-byte instructions. Using indexed addressing, however, the program in Example 4 accomplishes the same task with only five instructions. A flowchart for this program is shown in Fig. 8-1. Carefully study it and the program in Example 4 to see how the simplest form of the indexed addressing modes works. (The flowchart uses the notation "[A] → [TABLE + X]." Recall that this notation means "store the *contents* of A in the location whose address is symbolized by TABLE + X." Thus, the "[ ]" means "the contents of.")

In Example 5, we have implemented the simple memory test mentioned earlier. It begins with the same instructions as the program in Example 4, but it goes on to illustrate the CMP instruction in the absolute indexed addressing mode. A flowchart for the program is given in Fig. 8-2. Study the program and the flowchart to obtain a better understanding of the absolute indexed addressing mode. It is important that you realize that the calculated address of BASE + X may be used over and over again, as was the case for the STA TABLE,X and CMP TABLE,X instructions. Thus an address that was calculated in this way could be used by many different instructions in a program. The use of the indexed mode does not change the base address, or the contents of the index register, X or Y.

One other note about the program in Example 5. The use of $FF to test R/W memory is probably a poor choice. It is possible that

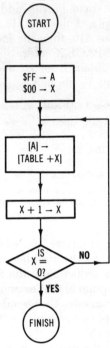

Fig. 8-1. Flowchart of program in Example 4. Recall that notation [A]→ [TABLE + X] means "the contents of the accumulator becomes the contents of the location symbolized by TABLE + X."

"empty" locations would not be discovered because the logic levels on the data bus might all be one for these locations. A better choice for a number is $55, or any other number containing both ones and zeros.

Example 4: Program to Illustrate Absolute Indexed Addressing Mode

Object: Load $FF in all page-three locations.
$0300 = TABLE

0200	A2 00	START	LDX $00	Initialize X index to $00.
0202	A9 FF		LDA $FF	Initialize A to $FF.
0204	9D 00 03	BACK	STA TABLE,X	Store $FF in location TABLE + X.
0207	E8		INX	Increment index X.
0208	D0 FA		BNE BACK	If X ≠ 0, branch back to load other locations.
020A	00		BRK	

Example 5: Simple R/W Memory Test

Object: Load each location in page three with $FF. Then read each location in page three to see if it still contains the number $FF. If it does not contain $FF, output the ADL of that location.

$0300 = TABLE
$A003 = PADD
$A001 = PAD

144

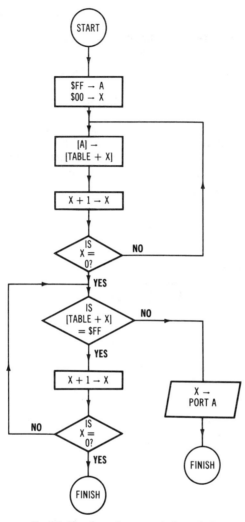

Fig. 8-2. Flowchart of program in Example 5.

0200	A2 00		START	LDX $00	The first five instructions of
0202	A9 FF			LDA $FF	this program were commented on
0204	9D 00	03	BACK	STA TABLE,X	in Example 4.
0207	E8			INX	
0208	D0 FA			BNE BACK	
020A	DD 00	03	CHECK	CMP TABLE,X	Compare A (still contains $FF with
020D	D0 04			BNE OUT	page three location. Branch to OUT
020F	E8			INX	if location does not contain $FF;
0210	D0 F8			BNE CHECK	otherwise return to read another
					location.

145

0212	00			BRK		Finish here when all locations are read.
0213	8D 03 A0	OUT	STA	PADD		Initialize Port A to be output port.
0216	8E 01 A0		STA	PAD		Output X for location where test fails.
0219	00			BRK		Then end here.

DATA TABLES

Indexed addressing provides an efficient technique for the manipulation of data stored in tables. This will be illustrated, along with the zero-page indexed addressing mode, in programming examples, Examples 6 and 7. The program in Example 6 locates the largest

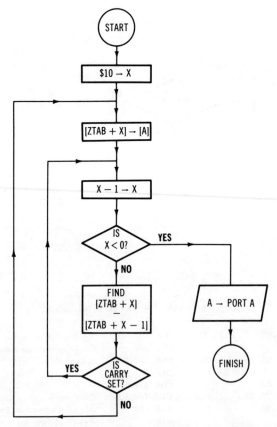

Fig. 8-3. Flowchart of the program in Example 6. Recall that carry flag is set if subtraction does not produce a borrow, that is, if [ZTAB + X] ⩾ [ZTAB + (X − 1)].

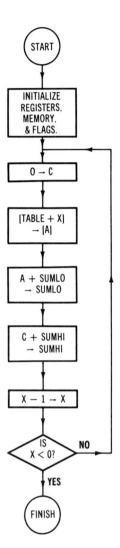

Fig. 8-4. Flowchart of program in Example 7.

number in a table, and the program in Example 7 adds all of the numbers in a table. The flowcharts for these two programs are shown in Figs. 8-3 and 8-4, respectively. In reference to the program in Example 6, you should realize, of course, that the largest value may be present in several locations. This program only finds the largest value. It does not note where it (they) are, or how many of them there are.

The program in Example 7 adds all of the numbers in a table. The largest value of the sum of all the numbers in the table would

Example 6: Program to Locate Largest Number in a Table

Object: Locate the largest number in a table that starts at location $00A0 and ends at $00B0. Output the largest number to Port A.

```
$00A0 = ZTAB
$A003 = PADD
$A001 = PAD
```

0200	A9 FF	START	LDA $FF	Initialize Port A DDR to make the
0202	8D 03 A0		STA PADD	port an output port.
0205	A2 10		LDX $10	Start X at $10 and get data
0207	B5 A0	AGAIN	LDA ZTAB,X	from the top of the table.
0209	CA	BACK	DEX	Decrement X; if X is less than
020A	30 07		BMI OUT	zero, task is finished.
020C	D5 A0		CMP ZTAB,X	Is [ZTAB + X] ≧ [ZTAB + (X — 1)]?
020E	B0 F9		BCS BACK	Yes, keep [ZTAB + X] as largest value and return to check the next location in the table.
0210	4C 07 02		JMP AGAIN	No, then use [ZTAB + (X — 1)] as largest value and return to check other locations in the table.
0213	8D 01 A0	OUT	STA PAD	Store largest value in Port A.
0216	00		BRK	Finished.

occur if each location had a $FF in it. Since $FF · $100 < $FFFF, a two-byte location for the sum will be sufficient as long as the table does not exceed $100 locations. That is why there is a high-order byte (SUMHI) and a low-order byte (SUMLO) for the sum of the numbers in the table. Although the table could have as many as $100 = 256 locations, our program illustrates a table with 16 entries. This program will be easier to test than one with 256 entries, while the basic principles remain the same.

Although these two examples of operating on data in tabular form may seem contrived, they are not. The author has used both ideas in working with computer applications. In fact, most of the programs given in this book have practical applications other than providing mental gymnastics for interested readers. Because information usually comes in large quantities, the importance of being able to work with tables can hardly be overemphasized. In fact, the ability to manipulate a large quantity of information quickly is one of the justifications for microprocessor-based instrumentation.

Example 7: Program to Add all Entries in a Table

Object: Add all the numbers in a table consisting of 16 locations in page zero, from $00A0 through $00AF.

```
$0000 = SUMLO
$0001 = SUMHI
$00A0 = TABLE
```

| 0200 | A9 00 | START | LDA $00 | |
| 0202 | 85 00 | | STA SUMLO | Clear SUMLO to zero. |

```
0204   85 01              STA  SUMHI       Clear SUMHI to zero.
0206   D8                 CLD              Clear decimal mode.
0207   A2 0F              LDX  $0F         Initialize X to start at the top
0209   18         BACK    CLC              of the table. Clear carry flag.
020A   B5 A0              LDA  TABLE,X     Load A with [TABLE + X].
020C   65 00              ADC  SUMLO       Add to SUMLO.
020E   85 00              STA  SUMLO       Result in SUMLO.
0210   A5 01              LDA  SUMHI       Get SUMHI.
0212   69 00              ADC  $00         Add carry, if any, from previous sum.
0214   85 01              STA  SUMHI       Result into SUMHI.
0216   CA                 DEX              Decrement X.
0217   10 F0              BPL  BACK        Keep adding until all the table entries
0219   00                 BRK              have been included in the sum. Then quit.
```

CODE CONVERSION PROGRAMS

Another important use of indexed addressing and tables is in converting one code into another. For example, refer to Example 8 in Chapter 6 in which a hexadecimal character represented by an ASCII value was converted into a hexadecimal number, and to Example 5 in Chapter 7 in which two hexadecimal numerals representing the contents of a memory location were converted to two ASCII characters. Tables and indexed addressing sometimes make the conversion task easier than when using arithmetic, logical, and shift instructions.

The program in Example 8 is a hex to ASCII conversion, the program in Example 9 converts two bcd digits to binary, and the program in Example 10 converts a hexadecimal number into the code necessary to display a hexadecimal numeral on a seven-segment LED display. Example 8 might be used to output information from a microcomputer to a video monitor, printer, typewriter,

Example 8: Hex-to-ASCII Conversion Program

Object: Convert the hex number representing the low-order nibble of a memory location into its ASCII equivalent. Refer to Table 8-2 for the location and contents of the conversion table. Output the ASCII character to Port A.

```
$0300 = TABLE
$A000 = PBD
$A001 = PAD
$A003 = PADD

0200   A9 FF        START   LDA  $FF        Initialize Port A to be an
0202   8D 03 A0             STA  PADD       output port by loading $FF
                                            into its DDR.

0205   AD 00 A0             LDA  PBD        Get data from Port B.
0208   29 0F                AND  $0F        Mask the high-order nibble.
020A   AA                   TAX             Put the low-order nibble in X.
020B   BD 00 03             LDA  TABLE,X    to be used as the index to look
                                            up the ASCII value in the table.
020E   8D 01 A0             STA  PAD        Output the ASCII value.
0211   00                   BRK             Finish.
```

or some other output device. Example 9 might be used to read bcd data from a voltmeter or other instrument and convert the data to binary for processing by the microcomputer. Example 10 could be used to display the contents of a register or memory location. Both the SYM-1 and KIM-1 use seven-segment displays to do this.

Because similar flowcharts have already been given, none will be drawn for Examples 8 through 10. In Example 8 note that the nibble to be converted to an ASCII value is used as the *index* to locate the ASCII character. The value TABLE points to the start of the code conversion table, while the hex value is actually used to locate the value in the table. In this way, the hex value was used to *address* the table, so that the corresponding ASCII value at the proper address could be retrieved. The contents of Table 8-2 must be loaded into memory in order for the program to work. The program could be expanded to output both nibbles of a memory location. Refer to Example 5 in Chapter 7 for details about how this might be accomplished.

The program in Example 9 assumes that two decimal digits are represented in bcd at Port B. For example, 95_{10} would appear as 1001 0101 at the Port B pins. Refer to Table 5-4 to find other decimal-to-bcd conversions. Also refer to Example 10 in Chapter 7 which accomplishes the same objective as the program in Example 9 in this chapter. Our task is to convert the bcd number to binary. Since the number in the ones place is the same in both bcd and hexadecimal, we may simply add it to the conversion of the number in the tens place. Thus,

$$95_{10} = (9 \cdot 10) + (5 \cdot 1) = (9 \cdot A) + (5 \cdot 1) = (9 \cdot A) + 5$$

Table 8-2. ASCII Character Look Up Table for Example 8

Hex Numeral	ASCII Character	Location	Contents
0	$30	$0300	$30
1	31	0301	31
2	32	0302	32
3	33	0303	33
4	34	0304	34
5	35	0305	35
6	36	0306	36
7	37	0307	37
8	38	0308	38
9	39	0309	39
A	41	030A	41
B	42	030B	42
C	43	030C	43
D	44	030D	44
E	45	030E	45
F	46	030F	46

will form the basis for the conversion. The bcd digit which appears in the high-order nibble must be multiplied by A and then added to the number in the low-order nibble. But the multiplication can be done ahead of time and the answers stored in a table in memory. Such a table is shown in Table 8-3. In order for the program in Example 9 to work, this table must be in memory.

Table 8-3. BCD to Binary Look Up Table for Example 9

BCD Number (Tens Place)	Hexadecimal Value (Number · $A)	Location	Contents
0	$00	$0000	$00
1	0A	0001	0A
2	14	0002	14
3	1E	0003	1E
4	28	0004	28
5	32	0005	32
6	3C	0006	3C
7	46	0007	46
8	50	0008	50
9	5A	0009	5A

Example 9: Decimal-to-Binary Conversion Program

Object: Convert bcd number (two digits) at Port B to a binary number and store the result in Port A.

$0000 = TABLE
$0010 = TEMP
$A003 = PADD
$A001 = PAD

0200	D8	START	CLD		Clear decimal mode
0201	AD 00 A0		LDA	PBD	Get two BCD digits from Port B.
0204	AA		TAX		Save in X.
0205	29 0F		AND	$0F	Mask high-order nibble.
0207	85 10		STA	TEMP	Store temporarily in TEMP.
0209	8A		TXA		Get both digits back in A.
020A	4A		LSR	A	Shift high-order nibble into low-
020B	4A		LSR	A	order nibble, and zeros into high-
020C	4A		LSR	A	order nibble.
020D	4A		LSR	A	
020E	AA		TAX		Use high-order nibble as index to
020F	B5 00		LDA	TABLE,X	look up conversion in TABLE.
0211	18		CLC		Clear carry for addition.
0212	65 10		ADC	TEMP	Add conversion of tens place to ones place.
0214	8D 01 A0		STA	PAD	Result into Port A.
0217	A9 FF		LDA	$FF	Configure Port A into output port.
0219	8D 03 A0		STA	PADD	$FF into DDR of Port A.
021C	00		BRK		Finished.

The program in Example 10 converts the low-order nibble of a location to the seven-segment code necessary to indicate the hexa-

Table 8-4. Data for Hex Numeral to Seven-Segment Display Program

Seven-Segment Display	Output Port Bit Assignments	
	Bit 7 6 5 4 3 2 1 0 Segment g f e d c b a	

Hexadecimal Character	Output Data-Table Contents	Location
0	$3F	$03F0
1	06	$03F1
2	5B	$03F2
3	4F	$03F3
4	66	$03F4
5	6D	$03F5
6	7C	$03F6
7	07	$03F7
8	7F	$03F8
9	67	$03F9
A	77	$03FA
B	7C	$03FB
C	39	$03FC
D	5E	$03FD
E	79	$03FE
F	71	$03FF

decimal numeral on a seven-segment LED display. Table 8-4 summarizes the segment-bit assignments for the output port, and it lists the table contents that are necessary to perform the conversion. It will be assumed that a logic one lights the segment, while a logic zero at the output port will turn the segment off. Each segment can be controlled individually by the computer in this application.

Example 10: Hex-to-Seven-Segment Conversion Program

Object: Convert the low-order nibble of a memory location into the seven-segment code necessary to display the hexadecimal numeral which represents the nibble. Output the code to Port A.

```
$03F0 = TABLE
$A003 = PADD
$A001 = PAD
$A000 = PBD
```

0200	A9 FF	START	LDA	$FF	Configure Port A to be an output
0202	8D 03 A0		STA	PADD	port by loading $FF into its DDR.
0205	AD 00 A0		LDA	PBD	Get data to be displayed from Port B.
0208	29 0F		AND	$0F	Mask high-order nibble.
020A	A8		TAY		Put low-order nibble in Y for index.

```
020B   B9 0F 03          LDA  TABLE,Y      Look up code for seven-segment display.
020E   8D 01 A0          STA  PAD          Output code to Port A.
0211   00                BRK               Finished.
```

MULTIPLE-BYTE ARITHMETIC

The indexed addressing modes are also useful for performing multiple-byte arithmetic operations, especially when three or more bytes are involved. This is illustrated with a triple-precision decimal-mode addition program, shown in Example 11. Double precision sums were illustrated in Chapter 5, and you may want to refer to those examples. The process of adding numbers that must be represented by more than one byte is shown in Fig. 8-5. The illus-

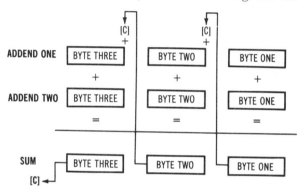

Fig. 8-5. Diagram of triple-precision sum.

tration applies both to binary numbers and decimal numbers. The only difference is that the decimal mode flag must be set to do decimal arithmetic, and it is assumed that in the decimal mode each byte represents a number no greater than 99. Note that this triple-precision addition program requires no more instructions than the double-precision program given in Example 6 in Chapter 5. If greater precision (more bytes) is required, then a savings in program bytes results from using the absolute indexed mode of addressing as illustrated by Example 11. The program in Example 11 is easily modified to add four-byte numbers, five-byte numbers, etc., simply by changing the LDY instruction to reflect the number of bytes used to represent the numbers being added. In Example 11, the *most-significant byte* of each of the numbers is stored in the location of the base address of NUM1, NUM2, and SUM, respectively. Thus, the most-significant byte of NUM1 is in location $0300, and the least-significant byte of NUM1 is in location $0302.

The program in Example 12 converts a four-digit hexadecimal number (16-bit binary number) to a decimal number. Since

Example 11: Triple-Precision Decimal Addition Program

Object: Perform a triple-precision decimal-mode addition. Use the Y register for the index. Y is the number of bytes used to represent the numbers involved in the sum.

$0300 = NUM1; most-significant byte of addend 1
$0310 = NUM2; most-significant byte of addend 2
$0320 = SUM; most-significant byte of sum

0200	18	START	CLC	Clear carry flag.
0201	F8		SED	Set decimal mode.
0202	A0 02		LDY $02	Initialize Y index to two.
0204	B9 00 03	BACK	LDA NUM1,Y	Get byte of NUM1.
0207	79 10 03		ADC NUM2,Y	Add to byte of NUM2.
020A	99 20 03		STA SUM,Y	Result into sum location.
020D	88		DEY	Decrement Y index.
020E	10 F4		BPL BACK	If Y $\geq$ 0, branch
0210	00		BRK	back to get other bytes.

the largest four-digit hexadecimal number is $FFFF, and since $FFFF $= 65535_{10}$, it is clear that five bcd nibbles are needed to represent the largest possible number. We will use three bytes of memory for the decimal number and two bytes for the hexadecimal number.

The conversion proceeds as follows. Let $PQRS be the four-digit hexadecimal number to be converted to bcd, in the sense that $P is the most-significant hexadecimal digit and $S is the least-significant hexadecimal digit. Using the base-16 place values, $PQRS can be expressed as follows:

$$\$PQRS = (\$P \cdot 4096_{10}) + (\$Q \cdot 256_{10}) + (\$R \cdot 16_{10}) + (\$S \cdot 1_{10}).$$

Thus, if we add 4096 to itself $P times, add 256 to itself $Q times, add 16 to itself $R times, and add 1 to itself $S times, *using the decimal mode,* then the conversion will be complete. Adding 4096 to itself and adding 256 to itself requires a double-precision (two-byte) sum, with the possibility of a carry into a third byte. That is the reason three bytes of memory, DCMLO, DCMMI, and DCMHI, are used in Example 12 to store the answer. The two-byte hexadecimal number to be converted to bcd will be stored in locations symbolized by PQ and RS. The numbers to be added, 4096, 256, 16, and 1, are stored in a table that is referenced using the absolute indexed addressing mode.

The program of Example 12 illustrates two indexed addressing techniques introduced in this chapter, namely:

- The use of tables for code conversions
- Multiple-precision arithmetic

Note that this four-hex-digit conversion program requires only three more instructions than its two-digit counterpart in Example 11 in

Chapter 7. The use of indexed addressing modes makes programming much more efficient.

One application of this program is related to the pulse counting mode of the 6522 versatile interface adapter that is described in Chapter 10. This integrated circuit is found on both the AIM 65 and the SYM-1. The 6522 has the ability to detect and count pulses on its PB6 pin. A 16-bit register keeps track of the number of pulses counted, and this register (occupying two memory locations)

Example 12: Four-Digit Hexadecimal to Five-Digit Decimal Conversion Program

Object: Convert $PQRS, a four digit hexadecimal number, to a five-digit decimal number. Assume $PQ is a location symbolized by PQ, and $RS is in a location symbolized by RS. The three-byte decimal number will be stored in three locations called DCMLO, DCMMI, and DCMHI.

$0001 = DCMLO; Low-order byte of decimal answer
$0002 = DCMMI; Middle-order byte of decimal answer
$0003 = DCMHI; High-order byte of decimal answer
$0010 = RS; Low-order byte of hexadecimal number
$0011 = PQ; High-order byte of hexadecimal number
$0300 = CNVLO; Four bytes, $96, $56, $16, $01, from $0300 to $0303, respectively
$0304 = CNVHI; Four bytes, $40, $02, $00, $00, from $0304 to $0307, respectively

0200	A9 00	START	LDA	$00	Clear the locations that will
0202	85 01		STA	DCMLO	contain the decimal answer.
0204	85 02		STA	DCMMI	
0206	85 03		STA	DCMHI	
0208	A2 03		LDX	$03	X will index number from the
020A	A5 10	MORE	LDA	RS	conversion table. Get $RS.
020C	29 0F		AND	$0F	Mask $R, leaving $S.
020E	F0 1A		BEQ	ARND	If $S = 0, skip the addition.
0210	A8		TAY		Otherwise transfer $S to Y to serve
0211	18		CLC		as a counter for $S additions.
0212	F8		SED		Clear carry and set decimal flags.
0213	A5 01	HERE	LDA	DCMLO	Get low-order byte of decimal number.
0215	7D 00 03		ADC	CNVLO,X	Add the two-digit number from the
0218	85 01		STA	DCMLO	conversion table.
021A	A5 02		LDA	DCMMI	Get the middle-order byte.
021C	7D 04 03		ADC	CNVHI,X	Add the most-significant digits of
021F	85 02		STA	DCMMI	the conversion numbers.
0221	A5 03		LDA	DCMHI	Get the high-order byte.
0223	69 00		ADC	$00	Add any carry from previous sum.
0225	85 03		STA	DCMHI	Result into high-order byte.
0227	88		DEY		Decrement Y before adding again
0228	D0 E9		BNE	HERE	to see when $S sums are complete.
022A	CA	ARND	DEX		The next higher place value will
022B	30 0C		BMI	FINISH	be converted by moving $PQRS four
022D	A0 04		LDY	$04	bits to the right. Y serves as the
022F	46 11	NIBRO	LSR	PQ	bit counter. Shift PQ right.
0231	66 10		ROR	RS	Rotate PQ into RS.
0233	88		DEY		Decrement bit counter until an
0234	D0 F9		BNE	NIBRO	entire nibble has been moved from
0236	4C 0A 02		JMP	MORE	PQ into RS. Jump back to convert
0239	00	FINISH	BRK		the next place value.

can be read by the 6502. Of course, the count is expressed in binary, but since human beings like their numbers in decimal, a conversion is necessary to produce a decimal representation on an output display.

INDIRECT ADDRESSING

The essential idea in indirect addressing is that the *location* referenced by the second byte of an instruction *does not* contain the data upon which the microprocessor operates. Instead, the zero-page location referenced by an instruction *contains the low address* (ADL) of the location of the data. The high address (ADH) of the location at which the data is to be found is in the next sequential zero-page memory location. Thus, the ADL and ADH address information is *pointed to* by the instruction.

Call the second byte of an instruction using the indirect addressing mode IAL, an acronym for indirect address low. The IAL is the low-order byte of the address of a *zero-page* memory location. Then the content of IAL is the ADL of the data to be operated on, and IAL + 1 contains the ADH of the data to be operated upon. A diagram of this is shown in Fig. 8-6. Symbolically,

$$[IAL] = ADL$$
$$[IAL + 1] = ADH$$
$$[ADL\text{-}ADH] = DATA$$

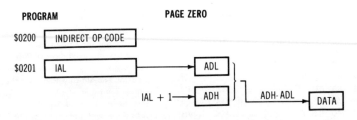

Fig. 8-6. Diagram of Indirect Addressing Mode.

Indirect addressing is always indicated by parentheses around the operand symbol. The parentheses are used to indicate that the *content* of the location symbolized is the *address* of the data to be operated on, rather than the data itself. It is worthwhile to ask what a hypothetical

LDA (MEM)

instruction would mean. This "instruction" would result in the accumulator being loaded with data from a location whose ADL was in MEM and whose ADH was in MEM + 1. The only instruction in

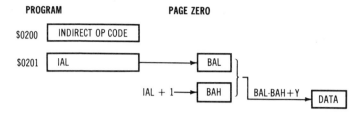

Fig. 8-7. Diagram of Indirect Indexed Addressing Mode.

the instruction set of the 6502 that uses indirect addressing is the JMP instruction. However, the indirect indexed addressing mode, studied next, is similar to the indirect addressing mode.

INDIRECT INDEXED ADDRESSING MODE

The *indirect indexed addressing mode* is similar to indirect addressing, except that it uses the Y register as an index. With indirect indexed addressing, the data to be operated on is found in a location identified by BAH-BAL + Y. Acronym BAL symbolizes "base-address low," and BAH symbolizes "base-address high." Thus the Y index has the same meaning as it did in the absolute indexed addressing mode. However, BAL and BAH are not given in the instruction. Instead, the second byte of an indirect indexed instruction is the low-order address of the page-zero location that contains BAL. As before, call the second byte of the indirect indexed instruction IAL. BAH is found in the location whose zero-page address is IAL + 1. Refer to the diagram in Fig. 8-7.

All indirect indexed instructions are two-byte instructions. The first byte is, as always, the op code. The second byte is the address-low (IAL) of the location in page zero that contains the base-address low (BAL) of the location that contains the data. The base-address high (BAH) is contained in location IAL + 1. When the microcomputer obtains BAL from location IAL in page zero, it *adds* the contents of the Y register to find the ADL of the data. Any carry from this result is added to the contents of location IAL + 1 to find the ADH of the data. Symbolically, the address of the location that contains the data is given by the expression:

$$ADH–ADL = BAH–BAL + Y$$

The fact that the carry from BAL + Y is added to BAH means that when an indexed address reaches $0AFF, the next sequential address is in the next page, namely $0B00. Example 13 illustrates how to calculate the address of the data referenced by an indirect indexed instruction.

Example 13: Calculating Address Referenced With Indirect Indexed Addressing Mode

In the following program, calculate the address of the location whose contents are transferred to the accumulator

```
[$00F0] = $67     [$00F1] = $03
0200   A0 23      LDY $23
0202   B1 F0      LDA (MEM),Y
```

Solution: Since MEM refers to location $00F0 and this location contains $67, the BAL is $67. The location MEM + 1 is $00F1, and it contains $03, so BAH–BAL = $0367. Then BAH–BAL + Y = $0367 + $23 = $038A, so the location referenced by the LDA (MEM),Y instruction is $038A.

If $Y = 0$, then the instruction

LDA (MEM),Y

works exactly like the hypothetical instruction described in the previous section. The data to be loaded into the accumulator is found in a location whose ADL is in the zero-page location MEM and whose ADH is in the zero-page location MEM + 1. The indirect indexed mode is frequently used with $Y = 0$. The diagram in Fig. 8-6 applies to this case. The instructions that have indirect indexed addressing capability include two data transfer instructions, the arithmetic and logical operations, and a comparison instruction.

The first programming example, given in Example 14, was inspired by the MEMORY TEST[1] program written by Butterfield. Readers who are interested in a good memory test program should consult the reference. We consider only the problem of loading the same number, say $FF, in all memory locations in page $PQ through page $RS of the address space. Refer to the detailed flowchart of this program given in Fig. 8-8. Locations $0001 and $0002 should

Example 14: Program to Load R/W Memory With a Number

Object: Load pages $PQ through $RS with $FF.
$0000 = TABLE
$0001 = START; [0001] = $PQ
$0002 = STOP; [0002] = $RS

0010	A0 00	ORIGIN	LDY $00	Initialize Y index to zero.
0012	84 00		STY TABLE	Initialize BAL of TABLE to zero.
0014	A6 02		LDX STOP	X register contains last page, RS.
0016	A9 FF		LDA $FF	Initialize A to $FF for load.
0018	91 00	BACK	STA (TABLE),Y	Store A in location BAH–BAL + Y. (BAH is in location $0001.)
001A	C8		INY	Increment index.
001B	D0 FB		BNE BACK	Branch back if Y ≠ 0; otherwise
001D	E6 01		INC START	page is filled so increment page number.
001F	E4 01		CPX START	Is page number [STOP] = RS?
0021	B0 F5		BCS BACK	No, fill another page. Yes, then task
0023	00		BRK	is finished.

---

[1]Butterfield, F. J., *The First Book of Kim,* Orb, Argonne, Illinois, 1977, p. 122.

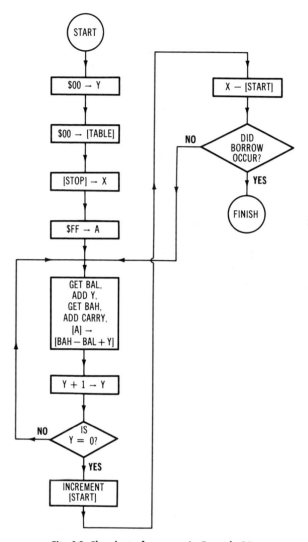

Fig. 8-8. Flowchart of program in Example 14.

contain the starting page number ($PQ) and the ending page number ($RS), respectively.

A SIMPLE MONITOR

Another example of the use of indirect indexing is shown in Example 15 which will be called the NIM-1 for Nibble Input Monitor. It allows the two I/O ports to be used to modify and display the contents of any location in memory. Data or address information is entered one nibble at a time using the switches on the I/O board. The contents of a location are displayed on the LEDs on the I/O board. Perhaps this simple monitor could be extended to initialize the program counter and execute programs, but our objectives were smaller in scope. We want to illustrate the indirect indexing mode, and we want to show how the most basic feature of a monitor could be implemented. To be precise, the program in Example 15 uses *indirect* addressing because the Y index is zero.

To use the NIM-1 and the I/O board to examine and modify a memory location, the NIM-1 program must be running, and these instructions must be followed.

- The four nibbles forming the address of the location to be modified are entered one nibble at a time, beginning with the high-order nibble and ending with the low-order nibble. PB5 is at logic one for an address nibble.
- The nibble value is determined by the settings of switches PB4, PB3, PB2, and PB1. PB4 is the high-order bit and PB1 is the low-order bit of the nibble.
- The two nibbles forming the data to be loaded are entered one nibble at a time using the same switches mentioned above. PB5 is at logic zero for a data nibble.
- When the switches are set (PB5 is at logic one for an address and at logic zero for data, and PB4, PB3, PB2, and PB1 represent the nibble), then changing the setting of the PB0 switch enters the information. Either a change from logic zero to logic one or a change from logic one to logic zero will enter the information. PB0 is debounced, so the nibble is only entered once.

A flowchart of the entire NIM-1 program is given in Fig. 8-9.

Example 15: Nibble-Input-Monitor: The NIM-1

Object: Use the I/O board to examine, modify, and display the contents of any location in memory.

```
$0000 = ADL
$0001 = ADH
$0002 = TEMP
$A003 = PADD
$A001 = PAD
$A000 = PBD
```

0010	A9 FF	ORIGIN	LDA	$FF	Load Port A data direction register
0012	8D 03 A0		STA	PADD	so it is an output port.
0015	B1 00	START	LDA	(ADL),Y	Output the data at the location
0017	8D 01 A0		STA	PAD	BAH–BAL + Y where BAL is [ADL]
					and BAH is [ADH].
001A	AE 00 A0		LDX	PBD	Read Port B.

001D	8A		CHECK	TXA	Save A in X.
001E	4D	00 A0		EOR PBD	Exclusive-OR with PBD to see if PB0
0021	29	01		AND $01	has changed. Mask all bits except PB0
0023	F0	F8		BEQ CHECK	Loop to CHECK if no transition occurred
0025	AD	00 A0		LDA PBD	Read Port B.
0028	29	3E		AND $3E	Mask bits not used for information.
002A	0A			ASL A	Move bit from PB5 into carry flag
002B	0A			ASL A	and the nibble into the high-order
002C	0A			ASL A	nibble of A. All other bits are zero.
002D	A2	04		LDX $04	Initialize X register to count four bits.
002F	85	02		STA TEMP	Store A temporarily.
0031	B0	0F		BCS ADDRSS	If carry was set, nibble was for address.
0033	A0	00		LDY $00	Set Y index to zero.
0035	B1	00	DATA	LDA (ADL),Y	Get contents of location to be modified.
0037	06	02		ASL TEMP	Shift high bit of nibble into carry.
0039	2A			ROL A	Rotate carry into A.
003A	91	00		STA (ADL),Y	Store modified data in location BAH–BAL.
003C	CA			DEX	Repeat four times to get entire nibble
003D	D0	F6		BNE DATA	into location.
003F	4C	15 00		JMP START	Go back to get more information.
0042	0A		ADDRSS	ASL A	Address information: Shift high bit
0043	26	00		ROL ADL	of nibble into carry flag. Rotate carry flag into ADL, high-order bit of ADL into carry flag, and carry
0045	26	01		ROL ADH	flag into ADH.
0047	CA			DEX	Repeat four more times to get entire
0048	D0	F8		BNE ADDRSS	nibble into the address.
004A	4C	15 00		JMP START	Go back to get more information.

INDEXED INDIRECT ADDRESSING

With *indirect indexing*, studied in the previous section, the index determined the location of the data. With *indexed indirect addressing*, the subject of this section, the *index determines the location of the address of the data.* The X register is the only register that may be used as an index in this mode.

The instruction

LDA (MEM,X),

where MEM is *zero-page* location whose low-order address is IAL, gets the ADL of the location of the data byte from the zero-page location IAL + X. The ADH of the data is found in the zero-page location IAL + (X + 1). Example 16 shows such a calculation, and Fig. 8-10 diagrams this addressing mode.

All indexed indirect instructions use the notation shown above for the LDA (MEM,X) instruction (see Table 8-1 for a list of instructions that have this mode available). They are two-byte instructions, the first byte being the op code, and the second byte being the IAL which, when added to X, gives the zero-page location where the ADL of the data byte is found.

Like indirect indexed addressing, indexed indirect addressing is useful in dealing with large quantities of information. Our last programming example illustrates how indexed indirect addressing

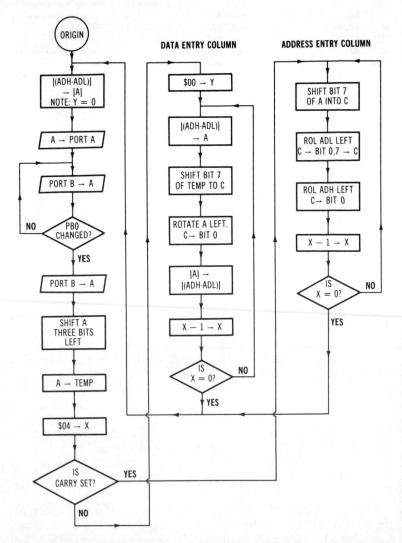

Fig. 8-9. Flowchart of NIM-1 Program. Notation [(ADH-ADL)] means "the contents of the location whose address is the contents of the locations ADH and ADL."

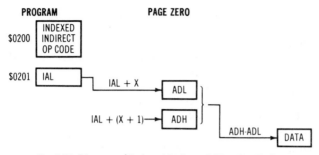

PROGRAM **PAGE ZERO**

Fig. 8-10. Diagram of Indexed Indirect Addressing Mode.

Example 16: Calculating the Address Referenced With Indexed Indirect Addressing Mode

Find the location referenced by the indexed indirect instruction in the following:

```
[$0017] = $FF       [$0018] = $A0
0200  A2 14   START   LDX $14
0202  E1 03   END     SBC (MEM,X)
```

Solution: The IAL is $03 + $14 = $17. Location $0017 contains $FF and location $0018 contains $A0, so the location referenced by the SBC (MEM,X) instruction is $A0FF.

can be used to input information from several sources. Suppose an instrument that collects data provides four output channels. (The author's application was a speech recognition circuit.) Assume that the four channels are multiplexed; that is, the data from a channel appears at a single I/O port on the computer, depending on the channel number (zero through three) that is loaded into another I/O port. The voltage level at the output of the multiplexer is converted to a 6-bit digital number by an analog-to-digital (A/D) circuit. When the circuit is busy making an analog-to-digital con-

Table 8-5. Multichannel Data Logging Program Information

Write Multiplexer Port		Read Data Port
$00	selects	Channel-0 Data
$01	selects	Channel-1 Data
$02	selects	Channel-2 Data
$03	selects	Channel-3 Data
[$0000] = [Base Address Low of Channel-0 Table] = $00.		
[$0001] = [Base Address High of Channel-0 Table] = $03.		
[$0002] = [Base Address Low of Channel-1 Table] = $40.		
[$0003] = [Base Address High of Channel-1 Table] = $03.		
[$0004] = [Base Address Low of Channel-2 Table] = $80.		
[$0005] = [Base Address High of Channel-2 Table] = $03.		
[$0006] = [Base Address Low of Channel-3 Table] = $C0.		
[$0007] = [Base Address High of Channel-3 Table] = $03.		

version, bit seven of the data port is one. When the conversion is complete, bit seven is zero. Table 8-5 summarizes the pertinent information for the system.

All four channels must be read and the data stored in a table, one table for each channel. After all four channels are read, a delay of 10 ms is inserted before they are read again, until $64_{10} = \$40$ data points have been read for each channel. The channel-zero data will be stored in locations $0300 through $033F, channel-one data in locations $0340–$037F, channel-two data in locations $0380–$03BF, and channel-three data in locations $03C0–$03FF. The machine language version is not given because it is unlikely that you would use exactly the same program.

Example 17: Logging Four Channels of Input Data

Object: Read and log the four-channel system described in the text.

$0000 = TABLE
$0000 = BAL0
$0002 = BAL1
$0004 = BAL2
$0006 = BAL3

```
ORIGIN    LDX  $00          Initialize X index to zero.
HERE      LDY  $00          Initialize Y index to zero, Y = Channel Number.
AGAIN     STY  MULTPLX      Store Y in multiplexer to select channel.
BACK      LDA  DATA         Get A/D data at data port.
          BMI  BACK         If bit seven is one, A/D is busy.
          STA  (TABLE,X)    Otherwise store data in table.
          INX               Advance X to select the BAL of
          INX               the next table.
          INY               Advance Y to get next channel.
          CPY  $04          If Y < 4, branch back to get data from
          BCC  AGAIN        another channel.
          INC  BAL0         Otherwise, the first data point for each
          INC  BAL1         channel has been logged. Next, increase
          INC  BAL2         the BAL of each table, so the next point
          INC  BAL3         will be stored in the next location.
          LDA  BAL3         If BAL3 is $00, the whole table has been
          BEQ  OUT          filled, so the task is finished.
            .
            .               Otherwise delay here with interval timer.
            .
          JMP  HERE         Then jump back to get more points.
OUT       . . . . . . . .
```

INTRODUCTION TO THE EXPERIMENTS

Having advanced to this stage in your knowledge of the 6502 instruction set, you should feel more like writing your own programs than repeating the ones in the text. The experiments that follow give you some experience with the programs we studied in this chapter; some experiments suggest another program to write, a program that is somewhat similar to the one being studied. You have probably thought of programs you want to write for yourself, and you should take the time to try a few of these. You have now learned all but a few instructions of the instruction set, so you should be able to write programs. If you cannot think of any programs of your own, here are a few ideas to try for programming experience:

- A program to load data from the I/O board Port B into a table
- A five-byte addition program
- A program to transfer one page of memory to another page of memory
- A program to relocate a program (difficult)
- A program to transfer a table in an input buffer to the top of an existing table someplace in memory
- A program to handle N input channels simultaneously, storing each channel in a separate page in memory
- A program to implement an FIFO (First-In, First-Out) memory for a given number of bytes, say N bytes
- A program to implement a LIFO (Last-In, First-Out) memory for 256 bytes.

EXPERIMENT NO. 1

Step 1

Load the program in Example 8-4, which is listed below for convenience.

```
0200   A2 00      START    LDX $00
0202   A9 FF               LDA $FF
0204   9D 00 03   BACK     STA TABLE,X
0207   E8                  INX
0208   D0 FA               BNE BACK
020A   00                  BRK
```

Step 2

Execute the program. Check a number of locations in page three of memory to see if the program worked. Change the byte at location $0203 to $00. Now what do you expect to find in page three locations?

(The first time the program is run should result in $FF being stored in every page three location. The second time the program is run should clear every location in page three.)

EXPERIMENT NO. 2

Step 1

Load the program in Example 6. It is listed here for convenience.

0200	A9	FF		START	LDA $FF
0202	8D	03	A0		STA PADD
0205	A2	10			LDX $10
0207	B5	A0		AGAIN	LDA ZTAB,X
0209	CA			BACK	DEX
020A	30	07			BMI OUT
020C	D5	A0			CMP ZTAB,X
020E	B0	F9			BCS BACK
0210	4C	07	02		JMP AGAIN
0213	8D	01	A0	OUT	STA PAD
0216	00				BRK

Step 2

Clear locations $00A0 through $00B0. Run the program. What do you expect to see at Port A?

(If all the locations are loaded with $00, the largest value in the table is $00. All the Port A LEDs should go out.)

Step 3

Put some other numbers in locations $00A0 through $00B0, noting the largest. Now run the program, and check to make sure it does find the largest number.

Step 4

Modify the program to find the smallest number in the same table, and to output this number to Port A. Check your program to see if it works.

EXPERIMENT NO. 3

Step 1

Load the program in Example 7, which is listed below for convenience.

0200	A9	00	START	LDA $00
0202	85	00		STA SUMLO
0204	85	01		STA SUMHI
0206	D8			CLD
0207	A2	0F		LDX $0F
0209	18		BACK	CLC

```
020A   B5  A0           LDA  TABLE,X
020C   65  00           ADC  SUMLO
020E   85  00           STA  SUMLO
0210   A5  01           LDA  SUMHI
0212   69  00           ADC  $00
0214   85  01           STA  SUMHI
0216   CA               DEX
0217   10  F0           BPL  BACK
0219   00               BRK
```

Step 2

Clear the locations $00A0 through $00AF. Execute the program. What do you expect to find in SUMLO and SUMHI, locations $0000 and $0001, respectively?

(You should find $00 in both locations.)

Step 3

Load all of the locations in the table with $FF. Now what do you expect to find in SUMLO and SUMHI?

(You should find $F1 in SUMLO, and SUMHI should contain $0E since $F · $FF = $0EF1.)

Step 4

Write a program to subtract the same number from all the numbers in a table. It will not look exactly like Example 7, but it should use Z-PAGE,X addressing. Assume the table is in locations $00A0 through $00AF.

EXPERIMENT NO. 4

Step 1

Load the program in Example 8, listed here for convenience. This experiment will use the I/O board, so attach it to the application port. Also load the conversion table, Table 8-2, into memory.

```
0200   A9  FF       START   LDA  $FF
0202   8D  03  A0           STA  PADD
0205   AD  00  A0           LDA  PBD
0208   29  0F               AND  $0F
020A   AA                   TAX
020B   BD  00  03           LDA  TABLE,X
020E   8D  01  A0           STA  PAD
0211   00                   BRK
```

Step 2

For convenience in running the program, change the BRK instruction to a JMP 0205 instruction, putting the program in a loop that runs continuously.

Step 3

Set up a hex nibble on the Port B switches PB3–PB0. For example, set the switches to $A. What should you observe at Port A?

(Since the program converts the hex number represented by the four switches to ASCII, you should observe $41 at Port A.)

Step 4

Alter the switches PB3–PB0, and check to see if the program is making the correct conversion. Use Table 8-2 to check your answers.

Step 5

Try writing a program to take an ASCII character from some location and convert it to the low-order nibble of another location. Table 8-2 should be useful. Use a table to perform the conversion.

EXPERIMENT NO. 5

Step 1

Load the program in Example 9. If you are not using an AIM 65, you may want to add an AND $BF instruction after the LDA PBD instruction to mask bit six.

0200	D8		START	CLD
0201	AD 00 A0			LDA PBD
0204	AA			TAX
0205	29 0F			AND $0F
0207	85 10			STA TEMP
0209	8A			TXA
020A	4A			LSR A
020B	4A			LSR A
020C	4A			LSR A
020D	4A			LSR A
020E	AA			TAX
020F	B5 00			LDA TABLE,X
0211	18			CLC
0212	65 10			ADC TEMP
0214	8D 01 A0			STA PAD
0217	A9 FF			LDA $FF
0219	8D 03 A0			STA PADD
021C	00			BRK

Step 2

Set up two bcd digits on the Port B switches. Make sure Table 8-3 is in memory. Run the program. Does the program convert bcd to binary correctly? For example, if the digits 95 are set up on the port input switches, what do you expect to see at Port A?

($95_{10} = \$5F$ so you should observe $5F at Port A.)

Step 3

Try writing a program to convert a hexadecimal number less than $64 = 100_{10}$ to two bcd digits and output them at Port A.

EXPERIMENT NO. 6

Step 1

Load the NIM-1, Example 15. The program is quite long, so it is not repeated here. Turn back to the original listing to load it into memory.

Step 2

Execute the program. Following the instructions for entering address and data information, enter $00 in location $0300. This is accomplished as follows:

- Set PB5 to 1 (address mode) and PB4–PB1 to represent $0. Change switch PB0.
- Set PB5 to 1 and PB4–PB1 to represent $3. Change switch PB0.
- Set PB5 to 1 and PB4–PB1 to represent $0. Change switch PB0.
- Enter the last zero in the address by leaving PB5–PB1 the same as in the previous step; then change switch PB0 to enter the nibble.

The address $0300 is now entered. To enter $00 as data:

- Set PB5 to 0. PB4–PB1 should represent $0. Change switch PB0.
- Change switch PB0 to enter the second nibble.

Now examine location $0300. It should contain $00, and all the Port A LEDs should be off.

Step 3

Enter $7F in location $0300. Since the monitor is already set up to modify location $0300, we can leave it in the data mode (PB5 at 0) and enter $7F with these steps.

- Set switches PB4–PB1 to represent $7. Change PB0.
- Set switches PB4–PB1 to represent $F. Change PB0.

Examine location $0300 to see if your I/O board and NIM-1 monitor did actually enter $7F in this location, and that Port A does represent the data found in a location.

EXPERIMENT NO. 7

Step 1

Breadboard the circuit shown in Fig. 8-11. The author used a ribbon cable from a 22/44-pin edge connector on the application port to a dip socket on an AP Products Superstrip. (These parts are available from JAMECO Electronics, 1021 Howard Ave., San Carlos, CA 94070.)

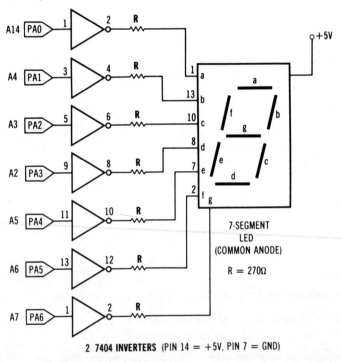

2 7404 INVERTERS (PIN 14 = +5V, PIN 7 = GND)

Fig. 8-11. Circuit diagram for Experiment No. 7. Pin numbers on application connector are given for each bit of Port A used.

Step 2

Load the program in Example 10. It is listed below for convenience. Also load Table 8-4 into memory.

```
0200   A9 FF      START    LDA  $FF
0202   8D 03 A0            STA  PADD
```

```
0205   AD 00 A0          LDA  PBD
0208   29 0F             AND  $0F
020A   A8                TAY
020B   B9 F0 03          LDA  TABLE,Y
020E   8D 01 A0          STA  PAD
0211   00                BRK
```

Step 3

Change the BRK instruction at location $0211 to a JMP 0205 so the program will run as a continuous loop.

Step 4

What is the status of the LEDs on the seven-segment display when the system is RESET?

Step 5

Now try to input various nibbles on the Port B switches. You should observe the hex numeral corresponding to the switch settings on PB3–PB0.

CHAPTER 9

Subroutines,
The Stack, and
Interrupts

OBJECTIVES

At the completion of this chapter you should be able to:

- Understand the function of subroutines and use them in programs.
- Understand how the stack is used in processing subroutines and interrupts.
- Use the JSR, RTS, CLI, SEI, RTI, PHA, PHP, PLA, PLP, TXS, TSX, BRK, and NOP instructions. See Table 9-1 for a summary.
- Write programs that make use of subroutines and interrupts.

INTRODUCTION

With few exceptions, the programs in this book that have been used to illustrate the 6502 instruction set would generally be part of larger programs with more elaborate objectives. For example, the program in Example 10 in Chapter 7 that converts two bcd digits to an 8-bit binary number might be part of a much longer data-logging program in which the input data is manipulated and displayed on an oscilloscope or output to a printer. As such, the bcd to binary program would be called a *routine*. Long programs can frequently be divided into groups of simpler programs, each of

Table 9-1. Summary of Instructions Introduced in Chapter 9

Instruction	Description	Addressing Mode Op-Codes	
		Implied	Absolute
BRK	Force Interrupt	00	
CLI	Clear Interrupt Disable Flag	58	
JSR	Jump to Subroutine		20
NOP	No Operation	EA	
PHA	Push Accumulator on Stack	48	
PHP	Push P Register on Stack	08	
PLA	Pull Accumulator from Stack	68	
PLP	Pull P Register from Stack	28	
RTI	Return from Interrupt	40	
RTS	Return from Subroutine	60	
SEI	Set Interrupt Disable Flag	78	
TSX	Transfer Stack Pointer to X Register	8A	
TXS	Transfer X Register to Stack Pointer	9A	

which is usually referred to as a routine. A 16-bit multiplication program might be part of the interpreter of a high-level language, such as FORTRAN. As such, it would be called a *multiplication routine*.

If a program requires the use of a particular routine in several different places in the program, then the instructions for that routine would have to be repeated. This is inefficient programming. It would be better if the routine could be written and stored once, and the program could *jump* to the routine whenever it was needed, followed by a *return* to the main program.

The 6502 microprocessor has two quite different, but extremely important, ways of jumping to and returning from routines. The first is through the use of the JSR (Jump to Subroutine) instruction and the RTS (Return from Subroutine) instruction. The second way of jumping to a routine is through the use of *interrupts*. In this case, an external circuit signals the microprocessor and requests that it jump to a particular routine, called an *interrupt routine*. These two techniques for calling a routine will be discussed in detail in this chapter. The various instructions that are used in calling and processing these two types of routines are summarized in Table 9-1.

SUBROUTINES

A routine that may be used at several points in a program through the use of the JSR instruction is called a *subroutine*. Like a program, a subroutine has a specific objective, such as multiplying two 8-bit numbers. Once designed as a subroutine, it cannot be used by itself. The program of which the subroutine is a part is called the *main program*. The main program can use (or call) the subroutine at any point through the use of the JSR instruction. On the other hand, the subroutine signals the main program that it has completed its objective with an RTS instruction. The main program then continues execution at the instruction following the JSR instruction. In this way, the instructions in the subroutine have been "inserted" in the main program, between the JSR instruction and the one that follows it.

The JSR instruction is a three-byte instruction. The first byte is the op code ($20), the second byte is the ADL for the location of the first instruction in the subroutine, and the third byte is the ADH for the location of the first byte in the subroutine. Consider the program excerpt shown in Table 9-2. The STA, LDA, and LDX are just "dummy" instructions used to illustrate the fact that the JSR instruction is usually found somewhere in the middle of a main program. It is also assumed in Table 9-2 that there are many instructions in the subroutine, only the first and last of which have been shown.

Referring to Table 9-2, the JSR MLTP instruction results in a jump to the subroutine labeled MLTP, and the op code of the first instruction in subroutine MLTP is located at address $0300. The instruction located at this address will be executed immediately following execution of the JSR MLTP instruction. Subsequent instructions in the subroutine will be executed until an RTS (Return from Subroutine) instruction is encountered.

The RTS instruction is a single-byte instruction, op code = $60. Execution of this instruction results in the main program continuing at the instruction following the JSR instruction. In the example shown in Table 9-2, the RTS instruction would result in the next op code being fetched from the location whose address is $0253; that is, the location immediately following the last byte of the JSR instruction.

The JSR instruction contains the information necessary to find the first instruction of the subroutine, but the RTS instruction is

Table 9-2. Example of Subroutine Call and Return from Subroutine

Location	Instruction	Label	Mnemonic	Operand	Comments
024D	8D 03 04	MAIN	STA	MEM	
0250	20 00 03		JSR	MLTP	Jump to subroutine labeled MLTP.
0253	AD 03 04		LDA	MEM	
0300	A2 FF	MLTP	LDX	$FF	
•			•		
•			•		
•			•		
0344	60		RTS		Return from subroutine

a single-byte instruction and contains no such information. How could it? Since, as indicated, a jump to a subroutine may occur anywhere in the main program, there will be a number of different "return locations."

How does the microprocessor know where to return to get the next instruction after a subroutine call has been completed? Before the microprocessor jumps to the subroutine, it stores the *address of the location of the third byte* of the JSR instruction in a special section of read/write memory called *the stack*. Execution of the RTS instruction results in a fetch of this address which is then loaded into the program counter. The program counter is then automatically incremented by one to identify the address at which the op code immediately following the JSR instruction is stored. In the example shown in Table 9-2, the address of the $03 byte is stored on the stack. That is, ADL $52 and ADH $02 are stored on the stack. Upon executing the RTS instruction, these two numbers are loaded back into the program counter of the microprocessor, the $52 is incremented by one, and the number $0253 becomes the new PCH-PCL and, thus, the address of the location of the next op code. Since both subroutines and interrupts, to be described in a subsequent section of this chapter, make use of the stack, we now turn to an explanation of the operation of the stack.

THE STACK

The stack is a series of read/write memory locations in page one of memory (addresses $0100–$01FF). The stack area starts at address $01FF and extends downward in memory, but no farther than address $0100. It is sometimes called a *push down* stack because locations are filled from the top location, whose address is $01FF, downward; but locations are emptied (loosely speaking) from the bottom upward. It could better be called *FILO* for "first-in, last-out" memory. The *first* byte placed on the stack by the microprocessor is the *last* byte taken off the stack.

All stack operations make use of the *stack pointer*, the only internal register of the 6502 that has not yet been mentioned. The stack pointer is an 8-bit register which contains the low-order address (ADL) of the next *empty* or available location on the stack. The location just above this may be called the *top* of the stack, since it was the last location filled by a stack operation. When the contents of the stack pointer are placed on the address bus, an ADH of $01 always appears along with the contents of the stack pointer as ADL. Thus, in a certain sense, the stack pointer is a 16-bit register with the most significant byte always being equivalent to $01. That is, the ADH of the location to be referenced by a stack operation is always $01, while the ADL for the location comes from the stack pointer. (If the address line A8 is not decoded, as in the case of some small microprocessor-based designs, then the stack will be in page zero.)

The stack pointer is always initialized to $FF by a RESET operation. You may check this by pressing the RESET button on your computer and then using the monitor to examine the contents of this register. There may be situations in which it is undesirable to have the stack near the top of page one in memory. Two instructions allow the stack pointer to be set to any page-one location or, if necessary, to be checked. The TSX instruction transfers the contents of the stack pointer to the X register. This may be used to see how much of the stack has been used. The TXS instruction transfers the contents of the X register to the stack pointer. This may be used to set the stack pointer to other locations in page one of memory for the stack. One could, with considerable care in programming, operate two or more stacks in page one through the use of the TXS and TSX instructions. However, great care must be exercised to make sure the stack does not wrap around, for when the stack pointer reaches $00, it will be decremented to $FF with the next stack operation, and then it will start writing over data at the bottom of the stack, address $01FF.

To understand how the stack is used for subroutine calls, consider again the program example in Table 9-2. Assume that the system has been RESET so that the stack pointer is $FF before the program is executed. Upon execution of the JSR MLTP instruction, the number $02, representing the ADH of byte three in the JSR MLTP instruction, is stored in the location with address $01FF. The stack pointer is then decremented by the microprocessor to $FE, and the number $52, representing the ADL of byte three in the JSR MLTP instruction, is stored at the location whose address is $01FE Again, the stack is decremented and it becomes $FD. Finally, the number $0300 is put in the program counter on the address bus to fetch the first op code in the subroutine. The subroutine is then executed.

The RTS instruction causes the stack pointer to be incremented from $FD to $FE, and the contents of the location with address $01FE is loaded into the PCL. The stack pointer is incremented again, and the contents of the location whose address is $01FF is put into the PCH. Next, the program counter is incremented, and the program counter contents, now $0253, are placed on the address bus to fetch the op code of the instruction following the JSR instruction in the main program.

The JSR and RTS instructions may be summarized briefly as follows:

- JSR—Push the address of the third byte of the JSR instruction on the top of the stack in the order ADH, ADL. Place the second and third bytes of the JSR instruction into the PCL and PCH, respectively. Continue execution.
- RTS—Pull the top two bytes off the stack and place them in the program counter in the order PCL, PCH. Increment the program counter and continue execution.

It is clear that the JSR and RTS instructions require the microprocessor to perform several operations, and, consequently, one would expect that these instructions take a lot of time. They do. An examination of the instruction set summary or the complete instruction set for the 6502 shows that they each take six clock cycles, whereas the shortest instructions only take two clock cycles. In applications where time is critical, it may be necessary to avoid subroutines; but, in many other applications, the expense in time is worth the programming convenience and savings in the memory space allotted to the program. Your microcomputer monitor is a good place to look for the applications of subroutines.

NESTED SUBROUTINES

To understand the idea of nested subroutines and how the stack works, consider Example 1. This program does nothing except demonstrate the concept of nested subroutines. The main program is simply a loop consisting of a subroutine call, namely JSR ONE. Note that subroutine ONE calls another subroutine, subroutine TWO. This represents a nested subroutine, because one subroutine is calling another. Finally, subroutine TWO calls subroutine THREE, which also does nothing, whereupon it returns to subroutine TWO. Subroutine TWO returns to subroutine ONE, and subroutine ONE returns to the main program. The sequence of instruction executions is illustrated in Table 9-3. We have, so to speak, subroutines nested three deep. In Example 9-1, observe that

Example 1: Demonstration of Nested Subroutines

MAIN PROGRAM

0010	20 00 01	MAIN	JSR ONE	Jump to subroutine ONE.
0013	4C 10 00		JMP MAIN	Loop back to jump to subroutine ONE.

SUBROUTINE ONE

0100	20 00 02	ONE	JSR TWO	Jump to subroutine TWO.
0103	60		RTS	Return to main program.

SUBROUTINE TWO

0200	20 00 03	TWO	JSR THREE	Jump to subroutine THREE.
0203	60		RTS	Return to subroutine ONE.

SUBROUTINE THREE

0300	60	THREE	RTS	Return to subroutine TWO.

Table 9-3. Instruction Execution Sequence and Stack Pointer Values for Example 1

Location	Instruction	Stack Pointer	Page One Memory Locations By ADL						
			$FF	$FE	$FD	$FC	$FB	$FA	$F9
(Initial Values)		$FF	XX	XX	XX	XX	XX	XX	XX
0010	20 JSR 0100		(XX means "don't care")						
		$FD	00	12	XX	XX	XX	XX	XX
0100	20 JSR 0200								
		$FB	00	12	01	02	XX	XX	XX
0200	20 JSR 0300								
		$F9	00	12	01	02	02	02	XX
0300	60 RTS								
		$FB	00	12	01	02	XX	XX	XX
0203	60 RTS								
		$FD	00	12	XX	XX	XX	XX	XX
0103	60 RTS								
		$FF	XX	XX	XX	XX	XX	XX	XX
0013	4C JMP 0010								
		$FF	XX	XX	XX	XX	XX	XX	XX
0010	20 JSR 0100								
		$FD	00	12	XX	XX	XX	XX	XX
.	.	.							
.	.	.							
.	.	.							

the subroutine label, TWO for example, also labels the starting location of the subroutine.

Although the program in Example 9-1 was introduced for the sole purpose of demonstrating nested subroutines and the operation of the stack with nested subroutines, you might want to make the program more useful by putting delay loops, see Chapter 6, in each of the subroutines. For example, suppose subroutine THREE produces a 10-millisecond delay. Subroutine TWO might produce a 100-millisecond delay by calling subroutine THREE ten times. If subroutine ONE called subroutine TWO ten times, then subroutine ONE would produce a delay of 1 second. Thus, the programmer would have a choice of three delays, 1 second, 100 milliseconds, or ten milliseconds, by calling subroutine ONE, TWO, or THREE, respectively.

The implementation is left to the reader. Precise delays are more easily programmed through the use of interval timers, the subject of the next chapter.

When the program in Example 1 is executed, the sequence of instruction executions is shown in Table 9-3. Also shown is the value of the stack pointer after execution of each instruction, and the contents of the stack locations used by the program are given on the right-hand side of the table. After executing the first JSR instruction, the stack pointer is $FD, meaning locations with addresses $01FF and $01FE have been filled. In particular, these locations contain the ADH and ADL of the last byte of the first JSR instruction, as can be seen from the contents of the stack. It can be seen that subroutines nested three deep will require at least six locations in the stack. The stack is said to be six locations deep. Observe that, as the RTS instructions are executed, the stack pointer is incremented until it is again $FF when all the subroutines have been executed.

USE OF THE STACK FOR STORAGE

A program that makes use of the X register, for example, may have a subroutine that also requires the use of this register. Furthermore, the contents of the processor status register (P register) will undoubtedly change during execution of the subroutine, but it may be necessary to preserve the flag settings in the P register for the part of the main program that follows the subroutine. Clearly, it is desirable to have some way of saving the contents of the 6502 internal registers so that a subroutine may use them and so that after execution of a subroutine the registers may be restored to the same value they had prior to the use of the subroutine. Of course, certain memory locations could be allocated for the purpose of saving registers, but there is a more efficient technique that makes use of the stack and several so-called stack operations.

Here we summarize the principal stack operations; S stands for the contents of the stack pointer, and M_S stands for a memory location in page one whose low address corresponds to the stack pointer.

- PHA—Push Accumulator on the Stack: place the contents of the accumulator on the stack, then decrement the stack pointer. Logically, $A \rightarrow M_S$, $S - 1 \rightarrow S$. See Fig. 9-1.
- PHP—Push the P register on the Stack: place the contents of the processor status register on the stack, then decrement the stack pointer. Logically, $P \rightarrow M_S$, $S - 1 \rightarrow S$. See Fig. 9-2.

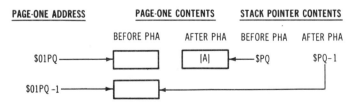

Fig. 9-1. Diagram of PHA Instruction. In this diagram, A symbolizes accumulator and PQ symbolizes any two-digit hexadecimal number.

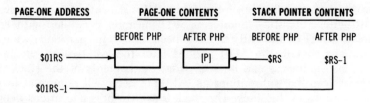

Fig. 9-2. Diagram of PHP Instruction. P symbolizes processor status register and RS symbolizes any two-digit hexadecimal number.

- PLA—Pull Accumulator from the Stack: increment the stack pointer, then load the accumulator with the contents of the stack. Logically, $S + 1 \rightarrow S$, $M_S \rightarrow A$. See Fig. 9-3.

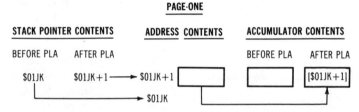

Fig. 9-3. Diagram of PLA Instruction. JK symbolizes any two-digit hexadecimal number.

- PLP—Pull the P register from the Stack: increment the stack pointer, then load the P register with the contents of the stack. Logically, $S + 1 \rightarrow S$, $M_S \rightarrow P$. See Fig. 9-4.

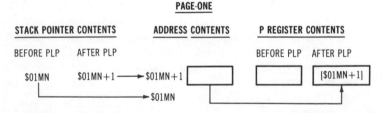

Fig. 9-4. Diagram of PLP Instruction. MN symbolizes any two-digit hexadecimal number.

Assume that the contents of both the accumulator and the P register are to be preserved during a subroutine jump. Before the JSR instruction, one would place a PHA and a PHP instruction. After the JSR instruction, still in the main program, one would have a PLP and a PLA instruction, *in that order*. Remember, the accumulator was "first in" so it will be "last out." It is very important to keep track of the order in which data to be saved is placed on the stack, because it is *taken from the stack in reverse order.* The "save" instructions could be in the subroutine instead, the PHA and PHP being the first two instructions in the subroutine instead, and the PLP and PLA the last two instructions before the RTS instruction.

It is also very important that these instructions occur in pairs. That is, for every PHA instruction there should be a PLA instruction, and for every PHP instruction there should be a PLP instruction. If this is not the case, then the stack pointer will not correctly point to the data that is to be transferred. There may be a few exceptions to the rule of having the save instructions occur in pairs, but it is a good rule to keep in mind when programming.

To save the X register, for example, during a subroutine jump, it is first transferred to the accumulator and then to the stack before the subroutine call. After the subroutine call the contents of the stack are placed in the accumulator, and the accumulator contents are transferred to the X register. The program in Example 2 illustrates these ideas.

Example 2: Saving X Register During Subroutine Call

Show how the X register may be preserved during a subroutine call.

Solution: The program listing for the main program would appear as follows:

TXA	Transfer the X register to the accumulator.
PHA	Push A on the stack.
JSR MLTP	Jump to subroutine MLTP.
PLA	Pull A from the stack.
TAX	Transfer the accumulator to the X register.

The contents of the internal registers of the 6502 may also be saved by putting the save instructions in the subroutine. Example 3 shows how the accumulator, X register, and Y register may be saved during a subroutine call by placing the save instructions in the subroutine.

Example 3: Saving X and Y Registers During Subroutine Call

Show how the accumulator, X register and Y register may be saved with stack operations placed in the subroutine.

Solution: The subroutine would appear as follows:

PHA	Transfer A to the stack.
TYA	Transfer Y to A.
PHA	Push A on the stack.
TXA	Transfer X to A.
PHA	Push A on the stack.
•	
•	Subroutine instructions.
•	
PLA	Pull A from the stack.
TAX	Transfer A to X.
PLA	Pull A from the stack.
TAY	Transfer A to Y.
PLA	Pull A from the stack.
RTS	

The stack operation instructions are not used exclusively with subroutines and interrupts. They may be used anywhere in a program or subroutine where a few simple instructions will save a byte of data momentarily. An examination of the instruction set will show that the stack operations are only one cycle longer than the necessary STA and LDA instructions, if one is saving data. Keep in mind, however, that if a subroutine requires several stack operations in addition to the JSR and RTS instructions, then it requires a great deal of time. This is of concern only in those applications where time is a critical factor. In many applications, this is not the case.

Another illustration of a situation in which a subroutine is useful is shown in Example 4. Suppose we have a rather extensive program such as a monitor, FORTRAN interpreter, or an assembler, all of which require lengthy communication with an input device and an output device. We will assume that both I/O devices use the ASCII format; that is, an ASCII character is read at the keyboard input port, and, when it is necessary to produce an output, an ASCII character is written to an output port. Clearly, programs such as this are required to input and output information at many places in the program, and subroutine calls provide a convenient way of accomplishing this. Furthermore, in certain cases the output should *mimic* or *echo* the input. For example, when an input key is pressed, the same character should appear on the video monitor or teletypewriter.

Example 4 is a partial *simulation* of such a situation. The main program is a "dummy" program that represents an interpreter, assembler, or a monitor. In our case, we just use an infinite loop containing three subroutine calls. The subroutines are more realistic, although in an actual case they might be more complicated. We assume the keyboard produces a 7-bit ASCII character at bits PB6–PB0 of Port B. Bit seven of Port B is used by the keyboard to signal the computer that a character is ready. The keyboard makes bit seven (PB7) of Port B logic zero if a character is ready (key depressed); otherwise it is at logic one. The INPUT subroutine simply loops until a character is entered from the keyboard; then it returns to the main program, which, in a real situation, would process the input until it was ready for another character from the keyboard. This type of keyboard operation is called *polling*. The program *polls* the keyboard until a character is ready. Observe that the accumulator serves to pass the character from the subroutine to the main program.

If it is necessary to output a character, the main program calls the OUTPUT subroutine. We have used Port A to simulate this output location. Finally, if the main program must "echo" the input to the output, it calls the ECHO subroutine. The ECHO subroutine not only passes an ASCII character to the main program, but it also outputs the same ASCII character to the output device. Again, the main program is not to be taken literally. It is meant to simulate a much longer program that calls these subroutines.

Example 4: Program to Simulate ASCII Input and Output Subroutines

Objective: Write a program to poll a keyboard with an "input" subroutine, write ASCII characters to an output device with an "output" subroutine, and write a subroutine that echos the input to the output.

$1700 = PAD; Port A Output Port
$1701 = PADD; Port A Data Direction Register
$1702 = KYBD; Keyboard Input

0200	20 00 03	START	JSR INPUT	Jump to INPUT subroutine.
0203	20 10 03		JSR OUTPUT	Jump to OUTPUT subroutine.
0206	20 20 03		JSR ECHO	Jump to ECHO subroutine.
0209	4C 00 02		JMP START	Loop to start over.
0300	AD 02 17	INPUT	LDA KYBD	Read data from keyboard.
0303	30 FB		BMI INPUT	If bit seven in one, wait until
0305	60		RTS	key is depressed. Otherwise, return with ASCII character.
0310	8D 00 17	OUTPUT	STA PAD	Write data to Port A.
0313	60		RTS	Return to main program.
0320	20 00 03	ECHO	JSR INPUT	Get data from keyboard.
0323	20 10 03		JSR OUTPUT	Write data to output port.
0326	60		RTS	Return to main program.

INTERRUPTS

Once a program has begun execution, nothing short of hitting the RESET button, pulling the plug, or dropping a hammer on the 6502 will stop it. The programs already described in this book either continued by jumping to the monitor (BRK instruction) or they ran continuously in some kind of loop with the use of a branch instruction or the JMP instruction. The program counter was under complete control of the program and the microprocessor, as opposed to outside or external influences. Even the monitor runs continuously, so in all cases the program flow was controlled by the software, that is, the program itself.

To allow external devices, for example, a keyboard, panic button, or interval timer, to exert control over the program flow, the 6502 has the capability of being *interrupted* by external circuitry. In particular, a logic-zero voltage level on the *interrupt request* (IRQ) pin on the microprocessor may cause an interrupt, or a logic one to logic zero (negative edge) transition on the nonmaskable interrupt (NMI) pin on the microprocessor can interrupt the program that is currently being executed.

What happens when an external device produces an interrupt by bringing the IRQ pin to logic zero or by producing a negative transition on the NMI pin? These are the events that follow an interrupt request on the IRQ pin.

- The instruction currently being executed by the processor is completed.
- If bit two in the processor status register (the IRQ disable flag) is a one, the interrupt request is ignored and program execution continues.
- Assuming that the IRQ disable flag in the P register was cleared that is, bit two has a value of zero, then the IRQ disable flag is set to prevent further interrupts while the existing one is being processed.
- After the instruction that was being executed at the time of the interrupt is completed, the current value of the program counter is stored on the stack in the order PCH first, PCL next.
- The contents of the P register are stored on the stack.
- The microprocessor reads the contents of the location whose address is $FFFE. The number found there becomes the *new* PCL.
- The number found in the location whose address is $FFFF becomes the *new* PCH.
- The next op code is fetched from the location whose address is the new PCH-PCL. That is, the microprocessor puts the contents of the program counter on the address bus to fetch the next op code. Program execution continues from this point.

In terms that neglect some of the more subtle events described above, an interrupt, produced by an external event, causes the program to jump to another location where it continues executing instructions. The address of the new location is stored in the locations with addresses $FFFE and $FFFF. The jump is actually like a jump to a subroutine, since the return addresses are placed on the stack.

The location whose address is $FFFE is called IRQL, and the loccation whose address is $FFFF is called IRQH. The numbers stored in these two locations are known as the *IRQ vector*. The IRQ vector *points* to a location where program execution is to begin when an interrupt request occurs and is recognized (IRQ disable is clear).

A *nonmaskable interrupt* differs from an *interrupt request* in the following ways:

- The NMI pin is *edge sensitive* rather than *level sensitive*. A nonmaskable interrupt is produced by a logic-one to logic-zero transition on the NMI pin, whereas an interrupt request is produced by a logic-zero level on the IRQ pin.

- The nonmaskable interrupt is recognized and processed no matter what the status of the interrupt disable flag. That is why it is called nonmaskable.
- The nonmaskable interrupt vector is fetched from the locations whose addresses are $FFFA and $FFFB. That is, the new PCL is stored in the location whose address is $FFFA, and the new PCH is stored in the location whose address is $FFFB. These locations are called NMIL and NMIH, respectively.

The setting and clearing of the interrupt disable flag occurs in exactly the same way with an NMI-type interrupt as with an IRQ-type interrupt. Although an NMI *sets* the interrupt flag, this only *prevents* further *IRQ-type interrupts*. The interrupt disable flag *does not* prevent NMI-type interrupts. The stack operations are the same for both types of interrupts, and the RTI operation (to be described in Example 5) is the same in both cases. A nonmaskable interrupt can interrupt an IRQ-type interrupt routine, but the inverse is not true. Thus, the nonmaskable interrupt has a *higher priority* than an IRQ-type interrupt, an important consideration for any decision involving the use of interrupts in a particular application.

The KIM-1 and AIM 65 microcomputers handle interrupts in similar ways. The IRQ vector and the NMI vector point to locations in ROM. These locations contain indirect jump instructions to locations in R/W memory. Thus, the user can vary the starting point of the interrupt routines by loading the proper R/W memory locations with the vectors that point to the start of *his* interrupt routine. An example will aid in your understanding. In the AIM 65, locations with addresses $FFFE and $FFFF contain $78 and $E0, respectively. The value $E078 becomes the new value of the program counter when an interrupt is recognized. The address $E078 is a location in ROM, and, as outlined above, the first op code in the interrupt routine is stored in this location. Examination of the location whose address is $E078 shows that it contains a $6C, which is the op code for an indirect jump. The next two bytes in memory are the ADL and the ADH of the location for the jump. These two bytes are $04 and $A4, respectively. The location with address $A404 is an R/W memory location. Recall that with the indirect jump instruction, it is this location that contains the new PCL, while the new PCH is in the location whose address is $A404 + 1, *or* $A405. The user loads these locations with the ADL and ADH of the first instructions of *his* interrupt routine. That is, the contents of the locations with addresses $A404 and $A405 become the value in the program counter. The KIM-1 works in the same way, but with different addresses. Tables 9-4 and 9-5 summarize the important locations for these two systems, and Example 5 traces the history

Table 9-4. AIM 65 Interrupt Structure and Important Addresses

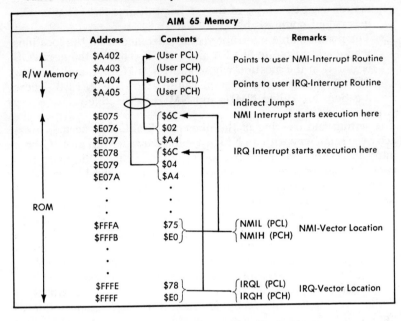

AIM 65 Memory			
	Address	Contents	Remarks
R/W Memory	$A402	(User PCL)	Points to user NMI-Interrupt Routine
	$A403	(User PCH)	
	$A404	(User PCL)	Points to user IRQ-Interrupt Routine
	$A405	(User PCH)	
			Indirect Jumps
	$E075	$6C	NMI Interrupt starts execution here
	$E076	$02	
	$E077	$A4	
	$E078	$6C	IRQ Interrupt starts execution here
	$E079	$04	
	$E07A	$A4	
ROM	.	.	
	.	.	
	.	.	
	$FFFA	$75	NMIL (PCL) NMI-Vector Location
	$FFFB	$E0	NMIH (PCH)
	.		
	.		
	$FFFE	$78	IRQL (PCL) IRQ-Vector Location
	$FFFF	$E0	IRQH (PCH)

Table 9-5. KIM-1 Interrupt Structure and Important Addresses

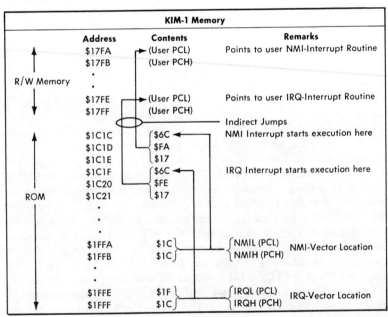

KIM-1 Memory			
	Address	Contents	Remarks
	$17FA	(User PCL)	Points to user NMI-Interrupt Routine
	$17FB	(User PCH)	
R/W Memory	.		
	.		
	$17FE	(User PCL)	Points to user IRQ-Interrupt Routine
	$17FF	(User PCH)	
			Indirect Jumps
	$1C1C	$6C	NMI Interrupt starts execution here
	$1C1D	$FA	
	$1C1E	$17	
	$1C1F	$6C	IRQ Interrupt starts execution here
	$1C20	$FE	
ROM	$1C21	$17	
	.		
	.		
	.		
	$1FFA	$1C	NMIL (PCL) NMI-Vector Location
	$1FFB	$1C	NMIH (PCH)
	.		
	$1FFE	$1F	IRQL (PCL) IRQ-Vector Location
	$1FFF	$1C	IRQH (PCH)

of the program counter subsequent to an interrupt request on the KIM-1.

In the SYM-1 microcomputer, addresses $FFFE, $FFFF, $FFFA, and $FFFB are all R/W memory locations. Thus, the user may place his own interrupt request vector or nonmaskable interrupt vector in these locations. That is, for an interrupt request, the new value of the PCL is in the location whose address is $FFFE, and the new value of the PCH is in the location whose address is $FFFF. The NMI vector is placed in $FFFA and $FFFB. The monitor of the SYM-1 will load all of these locations with its own interrupt routine vectors if the user does not load them. Table 9-6 summarizes the interrupt locations of importance to the SYM-1 microcomputer.

Table 9-6. SYM-1 Interrupt Structure and Important Addresses

SYM-1 MEMORY*			
	Address	Contents	Remarks
R/W MEMORY	$A67A† $A67B† • • • $A67E† $A67F†	(User PCL) (User PCH) (User PCL) (User PCH)	NMI-Vector Location. Points to user NMI-Interrupt Routine IRQ-Vector Location. Points to user IRQ-Interrupt Routine

*In order to modify these locations, the SYM-1 system requires that a JSR ACCESS instruction precede the instructions that load these locations. ACCESS = $8B86.
†According to to the SYM-1 manual, these locations are "echoed" at locations $FFFA, $FFFB, $FFFE, and $FFFF, respectively.

Although technically speaking, the interrupt request vector and the nonmaskable-interrupt vector are always found at the addresses $FFFE, $FFFF, $FFFA. and $FFFB, loosely speaking these vectors are found at $17FE, $17FF, $17FA, and $17FB in the KIM-1 and at $A404, $A405, $A402, and $A403 in the AIM 65, because the

Example 5: Tracing the Program Counter After an Interrupt Request
Trace the history of the program counter after an interrupt request on the KIM-1.
Solution: After finishing the instruction that was executing at the time of the interrupt, the program counter and the microprocessor behave as described in the following sequence:

PC	Microprocessor Activity
$FFFE	Fetch interrupt vector low = $1F.
$FFFF	Fetch interrupt vector high = $1C.
$1C1F	Fetch indirect jump op code = $6C.
$1C20	Fetch ADL of indirect jump = $FE.
$1C21	Fetch ADH of indirect jump = $17.
$17FE	Fetch new PCL from the location with address $17FE.
$17FF	Fetch new PCH from the location with address $17FF.
PCH-PCL	Fetch first op code in the user's interrupt routine.

actual interrupt vectors produce indirect jumps to these latter locations. Throughout the remainder of this book it will be assumed that the interrupt vectors are in these latter locations.

Both the interrupt-request routine and the nonmaskable interrupt routine must end with an RTI instruction. Execution of the RTI (Return from Interrupt) instruction causes the microprocessor to return to the main program, and it continues executing instructions immediately following the "interrupted" instruction. It does this by loading the program counter with the two numbers at the top of the stack, loading the P register with the third number down on the stack, incrementing the stack pointer once for each of the numbers (PCH, PCL, and P) mentioned, and clearing the interrupt disable flag in the P register. Examples 6 and 7 illustrate the stack operations that take place when an interrupt occurs and when an RTI instruction is executed.

Example 6: Tracing Stack Pointer After an Interrupt Request

Describe how the stack pointer and the contents of the stack register change as a result of an interrupt in the following program segment. Assume the interrupt occurs during execution of the LDA instruction.

```
0200   AD 00 03      LDA NUM1
0203   F0 05         BEQ THERE
```

Solution: Assuming the stack pointer was $FF before the interrupt, the number $02 representing the PCH will be stored on the stack at the location whose address is $01FF, and the stack pointer will be decremented to $FE. Next, the number $03, representing the PCL at the completion of the LDA instruction, will be stored on the stack. The stack pointer will be decremented again, and the contents of the P register at the completion of the LDA instruction will be stored on the stack at the location whose address is $01FD. The stack pointer will be decremented a third time to $FC.

Example 7: Tracing Stack Pointer Subsequent to RTI Instruction

Describe how the stack pointer and the contents of the stack change as a result of a return from interrupt in the same program segment shown in Example 6.

Solution: The stack pointer is first incremented to $FD, and the contents of the location whose address is $01FD are transferred to the P register. The contents of memory location $01FE are transferred to the PCL, and the contents of location $01FF are transferred to the PCH with suitable increments in the stack pointer. The stack pointer will be $FF at the completion of the RTI instruction, and the program continues with PCH-PCL = $0203, resulting in a fetch of the BEQ op code.

Fig. 9-5 illustrates the many activities that are taking place during the events described in Examples 6 and 7. This illustration shows the "flow" of the program counter during an IRQ-type interrupt and describes the "stack activities" as well.

The interrupt disable flag in the processor status register may also be set and cleared by the program in addition to being set by an interrupt and cleared by the execution of an RTI instruction. If it is imperative that a section of program not be interrupted by an interrupt request, then the interrupt flag may be set by the SEI

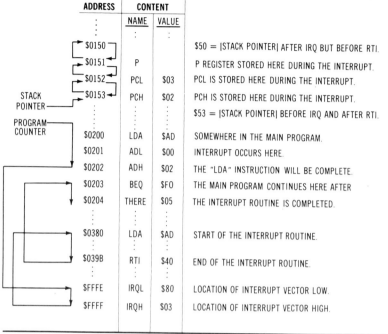

	MEMORY			REMARKS
	ADDRESS	CONTENT		
		NAME	VALUE	
	⋮	⋮	⋮	
	$0150			$50 = |STACK POINTER| AFTER IRQ BUT BEFORE RTI.
	$0151	P		P REGISTER STORED HERE DURING THE INTERRUPT.
	$0152	PCL	$03	PCL IS STORED HERE DURING THE INTERRUPT.
STACK POINTER	$0153	PCH	$02	PCH IS STORED HERE DURING THE INTERRUPT.
PROGRAM COUNTER	⋮	⋮	⋮	$53 = |STACK POINTER| BEFORE IRQ AND AFTER RTI.
	$0200	LDA	$AD	SOMEWHERE IN THE MAIN PROGRAM.
	$0201	ADL	$00	INTERRUPT OCCURS HERE.
	$0202	ADH	$02	THE "LDA" INSTRUCTION WILL BE COMPLETE.
	$0203	BEQ	$F0	THE MAIN PROGRAM CONTINUES HERE AFTER
	$0204	THERE	$05	THE INTERRUPT ROUTINE IS COMPLETED.
	⋮	⋮	⋮	
	$0380	LDA	$AD	START OF THE INTERRUPT ROUTINE.
	⋮	⋮	⋮	
	$039B	RTI	$40	END OF THE INTERRUPT ROUTINE.
	⋮	⋮	⋮	
	$FFFE	IRQL	$80	LOCATION OF INTERRUPT VECTOR LOW.
	$FFFF	IRQH	$03	LOCATION OF INTERRUPT VECTOR HIGH.

Fig. 9-5. Diagram representing the Program Counter and Stack Pointer changes that occur during an Interrupt Request (IRQ).

(set interrupt disable flag) instruction. Later in the program it may be cleared with the CLI (clear interrupt disable flag) instruction to allow further interrupts.

You should recognize that an interrupt request is like a JSR instruction. They both result in an exit from the main program in order to execute a subprogram. The subprogram is called an "interrupt routine" in the case of an interrupt request or a nonmaskable interrupt. In both cases, the information necessary to return to the main program is stored on the stack. One important difference is that an interrupt will result in the contents of the P register also being stored on the stack. If a programmer wishes to save the contents of the P register during a subroutine jump, then he *must* use the PHP and PLP instructions. The microprocessor takes care of saving the P register contents during an interrupt.

The reason for this important difference between an interrupt and a subroutine is simply that the programmer knows where he has placed a JSR instruction, but he never knows where an interrupt will occur in a program. If it occurs directly before a branch instruction, and the interrupt routine changes the flag settings in the P register (as it undoubtedly will) then a branch may be caused by the result of an operation in the interrupt routine rather than as a result of the operation in the main program that it was supposed to test. Clearly, the programmer put the branch instruction in the main program to test circumstances that develop there, rather than those in the interrupt routine. Since the 6502 saves the contents of the P register on the stack when an interrupt occurs, this allows the programmer to write programs without concerning himself with either *where* the interrupt might occur or *when* the P register is to be saved.

If other registers must be saved during an interrupt, then it is up to the programmer to use the necessary stack operations to save them. The accumulator is almost universally saved on the stack during an interrupt because almost every interrupt routine one could think of would use the accumulator. In fact, it would have been nice if the 6502 would take care of this responsibility, but the designers of the chip did not provide this feature. Note that all the register-save instructions *must* be included in the *interrupt routine*. If the X register is used in both the main program and the interrupt routine, then suitable instructions must be included in the interrupt routine to save and restore the X register. Example 8 illustrates the necessary instructions that must be included to save both the accumulator and the X register and then restore them.

Example 8: Saving Accumulator and X Register During an Interrupt

Show the instructions that will result in saving both the accumulator and the X register during an interrupt routine.

Solution:

Interrupt Routine

0300	48	BEGIRQ	PHA	Push accumulator on stack.
0301	8A		TXA	Transfer X to A.
0302	48		PHA	Push A on the stack.
0303	•		•	
	•		•	
	•		•	Interrupt routine instructions.
	•		•	—— (NOTE REVERSED ORDER)
	•		•	
	•		•	
0329	68		PLA	Pull A from the stack.
032A	AA		TAX	Transfer A to X.
032B	68		PLA	Pull A from the stack.
032C	40		RTI	Return to main program.

An interrupt request (IRQ) may also be forced with the use of the BRK instruction that is best described as a software-forced interrupt request. Note that a nonmaskable interrupt cannot be forced with any instruction. In those instances where one wants to enter the interrupt request routine without a "hardware-generated request," the BRK instruction is used to force a jump to the interrupt-request routine. Throughout this book we have been using this instruction to force the microprocessor to jump from the program we have written to the monitor. We have done this because, in this case, the monitor saves the register contents. Furthermore, in our use of the BRK instruction with the monitor, the microprocessor never returns from the interrupt. That is, the monitor avoids using the RTI instruction because that would cause execution to return to the next instruction in our program, an instruction that did not exist because we *ended* the program with a BRK instruction.

In general, when using the BRK instruction one must assume that an RTI instruction will be encountered and that the program will return from the interrupt routine. In this situation, it is important to realize that the BRK instruction results in an increment of the program counter by two. Thus, upon returning, the instruction immediately following the BRK instruction is *not* executed. If the break instruction op code is in the location ADH-ADL, then the next instruction to be executed after the return from the interrupt routine *must* be located with its op code in the location ADH-ADL + 2. For this reason, a *no-operation* instruction (NOP) with op code $EA is usually placed after a break instruction, that is, in the location ADH-ADL + 1. The reasons for this quirk in the BRK instruction are beyond the scope of this book and the author's comprehension.

Two examples of programs involving interrupts are given. The program in Example 9 illustrates how an FIFO (first-in, first-out) memory may be implemented. Originally it was part of a program to convert ASCII characters from a keyboard to Morse code, and it will be described in that context. Do not, however, consider that this example of data acquisition is unique to this application. There are other instances in which data must be read when they are produced, and stored in an FIFO memory to be processed on a first-in, first-out basis. The program in Example 10 is a 24-hour clock that uses a nonmaskable interrupt request. We turn first to the FIFO memory application.

Most operators can type faster than the Morse code is to be sent, so the keyboard must be read and stored in the FIFO (first-in, first-out) memory. In the program in Example 9, the keyboard is read with an interrupt request routine, and the ASCII character is placed in the FIFO memory. For the FIFO memory we used page two of memory. It is assumed that the keyboard produces a negative pulse of at least 10 microseconds on the IRQ pin when a key is depressed and the ASCII character is ready to be read. Many keyboards not only produce the 7-bit ASCII data for a particular key, but they also provide a positive- or negative-strobe signal when the data is ready. We assume the negative-strobe signal is connected to the IRQ pin, and the seven bits of ASCII data are available at Port A.

Space does not permit the listing of the complete conversion program. You are referred to a complete ASCII to Morse code conversion program in a reference[1]. Here we simply wish to show an example of an interrupt routine. The program is supposed to read the keyboard and store the ASCII character in the FIFO memory. Another part of the program reads the first character placed in the FIFO memory, converts it to Morse code, and "sends" it by keying a transmitter, and returns to see if another character has been placed in the FIFO memory. It continues to send as long as the FIFO memory is not empty. The keyboard continues to place characters in the FIFO memory as long as the typist continues. The typist may get up to $256 = \$FF + 1$ characters ahead of the sending routines before he begins to write over previously entered characters that have not yet been sent.

The Y register serves as an index for the FIFO memory whose base address is \$0200. The number in the Y register also points to the last location of the FIFO memory that was filled with the keyboard interrupt routine. In particular, the number in the Y register is the ADL of the last location in page two of memory that was filled by the keyboard interrupt routine. The number in the location labeled PNTR is the ADL of the location in page two of memory that contains the character being converted to Morse code and sent by the OUTPUT subroutine. If the contents of the Y register are identical to the contents of PNTR, then the OUTPUT subroutine has "caught up" with the keyboard input, and there is nothing to do but wait in a loop. The flowchart in Fig. 9-6 and the comments associated with the program should give you an understanding of the remaining details. Indexed addressing is used both to fill the FIFO memory using Y as an index and to empty the FIFO memory using X as an index.

The program in Example 10 is our second example of a program that uses an interrupt routine. It is a 24-hour clock program that may be used to display hours, minutes, and seconds. A number of clock programs have appeared in various sources.[2,3] These programs make use of the interval timers on the 6530 or 6522 integrated cir-

[1]De Jong, Marvin L., "The Best of Micro," *The Computerist*, Chelmsford, MA 01824, 1978, p. 38.

[2]Parsons, Charles, *The First Book of KIM*, ORB, Argonne, IL 60439, 1977, p. 52.

[3]Sullivan, Chris, "MICRO," *The Computerist*, Chelmsford, MA 01824, 1978, pp. 7-45.

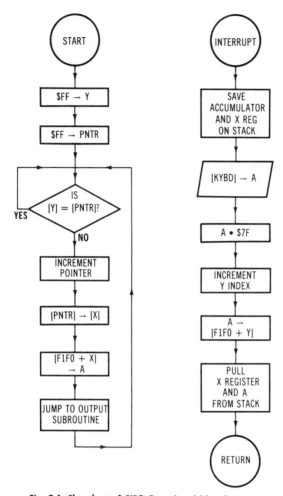

Fig. 9-6. Flowchart of FIFO Data Acquisition Program.

cuits and the system clock, a crystal-controlled oscillator. Although crystal oscillators are very accurate and stable, the precision necessary to keep good time over a long period (weeks) generally exceeds the capability of the microcomputer system's crystal oscillator. If we demand that there be an error of no greater than 1 second in 24 hours, then the crystal must be accurate to approximately 1 part in 100,000. Few microcomputer clocks guarantee this kind of accuracy, and, consequently, significant errors tend to accumulate over a period of days.

One approach to guarantee long-term (days) accuracy at the expense of short-term (seconds) accuracy is to use a signal from the

Example 9: First-in, First-out (FIFO) Data Acquisition Program

Objective: Read the data at an input port whenever an IRQ-type interrupt request occurs. Store this data in successively higher memory locations in page two of memory. Output data from the bottom of this table one location at a time until the highest filled location is reached. Wait there until more data is added to the table from the input port.

$0000 = PNTR; contains the ADL of the location in the FIFO memory that contains the data currently being processed by the output subroutine.

$0200 = FIFO; base address of the FIFO memory

$1700 = KYBD; input port for the data

$17FE = UIRQL; $00 = low order byte of user's interrupt vector

$17FF = UIRQH; $03 = high order byte of user's interrupt vector.

MAIN Program

0200	A0 FF	START	LDY	$FF	Initialize Y pointer.
0202	84 00		STY	PNTR	Initialize output pointer.
0204	C4 00	LOOP	CPY	PNTR	Is output pointer = Y pointer?
0206	F0 FC		BEQ	LOOP	Yes; wait in loop for more input data.
0208	E6 00		INC	PNTR	No; increment pointer to get data.
020A	A6 00		LDX	PNTR	PNTR contents will index FIFO memory.
020C	BD 00 02		LDA	FIFO,X	Get data from FIFO memory at FIFO + X.
020F	20 17 80		JSR	OUTPUT	Jump to subroutine to output data. (Not included in this program.)
0212	4C 04 02		JMP	LOOP	Return to see if there is more data.

Interrupt Routine

0300	48	NMIR	PHA		Save accumulator on the stack.
0301	8A		TXA		Transfer X to A.
0302	48		PHA		Save X on the stack.
0303	AD 00 17		LDA	KYBD	Read the keyboard.
0306	29 7F		AND	$7F	Mask bit seven. ASCII is a seven bit code.
0308	C8		INY		Increment Y to index next location in FIFO.
0309	99 00 02		STA	FIFO,Y	Store the keyboard data in the FIFO. memory at FIFO + Y.
030C	68		PLA		Get X back from the stack.
030D	AA		TAX		
030E	68		PLA		Get A from the stack.
030F	40		RTI		Return from interrupt.

60-Hz power line as the fundamental time unit. Whenever 60 cycles are counted a memory location that stores "seconds" is incremented. When the seconds location reaches 60, a "minutes" location is incremented, and when the minutes location reaches 60 an "hours" location is incremented. When the hours location reaches 24, the cycle begins again. The 60-Hz signal from the power line is first transformed down to 6.3 V ac and then conditioned with a 555 timer circuit acting as a Schmitt trigger to produce one negative transition for each cycle.[4] See Fig. 9-7 for details of the circuit.

---

[4]Jung, Walter G., *Popular Electronics*, January 1973, p. 73.

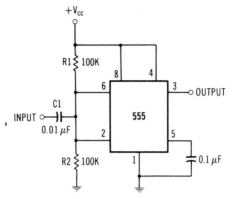

Fig. 9-7. A 60-Hz Signal Conditioner for 24 Hour Clock.

The 6.3 V ac is connected between the input and ground. The conditioned signal from the 555 circuit is applied to the NMI pin on the 6502 by way of pin 6 on the expansion port of the AIM 65, KIM-1, or SYM-1. Each time an interrupt occurs, a counter (location with address $0000 labeled CNTR) is incremented until 60 counts have accumulated. CNTR starts at $C4 and is incremented to $00 to give 60_{10} counts. Then the seconds counter (location with address $0001) is incremented. The "minutes" are stored in the location with address $0002, and "hours" are stored in the location whose address is $0003. The flowchart in Fig. 9-8 should help in understanding the nonmaskable interrupt routine.

The main program, associated with the 24-hour clock nonmaskable-interrupt routine, consists of loading the appropriate interrupt vectors into their locations and a routine to display the contents of SEC, MIN, and HRS on the microcomputer display. Do not connect the 60-Hz source to the NMI pin until these vectors have been loaded. The interrupt routine starts at the location whose address is $0300. It may be relocated anywhere in memory, but we will assume that the interrupt vector is $0300. The program in Example 10 shows the initialization instructions for the AIM 65. The same instructions are used with the KIM-1 and SYM-1, but the locations of the nonmaskable interrupt vector are different. See Tables 9-5 and 9-6 for the addresses of the appropriate locations for the KIM-1 and SYM-1 microcomputers. ($00 is loaded into $17FA on the KIM-1 or into $A67A on the SYM-1, while $03 is loaded into $17FB on the KIM-1 or into $A67B on the SYM-1.)

Each of the three microcomputer systems needs a different display routine to display the time, so we have included the necessary routine for each of the systems. Note that we have used the subroutine approach to display the time. Also observe that the routine for each system includes one or more subroutine calls to subroutines

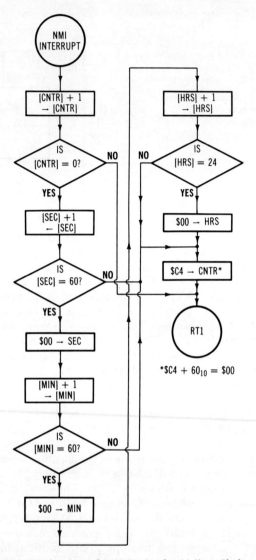

Fig. 9-8. Flowchart of NMI Routine for 24 Hour Clock.

included in the monitor. You are referred to your system manual for details of these subroutines.

Microcomputers are not used simply to keep time. There are much less expensive approaches to that problem. However, there are applications in which the time is important. If you are charging a client for the amount of time used to process his data, then a

Example 10. Twenty-Four Hour Clock Program

Objective: Calculate and display the time of day in hours, minutes, and seconds.

Main Program

$A402 = NMIVL; location of user interrupt vector, low-order byte
$A403 = NMIVH; location of user interrupt vector, high-order byte
$0000 = CNTR; location used to count 60 cycles

0200	A9 00	START	LDA	$00	
0202	8D 02 A4		STA	NMIVL	Load NMI vector, low-order byte.
0205	A9 03		LDA	$03	
0207	8D 03 A4		STA	NMIVH	Load NMI vector, high-order byte.
020A	A9 C4		LDA	$C4	CNTR counts from $C4 to $00 to give a
020C	85 00		STA	CNTR	total of $3C = 60 counts.
020E	20 03 40	LOOP	JSR	DISPLY	Jump to display subroutine at $0340.
0211	4C 0E 02		JMP	LOOP	Loop to display time continuously.

Nonmaskable Interrupt Routine

$0000 = CNTR; location used to count 60 cycles
$0001 = SEC; location used to store time in seconds
$0002 = MIN; location used to store time in minutes
$0003 = HRS; location used to store time in hours

0300	48	NMIR	PHA		Save accumulator on the stack.
0301	E6 00		INC	CNTR	Increment CNTR once for every interrupt.
0303	D0 33		BNE	DONE	Counter has not reached zero (60 counts) yet.
0305	F8		SED		Set decimal mode for subsequent additions.
0306	18		CLC		Clear carry flag for same reason.
0307	A5 01		LDA	SEC	Get time in seconds.
0309	69 01		ADC	$01	Add one to increment seconds counter.
030B	85 01		STA	SEC	Store in seconds counter.
030D	C9 60		CMP	$60	Has the seconds counter reached 60?
030F	90 22		BCC	RPT	No; Initialize CNTR, then return from interrupt.
0311	A9 00		LDA	$00	Yes; Initialize seconds to zero.
0313	85 01		STA	SEC	
0315	18		CLC		Clear carry flag to add one to minutes
0316	A5 02		LDA	MIN	counter. Get minutes counter.
0318	69 01		ADC	$01	Add one to minutes.
031A	85 02		STA	MIN	Result into minutes counter.
031C	C9 60		CMP	$60	Has the minutes counter reached 60?
031E	90 13		BCC	RPT	No; Initialize CNTR, then return from interrupt.
0320	A9 00		LDA	$00	Yes; Initialize minutes to zero.
0322	85 02		STA	MIN	
0324	18		CLC		Clear carry for next addition.
0325	A5 03		LDA	HRS	Get hours counter.
0327	69 01		ADC	$01	Increment by one.
0329	85 03		STA	HRS	Result into hours counter.
032B	C9 24		CMP	$24	Has the hours counter reached 24?
032D	90 04		BCC	RPT	No; Initialize CNTR, then return from interrupt.
032F	A9 00		LDA	$00	Yes; start new day.
0331	85 03		STA	HRS	
0333	A9 C4	RPT	LDA	$C4	Initialize CNTR for 60 more counts.
0335	85 00		STA	CNTR	
0337	D8		CLD		Clear decimal mode.

| 0338 | 68 | DONE | PLA | | Get Accumulator from stack. |
| 0339 | 40 | | RTI | | Return from interrupt. |

AIM 65 Display Subroutine

$0004 = TSEC; temporary storage of seconds
$0005 = TMIN; temporary storage of minutes
$0006 = THRS; temporary storage of hours

0340	A5 01	DISPLY	LDA	SEC	Get seconds.
0342	85 04		STA	TSEC	Store temporarily here.
0344	A5 02		LDA	MIN	Get minutes.
0346	85 05		STA	TMIN	Store temporarily here.
0348	A5 03		LDA	HRS	Get hours.
034A	85 06		STA	THRS	Store here temporarily.
034C	A2 13		LDX	$13	X identifies right-most display cell.
034E	8A	BACK	TXA		Save X by
034F	48		PHA		placing it on the stack.
0350	A0 04		LDY	$04	Initialize Y for a count of four.
0352	A5 04		LDA	TSEC	Get seconds.
0354	29 0F		AND	$0F	Mask high-order nibble.
0356	18		CLC		Clear carry flag for subsequent addition.
0357	69 30		ADC	$30	Add $30 to convert low-order nibble to ASCII.
0359	09 80		ORA	$80	Set bit seven to one for display.
035B	20 7B EF		JSR	OUTDD1	Use monitor subroutine to display ASCII.
035E	46 06	AGAIN	LSR	THRS	Shift hours right into carry flag.
0360	66 05		ROR	TMIN	Carry into minutes; minutes (bit 0) into carry.
0362	66 04		ROR	TSEC	Carry into seconds; shift one bit right.
0364	88		DEY		Repeat four times, moving a nibble
0365	D0 F7		BNE	AGAIN	at a time into the display routine.
0367	68		PLA		Get X back again (it was modified in
0368	AA		TAX		monitor subroutine).
0369	CA		DEX		Decrement X to identify next display
036A	E0 0E		CPX	$0E	cell, then return to display another
036C	B0 E0		BCS	BACK	nibble, until all six nibbles of time
036E	60		RTS		have been displayed. Then return to main program.

KIM-1 Display Subroutine

$00F9 = DISPS
$00FA = DISPM
$00FB = DISPH

0340	A5 01	DISPLY	LDA	SEC	Get seconds.
0342	85 F9		STA	DISPS	Store in KIM-1 display cell.
0344	A5 02		LDA	MIN	Get minutes.
0346	85 FA		STA	DISPM	Store in KIM-1 display cell.
0348	A5 03		LDA	HRS	Get hours.
034A	85 FB		STA	DISPH	Store in KIM-1 display cell.
034C	A2 FF		LDX	$FF	Initialize X for timing loop.
034E	8A	RPT	TXA		Save X on stack during subroutine.
034F	48		PHA		
0350	20 1F 1F		JSR	SCANDS	Jump to KIM-1 display subroutine.
0353	68		PLA		Restore X.

0354	AA		TAX		
0355	CA		DEX		Decrement X.
0356	D0 F6		BNE	RPT	Branch to display again until X = 0.
0358	60		RTS		Return from subroutine.

SYM-1 Display Subroutine

$A640 = DISBUF; base address of SYM-1 display buffer
$8C29 = TAB; base address of seven-segment code table in SYM-1 monitor

0340	A5 01	DISPLY	LDA	SEC	Get seconds.
0342	85 04		STA	TSEC	Store temporarily in TSEC.
0344	A5 02		LDA	MIN	Get minutes.
0346	85 05		STA	TMIN	Store temporarily in TMIN.
0348	A5 03		LDA	HRS	Get hours.
034A	85 06		STA	THRS	Store temporarily in THRS.
034C	20 86 8B		JSR	ACCESS	Jump to SYM-1 ACCESS routine to access RAM.
034F	A2 05		LDX	$05	Initialize X index to fill display table.
0351	A5 04	PRR	LDA	TSEC	Get seconds.
0353	29 0F		AND	$0F	Mask high-order nibble.
0355	A8		TAY		Transfer low-order nibble to Y index.
0356	B9 29 8C		LDA	TAB,Y	Get seven-segment code from table.
0359	9D 40 A6		STA	DISBUF,X	Store in display buffer.
035C	A0 04		LDY	$04	Initialize bit counter for one nibble.
035E	46 06	DGL	LSR	THRS	Shift hours into carry flag.
0360	66 05		ROR	TMIN	Carry into minutes; minutes (bit 0) into carry.
0362	66 04		ROR	TSEC	Carry into seconds; shift one bit right.
0364	88		DEY		Decrement Y until one nibble has
0365	D0 F7		BNE	DGL	been shifted right.
0367	CA		DEX		Decrement X.
0368	10 E7		BPL	PRR	Return to convert remaining nibbles.
036A	A2 FF		LDX	$FF	Initialize X for timing loop.
036C	8A	JAT	TXA		Save X.
036D	48		PHA		
036E	20 06 89		JSR	SCAND	Jump to SYM-1 monitor subroutine.
0371	68		PLA		Get X back.
0372	AA		TAX		
0373	CA		DEX		Decrement X for timing loop.
0374	D0 F6		BNE	JAT	Branch to display again until X = 0.
0376	60		RTS		Return from subroutine.

system clock is useful. In any application where the time at which a particular event occurred must be known, a 24-hour clock is useful. The program in Example 10 would be easily modified to display or store the time at which a logic-zero to logic-one transition occurred at one of the Port B input pins. For example, if you were monitoring the feeding habits of a laboratory animal, a suitable detector could be placed at the feeding station to produce a logic level transition on an input pin that, in turn, would result in the time being recorded. Many other applications suggest themselves in a brainstorm. The program in Example 10 should not be used in applications such as frequency counting or other short-term timing measurements because the short-term stability of the power-line frequency is inadequate. Experiments such as these require interval timers and a crystal-controlled time base, the subject of the next chapter.

To start the 24-hour clock, load the programs and wire the circuit shown in Fig. 9-7. Before applying the 60-Hz signal to the 555 timer, start the program and make sure it works. Next, load locations with addresses $0001, $0002, and $0003 with the seconds, minutes, and hours of the time you intend to start the clock. Put $C4 into the location with address $0000. At the instant the time corresponds to the time loaded into memory, apply the 60-Hz signal to the 555 input.

EXPERIMENT NO. 1

Step 1

Load the following program.

0200	4C 00 03	START	JSR	NOTHING	Jump to a subroutine that does nothing.
0203	00		BRK		Break to monitor.
0300	EA	NOTHING	NOP		No operation.
0301	40		RTS		Return from subroutine.

Step 2

There are two bugs in this program. Can you find the bugs without running the program? It always pays to search for bugs before running a program.

Step 3

If you found the bugs before running the program, then run the program with the bugs in it anyway. If you didn't find the bugs, then you have no choice but to run the program with the bugs in it.

Step 4

Assuming that there are no bugs in the program, what would you expect to observe when the program is executed?

(The program should execute the jump to subroutine, the NOP instruction, return to the main program and execute the BRK instruction, whereupon the display should light showing the address $0205 and the contents of that location.)

Step 5

What do you observe when the program is executed?

(We observed that the display did not light. The BRK command was not executed.)

Step 6

We will attempt to debug the program using the single-step mode and a trace of the 6502 internal registers. What registers would you suggest be traced?

(Only the S register and the program counter are used in the program. These are the registers we will trace.)

Step 7

Single step through the program and make a table showing the contents of the stack pointer (S register) and the program counter after the execution of each instruction.

(We obtained the following table. The stack pointer was $FF initially.

Instruction	Register Contents After Execution of the Instruction		
	Program Counter High	Program Counter Low	Stack Pointer
JSR	$03	$00	$FF
NOP	$03	$01	$FF
RTS	$31	$30	$02

Your table may not be identical in all respects.)

Step 8

What do you conclude from studying your table? Concentrate on the contents of the stack pointer.

(We reasoned as follows: The program does jump to the subroutine because the program counter becomes $0301 as it should. However, in a subroutine jump the stack pointer should decrement by two to store the return address. The program made the jump, but it did not provide a way to return. This suggests the JMP instruction was executed rather than the JSR. Check the op code and confirm this.)

Step 9

Can you find the other bug by studying the table?

(It's not as easy but the evidence is there. Note that on the RTS instruction the stack pointer increments by three, that is $00, $01, $02. But an RTS instruction should only result in the stack pointer being incremented by two. An RTI op code was substituted for the RTS op code.)

Step 10

Change the op codes to their correct values and verify that the program now runs correctly.

EXPERIMENT NO. 2

Step 1

Examine the following program, then load it into your micro-computer.

```
0200   A2 00      START      LDX  $00          Initialize X to $00.
0202   9A                    TXS               Transfer the contents of X to S.
0203   20 00 03             JSR  NOTHING       Jump to subroutine.
0206   00                    BRK               Break to the monitor.
0300   EA         NOTHING    NOP               No operation.
0301   60                    RTS               Return from subroutine.
```

Step 2

What will the value of the stack pointer be after execution of the TXS instruction?

(The stack pointer will be $00 because the value of X ($00) was transferred to the stack pointer by the TXS instruction.)

Step 3

Will this program work correctly? Remember the JSR instruction requires two locations on the stack. What do you predict will happen when the program is executed? Where will PCL and PCH be stored?

(The value of the program counter will be stored at locations whose addresses are $0100 and $01FF. After storing PCH = $02 at $0100, the stack pointer is decremented and becomes $FF. Thus, the PCL = $05 is stored at the location whose address is $01FF. The stack "wraps around." Recall that what is stored as the program counter is the address of the third byte in the JSR instruction which in this case is $0205. The program will work perfectly. The stack pointer may have any initial value the user desires.)

Step 4

You may want to check the operation of the stack pointer in this case by single stepping through the program and tracing the history of the stack. Also check the contents of the stack after each step.

EXPERIMENT NO. 3

Step 1

Breadboard the circuit of Fig. 9-7, but do not connect the 60-Hz signal to the 0.01-μF capacitor. Load the program for the 24-hour clock.

Step 2

Put $C4 into memory location with address $0000. Load locations with addresses $0001, $0002, and $0003 with the seconds, minutes, and hours, respectively, of the time at which you intend to start your clock. If you have a WWV receiver use it to set the time and start the clock.

Step 4

Start the program. The AIM 65 will display the time continuously, while the KIM-1 and SYM-1 multiplex the various segments giving what appears to be a continuous display. The time displayed should be the time you stored in Step 2.

Step 5

At the instant the time on WWV or a good electric clock coincides with the time stored in the display, connect the 60-Hz signal to the capacitor on the 555 timer input. If you do not succeed the first time, try again until you have a good match between your clock and some standard.

Step 6

Let your system run overnight or for a day. Does it keep good time? Keep your clock circuit and program. It will be used in the next experiment.

EXPERIMENT NO. 4

Step 1

How would you modify the main program of the 24-hour clock to display the correct time only when a transition occurs at PB0 (Bit 0 of Port B)? Try to write the modification yourself before looking at our answer.

(Here is how the main program would look after we modify it to display the time after a logic-level transition at PB0. Other answers are possible. Comments are provided for the added instructions.

```
START    LDA   $00
         STA   NMIVL
         LDA   $03
         STA   NMIVH
         LDA   $C4
         STA   CNTR
LOOP     LDY   PBD      Transfer data at Port B to the Y register.
PULSE    TYA            Transfer contents of Y to A.
         EOR   PBD      Exclusive OR produces a one in any bit that changed.
         AND   $01      Mask all except bit 0.
         BEQ   PULSE    Loop back to PULSE unless bit 0 changed.
         JSR   DISPLY   Display time.
         JMP   LOOP     Return to check Port B for more transitions.)
```

Step 2

Modify Example 10 to include the above instructions or the instructions you used to answer STEP 1.

Step 3

Execute the program. Remember to supply the 60-Hz signal after the program is running. The display should remain blank. Change the PB0 switch on the I/O board. You should observe the time. On the KIM-1 and SYM-1 the time will flash on the display momentarily. On the AIM 65 the time will be latched into the display, but the display will not change until another transition occurs.

Step 4

Try to think of at least one application where the ability to record the time when a particular event causes a logic-level transition on an input pin might be useful.

Step 5

About how much time does the NMI interrupt routine take? Why is this an important question?

(Consider first that an interrupt occurs 60 times every second. During 59 of those interrupts only five instructions are executed. They include the PHA, INC, BNE, PLA, and RTI instructions that take 3, 5, 3, 4, and 6 microseconds, respectively. (We are assuming a clock frequency of 1 MHz.) The interrupt itself takes 8 microseconds; that is, there are eight clock cycles between the completion of the last instruction in the main program and the fetch of the first op code in the interrupt routine. Thus, we have a total of 29 microseconds for the interrupt time. The AIM 65 and KIM-1 require an indirect jump for each interrupt, and that accounts for another 5 microseconds, giving a total of 34 microseconds. The remaining interrupt in the one-second interval requires 23 microseconds, in addition to the time mentioned above, to increment the seconds counter and attend to other details. Thus, in 1 second the microprocessor spends $(60 \times 34 + 23)$ microseconds processing the interrupts. The total is 2063 microseconds, so about 0.2063% of the time is devoted to maintaining the 24-hour clock. The additional time required to increment the minutes and/or hours counters is small enough to neglect because these instructions are used so seldom. The minutes counter is incremented only once every 3600 interrupts, and the hours counter is incremented once every 216,000 interrupts.

The question is important because a real time clock such as this must usually run concurrently with other programs. One must know whether the interrupt routine will adversely affect the operation of another program. In most cases the 0.2063% will not bother.)

Step 6

Try to write an interrupt routine that keeps time using ASCII rather than the decimal mode we used. This is useful in those microcomputers that must output the time to display devices such as line printers and terminals that require ASCII data.

EXPERIMENT NO. 5

Step 1

Breadboard the circuit shown in Fig. 9-9. It consists of a mechanical switch that is debounced by the cross-coupled NAND gates and a 74121 monostable multivibrator that gives a 10-microsecond pulse (one-zero-one) each time the mechanical switch is changed from logic one to logic zero as noted on the switch positions. (Note that a debounced signal is available on the I/O board. A small wire or clip connected to pin 9 (PB0) on the application connector will provide the necessary debounced signal from the switch associated with PB0.)

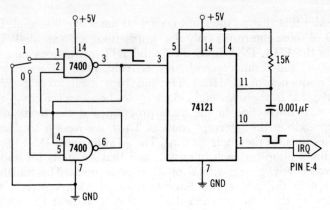

Fig. 9-9. Circuit to produce an Interrupt Request Signal on IRQ pin.

Step 2

Connect the output of the multivibrator to the IRQ line by connecting it to pin E-4 on the expansion connector. You will need a 22/44 pin edge connector to put on the expansion port.

Step 3

Load the following program.

0200	58	MAIN	CLI		Clear interrupt disable flag.
0201	A9 FF		LDA	$FF	Initialize Port A to be an output port
0203	8D 01 17		STA	PADD	by storing $FF in its DDR; KIM-1 address.
0206	4C 06 02	LOOP	JMP	LOOP	Loop here.
0300	48	INTERPT	PHA		Store accumulator on the stack.
0301	BA		TSX		Transfer stack pointer to X.
0302	8E 00 17		STX	PAD	Output X to Port A LEDs.
0305	68		PLA		Pull accumulator from the stack.
0306	40		RTI		Return from interrupt.

Step 4

The interrupt vector is $0300. Refer to Tables 9-4 to 9-6 and load the interrupt vector into the appropriate locations for your microcomputer.

Step 5

Describe what effect execution of the program will have on the Port A LEDs when the program is executed.

(When the program is started by initializing the program counter to $0200 (the starting address of the main program) we observed that the Port A LEDs did not glow.)

Step 6

What do you predict the Port A LEDs will show when an interrupt occurs by flipping switch PB0 from logic one to logic zero? Predict before you cause the interrupt, and give reasons for your prediction.

(The Port A LEDs should show $FB. In the interrupt routine the stack pointer is first transferred to the X register, then the X register is output to Port A. Thus, Port A displays the value of the stack pointer after the PHA instruction in the interrupt routine. Recall that an interrupt requires three locations on the stack, the PHA instruction will require one location, and then the stack pointer is decremented to point to the next empty location. Counting backward from an initial value of $FF to the first empty location gives $FB.)

Step 7

If the PHA and PLA instructions are replaced by NOP instructions, what will the stack pointer be during the interrupt as displayed by the Port A LEDs?

(Since only three locations on the stack are used, the stack pointer will be $FA.)

Step 8

Think carefully about what would happen if an interrupt routine had a PHA instruction but no corresponding PLA instruction. Experiment with the circuit and program if necessary.

EXPERIMENT NO. 6

Step 1

Write a program to display the time when an interrupt request occurs; that is, modify the 24-hour clock program to display the time when an interrupt from the circuit of Fig. 9-9 causes an interrupt. Try to write your own modifications before looking at the answer below.

```
0200   A9 00      START    LDA $00
0202   8D 02 A4            STA NMIVL
```

```
0205   A9 03                LDA $03
0207   8D 03 A4             STA NMIVH
020A   A9 40                LDA $40
020C   8D 04 A4             STA IRQVH      Load IRQ vector to point to DISPLY,
020F   A9 03                LDA $03        AIM 65 locations indicated.
0211   8D 05 A4             STA IRQVH      Load IRQ vector to point to DISPLY.
0214   A9 C4                LDA $C4        KIM and SYM users see Tables 9-5 and
                                           9-6.
0216   85 00                STA CNTR       Initialize CNTR for 60 counts.
0218   58                   CLI            Allow interrupts.
0219   4C 19 02   LOOP      JMP LOOP       Loop here.
```

Step 2

Load the program, initialize the time locations as described in the text, and start the program running. What should you observe on the display?

(The display should remain blank. The display subroutine has become an IRQ routine. The time will be displayed when an interrupt occurs.)

Step 3

With the circuit of Fig. 9-9, produce an interrupt. Does the time appear? If it does not, you have made a mistake with your program. Try again or use the answer given above.

EXPERIMENT NO. 7

Step 1

Study the program below and decide if it will execute properly. Explain your reasoning. The program has no objective or usefulness.

```
0200   A9 FF     START     LDA $FF        Initialize Port A to be an output port
0202   8D 01 17             STA PADD       by storing $FF in its DDR.
0205   48                   PHA            Save the accumulator on the stack.
0206   20 10 02             JSR TEST       Jump to subroutine TEST
0209   A9 F0                LDA $F0
020B   8D 00 17             STA PAD         Output accumulator contents to Port A.
020E   00                   BRK
0210   68        TEST       PLA            Get contents of stack.
0211   60                   RTS            Return from subroutine.
```

Step 2

What do you expect to observe if the program executes properly?

(Four of the lights on Port A should light and four should remain dark because after the program returns from the subroutine we load $F0 into Port A.)

Step 3

Execute the program, see if it works, and then explain why it doesn't work. Try tracing the program counter and the stack pointer.

(The program attempts to "pass a parameter" from the main program to the subroutine by means of the stack. The data is placed on the stack by the PHA instruction in the main program. It is pulled off the stack by the PLA instruction in the subroutine. If the stack pointer was $FF before the program was executed, then the PHA instruction will decrement it to $FE. The "return address" for the JSR instruction will be stored at $01FE and $01FD. The PLA instruction in the subroutine increments the stack pointer from $FC to $FD. The RTS instruction increments the stack pointer again, and reads the "return address" from locations with addresses $01FE and $01FF. Note that these are not the correct locations. It is good practice to make sure that PHA and PLA instructions always occur in pairs in subroutines and interrupts.)

CHAPTER 10

Interval Timers

OBJECTIVES

At the completion of this chapter you should be able to:

- Understand the use of interval timers in programming.
- Program the 6530, 6532, and 6522 interval timers.
- Write programs that use interval timers to implement delay loops, to measure time between events, and to count events.

INTRODUCTION

Computer systems that are designed mainly as "number crunchers" or data processors, and that operate primarily with high-level language interpreters such as BASIC, FORTRAN, etc., do not usually make much use of interval timers, except perhaps as a 24-hour clock. But in many cases where a computer is interfaced to some device in the real world, you are likely to find an interval timer.

One of the reasons for the popularity of the KIM-1 microcomputer in particular, and 6502-based designs in general, has to be the interval timers that are associated with these systems. An interval timer may replace software timing loops, freeing the computer for other tasks while the timing is taking place in external hardware. Interval timers may be used to implement 24-hour clocks. They can be used to make precise measurements of the times between events, and they can also be used as event counters. Almost any data logging problem requires a particular time to elapse between the points or values to be logged, and interval timers are ideal for implementing these time delays. Interval timers are used in music synthesis applications. The purpose of this chapter is to acquaint you with the basic programming techniques needed to operate an interval timer, and to give you some examples of simple applications that may give you ideas of your own.

In 6502 systems, an *interval timer* is a location in memory that may be loaded with a number like any other R/W memory location. After a number has been written into the location of the interval timer, the system clock decrements the number in the interval timer until the number is zero. At that time a flag in a register associated with the timer is set and/or an interrupt occurs, signaling the microprocessor that the "time is up." Details of how these events take place vary considerably, depending on the device involved. Interval timers are part of the logic circuitry found on integrated circuits known as the 6522 Versatile Interface Adapter (VIA), the 6530 RAM-ROM-I/O-Timer (RRIOT), and the 6532 RAM-I/O-Timer (RIOT). The 6530 is found exclusively on the KIM-1, while both the 6522 and the 6532 are found on the AIM 65 and the SYM-1. The specifications for these devices are found in Appendix C. After this brief introduction, we now proceed to examine the interval timing functions of each of these integrated circuits.

6530 INTERVAL TIMER

Although the integrated circuit known as the 6530 contains R/W memory locations, ROM memory locations, and I/O ports, in this section we are interested only in its interval timers. A model of the interval timer structure of the 6530 is shown in Fig. 10-1. The system clock decrements a number in the *timer register* at a rate determined by "divide down" logic. The clock signal may be divided by one, eight, 64, or 1024, depending on which divide circuit is selected. The divide circuits are selected by address lines A0 and A1. Thus, the two least-significant bits of the address of the counter register determine which divisor will be used to "predivide" the time base that is used to decrement the count. While the actual address may change; that is, 0000 0100 through 0000 0111, with the ADH fixed, the *same* register is addressed, but different count-down frequencies are selected by the programmable divide-down logic. If the divide-by-64 circuit is selected, then the timer register will be decremented once every 64 clock cycles.

When the number in the timer register reaches zero (an event that we will describe as "timing out"), a flag is set in a 1-bit register called the status register. The status bit is bit seven of a location in memory that is *read* to determine whether the timer has timed out. All the other bits (bit six through bit zero) of the status register

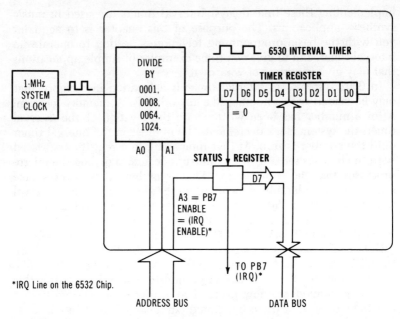

Fig. 10-1. Model of 6530 Interval Timer.

are always zero. A complete summary of the memory locations for the 6530 interval timer in the KIM-1 system is given in Table 10-1.

The time-out of a timer may also be used to cause an interrupt. This option is also selected by addressing. Refer to Table 10-1 and note that the divide-by-1024 circuit may be selected with either ad-

Table 10-1. The 6530 Interval Timer Read and Write Data

Address (KIM-1)	6530 Address Lines (Input) A3 A2 A1 A0				Function
$1704	0	1	0	0	Write to the T0001 Timer; PB7 Disabled
$1705	0	1	0	1	Write to the T0008 Timer; PB7 Disabled
$1706	0	1	1	0	Write to the T0064 Timer; PB7 Disabled
$1707	0	1	1	1	Write to the T1024 Timer; PB7 Disabled
$170C	1	1	0	0	Write to the T0001 Timer; PB7 Enabled*
$170D	1	1	0	1	Write to the T0008 Timer; PB7 Enabled*
$170E	1	1	1	0	Write to the T0064 Timer; PB7 Enabled*
$170F	1	1	1	1	Write to the T1024 Timer; PB7 Enabled*
$1706	0	1	1	0	Read Timer Register
$1707	0	1	1	1	Read Timer Status Register (Bit Seven)

Writing to or reading from any address after time-out clears the status register and sets PB7 to logic one.
*PB7 should be programmed as an input line.

dress $1707 or $170F. In using the first address, only the status flag will be set to one when the timer register reaches zero, while if the second address is used the status flag will be set *and* PB7 (pin seven of Port B) will make a logic-one to logic-zero transition. If PB7 is connected to either the IRQ pin or the NMI pin by means of an external wire, then an interrupt will result at the end of the timing period. However, PB7 must be programmed as an input line for this option to work. Table 10-1 and Fig. 10-1 show that address line A3 selects the interrupt mode.

The contents of the timer register may be read by reading the location whose address is $1706. The number in the timer will continue to decrement during and after a read operation. This read option is not used very frequently. In most programming situations, one is interested only in when the timer reaches zero, an event that is signaled by the status flag being set or by an interrupt.

Writing to or reading from any of the timer addresses *after* a time-out clears bit seven of the status register and sets PB7 to logic one. the latter being necessary to clear the interrupt.

The time duration, T, between the end of the last clock cycle in the write instruction (STA TIMER) and the setting of the status flag and/or the interrupt is given by the formula:

$$T = \left[(N \cdot D) + \frac{1}{2} \right] \cdot T_C \qquad (10\text{-}1)$$

where,

N is an 8-bit number written to the timer,
D is the divide ratio, for example, 64, 1024, etc., selected by addressing,
T_C is the system clock period (typically one microsecond).

The same formula applies to the timer on a 6532 integrated circuit. In fact, the timer on a 6532 has many features in common with the timer on a 6530.

For reference purposes (Table 10-1), we have included the states of the various address lines connected to the 6530 that identify which timer or feature is being used. Owners of other systems may use this information to help in interfacing a 6530.

The operation of the 6530 interval timer may be demonstrated with a few simple programs. Example 1 shows a simple delay loop implemented with an interval timer. The corresponding flowchart is shown in Fig. 10-2. Several modifications of this program are used in Experiment No. 1. The first instruction in Example 1 loads the accumulator with the number to be stored in the timer register. The next instruction stores this number in the timer register; the address chosen in this case calls for a divide-by-1024. At the conclusion of the fourth cycle in the STA instruction, the timer register begins

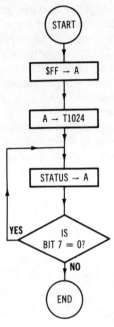

START

$FF → A

A → T1024

STATUS → A

IS BIT 7 = 0?

YES

NO

END

Fig. 10-2. Flowchart of Basic Interval Timer Delay Loop—Example 1.

to decrement. The status flag is read by the third instruction in the program, and bit seven is tested by the BPL instruction. If bit seven of the status register is zero, then the timer register has not yet reached zero. The program loops back to read the status flag until the flag is set, at which time the BRK instruction is executed, finishing the program. The total delay time produced by the interval timer delay loop is approximately

$$T = [255 \cdot 1024] \cdot 10^{-6} \text{ second} = 0.261 \text{ second},$$

where we have neglected the time for the STA and BPL instructions and the ½ cycle mentioned in Formula 10-1. The finer details will be considered when precision timing is required.

Example 1: Basic Interval Timer Delay Loop

Object: Produce a delay of approximately 0.261 second.

$1707 = T1024; location of divide-by-1024 timer. STATUS; Timer status register.

0200	A9 FF		START	LDA $FF	Get number to be stored in timer register.
0202	8D 07 17			STA T1024	Store it in /1024 timer.
0205	AD 07 17		LOOP	LDA STATUS	Read status.
0208	10 FB			BPL LOOP	Loop until timer times out.
020A	00			BRK	Finish.

The next program demonstrates how the interval timer may be used in an interrupt mode. Example 2 is not designed to do anything except generate equally spaced interrupts, the time between interrupts being determined by the timer chosen and the number loaded into the timer. The initialization sequence in Example 2 clears the interrupt flag to allow interrupts, then it forces an interrupt to get the timer started, and finally it waits in a "do-nothing" loop until the next interrupt occurs. In Experiment No. 3, some useful things will be done with this program. Here we simply demonstrate how to set up the interrupt mode. Note that for the KIM-1, output pin PB7 (pin 15 on the application connector) should be connected to the IRQ pin (pin 4 on the expansion connector).

Example 2: Demonstration of Interval Timer in Interrupt Mode

Object: Generate equally spaced interrupts with an interval timer.

$170E = T0064; divide-by-64 timer with interrupt enabled
$17FE = IRQL; Load with $06
$17FF = IRQH; load with $02

0200	58	START	CLI		Clear interrupt flag.
0201	00		BRK		Force interrupt.
0202	EA		NOP		No operation.
0203	4C 03 02	LOOP	JMP	LOOP	Loop here.
0206	A9 9C	INTRPT	LDA	$9C	Interrupt routine starts here.
0208	8D 0E 17		STA	T0064	Load divide-by-64 timer.
020B	40		RTI		Return from interrupt.

In order for the program in Example 2 to execute properly, an interrupt vector of $0206 must be loaded into locations whose addresses are $17FE and $17FF on the KIM-1. The time between interrupts will be $9C times 64 (timing interval) plus the time necessary to complete the JMP instruction in the main program and the LDA and STA instructions in the interrupt routine. Also, the time necessary to process the interrupt (seven clock cycles) and the indirect jump (five cycles) in the KIM-1 monitor must be included. Adding these periods gives a time interval between 10.002 milliseconds and 10.002 + 0.003 milliseconds as the time between interrupts. The +0.003 millisecond originates in the uncertainty of the location in the JMP instruction in the main program where the interrupt occurs. The JMP instruction requires three clock cycles, and it will be completed even though it is interrupted. Thus, the ability to generate equally spaced interrupts with the 6530 (or 6532) is made somewhat uncertain by the length of time required to complete the interrupted instruction. As we shall see below, one feature of the 6522 eliminates this uncertainty. In any case, the precision involved with the 6530 timer in the interrupt mode is sufficient for many experiments and designs.

6532 INTERVAL TIMER

The interval timer on the 6532 integrated circuit operates in almost the same way as the 6530 interval timer. The only significant difference is that the 6532 has an interrupt pin that is usually connected to the IRQ pin on the 6502 microprocessor. This is in contrast to the 6530 which uses the PB7 pin to signal an interrupt. The interval timer model shown in Fig. 10-1 for the 6530 will be identical in all respects to a model of the 6532 if the line labeled "TO PB7" is changed to "IRQ." The connection from the 6532 IRQ pin to the IRQ pin of the 6502 is usually internal to the microcomputer system; that is, a jumper wire is not necessary as in the case of the 6530 timer on the KIM-1. As in the case of the 6530, the control of the interrupt feature is implemented by addressing. If the address line A3 is at logic zero, then the interrupt feature is disabled. If address line A3 is at logic one, then the interrupt feature is enabled.

In Table 10-2 the various addresses used to select the timer functions are listed. Note that we have included addresses for the

Table 10-2. Equivalent Addresses for 6532 Timers on AIM 65 and SYM-1

Timer	KIM-1 Address	AIM 65 Address	SYM-1 Address
T0001	$1704*	$A494*	$A41C†
T0008	$1705	$A495	$A41D
T0064	$1706	$A496	$A41E
T1024	$1707	$A497	$A41F
READ STATUS	$1707	$A497	$A407
READ TIME	$1706	$A486	$A406

*Add eight (in hexadecimal) to the address to enable the interrupt feature on the KIM-1 and AIM 65.
†The interrupt line on the SYM-1 is not connected.

KIM-1 that actually address a timer on a 6530 chip rather than a 6532 chip. The reason is that these locations give timing intervals and interrupt behavior that is equivalent to the AIM 65. Since the interrupt pin of the 6502 on the SYM-1 is not connected to the IRQ pin on its 6532, the SYM-1 addresses are equivalent only in the sense that they produce identical timing intervals, *without interrupts*. The literature associated with the KIM-1 is far more extensive than that for the AIM 65 or SYM-1, and Table 10-2 is useful for writing new programs for the AIM 65 and SYM-1, if those programs make use of the 6532 interval timer. For purposes of illustration, Example 3 demonstrates the addressing required to implement a simple delay loop using the 6532 interval timer with the interrupt feature disabled. The program in Example 3 toggles bit zero of Port A (PA0) with a period equal to twice the length of the timing interval, producing a square waveform at PA0. See Experiment No. 3 for further details.

Example 3: Using an Interval Timer to Produce a Square Wave

Objective: Produce a square wave at PA0 with a programmable period.

$A001 = PAD; Port A
$A003 = PADD; Port A DDR
$A497 = T1024; Write to divide-by-1024 timer; read status

0200	A9 01	START	LDA $01	
0202	8D 03 A0		STA PADD	Make pin PA0 an output pin.
0205	A9 62	LOOP	LDA $62	Get number = ½ period of the square wave.
0207	8D 97 A4		STA T1024	Store in divide-by-1024 interval timer.
020A	A9 01		LDA $01	
020C	4D 01 A0		EOR PAD	Complement PA0.
020F	8D 01 A0		STA PAD	Result into PA0.
0212	2C 97 A4	TEST	BIT STATUS	Test status register for time out.
0215	10 FB		BPL TEST	
0217	4C 05 02		JMP LOOP	Repeat the process.

The frequency of the square wave produced by the timing variables chosen in Example 3 is about 5 Hz, corresponding to a period of approximately 0.20 second. Of course, higher and lower frequencies may be obtained by varying the byte in the location whose address is $0206 and/or by selecting a different divide-by ratio with another timer address. Example 3 uses AIM 65 addresses for the timer and for the output port. It may be converted to run on the SYM-1 by selecting the appropriate timer addresses with the use of Table 10-2. The output port addresses are the same for both systems. The program in Example 3 may be run on the KIM-1 by converting both the timer addresses and the output port addresses using Table 10-2 and Table 3-3, respectively. The square wave is produced by complementing the value of PA0 each time the interval timer is started. Complementation is produced by an

Table 10-3. Symbols for 6522 Timer Latches and Counters

Name	Symbol
Timer 1 Latch Low	T1L-L
Timer 1 Latch High	T1L-H
Timer 1 Counter Low	T1C-L
Timer 1 Counter High	T1C-H
Timer 2 Latch Low	T2L-L*
Timer 2 Counter Low	T2C-L
Timer 2 Counter High	T2C-H

*There is no corresponding Latch High.

Exclusive OR operation of PA0 with logic one. See Chapter 4 for a description of the logical operations.

6522 INTERVAL TIMERS

The 6522 Versatile Interface Adapter (VIA) is a complex but powerful integrated circuit. The purpose of this section is to describe the two interval timers on the chip. For a description of the other features of the 6522 refer to Appendix C. Do not expect to understand the many features of the interval timers with one reading. Study the descriptive material and experiments along with the programs that demonstrate the operation of the timers; then you will soon appreciate the versatility of this chip. One further note: the KIM-1 does not have a 6522, but an interface between the 6502 and a 6522 is described in Part II of this book, so that a 6522 could be added to a KIM-1 system very easily.

The 6522 has two interval timers referred to as T1 and T2. A model of the two 16-bit timers and their related control and interrupt registers is shown in Fig. 10-3. The basic principle of operation

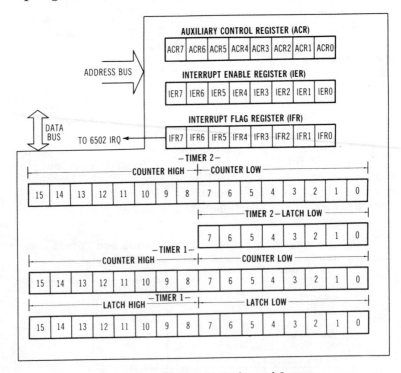

Fig. 10-3. The 6522 Registers, Latches, and Counters.

Table 10-4. Locations and Functions of 6522 Interval Timers on AIM 65 and SYM-1

Location	Timer	Write Function
A004	T1	Write data to timer 1 latch low (T1L-L).
A005	T1	Write data to timer 1 latch high (T1L-H) and counter high (T1C-H). Transfer the contents of T1L-L to T1C-L. Clear the T1 interrupt flag. Start timing.
A006	T1	Write data to timer 1 latch low (T1L-L).
A007	T1	Write data to timer 1 latch high (T1L-H). Clear the T1 interrupt flag.
A008	T2	Write data to timer 2 latch low (T2L-L).
A009	T2	Write data to timer 2 counter high (T2C-H). Transfer the contents of T2L-L to T2C-L. Clear the T2 interrupt flag. Start timing.
		Read Function
A004	T1	Read the contents of timer 1 counter low (T1C-L). Clear the T1 interrupt flag.
A005	T1	Read the contents of timer 1 counter high (T1C-H).
A006	T1	Read the contents of timer 1 latch low (T1L-L).
A007	T1	Read the contents of timer 1 latch high (T1L-H).
A008	T2	Read the contents of timer 2 counter low (T2C-L). Clear the T2 interrupt flag.
A009	T2	Read the contents of timer 2 counter high (T2C-H).

is similar to the 6530 and 6532 timers: a number loaded into a counter is decremented at the system clock rate until it reaches zero. At that time a flag is set in the interrupt flag register and, if the corresponding bit in the interrupt enable register is set, an interrupt will occur. The various features of the two timers are controlled by the status of various bits in the *Auxiliary Control Register* (ACR), the *Interrupt Flag Register* (IFR), and the *Interrupt Enable Register* (IER). In addition to studying Fig. 10-3, refer to Tables 10-3, 10-4, and 10-5 for the names, symbols, and addresses that will be used in describing the timers. Figs. 10-4, 10-5, and 10-6 supply the necessary information about the three registers (ACR, IFR, and IER) to select the various timing modes and interrupt conditions.

We will explain the functions of the various registers, latches, and timers in the context of demonstration programs. The program in Example 4 implements a simple delay loop, the most common function of an interval timer, using timer T2. The addresses used are the same for both the AIM 65 and SYM-1. The internal registers of the 6522 are cleared when a system RESET occurs, and we assume that is the state of the 6522 when the program in Example 3 is started. Refer to Fig. 10-4 and observe that when the IER is cleared, then the interrupt from timer T2 is disabled. The information in Fig. 10-6 indicates that since ACR5 = 0, then the T2 timer

Table 10-5. The 6522 Control and Interrupt Registers Used for the Timers

Register	Symbol	Address	Bits Used for Timers		
Auxiliary Control Register	ACR	$A00B	ACR7	ACR6	ACR5
Interrupt Flag Register	IFR	$A00D	IFR7	IFR6	IFR5
Interrupt Enable Register	IER	$A00E	IER7	IER6	IER5

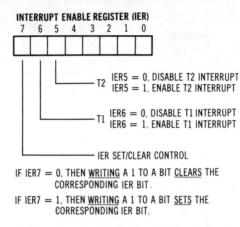

Fig. 10-4. Operation of 6522 Interrupt Enable Register.

is set to the mode in which a single time-out is generated. That is, the 16-bit number in the T2C-L and T2C-H is decremented at the clock rate until it reaches zero, at which time bit IFR5 is set (see Fig. 10-5).

The first two instructions in Example 4 load the Timer 2 Latch Low (T2L-L) with an 8-bit number. The next two instructions in

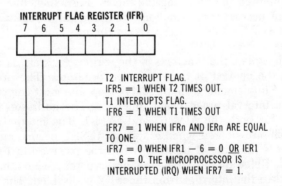

Fig. 10-5. Operation of 6522 Interrupt Flag Register.

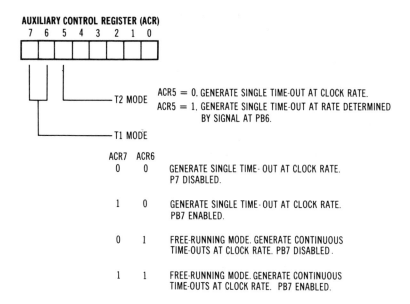

AUXILIARY CONTROL REGISTER (ACR)

7	6	5	4	3	2	1	0

T2 MODE

ACR5 = 0. GENERATE SINGLE TIME-OUT AT CLOCK RATE.
ACR5 = 1. GENERATE SINGLE TIME-OUT AT RATE DETERMINED BY SIGNAL AT PB6.

T1 MODE

ACR7	ACR6	
0	0	GENERATE SINGLE TIME-OUT AT CLOCK RATE. P7 DISABLED.
1	0	GENERATE SINGLE TIME-OUT AT CLOCK RATE. PB7 ENABLED.
0	1	FREE-RUNNING MODE. GENERATE CONTINUOUS TIME-OUTS AT CLOCK RATE. PB7 DISABLED.
1	1	FREE-RUNNING MODE. GENERATE CONTINUOUS TIME-OUTS AT CLOCK RATE. PB7 ENABLED.

Fig. 10-6. Operation of 6522 Auxiliary Control Register.

Example 4 load the Timer 2 Counter High (T2C-H) with an 8-bit number. At the completion of the STA T2C-H instruction, the number in the T2L-L is automatically transferred to the T2C-L, providing a 16-bit number in the T2 counter. There is no latch for the T2C-H. The number in the T2 counter, which we shall call N, is decremented at the system clock rate. Decrementing commences as soon as the T2 counter is loaded; that is, at the completion of the STA T2C-H instruction.

Later, after $(N + 1.5)$ microseconds have elapsed, bit IFR5 is set, signaling the time-out of the timer. If bit IER5 were set, enabling the interrupt feature, then an interrupt would also occur. However, in Example 4 we have assumed that the IER was cleared by a RESET operation prior to running the program. The last three instructions before the BRK instruction serve the purpose of testing bit IFR5 to see if a time-out has occurred. A one in bit five of the accumulator is ANDed with the IFR. If the result is zero, indicating that bit IFR5 has not yet been set, then the program loops back to test bit IFR5 again. Recall that the BIT instruction performs a logical AND operation. When the timer reaches zero, the program will detect the flag and exit the delay loop to execute the BRK instruction that will send it back to the monitor. The AIM 65 and SYM-1 displays will light after the BRK instruction is executed. By itself, the program in Example 4 is of little use except to demonstrate how to program timer T2 to produce a delay. Experiment No. 6 provides some variations of the program in Example 4 that might be useful in certain applications.

Example 4. Demonstration of T2 in Noninterrupt Delay Loop Mode

Objective: Generate a single delay using the system clock and the T2 timer.

```
$A008 = T2L-L
$A009 = T2C-H
$A00D = IFR
```

0200	A9 30	START	LDA	$30	Get number to be stored in T2L-L.
0202	8D 08 A0		STA	T2L-L	Store it in the timer.
0205	A9 99		LDA	$99	Get number to be stored in T2C-H.
0207	8D 09 A0		STA	T2C-H	Store it and start timing.
020A	A9 20		LDA	$20	Set bit five in A to one.
020C	2C 0D A0	DELAY	BIT	IFR	AND A with IFR to test bit IFR5.
020F	F0 FB		BEQ	DELAY	Wait here until bit IFR5 is one,
0211	00		BRK		then break to the monitor.

Example 5 demonstrates how the T2 timer may be programmed to operate in the interrupt mode. A program such as this could be used to produce interrupts for servicing some peripheral device, for example, but our purpose here is to demonstrate simply how the 6522 must be programmed to operate the T2 timer in this mode. Note in particular how the IER is programmed. Bit IER5 must be set by writing a one to *both* bit IER7, the IER set/clear bit, *and*

Example 5: Demonstration of 6522 Timer T2 in the Interrupt Mode

Objective: Produce a square wave of frequency 10 Hz on pin PA0.

```
$A001 = PAD; Port A
$A003 = PADD; Port A DDR
$A008 = T2L-L
$A009 = T2C-H
$A00E = IER; Interrupt Enable Register
$A404 = IRQL; Load with $15
$A405 = IRQH; Load with $02
```

0200	A9 A0	START	LDA	$A0	Set bits seven and five of A to one.
0202	8D 0E A0		STA	IER	Enable T2 interrupts.
0205	A9 FF		LDA	$FF	Set Port A DDR to make Port A an
0207	8D 03 A0		STA	PADD	output port.
020A	A9 00		LDA	$00	Initialize Port A LEDs to zero.
020C	8D 01 A0		STA	PAD	
020F	58		CLI		Clear interrupt flag to allow interrupts.
0210	00		BRK		Force the first interrupt.
0211	EA		NOP		No operation.
0212	4C 12 02	LOOP	JMP	LOOP	Idle here between interrupts.
0215	A9 50	IRQ	LDA	$50	Set up timer registers.
0217	8D 08 A0		STA	T2L-L	Initialize T2.
021A	A9 C3		LDA	$C3	
021C	8D 09 A0		STA	T2C-H	
021F	EE 01 A0		INC	PAD	Increment the contents of Port A.
0222	40		RTI		Return from interrupt.

bit IER5. The one in bit IER7 tells the 6522 that one or more bits of the IER are going to be *set*. The one in bit IER5 enables the interrupt feature of the T2 timer, as indicated in Fig. 10-4. A zero in the other data bits written to the IER leaves the corresponding IER bits unaffected.

The first two instructions in the program in Example 5 set the IER5 bit. Notice that $A0 corresponds to a one in bits seven and five. The CLI instruction clears the interrupt flag so that subsequent interrupts will work. The BRK instruction forces the first interrupt. In the interrupt routine, the T2 timer is loaded with $C350 = 50,000, so there will be slightly more than 0.05 second between interrupts. The voltage at pin PA0 will be a square wave with a frequency of 10 Hz, pin PA1 will produce a square wave of 5 Hz, pin PA2 will produce a square wave of 2.5 Hz, and so on. Note that in order for the program in Example 5 to work, an interrupt vector of $0215 is required, $0215 being the starting address of the interrupt routine.

USING T2 TIMER AS A COUNTER

To demonstrate how the T2 timer may be used to *count pulses from an external source*, we will describe a 24-hour clock with extremely low computer-time overhead. To simplify matters, our clock will keep time in hours and minutes, omitting seconds. In many applications such as security systems, oven timers, and punch clocks for timing in and out of work, the time to the nearest minute is sufficiently precise. Example 6 utilizes a conditioned signal from the 60-Hz power line, as outlined in Example 10 in Chapter 9. This signal is applied to pin PB6, which, in turn, is connected internally in the 6522 to the T2 timer. If bit ACR5 is set to one, then the number in the T2 timer is decremented once for each pulse on PB6, rather than being decremented by the system clock. If the T2 timer is loaded with 3600_{10}, then it will time out once every minute if 60-Hz pulses are applied to PB6. Timer T2 will be operated in the interrupt mode, so once every minute an interrupt occurs and locations in memory representing minutes and hours are incremented as necessary. You should compare this with the 24-hour clock program in Example 10 in Chapter 9 that required interrupts every $\frac{1}{60}$ second.

Examples 6 in this chapter and 10 in Chapter 9 are similar in several respects. The so-called "main" program initializes the interrupt vector and then breaks to the interrupt routine to start the timing. Both programs increment locations in memory corresponding to minutes and hours in the interrupt routine. The program then returns to the main program to display the time. Note that in

Example 6 we have used a JSR DISPLY instruction that jumps to the same display subroutine that was used in Example 10 in Chapter 9. This routine is not repeated here because of its length. The comments should provide enough information to understand the program, provided that you understood Example 10 in Chapter 9.

Example 6: Low Overhead 24-Hour Clock

Objective: Write a program to keep time in hours and minutes using the T2 timer.

$0340 = DISPLY; location of the first byte of the display subroutine described in Chapter 9, Example 10
$A00B = ACR; Auxiliary Control Register of the 6522
$A00E = IER; Interrupt Enable Register of the 6522
$A404 = IRQL; contains low-order byte of the interrupt vector
$A405 = IRQH; contains high-order byte of the interrupt vector

0200	78		MAIN	SEI		Set Interrupt Disable Flag.
0201	A9	00		LDA	$00	Load interrupt vector.
0203	8D	04 A4		STA	IRQL	
0206	A9	03		LDA	$03	
0208	8D	05 A4		STA	IRQH	
020B	A9	20		LDA	$20	Bit five of A is set to one, then it
020D	8D	0B A0		STA	ACR	is stored in the ACR to set the timer
0210	A9	A0		LDA	$A0	in the pulse counting mode.
0212	8D	0E A0		STA	IER	Enable interrupts from T2.
0215	58			CLI		Clear interrupt flag.
0216	00			BRK		Jump to the first interrupt.
0217	EA			NOP		No operation.
0218	20	40 03	IDLE	JSR	DISPLY	Jump to display subroutine.
021B	4C	18 02		JMP	IDLE	

$0002 = MIN; this location stores the time in minutes
$0003 = HRS; this location stores the time in hours
$A008 = T2L-L; low-order byte of the T2 timer
$A009 = T2C-H; high-order byte of the T2 timer

0300	48		IRQ	PHA		Push accumulator on the stack.
0301	A9	0F		LDA	$0F	Load T2 timer with 3600 = $0E10.
0303	8D	08 A0		STA	T2L-L	Since T2 counts through zero, use
0306	A9	0E		LDA	$0E	3599 = $0E0F.
0308	8D	09 A0		STA	T2C-H	Start counting pulses on PB6.
030B	F8			SED		Set decimal mode.
030C	18			CLC		Clear carry flag for next addition.
030D	A5	02		LDA	MIN	Get minutes.
030F	69	01		ADC	$01	Add one.
0311	85	02		STA	MIN	Result into minutes.
0313	C9	60		CMP	$60	Minutes equal 60?
0315	90	13		BCC	OUT	No. Prepare to leave interrupt routine.
0317	A9	00		LDA	$00	Yes. Set to zero then increment HRS.
0319	85	02		STA	MIN	
031B	18			CLC		Clear carry flag.
031C	A5	03		LDA	HRS	Get hours.
031E	69	01		ADC	$01	Add one.
0320	85	03		STA	HRS	Result into hours.
0322	C9	24		CMP	$24	Hours equal 24?

0324	90 04		BCC	OUT	No. Prepare to leave interrupt routine.
0326	A9 00		LDA	$00	Yes. Set hours to zero.
0328	85 03		STA	HRS	Result into hours.
032A	D8	OUT	CLD		Clear decimal mode flag.
032B	68		PLA		Pull accumulator from the stack.
032C	40		RTI		Return from the interrupt routine.

In order for the program in Example 6 to run, the program should be started with the contents of MIN equal to one less than the time at which you intend to start keeping time, and the contents of HRS should equal the correct time. Connect the circuit of Fig. 9-7 with the output of the 555 timer connected to PB6 (pin 17 on the application connector of the AIM 65). Connect the input of the 555 timer (Fig. 9-7) to the 6.3 V ac 60-Hz source at the instant at which the time exceeds the time loaded into MIN by one minute. Be sure that the computer and the 555 timer have common ground connections.

USING T1 TIMER

The T1 timer on the 6522 VIA may also be used to generate delays either with or without interrupts. In other words, Examples 4 and 5, described previously, will also work with the T1 timer. Changes to these programs to utilize the T1 timer would include writing the 16-bit number to T1L-L and T1L-H at addresses $A004 and $A005, respectively, instead of using T2L-L and T2C-H. Also, the time-out of timer T1 is flagged by bit IFR7 instead of bit IFR6. Thus, the BPL instruction, which tests bit seven, could be used to hold the timer in the delay loop until it times out. Then Example 4 should also be modified to include clearing bits ACR7 and ACR6, if the T1 timer is to be used. This last step would not be necessary after a system RESET because the registers are automatically cleared. Example 5 would also require bits ACR7 and ACR6 to be cleared, and, in addition, bit IER6 must be set to allow interrupts. Bit IER6 may be set by writing $C0 to the IER; that is, both bit IER7 and bit IER6 must be one to set bit IER6. Refer to Figs. 10-4, 10-5, and 10-6 for details. The T1 timer cannot be used to replace the T2 timer in Example 6 because it does not have an external pulse counting mode.

One of the most attractive features of the T1 timer is its ability to generate equally spaced interrupts in its "free-running" mode. In this mode, the timer is *automatically* restarted after each time-out. No write instructions are required to reset or restart the timer. This has the advantage of making the time between interrupts independent of the time necessary to process the interrupt routine instructions. For example, when an interrupt occurs, the instruction currently being executed is completed. Depending on the instruction being interrupted and the clock cycle in which it is interrupted, this time could vary from one to seven clock cycles. This might be a significant error in precision timing measurements, but it is eliminated with the free-running mode.

In the free-running mode it is also possible to invert the logic level of PB7 each time the counter reaches zero. Thus, a square wave output at PB7 may be obtained, the period of the square wave being twice the timing interval. The various modes are selected by bits ACR7 and ACR6 in the ACR. Refer to Fig. 10-6 for details. It is important to know that the time between interrupts or between inversions of PB7 is $N + 2$ clock cycles where N is the 16-bit number loaded into the T1 timer. Also, the T1 timer interrupt flag must be cleared after each interrupt. This is accomplished by reading T1C-L with an LDA T1C-L instruction. Even though we are not interested in the contents of this location, the reading operation clears the flag.

PRECISION TIMING PROGRAM

To demonstrate the operation of the T1 timer in its free-running mode, we have written three programs that also represent useful applications. The program in Example 7 measures the time interval, in units of 100 microseconds, between two successive negative pulses on pin PA7. A six-digit counter (three bytes of bcd data) is incremented every 100 microseconds after the first event produces a pulse on PA7 until the second event produces the second pulse on PA7. The display subroutine listed in Example 10 in Chapter 9 is used to display the result. Since the six-digit counter is incremented every 100 microseconds, the two most-significant digits give the time in seconds, the decimal point is between the second and third digits, and the remaining four digits give the time in units of ten-thousandths of a second. Time intervals between 0.0001 second and 99.9999 seconds may be measured with a precision of ±0.0001 second. The program in Example 7 is the basic ingredient for a large number of interesting applications that require precise measurement of the time between two events.

Example 7: Program to Measure Time Between Two Events

Objective: Measure the time between successive negative pulses on PA7 in units of 100 microseconds. Display the answer using the display subroutine of Example 10 in Chapter 9.

$0001 = CNTLO; contains the two low-order digits of the time interval
$0002 = CNTMI; contains the two middle-order digits of the time interval
$0003 = CNTHI; contains the two high-order digits of the time interval
$A001 = PAD; Port A, bit PA7 is used to detect the pulses.

$A004 = T1C-L; a location that is read to clear the T1 interrupt flag
$A005 = T1L-H
$A006 = T1L-L
$A00B = ACR
$A00E = IER
$A404 = IRQL; contains the low-order byte of the interrupt vector
$A405 = IRQH; contains the high-order byte of the interrupt vector

0200	A9 44	START	LDA $44	Get the low-order byte of the IRQ vector.
0202	8D 04 A4		STA IRQL	Store it in IRQL.
0205	A9 02		LDA $02	Get the high-order byte of the IRQ vector.
0207	8D 05 A4		STA IRQH	Store it in IRQH.
020A	F8		SED	Set decimal-mode flag for decimal addition.
020B	18		CLC	Clear carry flag for addition.
020C	A9 00	AGAIN	LDA $00	Clear counter locations.
020E	85 01		STA CNTLO	
0210	85 02		STA CNTMI	
0212	85 03		STA CNTHI	
0214	A9 40		LDA $40	Set bit six of A to one. Store the result in the ACR to put T1 in free-running mode.
0216	8D 0B A0		STA ACR	
0219	A9 C0		LDA $C0	Set bits six and seven of A to one. This result into IER enables T1 interrupts.
021B	8D 0E A0		STA IER	
021E	A9 62		LDA $62	The time between interrupts will be $62 + 2 = 100_{10}$ clock cycles.
0220	8D 06 A0		STA T1L-L	
0223	A9 00		LDA $00	Clear accumulator.
0225	2C 01 A0	WAIT	BIT PAD	Is PA7 at logic 1?
0228	30 FB		BMI WAIT	Yes; wait for a negative transition.
022A	2C 01 A0	IDLE	BIT PAD	No; then negative pulse has begun.
022D	10 FB		BPL IDLE	Wait for positive transition.
022F	8D 05 A0		STA T1L-H	Put $00 in T1L-H, then start timing.
0232	58		CLI	Clear interrupt flag to allow interrupts.
0233	2C 01 A0	LOAF	BIT PAD	Wait for next negative pulse.
0236	30 FB		BMI LOAF	
0238	2C 01 A0	BACK	BIT PAD	
023B	10 FB		BPL BACK	
023D	78		SEI	Pulse is complete; prevent further interrupts.
023E	20 40 03		JSR DISPLY	See Example 10, Chapter 9 for display subroutine
0241	4C 0C 02		JMP AGAIN	Return to make another measurement.
0244	48	IRQ	PHA	Save accumulator during the interrupt.
0245	A9 01		LDA $01	Increment counters during each interrupt, that is, every 100 microseconds.
0247	65 01		ADC CNTLO	
0249	85 01		STA CNTLO	Result into counter low-order byte.
024B	A9 00		LDA $00	Clear accumulator.
024D	65 02		ADC CNTMI	Add carry from previous add to

024F	85	02		STA CNTMI	middle-order byte of the counter.
0251	A9	00		LDA $00	Clear accumulator.
0253	65	03		ADC CNTHI	Add carry from previous add to the
0255	85	03		STA CNTHI	high-order byte of the counter.
0257	AD	04	A0	LDA T1C-L	Clear 6522 timer T1 interrupt flag.
025A	68			PLA	Restore accumulator.
025B	40			RTI	Return from interrupt.

A flowchart that presents most of the important features of the program in Example 7 is shown in Fig. 10-7. The instructions in Example 7 that relate directly to the operation of the T1 timer should be studied carefully. The instruction starting at address $0216 sets up the ACR for timer T1 to operate in the free-running mode with PB7 disabled. That is, PB7 will not toggle each time that an interrupt occurs. The instruction starting at the address $020B sets the IER to enable interrupts from the T1 timer. The low-order byte of the counter is loaded with the instruction starting at address $0220. Note that since the time between interrupts is to be 100_{10} clock cycles we loaded $62 = 98_{10}$ into the counter. Two additional cycles are used to reload the counter after each interrupt, giving exactly 100 clock cycles between interrupts. The high-order byte of the 16-bit number loaded into the counter is put there with the instruction starting at the address $022F, directly after the first negative pulse is detected. Recall that the timer starts counting down directly after T1L-H is loaded. Directly after that instruction, the 6502 interrupt flag is cleared to allow the 6522 VIA to interrupt it from timer T1. The six-digit counter is incremented in the interrupt routine once every 100 microseconds thereafter, until another negative pulse is detected. Note that one of the last instructions in the interrupt routine is used to clear the 6522 interrupt from the T1 timer.

To measure the time interval between positive pulses, change all of the BMI instructions to BPL instructions, and vice versa. The accuracy of the time measurements depends ultimately on the accuracy of the system clock. You should be aware that most crystal oscillators on microcomputers like the KIM-1, SYM-1, and AIM 65 are not accurate to six significant figures. For example, the crystal on the author's AIM 65 appears to have an error of 240 counts per million counts. If you want to do laboratory-standard timing, you will need laboratory-standard crystal oscillators.

The timer program may be used in many ways. We have used similar programs to measure muzzle velocities, the acceleration of gravity, the period of a square wave and to conduct simple stopwatch-type experiments. Note that mechanical switches are not suitable to provide pulses at PA7 unless they are debounced electronically. Refer to Fig. 3-2 for suitable debouncing circuitry. Photo-

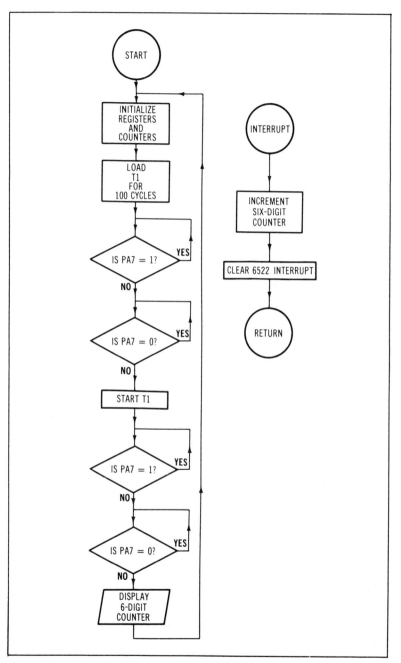

Fig. 10-7. Flowchart of Event Timing Program.

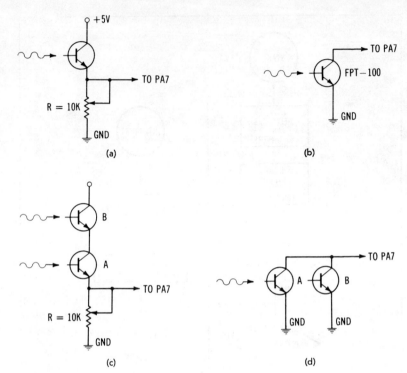

Fig. 10-8. Phototransistor Interface for Precision Timing Program of Example 7. Text describes difference in (a), (b), (c), and (d) circuits.

cells and phototransistors make excellent event detectors. Several possible interfaces involving phototransistors are shown in Fig. 10-8. The time between successive negative pulses produced by the phototransistor circuit is displayed by the program of Example 7.

Circuit (a) in Fig. 10-8 produces a negative pulse whenever the light to the phototransistor is interrupted. The 10K potentiometer is adjusted to give the necessary pulse depth. Circuit (b) produces a negative pulse when a light pulse strikes the phototransistor. Circuit (c) produces a negative pulse when the light to either phototransistor A *or* B is interrupted. Circuit (d) produces a negative pulse when a light pulse strikes either phototransistor A *or* B.

The program in Example 7 can be easily modified to measure the time for which pin PA7 is at logic zero. It can also be modified to start timing when a logic transition occurs at one pin of Port A and to stop timing when a logic transition occurs at another pin of Port A. The experiments at the end of the chapter go into some further details. Do not attempt to use other than incandescent light sources or LEDs operated from dc voltages, or you may find that you are timing the interval between ac pulses on the power line.

USING T1 TIMER TO IMPLEMENT FREQUENCY COUNTER

The second application of the T1 timer operating in the free-running mode is an event counter. It may be used to count the number of events that produce a positive pulse at pin PA7 in a programmed interval of time. As described here, the program is used as a frequency counter, and the number of positive pulses that occur in one second is displayed by the display subroutine of Example 10 in Chapter 9. However, the general principles are applicable to any kind of events-counting problem, such as radioactive decay, cars passing by a certain point, a laboratory animal going to his feeding station, the arrival of telephone calls, etc., provided that one can construct an interface circuit that produces a positive pulse on PA7 for each event.

Since the T1 timer is operating in the same mode as in Example 7, details regarding setting up the various timer registers will not be repeated. A flowchart of the program in Example 8 is shown in Fig. 10-9. Although the time between interrupts is independent of the time necessary to process the interrupt routine, this latter time must be taken into account in this program because time spent processing the interrupt routine is time *not spent* counting pulses. We decided on a basic time interval of 50,000 cycles. Twenty of these intervals gives a total counting time of 1 second, since each cycle is 1 microsecond. Each interrupt requires a total of 36 cycles (add the instruction cycles for each instruction in the interrupt routine, remembering that the interrupt itself takes seven cycles and the indirect jump required by the monitor takes five cycles). Thus, to obtain a total counting time of 50,000 cycles, we must set the timer for $50,000 + 36 - 2$ cycles $= 50,034$ cycles. Recall that the time between interrupts is $N + 2$, so we subtract two to get the correct number of cycles. So the timer should be loaded with $50,034 =$ $C372. Twenty of these intervals should give a total counting time of 1 second.

There is one additional minor complication. The first timing interval is not begun with an interrupt, but rather with an STA T1L-H instruction. To make sure all 20 intervals are the same length, we should, in principle, waste 36 cycles after the timer is started the first time. This is the reason that in Example 8 we have spent some time clearing counters and doing other odd jobs after starting the timer for the first time. In this way, we were able to take up 15 cycles leaving 21 cycles yet to waste. Instead of writing another delay loop taking 21 cycles, we chose to reduce the total

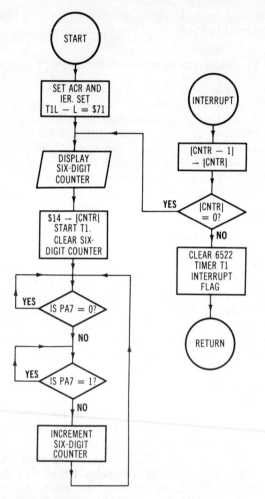

Fig. 10-9. Flowchart of frequency counter in Example 8.

counting time of each of the twenty 50,000-cycle intervals by one cycle. Thus, we used the number $C371 in the counter rather than $C372. We are now within 1 microsecond of 1 second for our total counting interval. This is more than sufficiently precise, and we could have decided not to worry about the 21 cycles.

The location with address $0000 is used as the count-to-twenty counter. It is loaded with $20 = 14 initially, and each interrupt decrements it until 20 interrupts have occurred. Then the program jumps to display the number of events counted. After displaying the number of events counted with a six-digit counter, the counter locations are initialized again and the process is repeated, giving a new measurement about once every second. If an event counting interval of ten seconds is desired, change the program byte at $021E to 200 = $C8.

Largely because of the time needed to increment the six-digit counter after each pulse is detected, there is a limit to the rate at which pulses may be counted without missing them. This limit is just above 20 kHz; in other words pulse rates of 20 kHz are acceptable, but rates above this result in pulses not being counted. To detect negative pulses, interchange the BMI and BPL instructions at $0233 and $0238.

Although the most obvious use of the frequency-counter program is to measure frequencies, there are other applications for an event counter. Experiments in nuclear physics, chemistry, biology, and medicine require nuclear-event counters. If some analog voltage signal needs to be integrated, for example, the output of a gas chromatograph, then a voltage-to-frequency converter connected to the frequency counter may be used to integrate the voltage waveform. Other things to count include rotations of a motor, heartbeats, rotation of a turnstile, arrival of cosmic rays, and many others. Of course, the timing interval may need to be changed, depending on the nature of the events that are counted.

Example 8: Frequency Counter

Objective: Count the number of events that take place in 1 second and display the result after each count.

$0000 = CNTR; contains number of 0.05-second intervals to be used in counting
$0001 = CNTLO; low-order byte of six-digit event counter
$0002 = CNTMI; middle-order byte of six-digit event counter
$0003 = CNTHI; high-order byte of six-digit event counter
$A001 = PAD; bit seven of Port A (PA7) is used as the input pin.
$A004 = T1C-L; this location is read to clear the 6522 interrupt flag
$A005 = T1L-H
$A006 = T1L-L
$A00B = ACR
$A00E = IER
$A404 = IRQL; contains low-order byte of interrupt vector
$A405 = IRQH; contains high-order byte of interrupt vector

0200	A9 50	START	LDA	$50	Set up interrupt vector.
0202	8D 04 A4		STA	IRQL	
0205	A9 02		LDA	$02	
0207	8D 05 A4		STA	IRQH	
020A	A9 40		LDA	$40	Set ACR so timer T1 operates in the
020C	8D 0B A0		STA	ACR	free-running mode.
020F	A9 C0		LDA	$C0	Set IER to enable T1 interrupts.
0211	8D 0E A0		STA	IER	
0214	20 40 03	DISP	JSR	DISPLY	Use display subroutine from Example 10 in Chapter 9.
0217	F8		SED		Set decimal mode for bcd addition.

```
0218  A9 71             LDA  $71      Set up T1 counter for 50,033 cycles
021A  8D 06 A0          STA  T1L-L    (see text).
021D  A9 14             LDA  $14      Set up 20₁₀ interval counter.
021F  85 00             STA  CNTR
0221  A9 C3             LDA  $C3      Start timer by loading its high-order
0223  8D 05 A0          STA  T1L-H    latch.
0226  A9 00             LDA  $00      Clear counters.
0228  85 01             STA  CNTLO
022A  85 02             STA  CNTMI
022C  85 03             STA  CNTHI
022E  58                CLI           Allow interrupts to start.
022F  EA                NOP           Use up two more cycles of time.
0230  2C 01 A0   WAIT   BIT  PAD      Is PA7 at logic zero?
0233  10 FB             BPL  WAIT     Yes. Then wait for it to go high.
0235  2C 01 A0   LOAF   BIT  PAD      No. Then wait for it to go low again.
0238  30 FB             BMI  LOAF     When it goes low, then a complete
023A  18                CLC           pulse has been detected so increment
023B  A5 01             LDA  CNTLO    the six-digit counter.
023D  69 01             ADC  $01      Add one to the low-order byte.
023F  85 01             STA  CNTLO    Result into low-order byte of counter.
0241  A5 02             LDA  CNTMI    Carry from previous addition is added
0243  69 00             ADC  $00      to middle-order byte of counter.
0245  85 02             STA  CNTMI    Result into middle-order byte.
0247  A5 03             LDA  CNTHI    Carry from previous addition is added
0249  69 00             ADC  $00      to high-order byte of the counter.
024B  85 03             STA  CNTHI    Result into high-order byte.
024D  4C 30 02          JMP  WAIT     Return to count the next pulse.
0250  48         IRQ    PHA
0251  C6 00             DEC  CNTR     Decrement count-to-twenty counter.
0253  F0 BF             BEQ  DISP     If count is zero, 1 sec interval is
0255  AD 04 A0          LDA  T1C-L    complete. Clear 6522 interrupt flag.
0258  68                PLA           Get accumulator back,
0259  40                RTI           then return from interrupt.
```

MAKING MUSIC USING T1 TIMER

A final program to demonstrate the T1 timer in the free-running mode with PB7 enabled is given in Example 9. This program generates a series of tones the frequencies of which are determined by numbers loaded into the T1 timer from a table, and the durations of which are determined by a number in a table that controls the number of times the T2 timer times out. The program could easily be modified to play simple songs. Simple programs like this may be used for sound effects in electronic games, alarms and alarm clocks, or music synthesis. A simple interface circuit is shown in Fig. 10-10.

The frequency of the tone is determined by the 16-bit number loaded into the T1 timer. PB7 is complemented each time T1 times out, so the number loaded into the T1 timer is ½ the period of the square wave at PB7, measured in microseconds. If 1000_{10} is loaded into T1, then the period will be 2000 microseconds, or the frequency will be 500 Hz. The desired periods are stored in a table in page

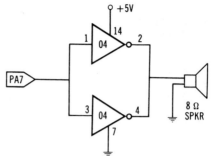

Fig. 10-10. Output Circuit for Tone Generation Program.

three. Starting at address $0300, the first two bytes of the table in page three contain the numbers to be loaded into T1L-L and T1L-H, respectively. The next byte contains a number that determines the duration of this tone. Timer T2 is loaded with $C34E corresponding to a time interval of about 0.05 second. The number in the third byte of the table in page three determines the number of 0.05-second intervals that the tone will play.

Information that determines the frequency and duration of the next tone is stored at addresses $0303, $0304, and $0305, and so on for as many tones as desired. The tone sequence or "song" will end when a $00 appears in a duration byte. Note that the Y register is used to index the tones and durations of the notes. Since each tone requires three bytes of page three, a total of 85_{10} notes are available if the song is confined to page three. Longer sequences of notes may be played if a new base address is chosen after 85_{10} notes are played, that is, if the song requires more memory space than page three. A short sequence of notes is provided in the program. The indirect indexed addressing mode was used so that a number of tone sequences could be played by changing the base-address low (BAL) and the base-address high (BAH) of the tone and duration tables.

Sirens, vibrato, or other sound effects may be created with similar programs by putting the frequency determining parameters in a loop where they are incremented or decremented in small amounts, and a single tone lasts for only a short period of time. You may wish to impress your wife by implementing a "wolf whistle" when she enters the room.

Example 9: Tone Generation Program

Objective: Use the PB7 toggle option of the T1 timer to generate tones.

$0000 = NOTLO; Contains $00, the BAL of the tone frequency table, low-order bytes

$0001 = NOTLO + 1; Contains $03, the BAH of the tone frequency table, low-order bytes

$0002 = NOTHI; Contains $01, the BAL of the tone frequency table, high-order bytes

$0003 = NOTHI + 1; Contains $03, the BAH of the tone frequency table, high-order byte

$0004 = DUR; Contains $02, the BAL of the tone duration table

$0005 = DUR + 1; Contains $03, the BAH of the tone duration table.

$A005 = T1L-H	
$A006 = T1L-L	
$A007 = T1L-H	
$A008 = T2L-L	
$A009 = T2C-H	
$A00B = ACR	
$A00D = IFR	

SIMPLE TONE TABLE

$0300	00 01 01 00
$0304	02 02 00 03
$0308	03 00 04 04
$030C	00 05 06 00
$0310	06 07 00 00

0200	A9 C0	START	LDA	$C0	Set up ACR for T1 to operate in
0202	8D 0B A0		STA	ACR	the free-running mode with PA7 enabled.
0205	A9 00		LDA	$00	Start T1 running.
0207	8D 06 A0		STA	T1L-L	
020A	8D 05 A0		STA	T1L-H	
020D	A0 00		LDY	$00	Initialize Y register.
020F	B1 00	OVER	LDA	(NOTLO),Y	Get low-order byte of half-period.
0211	8D 06 A0		STA	T1L-L	Result into timer.
0214	B1 02		LDA	(NOTHI),Y	Get high-order byte of half-period.
0216	8D 07 A0		STA	T1L-H	Result into timer.
0219	B1 04		LDA	(DUR),Y	Get duration of note.
021B	F0 1B		BEQ	OUT	Duration = zero means end of tone sequence.
021D	AA		TAX		Duration into X register.
021E	A9 4E	AGAIN	LDA	$4E	Total time = Duration × 0.05 second.
0220	8D 08 A0		STA	T2L-L	
0223	A9 C3		LDA	$C3	
0225	8D 09 A0		STA	T2C-H	Start timer T2.
0228	A9 20		LDA	$20	Check to see if time T2 flag is set.
022A	2C 0D A0	WAIT	BIT	IFR	
022D	F0 FB		BEQ	WAIT	
022F	CA		DEX		Decrement duration counter.
0230	D0 EC		BNE	AGAIN	
0232	C8		INY		Increment Y to get new tone parameters.
0233	C8		INY		
0234	C8		INY		
0235	4C 0F 02		JMP	OVER	Return to get another note.
0238	A9 00	OUT	LDA	$00	Clear ACR.
023A	8D 0B A0		STA	ACR	
023D	00		BRK		

EXPERIMENT NO. 1

Step 1

Load the following program. The timer addresses listed are for the KIM-1. See Table 10-2 to convert to the 6532 timers on the AIM 65 or SYM-1. This program is a modification of Example 1 in the text.

```
0200   A9 FF      START   LDA  $FF       Get number to be stored in the timer.
0202   8D 01 17           STA  PADD      Set Port A DDR to output data.
0205   8D 07 17           STA  T1024     Store in 1024 timer and start timer.
0208   AD 07 17   LOOP    LDA  STATUS    Read status flag of timer.
020B   8D 00 17           STA  PAD       Output status to Port A.
020E   10 F8              BPL  LOOP      Branch back to loop until time out.
0210   00                 BRK
```

Step 2

Press your system RESET key. Execute the program. What do you expect to observe on the Port A LEDs?

(The reset should cause all the LEDs to glow. When the program is in the delay loop, the LEDs should all go out. Note that while waiting for the timer to time out, bit seven and all the other bits of the status register are zero. When the timer goes through zero, bit seven is set to one. Storing this in the output port causes the PA0 LED to glow. All the other bits remain at zero. Thus, running the program should cause the PA0 LED to go out for about ¼ second and then it should light again.)

Step 3

Change the second byte of the program to something other than $FF, making sure that it is an odd number to ensure that PA0 remains as an output port. Rerun the program. What is the shortest pulse you can observe on PA0? Each count of the T1024 timer is 1.024 milliseconds, or approximately 1 millisecond.

EXPERIMENT NO. 2

Step 1

Load the following program. The timer addresses listed are for the KIM-1. See Table 10-2 to convert to the 6532 timer on the AIM 65 or SYM-1. This program is a modification of Example 1 in the text.

```
0200   A9 FF      START   LDA  $FF       Initialize Port A DDR so Port A is
0202   8D 01 17           STA  PADD      an output port.
0205   A9 00              LDA  $00       Initialize Port A pins to logic 0.
0207   8D 00 17           STA  PAD
020A   A9 FF      OVER    LDA  $FF       Get number for timer.
020C   8D 07 17           STA  T1024     Store in 1024 timer.
020F   EE 00 17           INC  PAD       Increment contents of Port A.
0212   2C 07 17   LOOP    BIT  STATUS    Test bit seven of status register.
0215   10 FB              BPL  LOOP      Loop until time out.
0217   4C 0A 02           JMP  OVER      Repeat timing loop.
```

Step 2

Before executing the program, predict what will happen with the Port A LEDs when the program is run. Then execute the program to verify your prediction.

(The Port A LEDs should toggle on and off at a rate determined by the number stored in the timer. PA1 toggles at ⅛ the frequency of PA0, PA2 at ½ the frequency of PA1, and so on.)

Step 3

Restart the program and predict how long it will take to light all the LEDs starting with them all dark. Use a stopwatch or sweep second hand to measure the time. Is this number consistent with the 0.261 second of each delay?

Step 4

Experiment with other values for the byte at $020B and other divide values; that is, with other timer locations.

(For step three above we obtained a time of 1 minute and 6 seconds. There are 254 delays and 254×0.261 second = 66.3 seconds. Step 4 may be used to test other values when they are loaded into the timer.)

EXPERIMENT NO. 3

Step 1

Load the following program. It is a variation of Example 2 described in the text. See Table 10-2 to convert the timer addresses for execution on the AIM 65 (select the interrupt mode). SYM-1 users will not be able to do this timing experiment because the 6532 on the SYM-1 is not connected to the IRQ line. Refer to Table 3-3 to find the AIM 65 Port A and Port A DDR addresses. Use a jumper cable to connect PB7 on the I/O board to pin four on the expansion connector on the KIM-1. The AIM 65 has the interrupt line connected internally.

0200	A9 FF	START	LDA $FF	Initialize the Port A DDR so
0202	8D 01 17		STA PADD	Port A is an output port.
0205	58		CLI	Clear interrupt disable flag.
0206	00		BRK	Force the first interrupt.
0207	EA		NOP	No operation.

0208	4C 08 02	LOOP	JMP LOOP	Loop here until interrupt.
020B	A9 FF	INTRPT	LDA $FF	Interrupt starts here.
020D	8D 0F 17		STA IT1024	Load divide-by-1024 timer; interrupt enabled.
0210	A9 01		LDA $01	
0212	4D 00 17		EOR PAD	Exclusive OR of $01 with contents of Port A.
0215	8D 00 17		STA PAD	Result into Port A.
0218	40		RTI	Return from interrupt.

Step 2

Load the interrupt vector ($020B) by putting $0B into location $17FE on the KIM-1 or $A404 on the AIM 65 and by putting $02 into location $17FF on the KIM-1 or $A405 on the AIM 65.

Step 3

Before running the program, analyze it and describe what you expect to observe on the Port A LEDs.

Step 4

Run the program, then explain what you observe.

(You should observe that the PA0 LED toggles; that is, it turns off and on at intervals of about 0.26 second. You have produced a square waveform with a period of approximately 0.52 second. Recall from the chapter on logical operations that an EOR with a logic 1 produces the complement. Each time an interrupt occurs, bit PA0 is complemented; that is, its logic level is changed causing the LED to switch.)

Step 5

What is the smallest number you can load into the timer register and still perceive the LED blinking as opposed to a continuous glow?

Step 6

Change the byte at the location whose address is $0211 to $05. Also, initialize Port A to $01 by loading $01 into the location with address $1700. Now run the program, using $FF as the number to be loaded into the timer register. Explain what you observe. Can you think of a use for this last result? The author couldn't; but he was fascinated by the blinking lights.

EXPERIMENT NO. 4

Step 1

In the program listed in Experiment 3 change the instructions from $0210 to the end of the interrupt routine to the instructions given below.

0210	EE 00 17	INC PAD	Increment the contents of Port A.
0213	CE 00 17	DEC PAD	Decrement the contents of Port A.
0216	40	RTI	Return from interrupt.

Step 2

Load the interrupt vectors as outlined in Step 2 of Experiment No. 3. Also, initialize the contents of PAD (Port A) to $00.

Step 3

Describe how you think this altered program will affect pin PA0 when the program is running.

(It should produce a positive pulse on pin PA0 of about six microseconds in duration. Review the INC and DEC instructions if necessary.)

Step 4

Attach a frequency counter to pin PA0. Then try the following numbers with the corresponding timer address:

1.	$50	$170C	T0001;	Divide by one timer.
2.	$7A	$170D	T0008;	Divide by eight timer.
3.	$9C	$170E	T0064;	Divide by 64 timer.
4.	$62	$170F	T1024;	Divide by 1024 timer.

Note what frequencies are produced at PA0 with the above values used in the program.

(We observed a frequency of 9.80 kHz for case 1, 1004 Hz for case 2, 99.9 Hz for case 3, and 9.98 Hz for case 4. These correspond to periods between pulses of 102 microseconds, 996 microseconds, 10.0 milliseconds, and 100 milliseconds, respectively. Note that for many applications these values are close enough to 100 microseconds, 1 millisecond, 10 milliseconds, and 100 milliseconds to make time measurements. No error is larger than 2%, and three errors were less than 1%.)

EXPERIMENT NO. 5

Step 1

In the program listed in Experiment No. 3, change the instructions from $0210 to the end of the interrupt routine with the instructions listed below.

```
0210   2E 00 17    ROL PAD    Rotate the contents of Port A to the left.
0213   40          RTI        Return from interrupt.
```

Step 2

Make sure the program loads the number $FF into the divide-by-1024 interval timer by checking the program bytes located at $020C and at $020E. Make sure the interrupt vectors are loaded.

Step 3

Before running the program, first load $FF into PADD, then load $01 into PAD. The PA0 LED should glow; all others should be dark.

Step 4

Execute the program and describe what you observe.

(We observed that the one in bit zero of Port A was shifted left at intervals of about 0.26 second, causing the LEDs to light. The lights to the left of the PA0 LED successively light and then go out as the one is shifted left. The peculiar thing is that the one does not reappear in bit zero as would be expected with a ROL instruction. Why does the one not reappear in bit zero of Port A?)

Step 5

Load all zeros into PAD after initializing PADD to $FF. All the LEDs should be out. Now set the carry flag by loading the P register with $01. Run the program and describe what you observe.

(We observed that when the program ran, the LEDs at Port A were turned on from right to left until they all glowed. They then remained glowing.)

Step 6

Modify the program listed in Experiment No. 3 again. Change the instructions from $0210 to the end of the interrupt routine with the instructions listed below.

0210	28		PLP	Get P register from the stack.
0211	2E 00 17		ROL PAD	Rotate the contents of Port A to the left.
0214	08		PHP	Place P register on the stack.
0215	40		RTI	Return from interrupt.

Step 7

Repeat Steps 2, 3, and 4 of this experiment. Compare the behavior of the modified program as observed on the Port A LEDs with the behavior of the unmodified program. Describe your results and then write an explanation. In your explanation tell how a PLP can be used before a PHP instruction, when the opposite order is the usual one. Why does the ROL instruction produce the expected results with the modified program? A good knowledge of the stack operation is necessary at this point. You may wish to refer to Chapter 9.

EXPERIMENT NO. 6

Step 1

Load the following program. It is very similar to Example 4 described in the text.

0200	A9 FF	START	LDA $FF	Load $FF into the Port A DDR
0202	8D 03 A0		STA PADD	to make it an output port.
0205	A9 30	BACK	LDA $30	Get data for T2L-L.
0207	8D 08 A0		STA T2L-L	Store it in the timer.
020A	A9 90		LDA $99	Get data for T2C-H.
020C	8D 09 A0		STA T2C-H	Store it in the timer and start the timer.
020F	A9 20	DELAY	LDA $20	Set bit five in A to one.
0211	2D 0D A0		AND IFR	AND A with bit five of the IFR.
0214	8D 01 A0		STA PAD	Output result to PAD.
0217	F0 F6		BEQ DELAY	Branch back if result is zero.
0219	00		BRK	Jump to monitor.

Step 2

Describe what you expect to observe on the Port A LEDs when this program is executed. Run the program and explain what you observe.

(You should observe that the LED associated with bit five, PA5, of Port A glows. The reason is that this bit is set to one by storing the contents of the IFR in Port A after time-out, that is, when bit IFR5 has been set to one by the timer timing out.)

Step 3

Modify the instructions starting at $020F in the program in Step 1 as shown next.

242

```
020F  EE 01 A0              INC  PAD        Increment the contents of PAD.
0212  A9 20                 LDA  $20        Set bit five of A to one.
0214  2C 0D A0    DELAY     BIT  IFR        AND with IFR.
0217  F0 FB                 BEQ  DELAY      Branch back until time-out.
0219  4C 05 02              JMP  BACK       Jump to delay again.
```

Step 4

Describe what you expect to observe on the Port A LEDs. Run the program and confirm your suspicions.

Step 5

With a stopwatch or sweep second hand, time the interval between the events when all the LEDs are dark. Compare this with the time you calculate 255 loops will take. They should be approximately the same.

EXPERIMENT NO. 7

Step 1

Load the following program.

```
0200  A9 20      START     LDA  $20        Set bit five of A to one.
0202  8D 0B A0              STA  ACR        Load A into the ACR of the 6522.
0205  A9 06                 LDA  $06
0207  8D 08 A0              STA  T2L-L       Store six in T2L-L.
020A  A9 00                 LDA  $00
020C  8D 09 A0              STA  T2C-H       Store zero in T2C-H.
020F  A9 20                 LDA  $20        Set bit five of A to one.
0211  2C 0D A0    CNT       BIT  IFR        AND A with the IFR.
0214  F0 FB                 BEQ  CNT        Branch back until IFR5 is set.
0216  00                    BRK            Then break to the monitor.
```

Step 2

Clearly we are using the T2 timer. What mode is it in? Check Fig. 10-6. What should the timer do in this mode?

(The timer is in the pulse counting mode. It should count pulses at pin PB6 until ($06 + 1) pulses have occurred; then it should set the interrupt flag and jump to the monitor.)

Step 3

Using the I/O board connected to the application port, carefully connect a jumper from pin 9 to pin 17, connecting PB0 to PB6. Note we are not using PB0, but we will use the PB0 I/O switch to pulse PB6. This can only be done on the AIM 65.

Step 4

Switch the PB0 switch from logic 1 to logic 0 after starting the program. What happens? Switch the PB0 switch several more times. How many times must you switch it before the program breaks to the monitor? Why?

(Since the T2 timer counts through zero, it will require N + 1 pulses at PB6 to decrement the timer through zero, where N is the number loaded into the timer.)

Step 5

Modify the bytes at addresses $0206 and $020B to be $10 and $0E, respectively, Connect the 60-Hz power line signal conditioner circuit of Fig. 9-7 to pin 17 of the application connector. Connect the input of the 555 to a 60-Hz source.

Step 6

When the second hand on your watch crosses 12, start the program running. How long will it be before it breaks to the monitor? Measure the time on your watch.

($0E10 = 3600$ so it should require $(3600 + 1)$ counts before the T2 timer counts to zero. At 60 counts/sec this should take about 60 sec = 1 min.)

Step 7

If you have a signal generator, set it to about 65 kHz. Instead of loading $0E10 into the counter, load $FFFF into it. Run the program. How long will it take to count to zero?

(It should take about one second.)

EXPERIMENT NO. 8

Step 1

To test the event timer and the frequency counter programs you will need a signal generator or some other source that produces positive or negative pulses. A simple 555 multivibrator circuit will do, and one is shown in Fig. 10-11. The frequency may be adjusted by changing the values of R_1, R_2, or C_T. The frequency f in Hz is determined from the formula

$$f = \frac{1.443}{(R_1 + 2R_2)C_T}$$

If you do not have a signal generator with a square-wave output, then breadboard the circuit shown in Fig. 10-11.

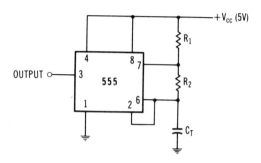

Fig. 10-11. Basic 555 Astable Multivibrator (Pulse Generator).

Step 2

Load the event timer program. Connect the square wave signal generator to PA7 (pin 8 of the application connector), making sure the computer and the signal generator have a common ground. Adjust the frequency of the signal generator to be about 100 Hz.

Step 3

What is the time interval between successive negative pulses with a frequency of 100 Hz? What number do you predict will show on the display?

(The interval between successive negative pulses with a 100-Hz square wave is 0.01 second, or 100×10^{-4} second. Since the time is given in units of 100 microseconds $= 10^{-4}$ second, the display should read about 000100.)

Step 4

Load the frequency counter program and measure the frequency of the same square wave. You should find that $f = 1/T$ where f is in hertz and T is the time interval measured in Step 3 in seconds.

Step 5

Increase the frequency of the signal to about 20 kHz. Does the frequency counter give correct results compared to the calibration of the signal generator? If you have another frequency counter available, check the computer measured frequency with the result of the frequency counter.

(We found that the laboratory frequency counter and the computer frequency counter were the same to within about 5 cycles. The 5 cycles was explained by a measurement of the crystal frequency of the author's computer that showed it to be running slow.)

Step 6

Increase the frequency of the signal generator to frequencies above 20 kHz, comparing the result given by the computer to either the dial value or to another measurement. What do you regard as the maximum frequency that may be measured with the computer?

Step 7

How would you modify the timing program to measure the time duration that PA7 is at logic zero? Flowchart your answer, then program and test it.

(The most important features of the flowchart are shown in Fig. 10-12.)

Step 8

Here are some further questions to consider: How could you measure very long (hours or days) intervals? Would a 24-hour

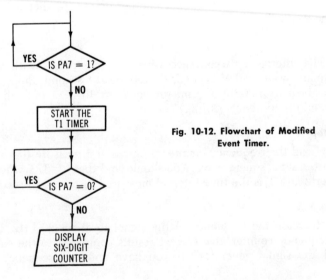

Fig. 10-12. Flowchart of Modified Event Timer.

clock be useful for this task? Can you modify the 24-hour clock program to produce a tone sequence at a preset time; that is, an alarm? In the tone sequence program, calculate the half-periods in microseconds that would be required to play several octaves of the equally tempered scale $(A = 440$ Hz$)$. Write a program to count events or frequencies using the PA6 pulse-counting mode of timer T2.

PART II

Interfacing the 6502

Introduction to Part II

The term *interfacing* means different things to different people in the world of microcomputers. For some it means connecting the computer to devices in the real world. A smoke detector, for example, may produce an input signal for a computer; a relay to drive a sprinkler system may act in response to a voltage level on an output pin of a computer. For others the term means connecting various integrated circuits and devices to make a microcomputer system. For example, how can additional R/W memory be added to an existing microcomputer system? For that matter, how could one build a microcomputer from scratch?

Both uses of the term "interfacing" are equally valid, but it is the latter interpretation of interfacing that will most correctly describe the position taken in Part II of this book. The microcomputer and any devices it controls should be regarded as a complete system, and developing and designing such a system would properly be described as interfacing. However, we have neither the time nor the space to describe the host of microcomputer-based designs, so we will concentrate on interfacing components up to and including I/O ports. In particular, the next three chapters have an underlying theme which is to configure several memory-mapped I/O ports. The principles learned in following this theme are generally applicable to interfacing problems. In Chapter 14 some designs that illustrate interfaces with the real world will be given.

Some background information and knowledge will be assumed. Experience with, and knowledge of, TTL or CMOS logic families will be extremely useful, if not necessary. In particular, the action of the various gates, flip-flops, and decoders should be understood. You should be able to read a truth table, understand binary and hexadecimal numbers, and know the most elementary Boolean operations. Readers not having this background may wish to study other books on these subjects in the Blacksburg Continuing Education Series™. The knowledge acquired in mastering Part I of this book will also be assumed. You are urged to re-read Chapter 1 of this book before beginning Part II.

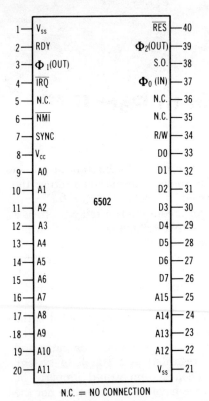

Fig. II-1. Pinout Diagram of 6502 Microprocessor.

N.C. = NO CONNECTION

The various pins of the 6502 microprocessor are conveniently divided into five groups. These five groups will help us to organize the subject matter in the next few chapters. A pinout diagram of the 6502 is shown in Fig. II-1.

- The pins used to supply power to the 6502. These include pin 8 for the +5.0 V dc ±5% (V_{cc}) supply and pins 1 and 21 for the ground (V_{ss}) connections.
- The address bus pins. There are 16 address bus pins, including pins 9 through 20 and pins 22 through 25. These are designated A15-A0.

- The bidirectional data bus pins. There are eight data bus pins from pin 26 through pin 33. These are designated D7-D0.
- The control bus pins. There are eight of these pins, including pin 2, RDY; pin 3, ϕ_1 (out); pin 7, SYNC; pin 34, R/W; pin 37, ϕ_0 (in); pin 38, S.O.; pin 39, ϕ_2 (out); and pin 40, $\overline{\text{RES}}$.
- The interrupt pins. There are two such pins, pin 4, $\overline{\text{IRQ}}$, and pin 6, $\overline{\text{NMI}}$. The function of these two pins has already been described in Chapter 9.

The next three chapters in this book are divided according to pin functions. In Chapter 11, we will deal with the address bus, including decoding and generating device select pulses. In Chapter 12, we will discuss the control bus, and in Chapter 13, we will deal with the bidirectional data bus. Of course, there will be some overlap. Our treatment of these topics is intended to be introductory rather than encyclopedic, since this book is intended for beginners more than for experts. When these chapters are completed, you should be able to understand how a microcomputer system works and, perhaps, you will be ready to create, add to, or remodel your own 6502-based microcomputer system.

Three final notes before beginning. First, you may wish to obtain a *TTL Data Book*, if you do not already have one. Either the data book published (1976) by Texas Instruments (P.O. Box 5012, Dallas, TX 75222), or the one published (1976) by National Semiconductor (2900 Semiconductor Drive, Santa Clara, CA 95051) will do. Second, complete pinout diagrams for the TTL integrated circuits used in the experiments are given in Appendix D. Finally, some of the material presented in the next few chapters was originally published in *MICRO*, a monthly journal devoted to 6502-based systems, and it is used with permission of the publisher.

CHAPTER 11

Address Decoding

OBJECTIVES

At the completion of this chapter you should be able to:

- Understand the need for address decoding circuits in a micro-computer system.
- Understand what the function of a device select pulse is, and how device select pulses may be generated.
- Design simple address decoding circuits to generate device select pulses for any memory location.

INTRODUCTION

While executing a program, the 6502 receives bytes of data from a variety of devices, and it sends bytes of data to one or more devices. Recall from Chapter 1 that a *READ* operation causes eight bits of data to be transferred from some location in memory to the microprocessor, while a *WRITE* operation causes eight bits of data to be transferred from the microprocessor to some location in memory. The locations in memory that supply data to the microprocessor may be R/W memory, ROM, a memory-mapped keyboard-input port, floppy-disc port, UART, A/D converter, or a variety of other devices. The 6502 processes the bytes of data it reads, and then writes data back either to R/W memory, to a teletypewriter output port, video monitor, relay, interval timer, D/A converter, or some other device.

It is the purpose of the address pins on the 6502 to place a set of *signals* on the address bus to *select* the memory location or the device that is going to either supply or receive eight bits of data. The set of *signals* that we speak of is a set of zero or one logic levels on the 16 address lines, A15-A0, that constitute the address bus. Typically, a logic zero or binary zero corresponds to a voltage level near zero, while a logic one or binary one corresponds to a voltage level near 5 volts. The logic levels on the 16-bit address bus are interpreted as a 16-bit binary number that we have been calling the *address* of a memory location, and that we have been representing by a four-digit hexadecimal number. Each memory location (and, hence, each device) in the computer system has a *unique address*, and when the 6502 places an address on the address bus, the uniquely addressed device or location must be activated.

Circuits that are connected to the address bus to produce a signal when a particular address appears on the address bus are called *decoders*. A decoding circuit may include one or more integrated circuits. When the correct address appears on the address bus, the output of the decoder changes to the logic level (usually zero) necessary to activate the device that is to supply or receive data. This signal is called a *device select pulse*, a *chip select pulse*, or a *port select pulse*. In this book, we will use the term "*device select pulse*," and the notation "DS" will be used to indicate device select pulses in diagrams. The bar over the "DS" means that the signal is "active low"; in other words, the device selected is activated by a logic-zero voltage level.

The READ and WRITE operations take place at regular intervals determined by the system clock frequency. Many 6502 systems use a 1-megahertz clock frequency, so each READ or WRITE cycle is 1 microsecond in duration. *Every* cycle of the clock corresponds to either *one* READ operation or *one* WRITE operation. (In some addressing modes the data that is read is discarded because the microprocessor is actually using that cycle for another purpose.) The memory locations in a 6502 system, including R/W memory, ROM, I/O ports, and interval timers, are accessed a million times every second. Since different memory locations are accessed on subsequent clock cycles, there is a different address on the address bus once every microsecond. That is the reason the device select signal is referred to as a *pulse*. The device select pulse is typically 1 microsecond in duration.

A schematic overview of the microcomputer system, as just described, is shown in Fig. 11-1. We shall refer to this figure again, but for now we will use it in conjunction with the following summary of the READ and WRITE operations:

- A READ cycle is 1 microsecond in duration. During the first part of that cycle, the microprocessor places the address of the memory location to be read on the address bus. The decoding

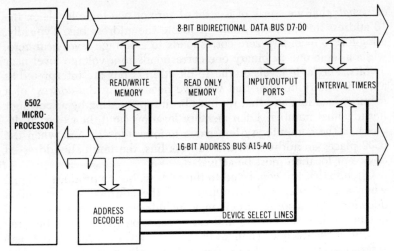

Fig. 11-1. Block diagram of 6502 System. Various memory locations, R/W Memory, ROM, etc., may decode some address lines internally, while highest-order address lines are decoded by decoding circuitry represented by ADDRESS DECODER block.

circuitry responds to that address by producing a device select pulse that activates *one* of the 65536 locations in the address space. The byte stored at that location is placed on the data bus, and the byte is stored in the 6502 microprocessor later in the 1-microsecond cycle.

- A WRITE cycle is 1 microsecond in duration. During the first part of that cycle, the microprocessor places the address of the memory location that is to receive the byte of data on the address bus. The decoding circuitry responds to that address by producing a device select pulse that activates one of the 65536 locations in the address space. Near the end of the cycle, the 6502 places the byte of data on the data bus, and the active memory location stores it at the end of the 1-microsecond cycle.

We now turn to a more elaborate description of address decoding.

ADDRESS DECODING

Fig. 11-2 indicates how a microprocessor with only one address line might generate device select pulses. When its single address line, called A0, is a logic one, then the device select line labeled $\overline{DS0}$ is at logic zero, and any device connected to it is activated. Meanwhile, the $\overline{DS1}$ signal is at logic one, so a device connected to it is disabled. We are assuming, unless otherwise stated, that all devices in the address space are activated by logic-zero signals. In

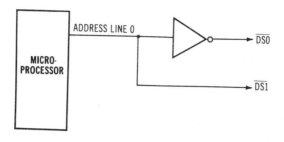

Fig 11-2. Hypothetical decoding scheme for one-address-line microprocessor.

any case, a one-address-line microcomputer can have only two memory locations. Table 11-1 is the decoder truth table.

Fig. 11-3 shows how a microprocessor with two address lines, A1 and A0, might be decoded. A 74139 decoder/demultiplexer could be used to generate four device select pulses, $\overline{DS3}$-$\overline{DS0}$. Refer to the truth table of the 74139 shown in Table 11-2. When both A0 and

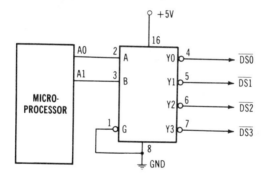

Fig. 11-3. Hypothetical decoding scheme for a two-address-line microprocessor (decoder shown is 74139).

Table 11-1. Truth Table for One Line Decoder

A0	DS0	DS1
0	1	0
1	0	1

Table 11-2. Truth Table for Two Line Decoder, 74139

A0	A1	DS0	DS1	DS2	DS3
0	0	0	1	1	1
0	1	1	0	1	1
1	0	1	1	0	1
1	1	1	1	1	0

A1 are at logic zero, then DS0 is at logic zero, and the device connected to it would be active. The truth table in Table 11-2 indicates the address line logic levels necessary to produce the other device selects. This kind of microprocessor system is not to be taken too literally, but it does illustrate the techniques necessary to produce a unique device select pulse for every possible address that is placed on the address bus.

A little inductive reasoning can be used to proceed further. If a microprocessor with one address line can be decoded to produce two device select pulses, and a microprocessor with two address lines can be decoded to produce four device select pulses, then it appears that the number of unique device select pulses that may be obtained from n address lines is 2^n. This is in fact the case and, consequently, the 16 address lines of the 6502 microprocessor may be decoded to give $2^{16} = 65536 = (\$FFFF + 1)$ device selects. This is the reason there are a total of 65536 memory locations in the memory space of the 6502.

Clearly, no single integrated circuit can be used to simultaneously decode all 16 address lines and provide an output pin for each device select pulse. Fortunately for the designer, it is usually not necessary to decode all 16 lines. Many R/W memory integrated circuits and ROM ICs decode the low-order address lines (A9-A0, for example) internally. The 6102 R/W memory integrated circuits and the 6530 ROM, R/W, I/O, and timer integrated circuits on the KIM-1 decode address lines A9-A0. Likewise, the 2104 R/W ICs on the AIM 65 and the SYM-1 decode the ten lowest-order address lines internally. The 2332 ROM chips on the AIM 65 or SYM-1 decode address lines A11-A0 internally. That is why in Fig. 11-1 we showed the address bus connected directly to the R/W memory locations as well as to the decoding circuitry. The decoding circuitry handles the high-order address lines for the various integrated circuits or other devices in the microcomputer system, while the low-order address lines are decoded by the integrated circuits themselves. Although in certain circumstances a designer may be required to decode all 16 address lines, there are numerous other circumstances in which only the highest-order address lines need to be decoded.

Consequently, our problem is to decode the highest-order address lines, at least initially. These lines are usually decoded to form *blocks* of address space. Before we see how this is done, some familiarity with the concept of address-space blocks is desirable. You may wish to refer again to Tables 1-2 and A-3 for this discussion.

Address line A15 is at logic zero for all addresses from $0000 through $7FFF, and it is at logic one for all addresses from $8000 through $FFFF, dividing the address space into two blocks each with $8000 = 32768_{10} memory locations. In most computer systems,

1024_{10} ($0400) memory locations are usually referred to as 1K of memory. Dividing 1024 into 32768 gives 32; thus address line A15 divides the address space into two 32K blocks. Table 11-3 indicates the logic level of A15 and the addresses associated with this level.

Table 11-3. Dividing Address Space Into 32K Blocks With Address Line A15

A15	Addresses
0	$0000–$7FFF
1	$8000–$FFFF

Fig. 11-4 shows how a 7404 inverter could be used to provide the necessary "decoding." In some microcomputer systems, A15 is used to divide the address space so that R/W memory is in the lower 32K locations, while ROM, I/O ports, and interval timers are in the

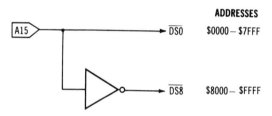

Fig. 11-4. Decoding circuit for dividing Address space into 32K blocks.

upper 32K locations. In many microcomputer systems, not all of the 64K "spaces" or locations are actually occupied by memory chips. Just because the address lines and decoders are available does not mean that they must be used.

Refer to Table A-3, or call on your knowledge of 16-bit binary numbers, and note that bit 14 of a 16-bit binary number is zero for half of the numbers between $8000 and $FFFF, while it is one for the other half of these numbers. Bit 14 similarly divides the hexadecimal numbers between $0000 and $7FFF into two groups. Thus, each 32K block of address space may be divided into two 16K blocks by the logic levels associated with A14. Table 11-4 illustrates how

Table 11-4. Dividing Address Space Into 16K Blocks With Address Lines A15 and A14

A15	A14	Addresses
0	0	$0000–$3FFF
0	1	$4000–$7FFF
1	0	$8000–$BFFF
1	1	$C000–$FFFF

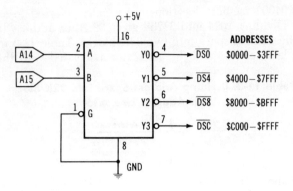

Fig. 11-5. Decoding circuit using 74139 to divide Address space into 16K blocks.

this works, and Fig. 11-5 shows a 74139 decoding address lines A15 and A14 to produce device select pulses for each 16K block. In Fig. 11-5 we indicate the range of addresses that will produce the corresponding device select pulse. For example, any address in the range $4000 to $7FFF will produce a device select pulse at the Y1 (pin 5) output of the 74139. The digit in the "$\overline{\text{DSn}}$" symbolism identifies the first digit in the lowest address that the decoder will enable.

Proceeding inductively again, if one address line (A15) divides the address space into two 32K blocks, and two address lines (A15 and A14) divide the address apace into four 16K blocks, then three address lines (A15, A14, and A13) could be decoded and used to divide the address space into eight 8K blocks, four address lines (A15, A14, A13, and A12) could be decoded and use to divide the address space into sixteen 4K blocks, and n address lines divide the address space into 2^n blocks. How many address lines must be decoded to divide the address space into 1K blocks? There are sixty-four 1K blocks in the address space of the 6502. Since $2^6 = 64$, six address lines (A15, A14, A13, A12, A11, and A10) are required. Many popular R/W memory chips decode the remaining ten address lines internally, as noted above.

In Fig. 11-6 we show how a 74138 Decoder/Demultiplexer may be used to divide the address space into 8K blocks. The logic levels of the address lines A15, A14, and A13 associated with each 8K block are presented in Table 11-5. Since we will refer to these blocks again, we have given each block of 8K memory locations a name, as indicated in Table 11-5. The names help to identify the location of the 8K block in the address space. The truth table of the 74138 given in Table 11-6 should be used in conjunction with Table 11-5 to verify the behavior of the 74138 decoding circuit shown in Fig. 11-6.

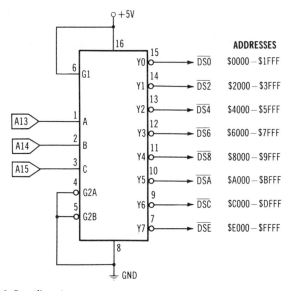

Fig. 11-6. Decoding circuit using 74138 to divide Address space into 8K blocks.

Table 11-5. Dividing Address Space Into 8K Blocks With Address Lines A15, A14, and A13

A15	A14	A13	Addresses	Block Name
0	0	0	$0000–$1FFF	8K0
0	0	1	$2000–$3FFF	8K1
0	1	0	$4000–$5FFF	8K2
0	1	1	$6000–$7FFF	8K3
1	0	0	$8000–$9FFF	8K4
1	0	1	$A000–$BFFF	8K5
1	1	0	$C000–$DFFF	8K6
1	1	1	$E000–$FFFF	8K7

Note that in Figs. 11-4, 11-5, and 11-6, the device select pulses are produced by *any* of the corresponding addresses given in these figures. Thus, in Fig. 11-6, for example, $\overline{DS6}$ will be at logic zero for

Table 11-6. Truth Table for 74138 Decoder

C	B	A	Y_0	Y_1	Y_2	Y_3	Y_4	Y_5	Y_6	Y_7
0	0	0	0	1	1	1	1	1	1	1
0	0	1	1	0	1	1	1	1	1	1
0	1	0	1	1	0	1	1	1	1	1
0	1	1	1	1	1	0	1	1	1	1
1	0	0	1	1	1	1	0	1	1	1
1	0	1	1	1	1	1	1	0	1	1
1	1	0	1	1	1	1	1	1	0	1
1	1	1	1	1	1	1	1	1	1	0

any address in the range $6000–$7FFF. Clearly, additional decoding is required if we demand that *each* address on the address bus produces a *unique* device select pulse that activates a *unique* location in memory.

ADDRESS DECODING FOR R/W MEMORY

To illustrate this idea begun in the previous paragraphs, let us examine a hypothetical but realistic design problem. Suppose we want the lowest 8K block of the address space to contain R/W memory. In other words, the 8K0 block with addresses from $0000 to $1FFF is to contain the R/W memory for our microcomputer system. Also assume that the R/W memory ICs we have chosen (2114 memory chips, for example) internally decode the ten lowest-order address lines, A9 through A0.

If the R/W memory chips decode address lines A9-A0, then we must decode the remaining six address lines, A15–A10. We could use a 74138 to decode the top three address lines, and another 74138 to decode address lines A12 through A10. The device select from the first 74138 will be used to activate the second 74138. Our final scheme is shown in Fig. 11-7. (Note that there is nothing inherently correct about one decoding scheme over another. There appear to be as many different ways of decoding as there are designers.)

Observe that in Fig. 11-7 we have not shown all the device select signals from the 74138 that decodes address lines A15–A13. The device select signal that is active for the 8K0 block of address space, addresses $0000–$1FFF, is connected to the G2A pin of the 74138 that decodes address lines A12 through A10. This 74138 works (supplies device select pulses) only if G2A is low, as is indicated by the inversion circle on the G2A pin. Otherwise this 74138 is disabled. Refer again to Fig. 11-6 and note that G2A will be at logic zero for all addresses from $0000–$1FFF, exactly the same addresses that are decoded by the second 74138 introduced in Fig. 11-7.

We have identified the device select pulses from the second 74138 by the first two digits of the lowest address in the 1K memory block that they enable. Thus, $\overline{DS04}$ is at logic zero for all addresses from $0400 through $07FF, a 1K block of address space.

For purposes of completeness, we conclude this little design problem by showing how the 2114 R/W memory chips would be connected to provide 1K of R/W memory. This is described by Fig. 11-8. Our main concern here is that the device select pulse $\overline{DS00}$ is connected to the so-called chip select pins of the two 2114 integrated circuits, enabling them for addresses $0000 through $03FF, while the 2114s themselves decode the lowest ten address lines, A9–A0. The addresses $0000 through $03FF are said to be *absolutely de-*

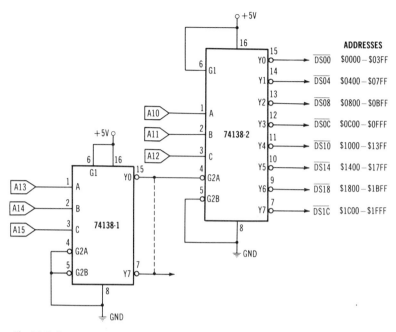

Fig. 11-7. Arrangement in which two 74138s are used to decode lowest 8K block of the address space for R/W memory.

coded because each memory location in this block is activated by *one* and *only one* address in the entire address space $0000-$FFFF of the 6502 microprocessor.

There are address decoding schemes in which one or more address lines are not decoded, and in those cases a particular memory location may be activated by several addresses rather than a single address, in contrast to absolute decoding. The KIM-1 does not decode address lines A13 through A15, which means that location $1FFF, for example, is also activated when addresses $3FFF, $5FFF, $7FFF, . . . , or $FFFF are on the address bus.

Note the data bus connections and the control line connections for the 2114 R/W memory chips in Fig. 11-8. Each chip provides 1K-by-four data bits, or a total of 4K *bits* of memory. Two chips give 1K-by-eight data bits, or a total of 8K bits of R/W memory. Since eight bits make one byte, two 2114s give 1K bytes of R/W memory. To provide a full 8K of R/W memory, the other seven device select lines in Fig. 11-7 must each be connected to two 2114 integrated circuits, requiring 16 2114 chips for 8K of memory. The R/W control line from the 6502 is connected to the write enable ($\overline{\text{WE}}$) pin of each 2114. An inverted ϕ_2 signal should also be connected to the

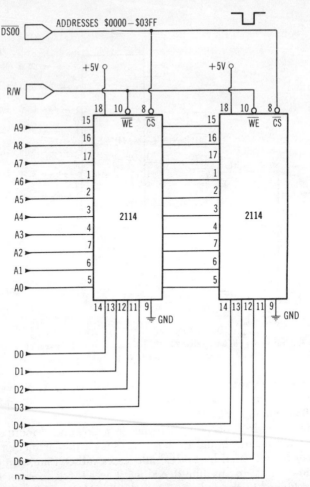

Fig. 11-8. Read/Write Memory Interface using two IC memory chips for memory locations with addresses $0000 - $03FF.

G2B pin of the 74138 decoder that supplies the $\overline{\text{DS00}}$ device select pulse. We shall postpone a more detailed discussion of the control bus and data bus interfaces until the next two chapters. In any case, you have enough information to provide your microcomputer system with 1K to 8K of R/W memory.

I/O PORT ADDRESS DECODING

As pointed out in the introduction to Part II of the book, the general theme of these chapters on interfacing the 6502 will be the configuration of several input/output ports. We will show how this may be done with standard 7400 series integrated circuits or, preferably, with the 74LS00 series integrated circuits. In addition to learning the fundamentals of interfacing, you will acquire the capability of adding several I/O ports with inexpensive, readily available integrated circuits.

Our first problem is to decide where in the address space of the microcomputer system to put the I/O ports. The general philosophy in 6502 systems is to put R/W memory at the low-order addresses, since page zero and page one should be R/W locations. Thus, the KIM-1, AIM 65, and SYM-1 all have 1K of R/W memory supplied and located at $0000 through $03FF. The three systems all make provision for additional R/W memory to be added from $0400 upward.

The KIM-1 provides device select pulses for an additional 4K of R/W memory from address $0400 to address $13FF. The SYM-1 provides device select pulses for an additional 7K of memory from address $0400 to address $1FFF. The AIM 65 provides device select pulses for an additional 11K of R/W memory, from address $0400 to address $0FFF and from address $8000 to address $9FFF. The address space on the AIM 65 from address $1000 to $7FFF is not decoded. but it is available for expansion.

In 6502 systems ROM is generally placed high in the address space. For example, the AIM 65 monitor is located at addresses $E000 through $FFFF. The KIM-1 has its monitor in the highest decoded locations (remember, the KIM-1 does not decode address lines A15–A13). The SYM-1 departs from this philosophy, and has its monitor located from address $8000 to $8FFF.

The 6502 address space allocation philosophy usually has I/O ports and interval timers somewhere between the R/W memory at the low end of the address space and the ROM at the high end of the address space. We decided to provide up to 16 I/O ports at addresses $9FF0 to $9FFF. These addresses correspond to "empty" memory locations in all three of the microcomputer systems. The added I/O ports, in addition to providing us with an interfacing problem, are also useful since the three microcomputer systems do not have many of these ports. If you want to add an ASCII encoded keyboard, video monitor, A/D converter, D/A converter, relays, sense switches, LED indicators, and other I/O devices to your system, you will soon find that two ports are inadequate. Also, by locating the I/O ports from addresses $9FF0 to $9FFF, we will have them out of the way of the other vital memory functions. The SYM-1 and AIM 65 have on-board decoders that will provide us with at least one device select pulse, and this will help to minimize the additional circuitry required to implement the I/O ports. On the other hand, the KIM-1 will require additional circuitry since it does not provide any device select pulses for these addresses, and since it does not fully decode all the address lines.

The circuit for providing the necessary device select pulses for 16 I/O ports is shown in Fig. 11-9. In the next few paragraphs, we will describe this circuit; do not expect to comprehend it with a single glance. The 74138 decodes the four highest address lines (A15–A12). Since address line A15 is connected to the G1 input of the 74138, it will provide no device selects for addresses below $8000. The truth table for the 74138 is shown in Table 11-7, and it gives the logic levels on the address lines A15 through A12 that produce the device select pulses on the output pins. Table 11-7 also indicates which addresses produce device select pulses. Note that the Y1 output pin of the 74138 is active (logic zero) for addresses $9000 through

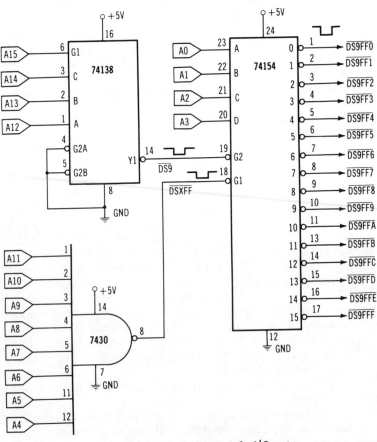

Fig. 11-9. Device select pulse circuit for I/O ports.

Table 11-7. Truth Table for 74138 in Fig. 11-9

A15	A14	A13	A12	Y0	Y1	Y2	Y3	Y4	Y5	Y6	Y7	Addresses
1	0	0	0	0	1	1	1	1	1	1	1	$8000–$8FFF
1	0	0	1	1	0	1	1	1	1	1	1	$9000–$9FFF
1	0	1	0	1	1	0	1	1	1	1	1	$A000–$AFFF
1	0	1	1	1	1	1	0	1	1	1	1	$B000–$BFFF
1	1	0	0	1	1	1	1	0	1	1	1	$C000–$CFFF
1	1	0	1	1	1	1	1	1	0	1	1	$D000–$DFFF
1	1	1	0	1	1	1	1	1	1	0	1	$E000–$EFFF
1	1	1	1	1	1	1	1	1	1	1	0	$F000–$FFFF

$9FFF; hence, that is the pin we will use for our device select pulse $\overline{DS9}$.

The 74138 decoder will produce device select pulses only when both pins G2A and G2B are at logic zero, and they are both permanently connected to logic zero (GND). The 7430 NAND gate output will be at logic zero only when all eight inputs are at logic one. The eight inputs are address lines A11 through A4. Recall that address bits A11 through A4 are the two "middle" nibbles of the address. Thus, the output of the 7430 NAND gate will be at logic zero for any address of the form $XFFX, where "X" is a "don't care" symbol for one hex digit. That is why we have labeled the device select signal from the 7430 NAND gate with $\overline{DSXFF}$.

Together the 74138 and the 7430 decode the 12 highest address lines, and the 74154 will decode the lowest four address lines, A3–A0. Note that the 74138 and the 7430 are connected to the G1 and G2 inputs of the 74154, enabling it only for addresses $9FF0 through $9FFF. The 74154 produces one active low output for each of these addresses, as indicated to the right of the 74154 in Fig. 11-9. Since all 16 address lines have been decoded, this is an absolute decoding scheme. Each of the logic-zero device select pulses from the 74154 may be used to activate an input port device or an output port device, as we shall see in the next two chapters. The decoding task has been completed, except for a few odds and ends that we now describe.

Both the AIM 65 and SYM-1 have device select pulses developed by their decoding circuitry that may be used instead of the 74138 in Fig. 11-9. The AIM 65 has a signal called $\overline{CS9}$ available at pin 19 on its expansion connector, and this may be connected to the G2 input (pin 19) of the 74154 decoder, completely omitting the 74138 shown in Fig. 11-9.

The SYM-1 has a device select pulse, labeled $\overline{98}$, available at jumper number 10. It is active for addresses $9800 through $9FFF. To eliminate the necessity for the 74138 in Fig. 11-9, connect this jumper to pin 19 on the 74154, and also connect a 3.3K pull-up resistor between pin 18 on the 74154 and the +5-V supply voltage.

The KIM-1 cannot dispense with the 74138, and, in fact, the additional circuit shown in Fig. 11-10 must be added. Since the KIM-1 does not decode address lines A15–A13, all of its locations in the lowest 8K block of the address space will be activated by several addresses on the address bus. For example, the memory location with address $1FFF will also be activated by the address $9FFF. To prevent this, the additional circuit shown in Fig. 11-10 disables the 74LS145 decoder on the KIM-1 board whenever address line A15 is at logic one. This is accomplished by bringing the D input of the 74LS145 on the KIM-1 to logic one by connecting it to pin four of the 7405 shown in Fig. 11-10.

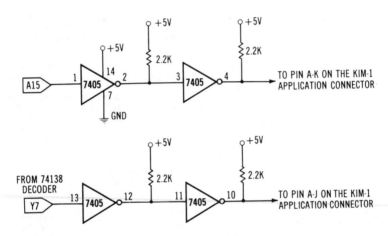

Fig. 11-10. Additional decoding circuit for KIM-1 I/O Port Device Selects.

The KIM-1 requires one other modification if it is to work properly with the circuit of Fig. 11-9. Recall from Chapter 9 that when an interrupt (or RESET) occurs two of the addresses $FFFA through $FFFF will appear on the address lines to fetch the interrupt (or RESET) vector. Since the KIM-1 system does not decode address lines A15 through A13, the interrupt (and RESET) vectors are actually located at addresses $1FFA through $1FFF. However, the modification introduced in the previous paragraph will deselect these locations whenever address line A15 is at logic one. To reselect the interrupt vectors located in the integrated circuit known as the 6530–002 on the KIM-1, we connect the Y7 output of the 74138 to the chip select on the 6530–002 through two open-collector 7405s. This modification is also shown in Fig. 11-10.

ADDRESS DECODING CIRCUIT FOR 6522 INTERFACE

In Chapter 10, we promised an interface circuit for the 6522 Versatile Interface Adapter so that KIM-1 owners could utilize the timers on this integrated circuit. The same decoding circuit used to enable the 74154 in Fig. 11-9 may be used to enable the 6522. The interface is shown in Fig. 11-11. The $\overline{DS9}$ device select pulse from the 74138 in Fig. 11-9 is connected to the $\overline{CS2}$ pin on the 6522. The $\overline{DSXFF}$ device select pulse shown in Fig. 11-11 is obtained from the 7430 in Fig. 11-9. If this pulse is first inverted and then connected to the CS1 pin on the 6522, then the 6522 will be addressed by addresses $9FF0 through $9FFF. (Note that the 74154 can no longer be used in this case.) Compare these addresses with the *on-board 6522* addresses for the AIM 65 and SYM-1, namely $A000 through $A00F. There is a one-to-one correspondence between the function of each $A00X address and each $9FFX address, where X is the same hex digit (0 through F) in both cases. Thus, in Chapter 10, the programs that used the interval timers will work in exactly the same way if all 6522 addresses with "A00" prefixes are replaced with "9FF" prefixes. Refer to Table 11-8 for additional details regarding addressing the 6522.

Table 11-8. Addressing Information for the 6522 Interface

Address	Function
$9FF0	Port B Output Data Register (PBD)
$9FF1	Port A Output Data Register (PAD), Controls handshake
$9FF2	Port B Data Direction Register (PBDD)
$9FF3	Port A Data Direction Register (PADD)
$9FF4	Write T1L-L; Read T1C-L; Clear Interrupt Flag
$9FF5	Write T1L-H and T1C-H; Transfer T1L-L to T1C-L; Clear Interrupt Flag; Start the T1 timer; Read T1C-H
$9FF6	Write T1L-L; Read T1L-L
$9FF7	Write T1L-H; Clear Interrupt Flag; Read T1L-H
$9FF8	Write T2L-L; Read T2C-L; Clear Interrupt Flag
$9FF9	Write T2C-H; Transfer T2L-L to T2C-L; Clear Interrupt Flag; Start the T2 timer; Read T2C-H
$9FFA	Shift Register (SR)
$9FFB	Auxiliary Control Register (ACR)
$9FFC	Peripheral Control Register (PCR)
$9FFD	Interrupt Flag Register (IFR)
$9FFE	Interrupt Enable Register (IER)
$9FFF	Port A Output Data Register (PAD), No effect on handshake

If, on the other hand, the $\overline{DSXFF}$ device select pulse is connected directly to the CS1 pin on the 6522, then the device selects from the 74154 may still be used because the 6522 is addressed with addresses $9000 through $900F. However, in this case the 6522 is not absolutely decoded, and it will be activated by any other set of addresses of the form $9XX0 through $9XXF except addresses $9FF0 through $9FFF, where X is a "don't care" hex digit. This will be of no consequence unless other memory locations in the range $9000 to $9FEF are to be utilized. The addresses $9FF0 through $9FFF enable the 74154 device selects, as before. Although it is generally good practice to absolutely decode the address lines, in certain cases no harm will result if this practice is not strictly followed.

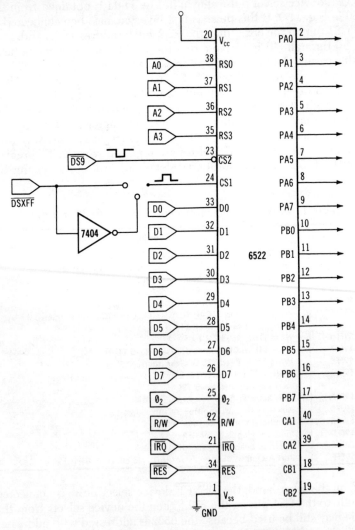

Fig. 11-11. Interface for 6522 Versatile Interface Adapter.

All the other input connections to the 6522 in Fig. 11-11 are found on the so-called expansion connectors on the KIM-1, SYM-1, and AIM 65. A pinout description of these connectors is given in Table 11-9. The functions of the various pins will be described in the next two chapters. Since you have enough detail in Fig. 11-11 to complete the interface and operate the chip, we will not return to the 6522 interface. This interface was introduced mostly as a service to KIM-1 users who do not have an on-board 6522.

Table 11-9. Pinout Description of Expansion Connector

Pin Number	Pin Function			Pin Number	Pin Function		
	AIM 65	SYM-1	KIM-1		AIM 65	SYM-1	KIM-1
1	SYNC	SYNC	SYNC	A	A0	A0	A0
2	RDY	RDY	RDY	B	A1	A1	A1
3	ϕ_1	ϕ_1	ϕ_1	C	A2	A2	A2
4	$\overline{IRQ}$	$\overline{IRQ}$	$\overline{IRQ}$	D	A3	A3	A3
5	S.O.	RO	RO	E	A4	A4	A4
6	$\overline{NMI}$	$\overline{NMI}$	$\overline{NMI}$	F	A5	A5	A5
7	$\overline{RES}$	$\overline{RES}$	$\overline{RES}$	H	A6	A6	A6
8	D7	D7	D7	J	A7	A7	A7
9	D6	D6	D6	K	A8	A8	A8
10	D5	D5	D5	L	A9	A9	A9
11	D4	D4	D4	M	A10	A10	A10
12	D3	D3	D3	N	A11	A11	A11
13	D2	D2	D2	P	A12	A12	A12
14	D1	D1	D1	R	A13	A13	A13
15	D0	D0	D0	S	A14	A14	A14
16	−12 V	$\overline{18}$	K6	T	A15	A15	A15
17	+12 V	DBOUT	SST OUT	U	ϕ_2	ϕ_2	ϕ_2
18	$\overline{CS8}$	POR	Unused	V	R/W	R/W	R/W
19	$\overline{CS9}$	Unused	Unused	W	$\overline{R/W}$	$\overline{R/W}$	$\overline{R/W}$
20	$\overline{CSA}$	Unused	Unused	X	TEST	TEST	TEST
21	+5 V	+5 V	+5 V	Y	$\overline{\phi_2}$	$\overline{\phi_2}$	$\overline{\phi_2}$
22	GND	GND	GND	Z	RAM R/W	RAM R/W	RAM R/W

6502 INSTRUCTIONS AND DEVICE SELECT PULSES

To understand a few more details related to device select pulses, we examine the execution of some 6502 instructions on a cycle-by-cycle basis. Table 11-10 describes the behavior of the address bus,

Table 11-10. Analysis of Microcomputer Buses by Clock Cycles During LDA Instruction in Absolute Addressing Mode

Cycle	Address Bus	R/W	Data Bus	Comments
1	$0200	1	$AD	The 6502 fetches the LDA op code.
2	$0201	1	$F0	The 6502 fetches the ADL of the memory location to be accessed.
3	$0202	1	$9F	The 6502 fetches the ADH of the memory location to be accessed.
4	$9FF0	1	DATA	The 6502 fetches the data in the location whose address is $9FF0.

the data bus, and the R/W control line during the execution of the LDA instruction in the absolute addressing mode, assuming that the LDA instruction op code is in the location with address $0200 and that the memory location referenced by the LDA instruction is $9FF0. Table 11-11 analyzes the STA instruction in a similar way, and Table 11-12 analyzes the ASL instruction by clock cycles.

Table 11-11. Analysis of Microcomputer Buses by Clock Cycles During STA Instruction in Absolute Addressing Mode

Cycle	Address Bus	R/W	Data Bus	Comments
1	$0200	1	$8D	The 6502 fetches the STA op code.
2	$0201	1	$F7	The 6502 fetches the ADL of the memory location to be referenced.
3	$0202	1	$9F	The 6502 fetches the ADH of the memory location to be referenced.
4	$9FF7	0	DATA	The 6502 is writing the contents of the accumulator to the location whose address is $9FF7.

Table 11-12. Analysis of Microcomputer Buses by Clock Cycle During Read-Modify-Write Instruction, e.g., ASL, DEC, or ROL Instruction

Cycle	Address Bus	R/W	Data Bus	Comments
1	$0200	1	$0E	The 6502 fetches the ASL op code.
2	$0201	1	$F5	The 6502 fetches the ADL of the memory location to be modified.
3	$0202	1	$9F	The 6502 fetches the ADH of the memory location to be modified.
4	$9FF5	1	DATA	The 6502 reads the contents of the location whose address is $9FF5.
5	$9FF5	0	DATA	The 6502 uses this cycle to modify the data.
6	$9FF5	0	MODIFIED DATA	The 6502 writes the modified data back to the location whose address is $9FF5.

In all three of these tables, note that each cycle is either a READ or WRITE cycle. Either an *instruction byte* is read, or a *data byte* is either read from memory or written to memory. Referring to Table 11-10, device select pulses corresponding to addresses $0200, $0201, $0202, and finally $9FF0 must be generated by the address decoding circuitry in order to execute this LDA instruction. Each device select pulse will last for about 1 microsecond. In Table 11-11, you see that similar events occur during an STA instruction. Finally, in Table 11-12, you can see that the data byte located at $9FF5 is first loaded into the microprocessor, then it is modified, and finally it is written back to the location whose address is $9FF5, during three successive cycles. The middle cycle of these three cycles is required to give the microprocessor time to modify the data. Although it, too, is a WRITE cycle, nothing new is written back to the location being modified. Finally, note that the device select pulse corresponding to $9FF5 will be generated three times during this Read-Modify-Write instruction. Consult your 6502 hardware manual for further details regarding bus activity during other instructions. We have chosen a few representative examples to illustrate the fact that each clock cycle in a 6502 system is either a READ or a WRITE cycle, and that device select pulses are generated during each clock cycle.

The address decoding circuit of Fig. 11-9 generates a 1 microsecond logic zero pulse when an LDA or STA instruction references one of the locations shown in the figure. This pulse may be used to preset or clear a flip-flop, as shown in the circuit in Fig. 11-12. The

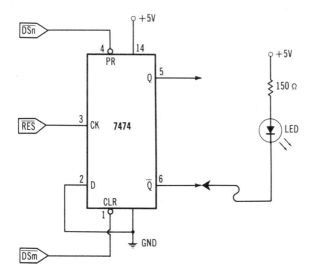

Fig. 11-12. Device select pulses used to preset and clear D-type flip-flop, and LED used as test probe.

LED probe will glow when it is connected to a logic-zero voltage level, and it can be used to test the logic levels of the Q or $\overline{Q}$ outputs. The probe will also be used in the experiments to detect device select pulses. We now describe the behavior of the circuit in Fig. 11-12, assuming the device select pulses from the 74154 in Fig. 11-9 are being used.

Suppose that the device select pulse $\overline{DS9FF0}$ is connected to the preset input of the 7474 and that device select pulse $\overline{DS9FF1}$ is connected to the clear input. When the microcomputer is RESET, as it usually is during "power up," then the $\overline{\text{RES}}$ control signal available at pin seven on the expansion connector will clock the logic level of the D input into the Q output. Thus, when power is first applied or the RESET button is pressed, the Q output will be low and the $\overline{\text{Q}}$ output will be high. The LED test probe connected to the $\overline{\text{Q}}$ output will glow, but an LED test probe connected to the $\overline{\text{Q}}$ output will not glow. Using an LDA $\overline{\text{DS9FF0}}$ will preset the flip-flop, making Q go to logic one and $\overline{\text{Q}}$ to logic zero. Using an LDA $\overline{\text{DS9FF1}}$ instruction in a program will clear the flip-flop to the same state it had after a RESET.

It should be clear that this scheme could be used to switch a motor, light, cassette recorder, or any other device, off and on with a computer program. Thus we have made a simple output circuit with no output port chips, control signals, or data bus lines involved. With interval timers, a square wave whose frequency and duty cycle may be programmed can be made to appear at either the Q or $\overline{\text{Q}}$ output of the 7474 flip-flop.

INTRODUCTION TO THE EXPERIMENTS

The experiments in the next few chapters will give you an opportunity to experiment with some of the circuits described in the text. Although a variety of techniques may be used to test the circuits, we have found that breadboarding on Proto Boards made by Continental Specialties, Super Strips made by A P Products, Inc., or the SK 10 made by E & L Instruments, Inc., is an excellent approach. In fact, we did all of the experiments in Part II on an A P Products Unicard. The Unicard has a 22/44 printed circuit pad just like the KIM-1, AIM 65, and SYM-1 edge connectors. We took a 22/44 pin edge connector with solder eyelets and soldered the eyelets to the Unicard pads. The edge connector may be connected directly to the expansion port and may be left in place for permanent applications, if desired. Photographs of this configuration before any experiments were begun and after a number of experiments were completed are shown in Fig. 11-13. The breadboards mentioned above are available from a variety of electronic parts mail-order houses. Consult the advertisements in any of the well known computer or electronics magazines for sources of parts.

Although we did not indicate in any of our circuit diagrams the particular variety of 7400-series integrated circuits to use, we strongly urge you to work with the 74LS00 variety. Ordinary 7400-series chips will work, but you run into buffering problems because of the higher power required to drive the logic inputs. The pins on the 6502 are rated at one standard TTL (7400 series) load, which means you can have four "LS" series inputs attached to a single 6502

(A) Before experiments.

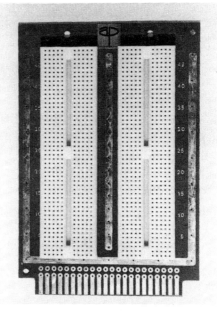

(B) After experiments.

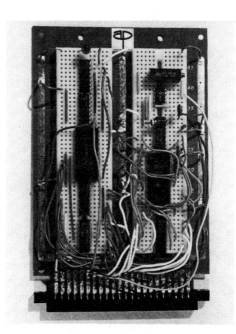

Fig. 11-13. Our breadboarding system.

output pin. Unless otherwise noted, the experiments were performed with the 74LS00 series. Do not attempt to use 74C00 or other CMOS circuits for the experiments.

Circuits that are breadboarded in one experiment will frequently be used in subsequent experiments. Do not, therefore, dismantle your circuits after each experiment.

EXPERIMENT NO. 1

Step 1

Breadboard the circuit shown in Fig. 11-6. Refer to Table 11-9 for the expansion connector pin description to connect the address lines. Use +5 V and GND from pins 21 and 22, respectively.

Step 2

Construct the simple LED probe shown in Fig. 11-12. It will be used to detect a series of device select pulses.

Step 3

Load the following program:

```
0200  AD F0 9F    START    LDA MEM      Fetch the contents of $9FF0.
0203  4C 00 02             JMP START    Loop back to START.
```

Note that this program is of no use except to demonstrate the generation of device select pulses. Refer to Table 11-10, and observe that the program simply repeats the LDA instruction analyzed in Table 11-10.

Step 4

Connect the LED probe constructed in Step 2 to each device select output of the 74LS138 in turn. Describe and explain what you observe.

(We observed that the LED glowed quite brightly on the Y0 (pin 15) output and less brightly on the Y4 (pin 11) output. On all the other outputs the LED did not glow. These observations may be explained by referring to Table 11-10 again. During three of the four clock cycles of the LDA instruction the address bus has an address in the lowest 8K block, that is, between $0000 and $1FFF. These addresses enable the DS0 device select pulse labeled in Fig. 11-6. During the fourth cycle of the LDA instruction the address $9FF0 appears on the address bus, and the decoding circuit produces a device select pulse on the $\overline{DS8}$ output, namely pin 11. The JMP instruction takes three cycles, all of which reference a memory location in the lowest 8K block. Thus, the entire program takes seven cycles. During six of those cycles the $\overline{DS0}$ pulse occurs, but during one cycle the $\overline{DS8}$ pulse occurs. Since the eye cannot perceive 1-microsecond flashes, we observe a bright glow when the LED is connected to the $\overline{DS0}$ line, and a faint glow when the LED probe is connected to the $\overline{DS8}$ line.)

Step 5

Replace the LDA instruction in the program of Step 3 with an STA instruction. Execute the program and use the LED probe to test the device select outputs of the 74LS138. Explain your results.

Step 6

Replace the LDA instruction in the program of Step 3 with an ASL $9FF5 instruction as analyzed in Table 11-12. Execute the program and describe and explain your results obtained by using the LED probe.

(The results are essentially the same as in Step 4, but the LED appears to glow more brightly. The ASL and JMP program takes nine cycles while the LDA and JMP program takes seven cycles. Refer to Table 11-12 and note that the location being modified has its address on the address bus for three of the six cycles required by the ASL instruction, or for a total of three of the nine cycles required for the program. In the LDA and JMP program the location being modified has its address on the address bus for only one cycle out of the seven cycles necessary to execute the program. Consequently, when the LED probe is connected to the $\overline{DS8}$ device select line, it appears to glow more brightly with the ASL and JMP program than with the LDA and JMP program.)

Step 7

If you have a frequency counter, connect it to pin 11 of the 74LS-138 while the program of Step 3 is running. What do you expect to measure? Repeat this experiment for the program of Step 6.

(In the first case you should measure $\frac{1}{7}$ of the clock frequency, or about 142.86 kHz.)

EXPERIMENT NO. 2

Step 1

AIM 65 owners may wish to repeat all of the steps in Experiment No. 1, using the device select pulse (called $\overline{CS9}$) made available at pin 19 on the expansion connector.

EXPERIMENT NO. 3

Step 1

SYM-1 owners may wish to repeat all of the steps in Experiment No. 1 using the device select pulse (called $\overline{98}$) made available at jumper number 10.

EXPERIMENT NO. 4

Step 1

Modify the circuit for the 74LS138 so that it is the same as shown in Fig. 11-9. AIM 65 and SYM-1 owners need not breadboard this integrated circuit. They can use the device select pulses mentioned in Experiments No. 2 and 3.

Step 2

Breadboard the 74LS30 8-input NAND gate shown in Fig. 11-9. Before connecting the output of the 74LS30 to the 74LS154, test it by loading the program given in Step 3 of Experiment No. 1. The LED should glow when the probe is connected to the output of the 74LS30. Why?

(The location referenced with the program is $9FF0. The output of the 74LS30 should go to logic zero whenever an address of the form $XFFX, where X is a "don't care" hex digit, is on the address bus.)

Step 3

Try the LED probe on the output of the 74LS30 when the same program is executed, but location $9550 is referenced. What should you observe?

(The LED probe should not glow, because the 74LS30 output goes to logic zero only when the middle two hex digits of the address are "FF".)

Step 4

Breadboard the 74LS154 circuit shown in Fig. 11-9. Connect the device select line from the 74LS30 to the G1 input (pin 18). AIM 65 users can omit the 74LS138 and connect their $\overline{CS9}$ device select pulse from pin 19 on the expansion connector to the G2 (pin 19) input of the 74LS154. If you have a SYM-1, connect the $\overline{98}$ device select pulse from jumper number 10 to the G2 input of the 74LS154.

Step 5

Refer to Experiment No. 1, Step 3, and load the same program. Execute the program and use the LED test probe to test the device select pulse outputs of the 74LS154. Which one should produce a glow on the LED?

(Since the location whose address is $9FF0 is referenced by the LDA instruction, the device select labeled $\overline{DS9FF0}$ should cause the LED to glow. None of the other outputs of the 74LS154 should affect the LED.)

Step 6

Change the address referenced by the LDA instruction to addresses $9FF1 through 9FFF, in turn, executing the program and testing the outputs of the 74LS154. You should observe that the correct address produces the corresponding device select pulse.

Step 7

Repeat Step 7 of Experiment No. 1 with the frequency counter connected to the output of the 74LS154 that is being enabled by the address referenced by the LDA instruction. What do you observe?

Step 8

Experiment with other instructions such as the STA, ROL, DEC, ADC, AND, and CMP instructions replacing the LDA instruction in the program described in Step 3 of Experiment No. 1. Do all of these instructions produce device select pulses on the 74LS154 when they reference the locations enabled by the 74LS154 outputs?

EXPERIMENT NO. 5

Step 1

Connect the circuit shown in Fig. 11-12. Connect the input labeled $\overline{DSn}$ to the $\overline{DS9FF0}$ device select pulse from the 74LS154 in Fig.

11-9. Connect the input labeled $\overline{DSm}$ to the $\overline{DS9FF1}$ device select pulse from the 74LS154. Construct two LED test probes and connect one to each of the outputs of the 7474.

Step 2

RESET your microcomputer by pressing the RESET key. Which LED glows?

(The LED connected to the Q output glows. The reason for making the RESET connection to the clock input of the 7474 is to bring up the Q outputs in known conditions when power is supplied. With motors, relays, or other devices connected to an output, it is very important to know the state of the outputs when power is first applied to a microcomputer system.)

Step 3

Load and execute the following program.

```
0200   AD F0 9F    START    LDA DS9FF0    Initiate device select pulse DS9FF0.
0203   00                   BRK           End of program.
```

What do you observe on the LEDs?

(The Q output LED should go out and the $\overline{Q}$ LED should glow.)

Step 4

Change the program above to initiate the $\overline{DS9FF1}$ device select pulse by using an LDA $\overline{DS9FF1}$ instruction. What happens to the LEDs?

(We observed that they switched back to their RESET condition.)

Step 5

Load and execute the following program.

```
0200   AD F0 9F    START    LDA DS9FF0    Initiate device select pulse DS9FF0.
0203   A9 FF                LDA $FF       Set up the T1024 interval timer.
0205   8D 97 A4             STA T1024
0208   2C 97 A4    WAIT     BIT STATUS    Time up?
020B   10 FB                BPL WAIT
020D   AD F1 9F             LDA DS9FF1    Initiate device select pulse DS9FF1.
0210   A9 FF                LDA $FF       Set up the interval timer again.
0212   8D 97 A4             STA T1024
0215   2C 97 A4    WAIT     BIT STATUS    Check the timer status again?
0218   10 FB                BPL LOAF
021A   4C 00 02             JMP START     Repeat entire program.
```

Step 6

The program in Step 5 initiates a device select pulse to preset the 7474, waits in a delay loop using the divide-by-1024 interval timer, clears the 7474, waits in a second delay loop, then repeats this process again and again. What do you expect to observe on the LED test probes connected to the Q and $\overline{Q}$ outputs of the 7474?

(The two LEDs should alternately blink on and off.)

Step 7

Experiment with the values loaded into the timers. You should be able to vary both the frequency of the pulsations and the duty cycle of the square wave at the Q output of the 7474. For example, change the byte at address $0204 to $01 and the byte at address $0211 to $05. Then connect a small speaker from the Q output to ground.

CHAPTER 12

Control Signals, Output Ports, and Applications

OBJECTIVES

At the completion of this chapter you should be able to:

- Describe the functions of each of the control pins on the 6502.
- Understand the timing requirements for interfacing the 6502 to R/W memory devices and TTL latches used as output ports.
- Construct up to 16 output ports using ordinary TTL integrated circuits.
- Design the control signal logic necessary to perform the READ and WRITE operations of the 6502.
- Construct a hexadecimal display port.
- Interface a digital-to-analog converter to an output port.

INTRODUCTION

In this chapter we will examine the functions of those pins on the 6502 that are classified as control pins. Although we will primarily be interested in the ϕ_2 and R/W signals, all of the control pins will be mentioned, if only to provide a brief summary of their function. The ϕ_2 and R/W signals are necessary to implement R/W memory, ROM, I/O ports, and interval timers, whereas some of the other control pins have more specialized functions.

CLOCK SIGNALS, Φ_0 (IN), Φ_1 (OUT), AND Φ_2 (OUT)

The heart of any microcomputer system is, of course, the microprocessor. What keeps the "heart" beating, so to speak, is the system clock. Although it is not absolutely necessary to have a *crystal controlled oscillator* for a clock, most microcomputer clocks are quartz crystals. Although crystal control of the clock frequency is commonplace, you should be cautioned against assuming that your clock frequency is absolutely accurate. The few measurements we have made suggest that the crystal frequencies may be in error by several hundred hertz relative to their specified frequency of 1 MHz. If precision timing is high on your list of applications, you may wish to purchase and install your own crystal. Consult the specification sheets in Appendix C for details on clock circuits.

In Fig. 12-1 we show the relationships between the ϕ_0 (IN) signal and the two clock signals that are produced by the microprocessor at the ϕ_1 (OUT) and the ϕ_2 (OUT) pins. We will assume that the clock frequency is 1 megahertz, making T_C 1 microsecond. Lower frequencies are not prohibited, and 2-MHz versions of the 6502 are available, but 1 MHz is currently the most popular frequency. There are many important properties of the three clock signals shown in Fig. 12-1, such as the pulse width, rise time, fall time, and the delay time between ϕ_1 and ϕ_2 that are described in detail in the specification sheets given in Appendix C, but we will be more concerned with the general features of these signals.

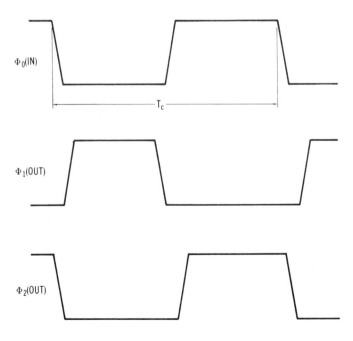

Fig. 12-1. Clock signals in 6502 Microcomputer System.

The clock system is called a *two-phase* system because the two clock signals ϕ_1 and ϕ_2 are out of phase. We will refer to the period when the ϕ_1 signal is at logic one as the ϕ_1 *phase* or simply as ϕ_1, while the period when ϕ_2 is at logic one will be called the ϕ_2 *phase* or simply ϕ_2. The periods when the two signals are at logic one are not allowed to overlap, although the transitions of these signals are extremely close. As we shall see, different events take place in the microcomputer system depending on whether ϕ_1 or ϕ_2 is at logic one.

R/W CONTROL SIGNAL

In a 6502 system, each clock cycle is either a READ cycle or a WRITE cycle. That is, the 6502 is either reading a memory location or writing to a memory location, but not both, during each and every clock cycle. The various components in the microcomputer system are "informed" about which of the two operations is taking place by the logic level on the R/W line. If the 6502 places a logic one on the R/$\overline{\text{W}}$ line, then a READ operation is taking place during that clock cycle. If the R/W line is at logic zero, then a WRITE operation is taking place. In some of the 6502 literature the R/W line is called the R/W line, indicating that the READ operation occurs on a logic one, while the WRITE operation occurs when the R/W line is at logic zero.

Fig. 12-2 shows the timing for reading a memory location. Let us use a concrete example and suppose that data is to be read from a 2114 R/W memory integrated circuit such as is found on the SYM-1 and AIM 65. (The specifications of the 2114 are in Appendix C.) Our reference point on the timing diagram in Fig. 12-2 will be the trailing edge of the ϕ_2 signal, as indicated by the left-most dashed line in Fig. 12-2. At the beginning of a new cycle, when ϕ_1 is at logic one, the 6502 places the address of the location to be read on the address lines, and the 6502 brings the R/W to logic one, informing the 2114 that *it* is to supply the data. The address lines and the R/W line do not change instantaneously, but the 6502 is guaranteed to have a stable address on the address bus and a stable logic one on the R/W line within 300 nanoseconds (ns) after ϕ_2. In Fig. 12-2, this time is labeled T_S, and it is referred to as the *set-up* time for the address bus and the R/W line. The cross-hatched areas in Fig. 12-2 indicate nonstable conditions. The two lines on the graph for the address bus indicate that some address lines are changing to logic one, while others are changing to logic zero. The high interval of ϕ_1 is that period when the address bus and the control lines are changing to select the operation (READ or WRITE) and the location to be accessed.

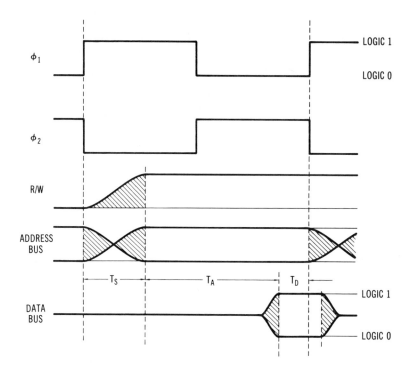

Fig. 12-2. Timing for a READ operation. T_S is set-up time for address lines and R/W line. T_D is time that data on data bus must be stable before end of ϕ_2. T_A is access time.

We now move our attention to the dashed line on the right-hand side of Fig. 12-2, which is the end of the read cycle. The 6502 requires that the data on the data bus be stable for at least 100 ns before the end of ϕ_2. We have labeled this period as T_D in Fig. 12-2. It is the trailing edge of the ϕ_2 signal that "clocks" or latches the data into the 6502. It is up to the device being read to have stable logic levels on the data bus at least 100 ns before the end of ϕ_2 and to hold the data lines stable for 10 ns after ϕ_2. The time between the address lines arriving at their stable levels and the point where the data lines must be stable is labeled T_A in Fig. 12-2. It is called the *access* time. Clearly

$$T_A = T_C - T_S - T_D$$

giving an access time for the 6502 of about 600 ns. We have neglected the rise time of the ϕ_1 signal in this equation, and in Fig. 12-2 we have shown ϕ_1 and ϕ_2 changing instantaneously, which is not the case. The rise time is about 25 ns, reducing the access time to 575 ns.

Recall that the address lines are connected to the decoding circuitry that produces a device select pulse and to the 2114 R/W memory chip that decodes the address lines A9 through A0. Because it takes time for the changing logic levels at the inputs of the decoding circuits to propagate to the outputs, the device select pulse will be delayed and will not begin until slightly after the address lines have reached their stable levels. With 7400 series or 74LS00 series chips this time is of little consequence since it is only a few nanoseconds, and we may regard the device select pulse as occurring simultaneously with the address lines reaching their stable values, sometime during ϕ_1.

Memory chips are usually a bit slower. While the address lines are changing, and for some time after they have become stable, the address decoding circuitry on the 2114 chip is actively responding to the address changes on its input lines. The 2114 must "decide" which four of its 4×1024 flip-flops will put data on the four output lines it has. The time it takes to "decide" is known as its *access* time. The access time of the memory chips used in a 6502 system *must be less* than the 6502 access time shown in Fig. 12-2 or the 6502 will read meaningless information. The 2114 chips have an access time of 450 ns, so there is a comfortable margin for which the data is stable. If the 2114 chip is selected by the device select pulse *and* its $\overline{\text{WE}}$ pin is at logic one, then after the access time has elapsed it puts its four bits of data on four lines of the data bus in the form of *stable* logic levels. The data will remain stable until shortly after the device select from the address decoding circuitry allows the chip select, $\overline{\text{CS}}$, on the 2114 to go high. This will occur after the trailing edge of ϕ_2, so the logic levels will be successfully read by the 6502, completing the read cycle. The logic circuit required to produce a "READ ENABLE" signal from the device select pulse and the R/W line is shown in Fig. 12-4.

We turn now to an analysis of a WRITE operation, the timing diagram being given in Fig. 12-3. The parameter T_S has the same meaning as before; namely it is the time required for the 6502 to produce stable logic levels on the address bus, and for the 6502 to change the R/W line to logic zero for a WRITE operation. The parameter T_{DS} is the amount of time, measured from the beginning of ϕ_2, required to produce stable logic levels on the data bus. The 6502 requires no more than 200 ns to produce stable data, giving a period of about 300 ns when the data are stable. Finally, the logic levels on the data bus remain stable for a short time after the conclusion of ϕ_2, called the data hold time and symbolized by T_H. For a 6502, T_H is typically 30 ns.

The peripheral that is to receive the data, the 2114 in our example, usually requires that the address be stable during the write time.

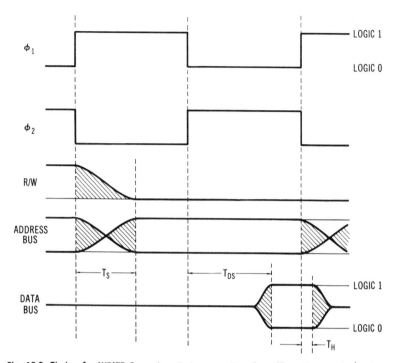

Fig. 12-3. Timing for WRITE Operation. T_S is set-up time for address lines and R/W line. T_{DS} is data set-up time from 6502. T_H is data hold time.

Thus, the $\overline{WE}$ pin on the 2114 is usually brought to logic zero *after* the addresses are stable, namely during ϕ_2. Thus, to activate the "write enable" ($\overline{WE}$) pin on the 2114, we would like the R/W line to be at logic zero *and* the ϕ_2 signal to be at logic one. We also want the chip to be selected by the $\overline{DS}$ pulse. The logic circuit shown in Fig. 12-4 produces the correct WRITE ENABLE signal for the conditions stated above. Furthermore, we must somehow signal the 2114 that the data is now stable and should be latched into whichever of the 4 × 1024 locations we have selected with the address. This is done by the trailing edge of the ϕ_2 signal at the end of the cycle. Note that at this time the data have been stable for almost 300 ns, a sufficient length of time for the 2114, which requires only 200 ns of stable data. The trailing edge of the ϕ_2 signal clocks the data into the 2114, completing the write cycle. Note that both the address lines and the data lines are still stable at the trailing edge of ϕ_2.

To conclude our discussion of the control signal interface required to correctly read the 2114 and to correctly write to the 2114, we note that some of the control line logic is located on the 2114 itself. In

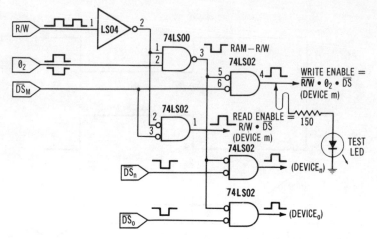

Fig. 12-4. Logic circuit to produce READ ENABLE and WRITE ENABLE signals.

Fig. 12-5 we show the control line logic that the designer must provide and the on-chip logic. Note that this is not the only way to interface the control signals to a 2114; in fact, the AIM 65 does not use this approach. The AIM 65 brings the R/W line directly to the $\overline{WE}$ pin on the 2114, and it effectively "ANDS" the ϕ_2 signal with the $\overline{DS}$ signal in the decoder, producing a chip select ($\overline{CS}$) signal that is at logic zero when ϕ_2 is at logic one and $\overline{DS}$ is at logic zero. It can be shown that this logic circuit is equivalent to the logic circuit shown in Fig. 12-5.

One final note on the control signals shown in Fig. 12-4: The signal labeled RAM R/W is generated on the KIM-1 and the SYM-1. Its logical expression is $\overline{R/W \cdot \phi_2}$, meaning that it is logic zero when the R/W line is at logic zero *and* ϕ_2 is at logic one. It is used to write to R/W locations, and it is made available at pin Z of the

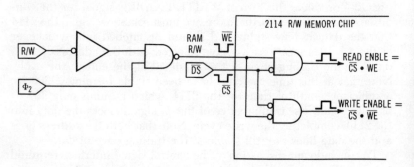

Fig. 12-5. Control Line Logic and On-Chip Logic for controlling 2114.

expansion connectors on these two systems. The AIM 65, on the other hand, generates a signal whose logical expression is $\overline{R/W} \cdot \phi_2$, a signal that is also called RAM R/W, and that is also brought to pin Z of the application connector. *The user should be aware of the fact that these are not equivalent signals.* The KIM-1 and SYM-1 RAM-R/W signals are useful for the WRITE operation. A future version of the AIM 65 will have the correct RAM-R/W signal. Current versions of the AIM 65 are marked near the crystal with a printed-circuit triangle. The new version of the AIM 65, with the correct RAM-R/W signal, will have a nontriangular-shaped symbol in the same place.

USING CONTROL SIGNALS FOR AN OUTPUT PORT

The circuit of Fig. 12-4, in addition to providing the necessary control signals for accessing R/W memory, may also be used to provide the necessary control signals for an output port. Recall that the write enable output of Fig. 12-4 is at logic one when the R/W line is at logic zero, ϕ_2 is at logic one, *and* the device select ($\overline{DS}$) is at logic zero. Apply this signal to the G input of either a 74100 or two 74LS75 integrated circuits, and connect the data bus to the D inputs of these chips, as shown in Figs. 12-6 and 12-7.

The 7475 and the 74100 integrated circuits are both bistable latches (or flip-flops), and they behave much like an R/W memory location during a WRITE operation. When the G inputs are at logic one, the Q outputs follow the logic levels at the D inputs. The D inputs are connected to the data bus of the 6502. Refer to Fig. 12-4 and notice that during a WRITE operation to the location whose address produces the $\overline{DS}$ pulse, a positive pulse, whose duration is the same as ϕ_2, is produced at the WRITE ENABLE output. If this pulse is applied to the G inputs of the 7475s or the 74100, then the Q outputs will correspond to the data on the data bus during the WRITE cycle, and, at the end of the WRITE cycle, the WE pulse ends while the data is still stable, clocking the data bus logic levels into the Q outputs. The $\overline{Q}$ outputs on the 74LS75 will have logic levels just opposite to their Q counterparts. The device select ($\overline{DS}$) pulses may be obtained from 74LS154 in the circuit of Fig. 11-9.

Note that only three instructions in the 6502 instruction set will write data to the output port we have just constructed. These are the STA, STX, and STY instructions. The output port only responds to a WRITE operation because the R/W line must be at logic zero for the WRITE ENABLE pulse to occur. Instructions such as LDA, LDX, LDY, or any other instruction that involves a READ operation from this address will produce meaningless data because nothing is read (no READ ENABLE pulse occurs). Instructions such as the

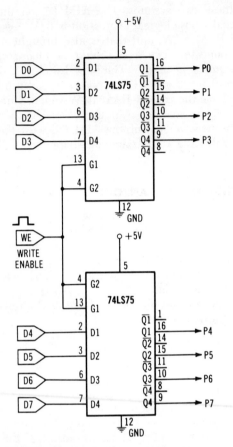

Fig. 12-6. Two 74LS75s used as Output Port. Circuit to generate WRITE ENABLE shown in Fig. 12-4.

ASL, DEC, and ROL instructions will not work because they require a READ cycle also. However, the use of only three of the nine instructions in the 6502 instruction set that involve the WRITE operation is no great handicap for an output port.

The output pins of the 6502, including the data bus pins, are rated for one TTL load. The 74100 in Fig. 12-7 represents such a load on the data bus. Since the data bus on your microcomputer will already have several devices loading it, the circuit in Fig. 12-7 will cause the data bus to be overloaded. The circuit *might* work with the data bus connected to the D inputs of the 74100, but it is a marginal situation. To solve the problem, the data bus must be buffered, one of the topics in the next chapter. The 74LS75s in Fig. 12-6 may be operated directly from the data bus, but if several output ports are desired, requiring that the data bus be connected to the inputs of several

290

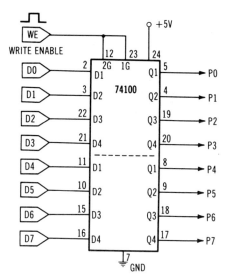

Fig. 12-7. A 74100 used as 8-bit output port. Circuit to generate WRITE ENABLE shown in Fig. 12-4.

74LS75s, then buffering will again be required. Refer to Chapter 13 for details. We will also postpone the discussion of input ports until Chapter 13, in which three-state devices are described. With suitable data bus buffering, the circuits shown in Figs. 11-9, 12-4, and 12-6 or 12-7 may be used to make up to 16 output ports with addresses \$9FF0 through \$9FFF. In the experiments at the end of this chapter, we will describe a simple buffer/driver that will allow you to experiment with these circuits, without going into a full discussion of data bus buffering. In Chapter 13 we will show how to make input ports. Some of the device select pulses from addresses in this range may be used for input ports.

MEMORY-MAPPED, LATCHED HEXADECIMAL DISPLAY

The address decoding circuit and the control line logic may be used to implement a memory-mapped, latched hexadecimal display. Assuming that the data lines at the expansion connector are adequately buffered (see the experiments section at the end of this chapter, or Chapter 13), two hexadecimal display chips with latches and drivers make a convenient and useful output display. The chips used were Texas Instruments TIL311s, but equivalent chips are made by other manufacturers. The circuit diagram is shown in Fig. 12-8. The write enable pulse from the circuit in Fig. 12-4 may be converted to the necessary strobe signal by the 74LS04 inverter. One of the device selects, $\overline{\text{DS9FF0}}$ for example, from the 74LS154 in Fig. 11-9 may be used to address the display.

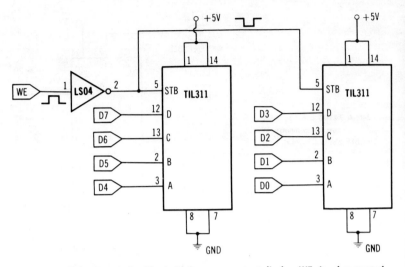

Fig. 12-8. Using hexadecimal latch-displays as an output display. WE signal generated with circuit shown in Fig. 12-4.

Assuming that this memory-mapped display is selected with the address $9FF0, one can view the contents of the accumulator, X register, or Y register with STA, STX, and STY instructions, respectively. This may be useful in debugging programs. For example, an STX $9FF0 instruction may be placed in a program loop that is giving trouble, and the program may be single-stepped to observe how the X register is changing. This is certainly much faster than using the register trace mode on the KIM-1. To observe the stack pointer, use a TSX instruction followed by an STX$9FF0 instruction. A latched hexadecimal display such as this is much more convenient (and more expensive) than the unlatched seven-segment displays that require constant refreshing. A program to demonstrate the display is given in the experiments.

MEMORY-MAPPED DIGITAL-TO-ANALOG CONVERTER AND AN APPLICATION TO MUSIC SYNTHESIS

The address decoding circuitry described in the last chapter, the control circuit logic, and the 74100 (or 74LS75s) may be used with a Motorola 1408L8 8-bit digital-to-analog converter to make a memory-mapped digital-to-analog converter circuit. The 1408L8 circuit is shown in Fig. 12-9, while the necessary control logic was shown in Fig. 12-4, the 74100 output latch circuit was given in Fig. 12-7, and the address decoding circuit was shown in Fig. 11-9. We used the $\overline{\text{DS9FF0}}$ device select pulse from the 74LS154 shown in Fig. 11-9.

Just as we did not attempt to explain how the various TTL gates and decoders worked, we will not attempt to explain how the DAC (digital-to-analog converter) works. Basically the 1408 is a system of resistors and "switches" that produce a current proportional to the 8-bit binary number represented by the logic levels on pins 5 through 12, pin 5 being the most significant bit. The outputs of the 74100 shown in Fig. 12-7 are connected to the inputs of the 1408 DAC. The CA3140 operational amplifier acts as a current-to-voltage converter, and the 10K feedback resistor (pin 6 to pin 2) may be adjusted to produce the desired proportionality between the 8-bit number on the input of the DAC and the voltage level at pin 6 of the CA3140 operational amplifier. You may wish to adjust the resistor so that with $FF as the digital signal you obtain 2.55 volts on the output. Then a simple hex-to-decimal conversion gives the correct output voltage, providing the decimal point is also shifted.

Although there are many uses for digital-to-analog converters, such as in controlling motor speed, analog-to-digital conversions, graphics on oscilloscopes or plotters, etc., the application we have chosen to illustrate the use of a DAC is from the area of music synthesis. If one cycle of a particular waveform is stored in a table in memory, and the computer writes the entries in the table to the

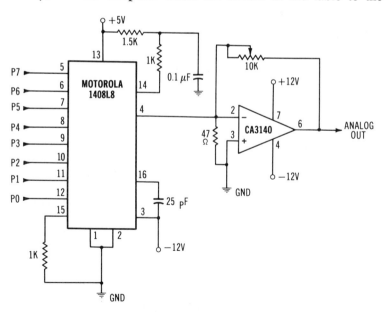

Fig. 12-9. Digital-to-analog converter circuit.

DAC as part of a continuously running loop, then the waveform appears as a voltage level at the output of the CA3140, and this voltage varies in exactly the same way as the stored waveform. If the entries in the table are written to the DAC at a fast enough rate, then the entire waveform stored in the table may appear at the DAC output at an audio frequency, say 440 Hz, that may then be amplified and connected to a speaker.

One advantage of this approach over the method of toggling an output, which we used in earlier tone generation programs, is that it is the waveform which affects the quality or timbre of the music; and, with the waveform in a table, we have complete control over the timbre. A toggled output is always a rectangular wave, and although the timbre may be altered somewhat by changing the duty cycle, the technique lacks the versatility of the sampled-waveform approach.

If the waveform table contains one cycle of the waveform, and if it is written to the DAC at the rate of 440 tables per second, then an "A" note (equally tempered scale) will be heard. If the same read-out rate were used, but only every other entry in the table were used, then we would hear a tone whose frequency is 880 Hz. Thus, by skipping a certain number of entries in the table the output frequency may be changed.

Chords (several simultaneous tones) may be produced by adding samples together in the microcomputer, and writing them to the DAC. For example, if we sample the table at every entry, every other entry, every third entry, and every fourth entry, add these samples together and output them continuously to the DAC, we will hear the fundamental, second harmonic, third harmonic, and fourth harmonic.

The equally tempered scale assigns the frequency of 440 Hz to the note A. Successively higher (or lower) notes are related to this frequency by multiplication by $2^{1/12}$. A table of note frequencies is provided in Table 12-1. Unfortunately, to play these frequencies we need to skip fractional numbers of entries in the waveform table. To handle this idea, we must look in a little more detail at how we

Table 12-1. Frequencies of Several Notes on Equally Tempered Scale

Note	Frequency (Hertz)	Note	Frequency (Hertz)
C	261.62	F♯	369.99
C♯	277.18	G	391.99
D	293.66	G♯	415.30
D♯	311.13	A	440.00
E	329.63	A♯	466.16
F	349.23	B	493.88

intend to accomplish the production of chords with our computer program.

For our waveform table, let us use one page of memory, or 256 entries. With a base address of $0300, for example, we can use indirect indexing to read the table. Keeping the base address high constant (BAH = $03), the program will continue to "wrap around" the table as the BAL (base address low) is incremented. Assume we can output a number to the DAC every 100 microseconds. Then the frequency we will hear is

$$f = \frac{1}{256 \times 100 \times 10^{-6} \text{ sec}} = \frac{10^4}{256} \text{ Hz} = 39.0625 \text{ Hz}$$

To produce higher frequencies, we must skip entries in the table so that we output the table more quickly. To hear middle C (f = 261.62), we must sample the waveform table every 261.62/ 39.0625 = 6.70 entries. The formula giving the number of table entries to skip is

$$S = \frac{256 \cdot f_T}{100 \times 10^{-6}}$$

where 256 represents the number of entries in the table, 100×10^{-6} is the time it takes to output the sum of the entries (loop time) to the DAC, and f_T is the frequency of the tone we wish to hear.

We decided to write a simple demonstration program to play the chord consisting of F and A (below middle C), middle C, and D♯. Thus, the chord consists of four tones, and the table must be sampled every 4.47 entries for the F note, every 5.63 entries for the A note, every 6.70 entries for the C note, and every 7.96 entries for the D♯ note. We begin by converting the fractional parts to hexadecimal. That is, for the F note,

$$0.47 = \frac{47}{100} = \frac{X}{256}$$

where X is the two-digit hexadecimal number to the *right* of the *hexadecimal* point. Solving for X gives X = $78 for the F note, $A2 for the A note, $B3 for the C note, and $F7 for the D♯ note. The intervals are then $4.78 for the F note, $5.A2 for the A note, $6.B3 for the C note, and $7.F7 for the D♯ note.

To sample the waveform table we may start by reading an entry, using indirect indexed addressing with the index set equal to zero, for each of the four notes. The samples are then added together and loaded into the DAC. Next, the base address low of each read operation is incremented by the numbers given in the preceding paragraph, and the next samples are taken from these new locations in the table.

To handle the fractional increments, a two-byte addition is performed. First the fractional part is added, then the integer part is added. Any carry from the fractional part will be added to the integer part. Only the integer part is used as the BAL for the table entry to be read. A close examination of the program in Example 1 will make this clear.

The program in Example 1 is very similar to the PLAY subroutine used by Hal Chamberlin[1] in his noteworthy article on computer music. There are many other important details, related to this sampled waveform approach to making music, that you may find in this reference or by obtaining a reprint from Micro Technology Unlimited, Box 4596, Manchester, NH 03108. Our coverage of this topic is intended only to stimulate your interest in this area of computer applications. Refer to the experiments for further details and other experiments with the DAC circuit of Fig. 12-9.

The waveform table we used was a triangular wave that produces a simple but mellow tone. A simple program for producing the waveform table is given in Example 2. Note that the largest amplitude in the table is $3F so that when four tones are added together the result will not exceed $FF, the largest number the DAC will accept. You may wish to experiment with other waveforms, such as a ramp or a rectangular waveform. To listen to the chord, we coupled the auxiliary input of our hi-fi to the output of the CA3140 using a 0.047-microfarad capacitor.

Example 1: Program to Produce Four Simultaneous Tones

$0000 = TN1L; Fractional part of waveform table address for tone one
$0001 = TN1H; Integer part of waveform table address for tone one (BAL)
$0002 = $03 = BAH of waveform table
$0003 = TN2L; Fractional part of waveform table address for tone two
$0004 = TN2H; Integer part of waveform table address for tone two (BAL)
$0005 = $03 = BAH of waveform table
$0006 = TN3L; Fractional part of waveform table address for tone three
$0007 = TN3H; Integer part of waveform table address for tone three (BAL)
$0008 = $03; BAH of waveform table
$0009 = TN4L; Fractional part of waveform table address for tone four
$000A = TN4H; Integer part of waveform table address for tone four (BAL)
$000B = 03; BAH of waveform table
$9FF0 = DAC; Digital-to-analog converter port

$0200	A2 00	START	LDY	$00	Set indirect index to zero.
$0202	D8		CLD		Clear decimal mode.
$0203	18		CLC		Clear carry for additions to follow.
$0204	B1 01	LOOP	LDA	(TN1H),Y	Get tone one sample from the table.
$0206	71 04		ADC	(TN2H),Y	Add tone two sample from the table.
$0208	71 07		ADC	(TN3H),Y	Add tone three sample from the table.

---

[1]Chamberlin, Hal, "A Sampling of Techniques for Computer Performance of Music," *BYTE*, V2, No. 9, Sept. 1977, p. 62.

$020A	71 0A	ADC (TN4H),Y	Add tone four sample from the table.
$020C	8D F0 9F	STA DAC	Output the result to the DAC.
$020F	A5 00	LDA TN1L	Calculate address of the next entry
$0211	69 78	ADC $78	by adding $4.78 to the previous address.
$0213	85 00	STA TN1L	Add fractional part first.
$0215	A5 01	LDA TN1H	Next add carry from this to integer
$0217	69 04	ADC $04	part of the low-order byte of the
$0219	85 01	STA TN1H	address.
$021B	A5 03	LDA TN1L	Repeat above process for remaining
$021D	69 A2	ADC $A2	three tones.
$021F	85 03	STA TN2L	
$0221	A5 04	LDA TN2H	
$0223	69 05	ADC $05	
$0225	85 04	STA TN2H	
$0227	A5 06	LDA TN3L	
$0229	69 B3	ADC $B3	
$022B	85 06	STA TN3L	
$022D	A5 07	LDA TN3H	
$022F	69 06	ADC $06	
$0231	85 07	STA TN3H	
$0233	A5 09	LDA TN4L	
$0235	69 F7	ADC $F7	
$0237	85 09	STA TN4L	
$0239	A5 0A	LDA TN4H	
$023B	69 07	ADC $07	
$023D	85 0A	STA TN4H	
$023F	A5 00	LDA DUM	The remaining instructions are
$0241	EA	NOP	"dummies." They take up time to
$0242	EA	NOP	make loop time 100 microseconds.
$0243	EA	NOP	
$0244	4C 04 02	JMP LOOP	Back to start over.

Example 2: Program to Place Triangular Waveform in Page Three of Memory

$0300 = Base Address of Waveform Table

$0250	A2 00	START	LDX $00	Initialize X register to zero.
$0252	A0 FF		LDY $FF	Initialize Y register to $FF.
$0254	8A	LOOP	TXA	Transfer X to A.
$0255	4A		LSR A	Divide by two.
$0256	9D 00 03		STA TAB,X	Store in table, beginning half.
$0259	99 00 03		STA TAB,Y	Store in table, ending half.
$025C	E8		INX	Increment X.
$025D	88		DEY	Decrement Y.
$025E	E0 80		CPX $80	Is X = $80?
$0260	D0 F2		BNE LOOP	No, continue filling table.
$0262	00		BRK	Yes, table is filled.

OTHER CONTROL PINS ON 6502

The control pins not yet mentioned include three input pins, $\overline{\text{RES}}$ (Reset), $\overline{\text{RDY}}$ (Ready) and S.O. (Set Overflow), and one output pin, SYNC (Synchronization). We will discuss these briefly. The

$\overline{RES}$ pin is usually used under "power up" conditions or at other times when it is desired that the microcomputer "restart." When power is applied to the 6502, or when the RESET key is depressed, the $\overline{RES}$ pin is held at logic zero. Suitable delay circuits hold the $\overline{RES}$ pin at logic zero during power-up conditions, while the RESET key is usually connected to a 555 timer to produce a logic-zero signal at the $\overline{RES}$ pin. After the $\overline{RES}$ line goes high, the 6502 waits for six clock cycles; then it fetches the new PCL from the location with the address $FFFC and the new PCH from the location with the address $FFFD. The next cycle sees PCH-PCL on the address bus to fetch the *first* op code in the program. In the case of the KIM-1, AIM 65, and SYM-1, this address is the starting point of the monitor.

The Ready ($\overline{RDY}$) pin is used to interface slow memory devices. If the ready line is brought to logic zero during ϕ_1 of any READ cycle, the R/W line remains at logic one and the address lines maintain their logic levels. In that case, slow memory devices may be given a longer access time. When the ready line is allowed to return to logic one, then the microprocessor will simply complete the second half of the clock cycle begun when the ready line was pulled low. That is, the slow memory device will be read. The $\overline{RDY}$ pin is also used in direct-memory-access (DMA) applications, a topic beyond the scope of this book.

The S.O. pin might be a useful pin, but it appears to have found few applications. Basically it could serve as a kind of "hardware flag," since a positive-to-negative transition on the S.O. pin sets the overflow flag. This flag may be tested with the BVC and the BVS instructions. Note that arithmetic operations also affect this flag.

Finally, the SYNC pin produces a logic-one pulse during the entire cycle in which an op code is being fetched. In the SYM-1, KIM-1, and AIM 65, the SYNC pulse is used to pull the $\overline{NMI}$ pin low when these microcomputers are in the single-step mode. This produces a nonmaskable interrupt. The instruction currently being executed is completed; then the processor jumps to the nonmaskable-interrupt routine. This monitor routine saves the processor registers and returns control of the program to the monitor. The user can, therefore, execute his program one instruction at a time, and the various registers may be examined after each instruction. The monitor routine contains no RTI instruction, so a key depression or some other signal is required to execute the next instruction in the user's program.

EXPERIMENT NO. 1

Step 1

Using the breadboard begun during the experiments at the end of Chapter 11, add the circuit shown in Fig. 12-4. KIM-1 and SYM-1 users may omit the 74LS04 and the 74LS00 and use the RAM-R/W signal available at pin Z of the expansion connector. Use the $\overline{\text{DS9FF0}}$ device select pulse from the 74LS154 shown in Fig. 11-9.

Step 2

Load the following program.

```
0200   8D F0 9F    START   STA MEM    Write to address $9FF0
0203   4C 00 02            JMP START  Loop back to START
```

Step 3

With the test probe shown in Fig. 12-4, test the WRITE ENABLE output and the READ ENABLE output. Describe and explain what you observe.

(You should observe that the LED glows when it is connected to the WRITE ENABLE, but it does not glow when it is connected to the READ ENABLE. Refer to Table 11-11 and note that during the fourth cycle of the STA $9FF0 instruction the device select pulse $\overline{\text{DS9FF0}}$ will occur. Since this is a WRITE operation, the R/W line will be at logic zero. During the last half of this cycle, ϕ_2 will be at logic one, and a WRITE ENABLE pulse will occur. The READ ENABLE requires that the R/W line be at logic one when the $\overline{\text{DS9FF0}}$ pulse occurs, but during the last cycle of the STA $9FF0 instruction the R/W line is at logic zero. Thus, no READ ENABLE pulse occurs.)

Step 4

How could you modify the program in Step 2 to produce a READ ENABLE pulse but not a WRITE ENABLE pulse? Use the LED test probe to verify your hypothesis.

EXPERIMENT NO. 2

Step 1

Breadboard the data bus buffer shown in Fig. 12-10. The 81LS97 is an octal version of the 74LS367, and two 74LS367s may be used instead. Other data bus buffers will also work. Keep this circuit for Experiments No. 3, 4, and 5.

Step 2

Breadboard the hexadecimal display circuit of Fig. 12-8. Connect the buffered data bus outputs to the data inputs of the two display

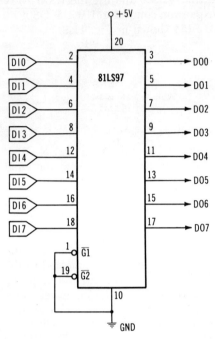

Fig. 12-10. Temporary data bus buffer for experiments in Chapter 12. Two 74LS367s (Hex Buffer/Drivers) will also serve for this purpose.

chips, as indicated in the figure. For the WRITE ENABLE pulse use the circuit of Experiment No. 1. The address of the display will be $9FF0, although any other of the addresses $9FF0 through $9FFF could also be used.

Step 3

To test the display, load the following program and execute it.

```
0200   A5 00      START   LDA  MEM      Load A with the contents of $0000.
0202   8D F0 9F           STA  DISP     Store A in the display.
0205   A9 FF              LDA  $FF
0207   8D 97 A4           STA  T1024    Store $FF in 1024 timer.
020A   2C 97 A4   WAIT    BIT  STATUS   Wait for time out.
020D   10 FB              BPL  WAIT
020F   E6 00              INC  MEM      Increment contents of $0000.
0211   4C 00 02           JMP  START    Loop to beginning of the program.
```

What effect do you expect this program will have on the display?

(The display should "count" through all possible (256) two digit hexadecimal numbers. The time delay simply gives enough time for human beings to observe the count.)

EXPERIMENT NO. 3

Step 1

Remove the display chips, and replace them with a 74100, as shown in Fig. 12-7.

Step 2

Connect the outputs of the 81LS97 to the D inputs of the 74100 shown in Fig. 12-7. Connect the WRITE ENABLE output of Fig. 12-4, that you wired in Experiment 1, to the G inputs of the 74100 as shown in Fig. 12-7.

Step 3

Wire a test probe like the one shown in Fig. 12-4. Check all eight outputs of the 74100. Some of them will be at logic one (the LED glows) and some of them will be at logic zero. This output port has random output logic levels when power is first supplied.

Step 4

Load and execute the following program.

```
0200  A9 FF      START    LDA  $FF      Put logic one into each bit of A.
0202  8D F0 9F             STA  PORTP   Store A in output port $9FF0.
0205  00                   BRK          Break to the monitor.
```

What do you expect the test probe LED to indicate when you test the output pins of the 74100?

(The LED should glow when it is connected to any of the 74100 output pins.)

Step 5

Change the byte to be stored in the output port to $00 by changing the program byte at address $0201 to $00. Execute the program again. What do you expect will appear on the output pins of the 74100? Experiment with other values of the byte located at $0201, and test the output port pins with the LED test probe. Your 74100 should work perfectly before you proceed.

EXPERIMENT NO. 4

Step 1

Add the circuit shown in Fig. 12-9 to your breadboard. Connect the outputs of the 74100 (or 74LS75s) to the Motorola 1408L8 DAC. Adjust the 10K resistor to be approximately 1000 ohms.

Step 2

Connect a vom or vtvm between ground and the output (pin 6) of the CA3140 operational amplifier.

Step 3

Using the "examine and modify memory" feature of your microcomputer, load $FF into the location whose address produces the device select pulse to write to the 74100. We have been using DS9FF0 in previous experiments. Your voltmeter should read, very approximately, three volts. Adjust the 10K feedback resistor so that the voltage is about 2.55 V.

Step 4

Now load the location whose address is $9FF0 with $00. Your voltmeter should read zero.

Step 5

Now load $80 into the DAC output port, $9FF0. You should read about 1.28 V on your voltmeter. If you do not get this value, you might check to see if bit seven is connected to pin five of the DAC. Pin five of the DAC input should be a logic one; all the other pins should be at logic zero.

Step 6

In turn, load $01, $02, $04, $08, $10, $20, $40, and $80 into the DAC and measure the logic levels on the input pins and the voltage output from the operational amplifier. The values given above to load into the DAC produce, in turn, a logic one on pins 12, 11, 10, 9, 8, 7, 6, and 5, leaving the other input pins at logic zero. In this way you can make sure all the output bits are properly ordered. Your DAC is now working properly. Compare your output voltages, given the DAC inputs, with what you would expect.

(You should obtain the following output voltages with the given inputs, provided the 10K feedback resistor was adjusted to give an output voltage of 2.55 volts with $FF loaded into the DAC. A DAC input of $01 gives 0.01 V, $02 gives 0.02 V, $04 gives 0.04 V, $08 gives 0.08 V, $10 gives 0.16 V, $20 gives 0.32 V, $40 gives 0.64 V, and $80 gives 1.28 V.)

EXPERIMENT NO. 5

Step 1

Load the programs given in Examples 1 and 2. Execute the program given in Example 2 first. This loads the waveform table needed for the tone generation program. After executing the program in Example 2, check page three of memory to see that it contains a triangular waveform.

Step 2

Load $03 into locations with addresses $0002, $0005, $0008, and $000B. These locations contain the high-order byte of the addresses of the entries in the waveform table.

Step 3

Connect a 0.047-microfarad capacitor from the output of the CA3140 to the input of your hi-fi or some other audio-amplifier–speaker system.

Step 4

In the program listed in Example 1, replace the instruction bytes from $0206 through $020B with $EAs. In other words, six bytes are changed to NOP instructions.

Step 5

Run the program. You should hear a mellow tone from your audio system. The program is now playing only one note.

Step 6

Remove the first two NOP instructions you inserted, and put the correct instruction bytes back into the program. Now execute the program. You should hear two tones that are harmonious.

Step 7

Remove the second two NOP instructions you inserted, and put the correct instructions back into the program. Execute it. What do you expect to hear?

Step 8

Add the final two correct instructions. Run the program. You should hear four tones. See reference 1 if you want to play the Star Spangled Banner in four-part harmony. Keep your DAC circuit; it will be used in the next chapter.

CHAPTER 13

Data Bus, Buffering, and Applications

OBJECTIVES

At the completion of this chapter you should be able to:

- Understand the necessity for buffering the various microcomputer buses.
- Understand and use three-state buffer/drivers to buffer the bidirectional data bus.
- Construct a 1-bit or an 8-bit input port using three-state buffer/drivers.
- Build and operate a memory-mapped analog-to-digital converter circuit.
- Design and construct latched input ports using the 8212 I/O integrated circuit.

INTRODUCTION

The general topic of this chapter will be the subject of buffering, but it will include a more complete discussion of the data bus than has been heretofore given in this book; several interfacing applications will also be mentioned. The control bus and the address bus are "one-way," or unidirectional, buses; that is, *one* device in the microcomputer system controls the logic level of the line. For example, the 6502 controls the logic levels on the address bus (unless the microcomputer system utilizes direct memory access techniques). The R/W line is also controlled by the 6502, and no other component in the microcomputer system can be allowed to affect this control line. On the other hand, logic levels on the data bus are controlled by the 6502 only during a WRITE operation. During a READ operation, the data bus logic levels are determined by the device that was addressed by the 6502. This might be a R/W memory chip, an input port, an interval timer, or a ROM chip. Since the data bus carries information *to* and *from* the 6502, it is called a *bidirectional* bus. We will look first at the need to buffer any kind of bus in a 6502 system; then we will examine the special requirements of a bidirectional bus.

WHY BUFFER?

There are two reasons for buffering any bus:

- The pins on the 6502 that control a bus line are rated to drive one standard TTL load. In many microcomputer systems there will be heavier loading than this; that is, the computer will have to "drive" more than one TTL-type input.
- The conductors in any bus system have capacitance. Capacitors require time to charge and discharge, and, consequently, they can distort the rapidly changing waveshapes one encounters on the buses. Buffers can drive a much larger capacitance than can the 6502, and, consequently, they are used to preserve the integrity of the waveshapes over long path lengths.

In addition, the data bus requires a special kind of buffer. Recall that the microprocessor is capable of reading data from any of 65536 devices. However, *only one* of these devices should control the data bus during any particular READ cycle. All the others should act as if they are not there. If two devices are trying to take a data bus line to opposite logic levels, not even a prophet can predict what data the 6502 will read. Furthermore, during a WRITE cycle all the devices in the memory space should be isolated from the data bus as far as their control of it is concerned, while the 6502 controls the logic levels on the data bus. This brings us to the third reason for buffering:

- Buffers must be capable of isolating the data bus from all of the devices connected to the data bus, except the device being addressed.

All the control pins, the address pins, and the data pins on the 6502 are capable of driving one standard TTL load. This means that only one standard 7400-series chip may be connected to an output pin on the 6502, if the 6502 is to operate properly. You could connect four 74LS00-series chips to a bus line, but if you tried to connect additional chips to these lines, the circuit might not operate.

One solution to the problem of connecting many devices to a single line, in the case of the control bus or the address bus, is to connect the pins of the 6502 directly to two 7404 inverters in series. Two inverters in series results in no *net* inversion. A 7404 can drive ten standard TTL loads and about 40 LS loads, while a 74LS04 can drive 20 74LS00 loads. This kind of buffering would be adequate for most systems provided the bus length is not too great. The AIM 65, KIM-1, and SYM-1 all buffer the ϕ_2 and R/W control lines with two 7404 inverters in series. Refer to the schematic of your system for details. The address lines in these three microcomputer systems are not buffered because they only drive a few MOS R/W memory and ROM chips that require almost no driving power. However, if any of these microcomputer systems are expanded, using the expansion connector for example, some or all of the address lines will have to be buffered. A popular technique is again to use two "head to tail" 7404 or 74LS04 inverters in series for each address line to be buffered. For an example, check Pollock's KIM-1 to S-100 bus circuit.[1]

There are other integrated circuits, called *bus buffer/drivers* that either may be used on a unidirectional bus, such as the control bus, or they may be used on a bidirectional bus. These integrated circuits have four (quad), six (hex), or eight (octal) buffer/drivers per chip. Some of the more popular chips are listed in Table 13-1. The logic symbols for some typical buffer/drivers are shown in Fig. 13-1. A truth table for the buffer/drivers used in this chapter is provided in Table 13-2. Study the function of the G (gate) input. Note that when the G input is low, then the output logic level of the buffer is the same as the input logic level. In that case, the buffer/driver is driving the particular bus line to which it is attached. An inversion circle on a G input indicates that the buffer/driver is active when the G input is at logic zero. Other buffers are active when their G inputs are at logic one, and their logic symbols will not have inversion circles at the G inputs.

Perhaps the most important feature is the third state in the truth table, the one labeled "disabled." When the gate is at logic one, the buffer/driver acts as if it were disconnected from the bus; that is, it behaves as if a switch in series with the output had been opened. In effect, the buffer is "disconnected" from the bus. This property of the buffer/driver is the reason for calling these devices "three-state buffer/drivers" or "TRI-STATE buffer/drivers." (TRI-STATE is a trademark of National Semiconductor Corporation.) Observe that the third state, or the disabled state, is exactly what is required

---

[1]Pollock, Jim, "KIM-1 to S-100 Bus Adapter," *6502 User Notes*, #7-8, p. 7.

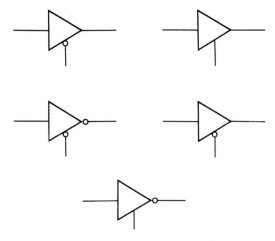

Fig. 13-1. Logic symbols for typical Buffer/Drivers.

when many devices are to be connected to the same bus. The bus buffer/driver can be enabled whenever the device to which its input is connected is addressed. It can be disabled, or disconnected from the bus in effect, whenever the device to which its input is connected is not addressed.

Fig. 13-2 shows how one bit of data might be input to the 6502 using some simple control logic and a three-state buffer/driver. Suppose the address on the address bus produces a device select pulse as indicated in Fig. 13-2. If the R/W line is at logic one, as it is during a READ cycle, then the output of the 74LS00 will go to logic zero during this cycle, enabling the three-state buffer/driver. The input labeled D7 will then control the logic level of the seventh bit of the data bus, and at the conclusion of the READ cycle the 6502 will read this logic level. Whenever the R/W line is low, *or* the

Table 13-1. Some Popular Buffer/Driver Integrated Circuits

74125 QUAD	DM8093 QUAD	DM8097 HEX	74LS241 OCTAL
74126 QUAD	DM8094 QUAD	74LS367 HEX	81LS97 OCTAL

Table 13-2. Typical Buffer/Driver Truth Table

Gate	Input	Output
0	0	0
0	1	1
1	X	DISABLED
X = DON'T CARE		

307

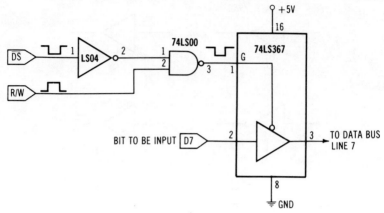

Fig. 13-2. Using Three-State Buffer/Driver to input one bit to data bus.

device select pulse is not present, then the three-state buffer/driver will be "disconnected" from the data bus, allowing other devices in the system to control this bus.

Note that the data must be stable at the input to the 74LS367 during the READ cycle. Clearly, the idea expressed in Fig. 13-2 may be extended to include the other seven lines of the data bus. Since the 74LS367 is a hex buffer/driver, two of them would be required to make an 8-bit input port. Alternatively, an octal device, such as the 81LS97, could be used to provide a single-chip 8-bit input port. An example of such an input port is given in Fig. 13-3. Note that we have changed the control signal logic slightly to illustrate that different possibilities exist, and the designer has a certain amount of freedom in this area. However, we are assuming that an $\overline{R/W}$ (inverted R/W) signal is available, and it will be if two 7404s in series are used to buffer this control line.

The circuit of Fig. 13-3 is not only useful as an input port, but it is also useful to interface some devices to the data bus. For example, on the KIM-1 we find two 74125 buffer/drivers used to interface the 6102 R/W memory chips to the data bus. Some memory chips lack the necessary drive to control the data bus, so buffer/drivers are used to provide the drive, and to isolate the memory chips from the bus when they are not being addressed. The 2114 R/W memory chips on the AIM 65 and SYM-1 have three-state data bus drivers. These on-chip buffer/drivers are capable of driving two TTL loads, and the AIM 65 and SYM-1 do not, therefore, buffer the R/W memory chips.

An important restriction on the use of the circuit in Fig. 13-3 must be observed if it is to be used as an input port. The data logic levels at the input to the 81LS97 must be stable, at least during the READ

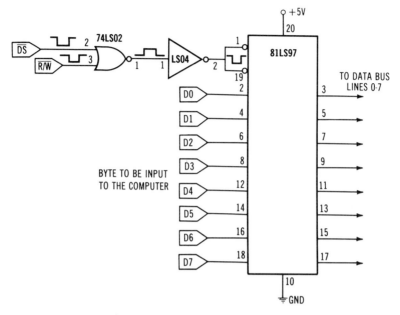

Fig. 13-3. Using 81LS97 as 8-bit Input Port.

cycle in which the port is being read, or else the 6502 will read incorrect data. In other words, an 81LS97 is not a latch. The logic
levels at the output follow the logic levels at the input anytime the
G inputs are at logic zero. A latched input port will be discussed
later in this chapter. We turn first to an application where the circuit of either Fig. 13-2 or 13-3 is suitable for reading data.

MEMORY-MAPPED ANALOG-TO-DIGITAL CONVERTER

The one-bit input port of Fig. 13-2 and the digital-to-analog converter circuit shown in Fig. 12-9 can be used to make an analog-to-
digital converter. The complete circuit is shown in Fig. 13-4. Several
parts of this circuit have already been described. For example, the
74100 latch was described in Chapter 12, Fig. 12-7. The WRITE
ENABLE pulse is generated by the circuit in Fig. 12-4. Any convenient device select pulse generated by the 74LS154 in Fig. 11-9
may be used. For the experiments, we used DS9FF0. The 74LS04
and the 74LS00 perform the same function as described in Fig. 13-2;
that is, they enable the buffer/driver on the 74LS367 during a READ
cycle. The 1408 is a digital-to-analog converter; it was described in
Fig. 12-9. Note that we have shown the data bus lines connected
directly to the 74100. Since the 74100 represents one TTL load on

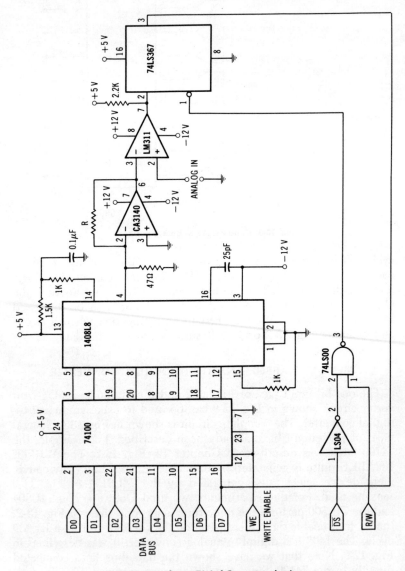

Fig. 13-4. Analog-to-Digital Converter circuit.

these lines, and there may well be other loads on the data bus in your microcomputer, it would be wise to use the buffer circuit shown in Fig. 12-10 between the data bus and the 74100. In that case, the output line from the 74LS367 1-bit input port should be connected directly to data bus line 7, and not to the input of the 74100. Now you should see that almost all of the circuit shown in Fig. 13-4 has already appeared in one form or another in previous circuit diagrams and, therefore, its complexity should not disturb you. The only new component is the LM311 voltage comparator whose significance in this circuit will now be explained.

To see how the analog-to-digital converter works, suppose that the microcomputer program starts by loading $00 into the 74100 output port that drives the 1408L8 DAC. Then the output of the CA3140 operational amplifier, which is converting the DAC current to a voltage level at pin 6 of the CA3140, should be zero. Assume also that the CA3140 feedback resistor, R, has been adjusted to give 10 volts at pin 6 when $FF is stored in the DAC port. Let the microcomputer program increment, in steps of one, the number being output to the DAC port. The voltage level at pin 6 of the CA3140 should increase from zero to ten volts in 255 steps of 39 mV/step during the incrementing process. If, after reaching $FF, the number loaded into the DAC port is incremented once more, then the voltage will suddenly drop to zero again. If this entire sequence of instructions is put into a program loop, then a ramp waveform will appear at the output of pin 6 of the CA3140. A photograph of an oscilloscope measurement of this waveform from our circuit is shown in Fig. 13-5.

Next, turn your attention to the LM311 voltage comparator. It compares the voltage at pin 3 with the voltage at pin 2. If the former is larger than the latter, then the output of the comparator, pin 7,

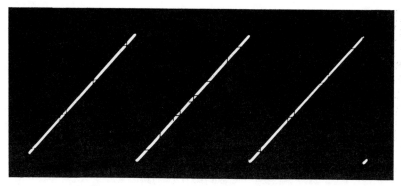

Fig. 13-5. Photograph of ramp waveform produced by DAC circuit. Sweep time is approximately 12 milliseconds, voltage rises from 0 to 10 volts.

will be at logic zero. If the voltage at pin 3 is less than the voltage at pin 2, then the output of the comparator is at logic one.

Suppose that the analog voltage at pin 2 of the comparator is 5 volts. Then, as the computer program increments the DAC output from 0 volts to 10 volts, the comparator output voltage will correspond to a logic one during that period when the DAC output is less than 5 volts. As soon as the DAC output exceeds 5 volts, the comparator output corresponds to a logic zero. Thus, by "watching" bit seven of the 1-bit input port, we can see when the comparator went from logic one to logic zero. It did this, of course, when the output of the DAC *was equal* (or slightly larger) to the analog input voltage. Fig. 13-6 is a photograph of both the DAC output and the comparator output with the program running. Observe that the comparator output drops to zero whenever the DAC output reaches a certain level.

Suppose that the DAC output was adjusted, by means of the feedback resistor (R), so that when $FF was loaded into the DAC port the voltage level at the output of the CA3140 was 2.55 volts. Further, suppose that the microcomputer program continually increments the number loaded into the DAC port. If the comparator switches from logic one to logic zero when the number loaded into the DAC port increments from $XY to $XY + 1, then the analog voltage is somewhere between $XY and $XY + 1. We, therefore, have succeeded in finding a hexadecimal representation of the analog voltage. To get a decimal representation, we must convert the hexadecimal number, $XY, to a base-ten number, and then move the decimal point two

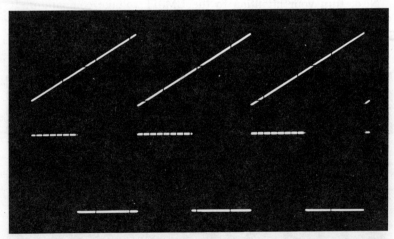

Fig. 13-6. Ramp waveform from DAC and LM311 Comparator output. Sweep time is 12 milliseconds; ramp voltage waveform (top) goes from 0 to 10 volts, while comparator output switches between 0 and 5 volts.

places to the left. Thus, $F0 corresponds to a voltage between 2.40 and 2.41 volts, and $C0 corresponds to a voltage between 1.20 and 1.21 volts.

A program to convert the analog voltage to a hexadecimal representation is presented in Example 1. We assume that the $\overline{DS9FF0}$ device select pulse is used to write to the DAC and to read the 74LS367. The 74LS367 represents the logic level of the comparator output. It will only be connected to the data bus (line seven) when the $\overline{DS}$ pulse is present and the R/W line is at logic one. Otherwise, it will be disabled. Note that the data at the output of the 74LS367 will be stable during the time when it is read because the comparator would only change its state after a new "voltage" had been output to the DAC by a new 8-bit representation from the computer. This takes only a few microseconds. Thus, there is no need to latch the data that we are going to read. Since we are only interested in the logic level of bit seven of the data bus, a BPL instruction is used to test the status of this bit.

When the program in Example 1 was run, the photograph shown in Fig. 13-7 was obtained from an oscilloscope used to measure the DAC output. Compare this photograph with the one shown in Fig. 13-6, and note that in Fig. 13-7 the ramp waveform stops as soon as the comparator switches from logic one to logic zero, indicating that the conversion has been completed. At that time, the number written to the DAC, which was also stored in the location whose address is $0000, is stored in the output Port A. If you have the I/O board used for the experiments at Port A, then the LEDs will indicate the hexa-

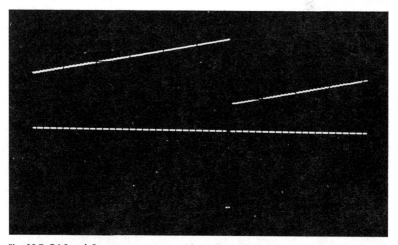

Fig. 13-7. DAC and Comparator outputs with Analog-to-Digital Converter program executing. Sweep time is 3 milliseconds, ramp waveform (top) peaks at 4 volts when comparator waveform (bottom) switches to 0 volts.

decimal number that represents the analog voltage. To generate an "unknown" analog voltage, a 10K potentiometer connected between +12 V and ground may be used, with the tap going to pin 2 of the comparator.

We were able to assemble all of the components, including the necessary decoding circuits described in Chapter 11, the control signal logic described in Chapter 12, and the components in Fig. 13-4 on a single AP Unicard, but it was a close fit. If you want a more permanent analog-to-digital converter, you might try a wire-wrap approach. Users of KIM-1 must be sure to include the circuit shown in Fig. 11-10, or they will have two devices trying to control the logic levels on the data bus simultaneously. (An oscilloscope is indispensable for getting this circuit adjusted properly. The layout, grounding, and general construction practices may affect its operation. Voltage comparators sometimes oscillate near the point where they make the transition from one logic level to the other.) More details on analog-to-digital conversions, including a much faster conversion routine, are provided in Chapter 14.

Example 1: Analog-to-Digital Conversion Program—Ramp Approximation

$0000 = DIGITL; digital representation of analog voltage
$9FF0 = DAC; output port to load the DAC and input port to test comparator
$A001 = PAD; output port to display result
$A003 = PADD; data direction register for PAD

$0200	A9 FF	START	LDA $FF	Set up data direction register.
$0202	8D 03 A0		STA PADD	
$0205	A9 00	AGAIN	LDA $00	Start generating DAC output voltage
$0207	85 00		STA DIGITL	by loading $00 into DIGITL.
$0209	A5 00	RAMP	LDA DIGITL	Get DIGITL and store it in the DAC port.
$020B	8D F0 9F		STA DAC	
$020E	AD F0 9F		LDA DAC	Test the comparator output level.
$0211	10 05		BPL DONE	If it is logic zero, conversion is finished.
$0213	E6 00		INC DIGITL	Otherwise, increment number and
$0215	4C 09 02		JMP RAMP	return to try again.
$0218	A5 00	DONE	LDA DIGITL	Now output the result to the I/O
$021A	8D 01 A0		STA PAD	port for display purposes.
$021D	4C 05 02		JMP AGAIN	Repeat the conversion process.

AN ASCII KEYBOARD INPUT PORT

One of the problems with the input port shown in Fig. 13-3 is that the data must be stable at the inputs to the port during the READ operation, and the data must be available when the computer is ready to "read" the port. In many instances, it is desirable to be able to latch a byte of data that is being input to the computer. For example, suppose two 7490 decade counters provide eight bits of counting data; at the end of a counting period we would like to store the result and then continue counting while the computer reads the byte of counting data just obtained. Clearly, using a three-state buffer/driver as an input port would not allow us to save the counting data because the outputs of the 7490s change constantly while counting.

Another example in which it is sometimes desirable to be able to latch the data byte to be input to the microcomputer is an ASCII keyboard. Many computer systems utilize a keyboard as an input device to get data or instructions from the outside world. The KIM-1 and SYM-1 systems interface with a teletypewriter keyboard with which seven bits of ASCII code are sent one bit at a time to the computer. This is called *serial input* and it is quite common. Of course, the computer is capable of reading seven bits of ASCII code in one byte. When operated in this way, the keyboard input is just another location in memory, and the mode is sometimes referred to as the *parallel* I/O mode.

To implement a parallel keyboard input port we will use the following:

- A device select pulse, $\overline{DS}$, for the memory location of the keyboard input port.
- A three-state buffer/driver connecting the keyboard to the data bus when the device select pulse occurs, but disabling it otherwise.
- A means for the keyboard to communicate with the computer; that is, the keyboard must inform the computer that a key has been depressed.
- A means to store the byte of ASCII code until the computer reads it into the accumulator.

Techniques for generating a device select pulse were described in Chapter 11. A single Intel 8212 8-bit I/O will be used. In this application the 8212 will be used for an input port. (It makes a suitable output port also, but it is more expensive than a 74100, for example.) In its input mode, the main advantages of the Intel 8212 are that it has some control-signal logic circuitry available on the chip, it has the ability to latch the input data, and it has three-state outputs that can be connected to the data bus.

The logic diagram of the 8212 is shown in Fig. 13-8. We may divide the chip circuitry into three subsystems; the control logic, including the $\overline{DS1}$, DS2, MD, STB, $\overline{CLR}$ inputs and the $\overline{INT}$ output; the eight data latches connected to the eight data inputs; and the eight three-state buffer/drivers. Consider first the control logic shown in Fig. 13-8. The $\overline{CLR}$ input will be tied to logic one to disable it, although it might be connected to the system $\overline{RES}$ line to

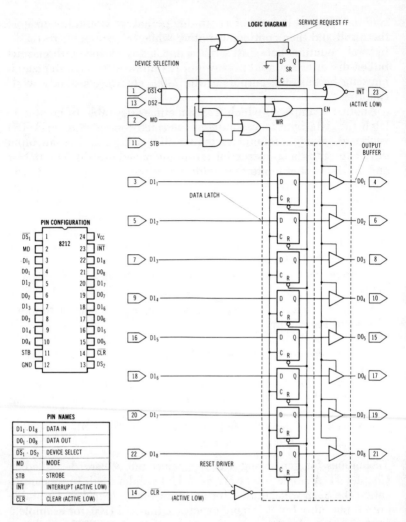

Courtesy Intel Corp.

Fig. 13-8. Logic diagram of Intel 8212 I/O Port.

bring up the inputs in a known logic-zero state. The MD input is tied to logic zero for the input mode. This step disables the top AND gate in the cluster of two AND gates and one OR gate, and it enables the lower AND gate in this same cluster. Then the STB (for strobe) line is connected directly to the C inputs of the data latches. When the STB line is at logic one, then the Q outputs of the latches follow the D inputs. When the strobe line goes to logic zero, then the data are latched; that is, they are *stored* at the Q outputs of the eight data latches. Associated with most ASCII keyboards is a strobe signal that consists of a positive pulse that occurs with each key depression and only occurs when the ASCII word is available at the parallel output of the keyboard. Many keyboards produce only a 7-bit word. Thus, a single key depression results in the ASCII data being stored in the 8212, with one bit (bit seven) left over. A 10-microsecond strobe pulse will be adequate for our purposes.

Note that the STB input is also connected to the C input on the service request flip-flop. The trailing edge of the strobe latches a logic zero into the Q output of the flip-flop because the D input of the service request flip-flop is connected to logic zero. Following the Q output of the flip-flop, we see that it is inverted, ored, and inverted again to produce a logic zero output at $\overline{\text{INT}}$ *whenever* the strobe pulse occurs. The output at the $\overline{\text{INT}}$ pin on the 8212 is used to communicate with the microcomputer, informing it that data is available. It might be used to cause an interrupt (either $\overline{\text{IRQ}}$ or $\overline{\text{NMI}}$), and the interrupt vector would point to a routine to read the keyboard with an LDA KEYBOARD instruction. Assume that KEYBOARD is a symbol for the address of the memory location of this input port.

Continuing, we note that the address of KEYBOARD appears on the address bus during the third cycle of the LDA KEYBOARD instruction. The address lines must be decoded to produce a device select pulse, $\overline{\text{DS}}$, for this address, and this device select pulse goes to pin $\overline{\text{DS1}}$ on the 8212. The R/W line is connected to the DS2 pin on the 8212. Thus, at the same time that $\overline{\text{DS1}}$ is brought to logic zero by the device select pulse, the DS2 pin is a logic one. When $\overline{\text{DS1}}$ is at logic zero *and* DS2 is at logic one, then the three-state buffers are enabled, as an examination of Fig. 13-8 will reveal. This action places the byte of data on the data bus.

Also observe that when $\overline{\text{DS1}}$ is at logic zero *and* DS2 is at logic one, then the *set* input of the service request flip-flop is at logic zero, setting it. A logic zero appears at the Q output of the service request flip-flop, clearing the interrupt request. In other words, $\overline{\text{INT}}$ goes to logic one. The data has now been read and the interrupt has been cleared, freeing the computer to go on its way until another key is depressed and the entire process is repeated.

In Fig. 13-9, we show a complete 8-bit input port utilizing the 8212. The device select pulse, $\overline{\text{DS9FFF}}$, is assumed to originate in the 74LS154 in Fig. 11-9. The R/W line comes from the 6502, while the keyboard strobe and the data originate in an ASCII encoded keyboard. Obviously there are other uses for an input port such as this, other than obtaining information from a keyboard. The data input pins might be connected to two 7490s in a decade counter configuration. A positive strobe might be generated by the same circuit

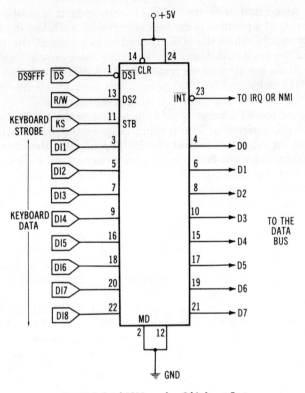

Fig. 13-9. Intel 8212 used as 8-bit Input Port.

that gates the pulses going to the first 7490 counter. When the gate closes, counting stops, a strobe occurs, and the data at the Q outputs of the 7490s is latched into the 8212. This would make a simple two-digit bcd pulse counter or timer. You can use your imagination to think of some other applications.

Let us produce the software necessary to utilize this input port. First assume that the INT is connected to the IRQ pin on the 6502. Note that the IRQ and NMI pins both require a pull-up resistor, but these are already connected on the AIM 65, KIM-1 and SYM-1 systems. The program offered in Example 2 illustrates how the input port would work in the interrupt mode. The main program is simply intended to simulate a much longer, more complex, and more useful program. The main program in Example 2 outputs the contents of the location with address $0000 to Port A, and in the experiments section of this chapter it will be used to test the input port. The main program is also an infinite loop. The interrupt routine reads the keyboard and stores the result in the location whose address is $0000.

Thus, the keyboard data is passed to the main program by using this zero-page memory location. Of course, the interrupt vector ($\overline{\text{IRQ}}$) must point to $0300 in order for the program to work. The same program could be used with $\overline{\text{INT}}$ connected to the $\overline{\text{NMI}}$ pin if the $\overline{\text{NMI}}$ interrupt vector points to $0300. The hardware in Fig. 13-9 and the software given in Example 13-2 constitute an interrupt driven keyboard.

There is another mode in which an input port may be operated without using interrupts. If the $\overline{\text{INT}}$ output is connected to the D7 input of our 1-bit port described in Fig. 13-3, then the strobe pulse will cause this input to go to logic zero. Assume another device select pulse, $\overline{\text{DS9FFE}}$, for example, is used to read this 1-bit input port. When it shows a logic zero in bit seven, then the computer knows that a key has been depressed and it should read the input port. In this case, the software is said to *poll* the keyboard. After the program

Example 2: Software for Interrupt Driven Input Port

```
$0000 = DATA
$1700 = PAD; Port A, an output port
$1701 = PADD; Port A data direction register
$17FE = IRQL; Contains $00
$17FF = IRQH; Contains $03
$9FF0 = KYBD; Keyboard input port
```

0200	A9 FF	MAIN	LDA $FF	Initialize Port A to be an output
0202	8D 01 17		STA PADD	port
0205	A5 00	LOOP	LDA DATA	Get data from address $0000.
0207	8D 00 17		STA PAD	Store it in the output port.
020A	4C 05 02		JMP LOOP	Loop here unless interrupt occurs.
0300	AD FF 9F	IRQST	LDA KYBD	Get data from keyboard input port.
0303	85 00		STA DATA	Store it at address $0000.
0305	40		RTI	Return from interrupt.

reads the input port, $\overline{\text{INT}}$ goes to logic one, indicating that the keyboard has been serviced. The software for this mode of operation is given in Example 3. Note that two distinct device select pulses are required. We have placed the polling software in a subroutine. Again, our main program is not to be taken literally. Rather, it is intended to simulate a more useful program. The subroutine INPUT stores the keyboard data in Port A. We will use this feature to test the program and the ports.

Example 3: Program to Poll Keyboard Input Port

```
$1700 = PAD; Port A, an output port
$1701 = PADD; Port A data direction register
$9FFE = POLL; Bit seven at logic zero indicates a keystroke
$9FFF = KYBD; Keyboard input port
```

0200	A9 FF	MAIN	LDA $FF	Set up data direction for Port A.
0202	8D 01 17		STA PADD	

0205	20 00 03	HERE	JSR INPUT	Jump to test if data from keyboard is ready.
0208	4C 05 02		JMP HERE	
0300	2C FE 9F	INPUT	BIT POLL	Is bit seven at logic zero?
0303	30 FB		BMI INPUT	No; loop here until it is zero.
0305	AD FF 9F		LDA KYBD	Yes; read the keyboard.
0308	8D 00 17		STA PAD	Output result to Port A.
030B	60		RTS	

EXPERIMENT NO. 1

Step 1

Connect a 74LS367 three-state buffer/driver as shown in Fig. 13-10. You can do this on a breadboard other than the AP Unicard.

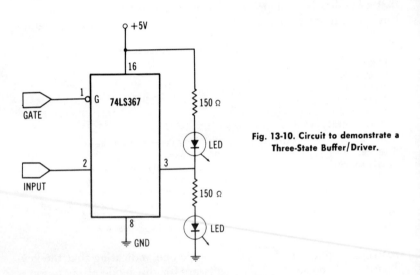

Fig. 13-10. Circuit to demonstrate a Three-State Buffer/Driver.

Step 2

Connect the gate, G, input to ground; then try connecting the input pin to logic one (+5 V) and next to logic zero (GND). What do you expect the LEDs will show?

(The top LED should glow when the input is connected to logic zero, because then current can flow from the +5-volt source through the LED and through the output pin of the 74LS367 to ground. The lower LED lights when the input is at logic one.)

Step 3

Now connect the gate, G, to logic one (+5 V) and repeat Step 2. What do you expect to observe? Refer to the truth table in Table 13-2 to explain your observations.

(Both LEDs will be lit since there is no longer a path to +5 V (through pin 3) or GND through the 74LS367.)

EXPERIMENT NO. 2

Step 1

In this experiment we will construct a 1-bit input port on the AP Unicard. The control-logic circuit will be similar to the one shown in Fig. 13-3. However, since the board is becoming crowded we will use a slightly modified version shown in Fig. 13-11. Note that the 74LS00 NAND gate is used as an inverter. Connect this circuit. The 74LS02 and 74LS00 are already on the breadboard.

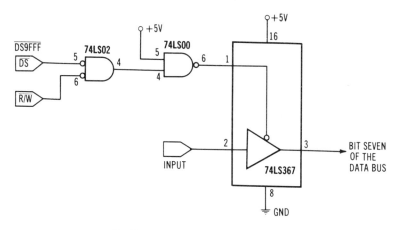

Fig. 13-11. One-Bit (Bit Seven) Input Port.

Step 2

Test the input port to see if it works. Connect the input (pin 2) of the 74LS367 to logic zero. Then load and execute the following program.

```
0200  2C FF 9F    START    BIT  PORT    Test bit seven of the input port.
0203  10 FB                BPL  START   If bit seven = zero, branch back.
0205  00                   BRK
```

What do you expect to observe?

(If bit seven is at logic zero, then the program should stay in the loop. Otherwise, it will exit the loop and jump to the monitor, lighting the display.)

Step 3

While the program is running, change the input pin from logic zero to logic one. What do you observe?

(You should observe that the program jumps to the monitor as soon as the input pin is lifted from its ground connection.)

Step 4

With the input pin connected to logic one, load and execute the same program as in Step 2, but with the BPL instruction replaced by a BMI instruction (op code $30). Describe and explain your results.

EXPERIMENT NO. 3

Step 1

Breadboard the analog-to-digital converter circuit of Fig. 13-4. Use the 1-bit input port constructed in the previous experiment; that is, connect the output of the LM311 comparator to the input of the 74LS367, and connect the output of the 74LS367 to bit seven of the data bus.

Step 2

Connect a 10K potentiometer between +12 V and ground, with the wiper of the potentiometer going to the analog input (pin 2) of the comparator.

Step 3

Write, load, and execute a short program to load $FF into the DAC output port, address $9FF0. Adjust the feedback resistor on the CA3140 to give about 10 V output at pin 6. Adjust the potentiometer to produce about 5 V at the pin 2 input of the comparator. What logic level should you measure with your voltmeter on the output of the comparator?

(You should measure a logic zero (zero voltage) since the output of the CA3140 exceeds the analog input to the comparator.)

Step 4

With the same program load $00 into the DAC output port. A simple program of the form:

```
LDA $00
STA DAC
BRK
```

will work. Now measure the output of the LM311 comparator. What do you expect to read?

(Your voltmeter should read +5 V because the output from the CA3140 is less than the potentiometer input to the comparator. Do not proceed to the next parts of this experiment unless your experiments this far have been successful.)

Step 5

Load and execute the following program:

```
0200   A5 00      START   LDA DIGIT
0202   8D F0 9F            STA DAC
0205   E6 00              INC DIGIT
0207   4C 00 02           JMP START
```

What do you suppose is the output of the CA3140?

(It should be a ramp waveform, since the input to the DAC is continually being incremented. If you have an oscilloscope, connect it to the output of the CA3140 (pin 6) and observe this waveform. A photograph of our results is shown in Fig. 13-5.)

Step 6

Connect the oscilloscope to pin 7 of the comparator. Describe and explain what you observe. Compare it with the photograph in Fig. 13-6.

EXPERIMENT NO. 4

Step 1

In this experiment, we will make some final tests of the analog-to-digital circuit. With the same circuit used in Experiment No. 3, load and execute the program given in Example 1. Connect the I/O board to the application connector.

Step 2

With the program running, reduce the potentiometer setting until the voltage at pin 2 of the LM311 voltage comparator is zero. If you cannot make this voltage zero with the potentiometer, connect pin 2 directly to ground. The LEDs at Port A should all be out, although in certain cases the op amp might have some offset voltage that will cause a one or a two to appear at Port A.

Step 3

Increase the potentiometer setting. What happens to the LEDs at Port A?

(You should observe that as the potentiometer setting is increased the number represented by the glowing LEDs at Port A increases. It should be possible to increase the potentiometer until $FF appears on the Port A LEDs. You have now successfully completed the A/D converter. Congratulations! The proportionality between the analog voltage level and the digital number is determined by the feedback resistor, R, in the operational amplifier circuit. For a much faster conversion scheme, refer to Chapter 14.)

EXPERIMENT NO. 5

Step 1

In this experiment we will test the 8212 I/O chip. There will be no room on the AP Unicard, if you have built the DAC and the A/D converter on this board. If you do not want to dismantle that circuit, you will need another breadboard. In any case, you will need the device select circuitry of Fig. 11-9. Connect the $\overline{\text{DS9FFF}}$ device select pulse to the $\overline{\text{DS1}}$ pin of the 8212 and connect the R/W line to DS2. Connect the output pins of the 8212 to the data bus, using the expansion connector as before. Connect the $\overline{\text{IRQ}}$ pin on the expansion connector to the $\overline{\text{INT}}$ pin on the 8212.

Step 2

Breadboard the circuit of Fig. 9-9. It is used to produce a strobe pulse. Instead of connecting the $\overline{\text{Q}}$ output of the 74121 to the $\overline{\text{IRQ}}$ line, connect the Q output (pin 6) to the strobe input of the 8212.

Step 3

With suitable jumper wires, connect the DI inputs of the 8212 to either +5 V or ground, producing logic one or logic zero signals, respectively.

Step 4

Load and execute the following program:

0200	A9 FF	MAIN	LDA $FF	Initialize Port A to be an output
0202	8D 01 17		STA PADD	port.
0205	A5 00	LOOP	LDA DATA	Get data from address $0000.
0207	8D 00 17		STA PAD	Store it in the output port.
020A	4C 05 02		JMP LOOP	Loop here unless interrupt occurs.
0300	AD FF 9F	IRQST	LDA KYBD	Get data from keyboard input port.
0305	40		RTI	Return from interrupt.

What do the Port A LEDs indicate?

(They should show whatever random data happened to be at address $0000.)

Step 5

Note the logic levels you have set up at the inputs to the 8212; then strobe the 8212 with the circuit of Fig. 9-9. What do you observe at the Port A LEDs?

(You should observe that they show the same logic levels as you input to the 8212. If they do not, check your interrupt vector and try again.)

Step 6

Now change the inputs to the 8212 by connecting some to +5 V and some to ground. What do you observe at the Port A LEDs?

(You should observe no change at these LEDs because the data has not yet been strobed into the outputs, nor has the 8212 been read.)

Step 7

Strobe the 8212 and observe that the Port A LEDs indicate the same data as are found at the inputs on the 8212.

Step 8

Design your own experiment to test the polled-service routine described in Example 3.

CHAPTER 14

Applications

INTRODUCTION

In this chapter we have collected several articles, already published or in press, that will give you an idea of what a finished microcomputer project is. Of course, the projects described represent only a small sample of the possibilities, and the projects would generally be regarded as "minimal" designs. That is, much more elaborate and sophisticated instruments and programs are possible. The articles also reflect the author's interests.

Two important sources of information for 6502 software and hardware are:

- *MICRO*—Published monthly by The Computerist, Inc., P.O. Box 3, S. Chelmsford, MA 01824.
- *Compute*—P.O. Box 5119, Greensboro, NC 27403.

These two journals are devoted to 6502-based systems. Of course, articles about 6502-based designs are often published in other journals as well.

Although the application programs described in this chapter were written for the KIM-1, they may be easily converted to run on other microcomputers once you understand both the basic elements of programming and the features of your microcomputer. We begin by giving a brief description of each application; the articles then follow to complete the chapter.

- "Digital-to-Analog and Analog-to-Digital Conversion Using the KIM-1." This article first appeared in *MICRO*, December 1977-January 1978, page 11. It is reprinted with permission. The article gives several experiments with the Motorola 1408L8 digital-to-analog converter. It also describes a storage scope application. The storage scope program and interface have been corrected and improved by including suggestions made in the article "Storage Scope Revisited," by Joseph L. Powlette and Donald C. Jeffery in the December 1978-January 1979 issue of *MICRO*.

- "Employing the KIM-1 Microcomputer as a Timer and Data Logging Module." This article first appeared in *MICRO*, February-March 1978, page 3. It shows how to measure the times at which a series of events occur, and how to store the times of the events for later display.
- "Employing the KIM-1 as a Precision Keyer and Automatic Message Sender." This article is to appear in *73 Magazine*. The article is of particular interest to amateur radio operators. Code speed is controlled digitally, and the program has the ability to send three standard code messages automatically.
- "Catching Bugs With Lights—A Program Debugging Aid." *Kilobaud Microcomputing* intends to publish this article. Some of the interfacing techniques introduced in the last few chapters of this book are used to display the contents of the various registers of the 6502.
- "Lunar Occultation of a Star." This program was written by Dr. Thomas D. Strickler, Jesse Maupin, and John Drake of Berea College. A technique to measure the precise time at which an analog voltage is changing is described. Although they were interested in timing occultations of stars by the moon, the techniques are applicable to a number of scientific problems, so the article is included.

DIGITAL-ANALOG AND ANALOG-DIGITAL CONVERSION USING THE KIM-1*

A Motorola 1408L8 8-bit digital-to-analog converter is connected as shown in Fig. 14-1. (The 1408L8 is available from James Electronics, 1021 Howard Ave., San Carlos, CA 94070, as are the op amps used in these experiments.) The PAD port of the KIM-1 is used to provide the digital input to the 1408L8. The analog output of the 1408L8 is a current sink at pin 4, which we converted to a voltage by means of the RCA CA3140 operational amplifier. The feedback resistor R is adjusted to give the desired voltage output. For example, a value of about 6500 ohms for this resistor results in a voltage range from 0 volts when PAD is 0000 0000 to 10 volts when PAD is 1111 1111.

---

*Copyright © 1977, The Computerist, Inc., All rights reserved.

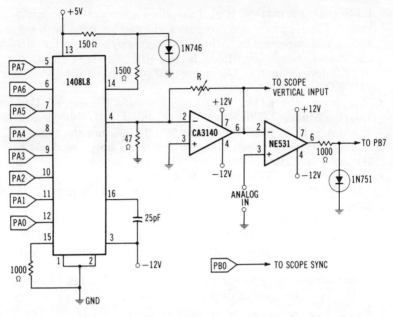

Fig. 14-1. Circuit diagram for Digital-to-Analog Converter and Analog-to-Digital Converter. See text for values of R; 1N746 is 3.3 V zener diode and 1N751 is 5.1 V zener diode.

For the first experiment do not connect the second op amp; simply connect the output of the first op amp to an oscilloscope as shown. Load the program given in Example 1.

Example 1: Program to Generate a Ramp Voltage Waveform

0300	A9 FF	START	LDA $FF	255 in accumulator.
0302	8D 01 17		STA PADD	Port A is the output port.
0305	EE 00 17	BACK	INC PAD	Increment number in PAD.
0308	4C 05 03		JMP BACK	Increment in a loop.

Running this program should cause a ramp waveform to be observed on the oscilloscope screen. A close examination of the ramp will show that it consists of $2^8 = 256$ steps, rather than a straight line.

Next, connect the 531 op amp. It acts as a comparator. It compares the voltage from the output of the first op amp (which we shall call the digital signal) with a voltage from some source to be applied to pin 3 (which we shall call the analog signal). The output of the 531 is connected to PB7 on the KIM. If PB7 = 1, the analog signal is greater than the digital signal. If PB7 = 0, the analog signal is less than the digital signal. The digital signal is, of course, produced by the contents of PAD.

A flowchart showing what we intend to do is shown in Fig. 14-2, and the corresponding program is given in Example 2. Output port

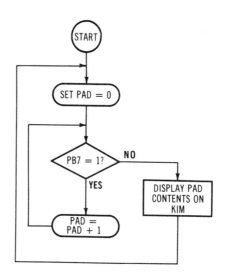

Fig. 14-2. Flowchart for Analog-to-Digital Converter: Ramp Approximation.

PAD is set to zero. If the analog signal is positive, then PB7 = 1. PAD is now incremented until the comparator indicates that the analog signal is less than the digital signal, i.e., PB7 = 0. At that instant, the digital and analog signals are the same to within one bit, the least significant bit, in PAD. The contents of PAD are then displayed and the cycle continues.

If the feedback resistor is adjusted so that a value of $PAD = 255_{10}$ = $\$FF_{16}$ produces a voltage of 2.55 volts, then we have constructed a simple digital voltmeter with a full-scale reading (in hex) of 2.55 volts. A simple program to convert from hex to base ten would make the meter easier to read.

The ramp approximation is quite slow, and there is a faster technique known as "successive approximation." It works as follows: the most significant bit in the DAC is set to one, and all the others are set to zero. If the comparator indicates that the analog signal is greater than the digital signal, then the highest bit is made zero, and

Example 2: Program for Analog-to-Digital Converter (Ramp Approximation)

0300	A9 FF	START	LDA $FF	255 in accumulator.
0302	8D 01 17		STA PADD	Make Port A an output port.
0305	A2 00	AGN	LDX $00	Start PAD at zero.
0307	8E 00 17	RAMP	STX PAD	Output value of X register.
030A	AD 02 17		LDA PBD	Read Port B.
030D	10 04		BPL DISP	Branch if bit 7 = 0.
030F	E8		INX	Increment X register.
0310	4C 07 03		JMP RAMP	Continue loop.
0313	86 F9	DISP	STX INH	Put X into display register.
0315	20 1F 1F		JSR SCANDS	Use KIM-1 display subroutine
0318	4C 05 03		JMP AGN	and start again at zero.

the next lower bit is set to one and the test is repeated. This iterative process is repeated until all eight bits have been tested, starting with the MSB and ending with the LSB. The flowchart shown in Fig. 14-3 indicates how this will be accomplished.

This analog-to-digital conversion scheme will be used in a program which digitizes 256 points on a waveform and then stores the results, to be displayed on an oscilloscope at a convenient time and with as many repetitions as desired. This program is useful for examining slow waveforms with an oscilloscope with a low persistence screen, for example, ECG waveforms, and it is useful for examining non-periodic waveforms, such as a one-shot impulse from an accelerometer. The program has triggering built in, and the output scan portion synchronizes the oscilloscope with a SYNC signal, turning an inexpensive scope into something more useful. Flowcharts for the storage scope program are presented in Figs. 14-4 and 14-5.

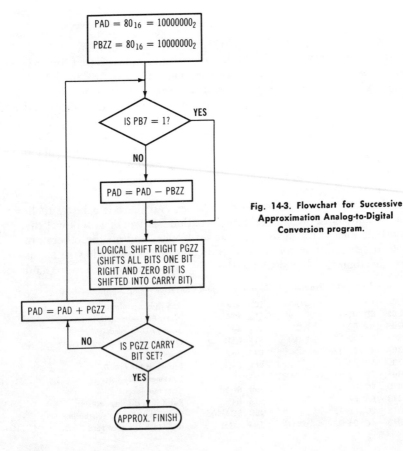

Fig. 14-3. Flowchart for Successive Approximation Analog-to-Digital Conversion program.

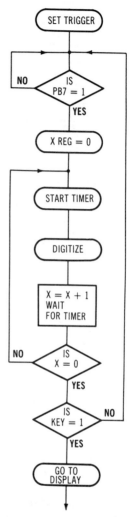

Fig. 14-4. Flowchart for Storage
Scope Program.

A short description of the behavior of the circuit and program follows. The experimenter chooses the desired trigger level and loads this into location $0306. When the analog signal is greater than this, the comparator makes PB7 go high and the scan begins. The sampling rate and the scan time are determined by the number loaded into the timer and the timer used, locations $0314 and $0316, respectively. It takes about 300 microseconds to digitize, so there is no point in choosing time intervals smaller than this. The X register is used as an index to identify each of the 256 points on the scan. After

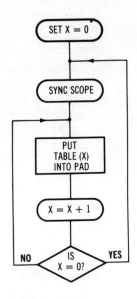

SET X = 0

SYNC SCOPE

PUT
TABLE (X)
INTO PAD

X = X + 1

NO — IS X = 0? — YES

Fig. 14-5. Flowchart for Waveform
Display program.

the timer is started, the analog signal is digitized and the timer is watched until it is finished. The X is then incremented and a new point is digitized until all 256 points are finished and stored in TABLE,X.

The X is then zero again. This entire process will repeat unless the "1" key is depressed, in which case the program displays the data on the oscilloscope, connected as before to the output of the first op amp. The display will repeat, complete with a SYNC signal output from PB0, until the program is halted. In our case we loaded the vector $17FA and $17FB with the starting address of the program ($0300) so a depression of the ST key caused the entire program to start over.

A listing of the program is shown in Example 3. Notice that the data is stored in TABLE,X located in page two of memory, PGZZ is at location $0000, the trigger level is in $0306, and the scan time variable is in $0314 and $0316. The scan time should not be shorter than 300 microseconds. As far as display is concerned, we found that a sweep rate of 200 to 500 microseconds per cm gave good results. Two photographs, showing the results obtained by converting two 14-Hz waveforms to digital levels and then displaying them on an oscilloscope with the storage scope program, are shown in Figs. 14-6A and B.

A few other comments may be in order. First, most of the ideas for this project were obtained in a KIM workshop offered by Dr. Robert Tinker. The software implementation is the author's work.

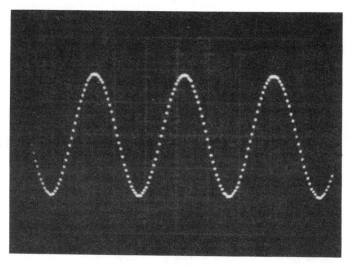

(A) Sine Wave.

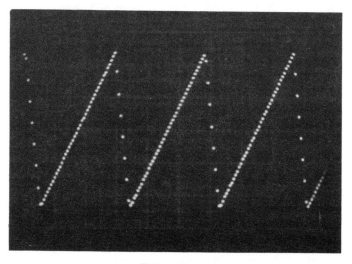

(B) Ramp Wave.

Fig. 14-6. Storage Scope reconstruction of 14-Hz Sine and Ramp Waveforms. Photographs made by Joseph L. Powlette and Donald C. Jeffery of Moravian College.

There are some obvious improvements, such as a sample-and-hold device between the analog source and the comparator or a faster approximation routine. These improvements are left for the reader to implement. Fast A/D converter circuits can be difficult to adjust.

I am indebted to Joseph L. Powlette and Donald C. Jeffery[1] of Moravian College for pointing out the necessity for the high-speed 531 op amp, and for providing the photographs.

Example 3: Program for Storage Scope

0300	A9 FF		BEGIN	LDA $FF	Initialize Port A to be an output port.
0302	8D 01 17			STA PADD	
0305	A9 10		START	LDA TSET	Trigger voltage set.
0307	8D 00 17			STA PAD	
030A	A2 00			LDX $00	Initialize X register.
030C	EA			NOP	
030D	EA			NOP	
030E	AD 02 17		TRIG	LDA PBD	Test PB7 for trigger level.
0311	10 FB			BPL TRIG	Wait if PB7 = 0.
0313	A9 C0		STIME	LDA $C0	Set scan time here.
0315	8D 05 17			STA TIMER	Select interval timer.
0318	A9 80			LDA $80	Start digitize sequence.
031A	85 00			STA PGZZ	Store initial value.
031C	8D 00 17		TEST	STA PAD	Output value.
031F	AC 02 17			LDY PBD	Test PB7.
0322	30 03			BMI FWRD	Branch if PB7 = 1.
0324	38			SEC	Clear borrow flag.
0325	E5 00			SBC PGZZ	Subtract bit seven.
0327	46 00		FWRD	LSR PGZZ	Set PGZZ for next lower bit.
0329	B0 05			BCS OUT	Out of digitize loop if finished.
032B	65 00			ADC PGZZ	Set next lower bit = 1.
032D	4C 1C 03			JMP TEST	Return to test all lower bits.
0330	8D 00 17		OUT	STA PAD	Final approximation in PAD
0333	9D 00 02			STA TABLE,X	and in TABLE(X) in page 2.
0336	E8			INX	Bump table index.
0337	F0 08			BEQ DISPLY	Go to display if table is complete.
0339	AD 07 17		CHEK	LDA TCHEK	Test if timer is finished.
033C	10 FB			BPL CHEK	If not, wait in loop.
033E	4C 13 03			JMP STIME	Digitize another point.
0341	20 6A 1F		DISPLY	JSR GETKEY	Is key "1" depressed?
0344	C9 01			CMP $01	
0346	F0 03			BEQ SYNC	Yes. Display the data.
0348	4C 05 03			JMP START	No. Return to start.
034B	A9 01		SYNC	LDA $01	Set up PB0 as SYNC output pin.
034D	8D 03 17			STA PBDD	
0350	A2 00			LDX $00	Initialize X to display table.
0352	AD 02 17		RPT	LDA PBD	Toggle PB0 for SYNC.
0355	49 01			EOR $01	Signal to scope.
0357	8D 02 17			STA PBD	
035A	BD 00 02		SCAN	LDA TABLE,X	Output TABLE(X) for
035D	8D 00 17			STA PAD	display on scope.
0360	E8			INX	Increment X register.
0361	D0 F7			BNE SCAN	Continue until all points are out,
0363	4C 52 03			JMP RPT	then repeat.

---

[1]"Storage Scope Revisited," Powlette, Joseph L., and Jeffery, Donald C., *MICRO*, December 1978-January 1979, p. 29.

EMPLOYING THE KIM-1 MICROCOMPUTER AS A
TIMER AND DATA LOGGING MODULE*

The interval timers on the 6530 on the KIM-1 microcomputer provide a convenient way to measure the time between two or more events. Such events might include the start and end of a race, the exit of a bullet from a gun and its arrival at a measured distance along its trajectory, the interruption of light to a series of phototransistors placed along the path of a falling object, an animal arriving at a feeding station, cosmic rays striking a detector, etc. Some of these measurements will be described in more detail below. Each event must produce a negative pulse that the microcomputer detects. The microcomputer also records the time at which the event occurred. The time is stored in memory, and later it may be displayed on the six-digit KIM-1 display.

The data logging, timer, and display programs are listed in Examples 4, 5, and 6, respectively. The programs must be used together for the applications described in this article, but each might be used with other applications, for example, pulse generators, Geiger counters, temperature logging, etc. The events to be timed must produce either a one-shot pulse (positive-zero-positive) whose duration is at least 50 microseconds, or a zero-to-positive transition which must be reset to zero before the next event. These signals are applied to pin PA0 accessed on the KIM-1 applications connector. The programs may be easily modified to detect positive pulses.

The first pulse starts the timer which continues to operate on an interrupt basis. The time at which the first pulse occurs is not recorded by the data logging program since it corresponds to $t = 0$. Successive pulses cause the data logging program to store the six-digit time counter in memory. The number of events (not counting the first event), N, to be timed must be stored in location $0003. Remember to convert the number of events, N, to base 16 before entering it in memory. As the program is written, N must be less than $75 = $4B$.

The function of the timer program is to load the interval timer, increment the six-digit time counter, and return to the data logging program. At the end of each timing period the timer causes an interrupt to occur (pin PB7 on the application connector must be connected to pin 4 on the expansion connector), the computer jumps to the timer program, does its thing, and returns to the main data logging program to wait for events.

Table 14-1 lists several timing intervals which are possible and the numbers which must be loaded into the various timers to produce

---

Table 14-1. Timing Intervals for Example 4

Time Interval	Value	Address	Measured Interval	% Error
100 microsec	49	170C	99.98 microsec	0.02%
1 millisec	7A	170D	0.9998 millisec	0.02%
10 millisec	9C	170E	10.007 millisec	0.07%
100 millisec	62	170F	100.5 millisec	0.5%

the given interval. For example, if one wishes to measure time in units of 100 microseconds, then $49 must be stored in the divide-by-one counter whose address is $170C. In this case. the numbers which appear on the display during the display portion of the program represent the number of 100 microsecond intervals between the first event and the event whose time is being displayed To put it another way, multiply the number on the display by 0.0001 to get the time in seconds. The other possibilities listed in the table are treated in the same way.

When all N events have been logged, the program automatically jumps to the display program. When one is ready to record the data, key "1" on the keyboard is depressed. The time of each event, excepting the first which occurred at $t = 0$, is displayed on the six-digit readout for several seconds before the display moves to the time of the next event. This gives the experimenter time to record the data on paper. If more time is required, increase the value of the number stored in location $0289.

Example 5 also lists the measured time interval and gives the percent error between the stated interval (say 100 microseconds) and the actual measured interval (99.98 microseconds). The measurements were made by connecting a frequency counter (PASCO Scientific Model 8015) to pin PB7 while the program was running and after the first event had started the timer. If greater accuracy is required for the 10-millisecond and 100-millisecond intervals, then experiment with putting NOP instructions between the PHA instruction and the LDA TIME instruction in the timer program.

The simplest application for the program is a simple stopwatch with memory. Any suitably debounced switch can be used. See pages 213 and 280 in *CMOS Cookbook* by Don Lancaster, published by Howard W. Sams & Co., Inc., 4300 West 62nd Street, Indianapolis, Indiana 46268 for several suitable switching circuits. The circuit of our Fig. 9-9 may also be used to construct a stopwatch.

Being a physics teacher, I originally designed the program to collect data for an "acceleration of gravity" experiment in the introductory physics lab. The technique may be applicable to other problems, so it is described herein. Nine phototransistors (Fairchild FPT 100 available from Radio Shack) were mounted on a meter stick at

10-cm intervals. Two incandescent (do not try fluorescent lighting) 150-watt flood lamps provided the illumination. The interface circuit is shown in Fig. 14-7.

The 555 timer serves as a Schmitt trigger and buffer which produces a negative pulse when an object passes between the light and the phototransistor. The 500K potentiometer is adjusted so that an interruption of the light to any of the phototransistors increases the voltage at pin 2 of the 555 from about 1.5 volts to at least 3.5 volts; this is a very simple adjustment that should be made with a vtvm or other high impedance meter, not a vom.

In the case of a simple pendulum, the relationship between the period and the amplitude can be investigated by allowing the pendulum to "run down" while logging the times when the bob interrupts the light to a single phototransistor. With only one phototransistor the timer-data logging program can also be used as a tachometer, if a rotating system of some kind is involved.

Lancaster, in the *CMOS Cookbook*, describes a tracking photocell pickoff which could be used in conjunction with the program for outdoor races and other sporting events. See page 346 in the "Cookbook." A simple light-beam–phototransistor system could be placed in a cage, and the apparatus would record the times at which an animal interrupted the beam, giving a measurement of animal activity.

If you want to measure the muzzle velocity of your rifle or handgun, you will have to be more creative. First, I would modify the

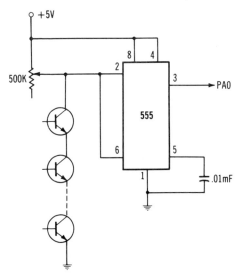

Fig. 14-7. Interface circuit for Timer-Data Logging program. Up to ten phototransistors (FPT-100) may be connected in series as indicated by dashed line.

program so that one pin, say PA0, is used to start the timing while another pin, say PB0, is used to stop the timing. This can be accomplished by changing the instructions at addresses $0226 and $022D in Example 4 from AD 00 17 to AD 02 17. Then I would use a fine wire foil to hold the clock input of a 7474 flip-flop low until the wire foil was broken by the exit of the bullet from the gun. The Q output going high would start the timing, so it would be connected to PA0. To end the timing, one could use a microphone to detect a bullet hitting the backstop. Of course, the microphone signal would have to to be amplified and used to clock the other flip-flop on the 7474 to signal the second event. Another approach would have the arriving bullet smash two pieces of aluminum foil together, closing a switch. The distance between start and stop should be at least 10 feet. Please be extremely careful with all muzzle velocity measurements.

Example 4: Data Logging Program

```
$0000 = LOW
$0001 = MID
$0002 = HIGH
$0003 = N
$0053 = LO
$0053 = MI
$00A3 = HI
$00F9 = INH
$00FA = POINTL
$00FB = POINTH
$0271 = KEY
$1700 = PAD
$1F6A = GETKEY
$1F1F = SCANDS
```

0200	78		INITIAL	SEI	Disable interrupt.
0201	F8			SED	Set decimal mode for addition.
0202	A2	00		LDX $00	Set X register to zero.
0204	A9	50		LDA $50	Locate interrupt vector $0250 at
0206	8D	FE	17	STA 17FE	addresses $17FE and $17FF.
0209	A9	02		LDA $02	
020B	8D	FF	17	STA 17FF	
020E	A9	99		LDA 99	Clear counter by storing 99
0210	85	00		STA LOW	in the three two-digit memory
0212	85	01		STA MID	locations of the counter.
0214	85	02		STA HIGH	
0216	AD	00	17	START	LDA PAD	Read input pin PA0.
0219	29	01		AND $01	Logical AND with input pin.
021B	D0	F9*		BNE START	If pin is 1, loop to START; if 0, continue.
021D	AD	00	17	FLIP	LDA PAD	Read input pin again.
0220	29	01		AND $01	Logical AND with input pin.
0222	F0	F9*		BEQ FLIP	If pin is 0, loop to FLIP.
0224	58	18		CLI CLC	Enable interrupt, go to interrupt
0226	00	EA		BRK NOP	to start timer, then return.

0228	AD 00 17	CHEK1	LDA	PAD	These instructions are the same
022B	29 01		AND	$01	as the START and FLIP sequence.
022D	D0 F9*		BNE	CHEK1	They sense a logic 0 to logic 1
022F	AD 00 17	CHEK2	LDA	PAD	transition at pin PA0 on the
0232	29 01		AND	$01	application connector.
0234	F0 F9*		BEQ	CHEK2	
0236	E8		INX		Increment X for each point.
0237	A5 00		LDA	LOW	Counter contents are stored in
0239	95 03		STA	LO,X	a sequence of locations indexed
023B	A5 01		LDA	MID	by the X register.
023D	95 53		STA	MI,X	
023F	A5 02		LDA	HIGH	
0241	95 A3		STA	HI,X	
0243	E4 03		CPX	N	Compare X to N. Return to CHEK1
0245	D0 E1		BNE	CHEK1	if X is less than N. Otherwise,
0247	78	DISPLAY	SEI		go to DISPLAY; disable interrupt.
0248	4C 71 02		JMP	KEY	Jump to display program at $0271

*To trigger on negative transitions change D0 instructions to F0 instructions and vice versa in the asterisked statements.

Example 5: Timer Program

$0049 = TIME
$170C = TIMEX
$0000 = LOW
$0001 = MID
$0002 = HIGH

0250	48	INTRPT	PHA		Push accumulator on stack.
0251	A9 49		LDA	TIME	Start timer for 49_{16} cycles.
0253	8D 0C 17		STA	TIMEX	
0256	A9 01		LDA	$01	Increment counter by adding 1
0258	65 00		ADC	LOW	to the two low digits;
025A	85 00		STA	LOW	and store result.
025C	A9 00		LDA	$00	Add carry from previous
025E	65 01		ADC	MID	addition to mid digits. If
0260	85 01		STA	MID	carry occurs from the two mid
0262	A9 00		LDA	$00	digits, then add this to the
0264	65 02		ADC	HIGH	two high digits.
0266	85 02		STA	HIGH	
0268	68		PLA		Pull accumulator from stack.
0269	40		RTI		Return to data logger.

Example 6: Display Program

$0003 = N
$0003 = LO
$0053 = MI
$00A3 = HI
$00F9 = INH
$00FA = POINTL
$00FB = POINTH
$0200 = INIT
$1707 = TIME
$1F6A = GETKEY
$1F1F = SCANDS

0271	20 6A 1F	KEY	JSR	GETKEY	Jump to KIM-1 keyboard monitor.
0274	C9 01		CMP	$01	Test valid input.
0276	D0 F9		BNE	KEY	If not, wait for input.
0278	A2 01		LDX	$01	Initialize X register to index
027A	B5 03	NXPNT	LDA	LO	data points.
027C	85 F9		STA	INH	Put in KIM-1 display registers.
027E	B5 53		LDA	MI	
0280	85 FA		STA	POINTL	
0282	B5 A3		LDA	HI	
0284	85 FB		STA	POINTH	
0286	8A		TXA		Save X while in subroutine by
0287	48		PHA		pushing it on the stack.
0288	A0 10		LDY	$10	Time to display each point.
028A	98	AGN	TYA		Save Y while in subroutine by
028B	48		PHA		pushing it on the stack.
028C	A9 FF		LDA	$FF	
028E	8D 07 17		STA	TIME	
0291	20 1F 1F	REPEAT	JSR	SCANDS	SCANDS is KIM-1 routine which
0294	AD 07 17		LDA	TIME	displays data in $00F9, $00FA,
0297	30 03		BMI	OVER	and $00FB. Repeated jumps to
0299	4C 91 02		JMP	REPEAT	SCANDS produce a constant display.
029C	68	OVER	PLA		Restore Y register.
029D	A8		TAY		
029E	88		DEY		Decrement Y by 1 and repeat
029F	F0 03		BEQ	HOP	display until Y = 0.
02A1	4C 8A 02		JMP	AGN	
02A4	68	HOP	PLA		Restore X register.
02A5	AA		TAX		
02A6	E4 03		CPX	N	Compare X with N. If X is less
02A8	F0 04		BEQ	BEGIN	than N increment X and display
02AA	E8		INX		next point. Otherwise, return
02AB	4C 7A 02		JMP	NXPNT	to the beginning.
02AE	4C 00 02	BEGIN	JMP	INIT	

EMPLOYING THE KIM-1 AS A PRECISION KEYER AND AUTOMATIC MESSAGE SENDER*

The short application program listed in Example 7 allows the KIM-1 to send any of three messages by pressing one of three keys, A, B, or C, on the KIM-1 keyboard, and with the interface circuit shown in Fig. 14-8 the KIM-1 becomes an electronic keyer as well. Any microcomputer with a 650X microprocessor and one of the MOS Technology PIA or VIA chips may be used with only minor modifications to the program. An important feature of the program is the ability to precisely set the code speed between 5 and 99 words per minute by entering the speed, in decimal, at storage location $0000 in memory. The program converts this decimal number to hexadecimal, then does a division routine to convert the speed to a

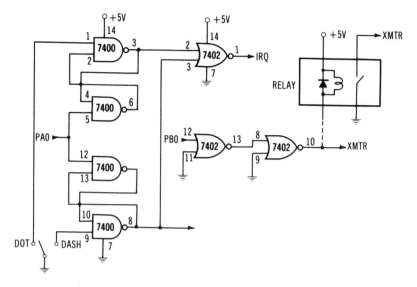

Fig. 14-8. Interface circuit for Keyer and Message Sender. Some transmitters may require optional relay for keying, with 1N914 diode across coil for protection against voltage transients. All grounds should be same as KIM-1 ground.

time duration of the basic dot element, and the interval timers on the 6530 PIA do the rest.

Anyone who does much contest operating will realize how useful an automatic message sender is. Even the casual cw operator can use it for sending CQ or other routine messages. Code tests for novices can be programmed and sent at precisely 5 wpm by storing the entire test in memory. At 5 wpm at least five minutes of code may be sent. For field day (1977) we used a similar program to send CQ CQ CQ FD DE KØEI KØEI K as message A; then when a station responded we sent _____ DE KØEI UR 599 MO 599 MO K where the blank was the call of the station to be keyed by the operator, after which he hit key B to give the remainder of the message. It worked very smoothly with no discernible pause between the call letters and the message. (Don't try to look up the score because K0EI was not the call we used.) The operation of the keyer is exactly like most electronic keyers; holding the paddle in the dot position will cause a series of dots and spaces to be sent. Dashes occur with the paddle in the dash position, and the timing of all the characters is controlled by the program and the crystal on the microcomputer.

Assuming the program has been loaded and the interface circuit connected, operation proceeds as follows. The code speed at which you wish to operate is loaded into storage location $0000. Any decimal number from 05 to 99 may be put into this location. Next the starting and ending addresses of each message must be loaded into memory. Since all three messages are in page two of memory, only the low-order bytes of the starting and ending addresses need be given. Suppose message A starts at $0200 and ends at $0251, message B starts at $0252 and ends at $0265, while message C starts at $0278 and ends at $02FF. Then one would load $00, the starting address of message A, at location $0001; $52, the starting address of message B goes in at $0002; and $78 is entered at $0003. The respective ending addresses go into memory locations $0004 to $0006; that is, $51 goes into $0004, $65 goes into $0005, and $FF goes into $0006.

How do you load the messages themselves? For each character you want to send you must load the corresponding hex number shown in Table 14-2. Suppose message A is to be "DE K0EI K," and is to start at $0200. Then you load the hex numbers $90, $40, $00, $B0, $FC, $40 $20, $00, $B0 from locations $0200 through $0208; $00 goes into $0001 and $08 goes into $0004.

Probably the best way to proceed is to first load the three messages including spaces, noting the starting and ending addresses of each message on a piece of paper. Then go back to page zero and put the starting and ending addresses in their proper locations (Table 14-3). Go to location $0300 and hit the go button to start the program running. Test to make sure everything is working before you put it on the air.

Table 14-2. Morse Character to Hex Conversion Table

Morse Character	Hex	Morse Character	Hex	Morse Character	Hex
A	60	S	10	Word space	00
B	88	T	C0	S̅K̅	16
C	A8	U	30	B̅T̅	8C
D	90	V	18	A̅R̅	54
E	40	W	70	/	94
F	28	X	98	.	56
G	D0	Y	D8	,	CE
H	08	Z	C8	?	32
I	20	1	7C		
J	78	2	3C		
K	B0	3	1C		
L	48	4	0C		
M	E0	5	04		
N	A0	6	84		
O	F0	7	C4		
P	68	8	E4		
Q	D8	9	F4		
R	50	0	FC		

Table 14-3. Storage Locations to Be Loaded by Operator

Location	Contents
0000	Speed in decimal (words per minute)
0001	Starting address of message A (low-order byte)
0002	Starting address of message B
0003	Starting address of message C
0004	Ending address of message A (low-order byte)
0005	Ending address of message B
0006	Ending address of message C
00F1	$04 prevents interrupts while in the monitor program

The flowchart shown in Fig. 14-9 and the comments in the program should give the reader a good feeling for the structure of the program. It consists of three principal parts, the main program, subroutine SEND, and the interrupt routine, all of which have individual flowcharts shown. Minor components are subroutine DIT which holds PB0 at logic zero for the dot length followed by a logic one for the space length, subroutine DAH which holds PB0 at logic zero for three dot lengths (1 dah = 3 dits) followed by a space, and subroutine TIMER which loads the timer on the KIM-1 with the precise length of one dot and then waits for this time to elapse.

We now look at some specific details of the program. The speed in words-per-minute must be converted to hex before the computer can do any further calculations with it. This conversion may best be explained with an example. Suppose we wish to operate at 20 wpm, so 20 is entered into location $0000. What we mean by 20 is 2 in the tens place and 0 in the ones place, but what the computer thinks this means is 2 in the sixteens place and 0 in the ones place. At least we agree on the ones place, so initially we mask the ones place out with an AND instruction; later we retrieve it and simply add it to the result of our decimal-to-hex conversion of the 2. To trick the computer into thinking the 2 in the sixteens place is the 2 in the tens place we intended it to be, we change the sixteen to a ten with this trick,

$$10 = \frac{16}{2} + \frac{16}{8}$$

The sixteens place divided by two is accomplished by one shift right instruction (LSR), while the sixteens place divided by eight is accomplished by three shift right instructions. So, the two in the sixteens place is shifted right once, stored, shifted right two more times, and these two results are added. We now have 2 × 10 in the computer (in hex, of course) rather than 2 × 16. Adding the results from the ones place completes the conversion.

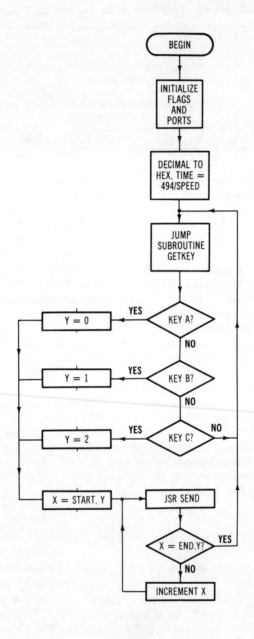

(A) Keyer.

Fig. 14-9. Flowchart for

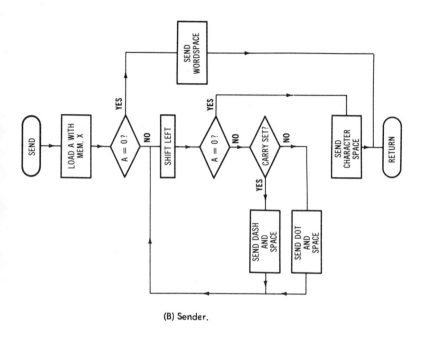

(B) Sender.

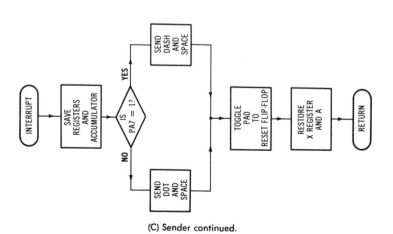

(C) Sender continued.

Keyer and Message Sender.

Using the keying speed definitions from *The Radio Amateur's Handbook,* one can calculate that the dot length in milliseconds is 1200/S where S is the code speed in words per minute. If the divide-by-1024 timer on the KIM-1 is used, one count corresponds to 1.024 milliseconds. Converting the dot length to timer counts gives

$$\text{TIME} = \frac{(1172)}{S} \text{ base } 10 = \frac{(494)}{S} \text{ hex}$$

where TIME is the number to be loaded into the divide-by-1024 timer to give a code speed of S wpm. So the computer must divide S into 494. This is determined by successively subtracting S from 494 until the result becomes negative. The number of subtractions is the quotient of 494/S.

Pin PB0 on the KIM-1 is used as the keying output from the computer. When power is applied to the computer and the reset button is depressed, PB0 comes up in a logic-one state. This dictates that logic one corresponds to the transmitter being off. Consequently, PB0 is buffered and inverted twice by the NOR gates. Inverters such as the 7404 would work, but since I needed a NOR gate in the keyer interface, I simply used the other NOR gates on the same chip. If PB0 could sink enough current it might drive the relay directly, but I perferred the buffering shown in Fig. 14-8. Mark elements of the Morse code are sent by decrementing (DEC) PB0 for the appropriate length of time, while space elements are sent by leaving PB0 at logic one.

The program idles in the loop starting with JSR GETKEY and ending with BNE RPT, testing each of three keys (A, B, and C) to see if they were depressed. Refer to flowcharts for the keyer and message sender shown in Figs. 14-9A, B, and C. If no key is depressed, the program remains in this loop. If a key is depressed, register Y is set to zero, one, or two, depending on which key was struck. The Y is then used as an index to look up the starting address (low-order byte of page two of memory) of the message (STRT,Y) and later the ending address (END,Y) of the message. The starting address is used as an index to find the first code element of the message (MEM,X), and it is incremented until the ending address is encountered.

The conversion of an 8-bit word of memory to a Morse code character has been described in other references in detail and will not be repeated here. There are a number of schemes available[1,2,3,4], but

---

[1]Pollock, James W., "1000 WPM Morse Code Typer," 73, January 1977, p. 100.

[2]De Jong, Marvin L., "A Complete Morse Code Send/Receive Program for the KIM-1," *MICRO*, April-May 1978, p. 7.

the most efficient schemes appear to be those in references 3 and 4, and that was the technique used here.

The keyer is implemented by the interrupt routine which in turn uses subroutines DIT, DAH, and TIMER. It will send at exactly the same speed as the messages. The keyer interface circuit is simply debouncers that are reset at the end of an interrupt. If the key is still in the dot or dash position, the reset has no effect and another interrupt occurs. The flowchart indicates that the state of PA7 determines which element is to be sent.

One last thought: if you want to be able to key in a few characters in the middle of a message, just load a few word spaces there and key the characters in when the blank occurs. This is handy for giving signal reports and also in some contests where the number of contacts is updated after each QSO.

Example 7: Source Listing for Message and Keyer Program

```
0300   78            BEGIN   SEI              Prevent interrupts.
0301   D8                    CLD              Binary mode.
0302   A9 C9                 LDA   $C9        Set interrupt vectors.
0304   8D FE 17              STA   IRQL
0307   A9 03                 LDA   $03
0309   8D FF 17              STA   IRQH
030C   A9 01                 LDA   $01        Initialize I/O Ports A
030E   8D 02 17              STA   PBD        and B.
0311   8D 03 17              STA   PBDD       PB0 is output pin.
0314   8D 01 17              STA   PADD       PA0 is output pin.
0317   8D 00 17              STA   PAD
031A   CE 00 17              DEC   PAD        Toggle PA0 to reset debounce
031D   EE 00 17              INC   PAD        circuit.
0320   A5 00                 LDA   SPEED      Get decimal value of speed
0322   48                    PHA              from location $0000 and
0323   29 F0                 AND   $F0        convert it to hex.
0325   4A                    LSR   A          Multiply tens digit by ten.
0326   85 10                 STA   SCRATCH
0328   4A                    LSR   A
0329   4A                    LSR   A
032A   18                    CLC
032B   65 10                 ADC   SCRATCH
032D   85 10                 STA   SCRATCH    Result of multiplication here.
032F   68                    PLA              Get SPEED again.
0330   29 0F                 AND   $0F        Add ones digit to SCRATCH.
0332   65 10                 ADC   SCRATCH
0334   85 10                 STA   SCRATCH    Decimal to hex complete.
0336   38                    SEC              Division routine begins here.
0337   A2 00                 LDX   $00
0339   A9 94                 LDA   $94
```

---

[3]Pollock, James W., "A Microprocessor Controlled CW Keyboard," *Ham Radio*, January 1978, p. 81.

[4]Ockers, Stan, "Code Test" *The First Book of KIM*, ORB, Argonne, Illionis, 1977, p. 56.

033B	85 08		STA	LO	
033D	A9 04		LDA	$04	
033F	85 09		STA	HI	
0341	A5 08	UP	LDA	LO	
0343	E5 10		SBC	SCRATCH	
0345	85 08		STA	LO	
0347	A5 09		LDA	HI	
0349	E9 00		SBC	$00	
034B	85 09		STA	HI	
034D	E8		INX		
034E	B0 F1		BCS	UP	
0350	86 07		STX	TIME	Division complete.
0352	20 6A 1F	RPT	JSR	GETKEY	Read keyboard subroutine.
0355	58		CLI		
0356	A0 00		LDX	$00	Test keys.
0358	C9 0A		CMP	$0A	
035A	F0 0A		BEQ	MESSA	
035C	C9 0B		CMP	$0B	
035E	F0 05		BEQ	MESSB	
0360	C9 0C		CMP	$0C	
0362	D0 EE		BNE	RPT	
0364	C8		INY		
0365	C8	MESSB	INY		
0366	BE 01 00	MESSA	LDX	STRT,Y	Start message.
0369	20 76 03	CNT	JSR	SEND	
036C	8A		TXA		
036D	D9 04 00		CMP	END,Y	End message?
0370	F0 E0		BEQ	RPT	
0372	E8		INX		
0373	4C 69 03		JMP	CNT	
			SUBROUTINE SEND		
0376	8A	SEND	TXA		
0377	48		PHA		
0378	BD 00 02		LDA	MEM,X	Get code element.
037B	F0 1E		BEQ	WDSP	
037D	0A	HERE	ASL	A	
037E	F0 10		BEQ	FINSH	
0380	48		PHA		
0381	B0 06		BCS	DASH	
0383	20 A0 03		JSR	DIT	Send dot.
0386	4C 8C 03		JMP	ARND	
0389	20 B9 03	DASH	JSR	DAH	Send dash.
038C	68	ARND	PLA		
038D	4C 7D 03		JMP	HERE	
0390	A2 02	FINSH	LDX	$02	
0392	20 BE 03	AGN	JSR	TIMER	Character space.
0395	CA		DEX		
0396	D0 FA		BNE	AGN	
0398	68		PLA		
0399	AA		TAX		
039A	60		RTS		
039B	A2 04	WDSP	LDX	$04	Word space.
039D	4C 92 03		JMP	AGN	
			SUBROUTINE DIT		
03A0	A2 01	DIT	LDX	$01	

```
03A2   CE 02 17   BACK      DEC  PBD
03A5   20 BE 03   SPA       JSR  TIMER
03A8   CA                   DEX
03A9   D0 FA                BNE  SPA
03AB   AD 02 17             LDA  PBD
03AE   4A                   LSR  A
03AF   B0 07                BCS  DONE
03B1   EE 02 17             INC  PBD
03B4   E8                   INX
03B5   4C A5 03             JMP  SPA
03B8   60         DONE      RTS
                           SUBROUTINE DAH
03B9   A2 03      DAH       LDX  $03
03BB   4C A2 03             JMP  BACK
                           SUBROUTINE TIMER
03BE   A5 07      TIMER     LDA  TIME      Delay for the number of
03C0   8D 07 17             STA  TIMER     1.024-millisecond units
03C3   2C 07 17   CHK       BIT  TIMER     stored in TIME.
03C6   10 FB                BPL  CHK
03C8   60                   RTS
                           INTERRUPT ROUTINE
03C9   48         INTRPT    PHA            Save registers.
03CA   8A                   TXA
03CB   48                   PHA
03CC   AD 00 17             LDA  PAD       Is PA7 = logic one?
03D0   30 06                BMI  PAST      Yes, dah. No, dit.
03D2   20 A0 03             JSR  DIT       Send dot.
03D5   4C DA 03             JMP  ACRS
03D8   20 B9 03   PAST      JSR  DAH       Send dash.
03DB   CE 00 17   ACRS      DEC  PAD       Toggle debounce circuit.
03DD   EE 00 17             INC  PAD
03E0   68                   PLA            Restore registers.
03E1   AA                   TAX
03E2   68                   PLA
03E3   40                   RTS            Return from interrupt.
```

CATCHING BUGS WITH LIGHTS—
A PROGRAM DEBUGGING AID*

In debugging a program, how often have you wished you could *see* the contents of the accumulator or the status register at each step *without* pushing all those buttons? If you are interested in a simple hardware solution to this problem, read on.

Although my circuit was designed for the KIM-1, the idea certainly is applicable to other systems. Even if you're not interested in my Bug-Light circuit for programming purposes, it gives you one or more output ports in page zero of memory, and it makes a useful tool for teaching programming.

The KIM-1 monitor and a little hardware provide you with a single-step mode in which the program may be executed one instruction

---

*Courtesy of *Kilobaud Microcomputing.* Copyright © 1979 by 1001001, Inc., Peterborough, NH. All rights reserved.

at a time. After each instruction is executed, the resident monitor program stores the contents of the accumulator, the status register, X register, Y register, and other registers. (See Table 14-4 for the locations of each register.) The important registers are also saved in zero page when a break (BRK) command is placed in a program and the IRQ vector is $1C00. Both the single-step (SST) mode and the break-to-KIM monitor are used extensively in debugging programs.

Table 14-4. Zero-Page Memory Locations of Various Registers

Address	Label	Contents
00EF	PCL	Program Counter Low
00F0	PCH	Program Counter High
00F1	P	Status Register (Flags)
00F2	SP	Stack Pointer
00F3	A	Accumulator
00F4	Y	Y Register
00F5	X	X Register
00F6	CHKHI	Cassette Checksum High
00F7	CHKSUM	Cassette Checksum Low

Use of the SST mode is explained in the KIM-1 User Manual, while the break-to-KIM monitor technique is explained in *The First Book of KIM*. With either technique, the contents of the various registers may be read by using the keyboard to look up the locations in zero page where their contents are stored. For example, to see what the contents of the accumulator are after an instruction, simply address location $00F3 with the keyboard to display it on the seven-segment display.

It's a great feature, but it's slow. At least six consecutive key depressions must take place to examine a register, restore the program counter, and execute the next instruction in the program. If you're following your program around some crazy loop to see why it never comes out, this procedure can take a lot of time. Perhaps my arthritic fingers and bouncy keys are the problem. There has to be a faster approach to the register display problem. A reasonable objective, I decided, was an LED display of each bit in a particular register, with no extra key depressions.

To accomplish this objective I designed a circuit to decode the addresses of the locations where the various register contents were stored and allow the microprocessor to WRITE the same data to output ports with LEDs to represent each bit. Thus, when the monitor stores the contents of the status register at location $00F1, it also writes the same data to an output port whose address is $00F1. In this case the LEDs indicate the state of the various flags. If the output port has address $00F3, then the LEDs will show the contents of the accumulator, in binary, of course.

Bug-Lights comes in three versions. The basic circuit is shown in Fig. 14-10. It will display one register only. A modification that increases the utility of the basic circuit is shown in Fig. 14-11. The DIP switch allows you to select which register you want to follow as you step through your program. If you really like blinking lights and/or do a lot of programming, see the chrome-plated modification to display up to eight registers simultaneously, as outlined in Fig. 14-12.

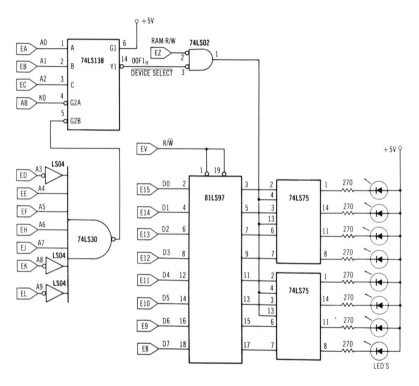

Fig. 14-10. Basic Bug-Lights circuit.

Of course, the most important registers to display are the accumulator, the status register, the X and Y registers and, perhaps, the stack pointer. These displays would make an impressive yet functional front panel. My personal version has the DIP switch modification shown in Fig. 14-11. (The program counter low, PCL, is stored at address $00EF and cannot be observed with the Bug-Light circuit. I cannot recall ever using this register to debug a program.)

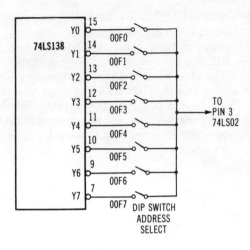

Fig. 14-11. Use of DIP Switch to select register to be displayed by Bug-Lights circuit.

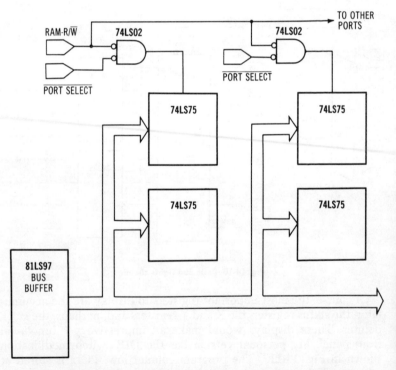

Fig. 14-12. Bug-Lights circuit expanded to output several registers simultaneously. Each pair of 74LS75s makes one 8-bit output port. Port selects are from 74LS138 decoder.

We will begin with the address decoding circuitry. The 74LS138 decoder/demultiplexer will decode the lowest three address lines (A0, A1, A2) when G1 is at logic one and G2A and G2B are at logic zero. G1 is tied high, eliminating any further consideration of it.

In order to have both G2A and B at logic zero, the $\overline{K0}$ select from the KIM-1 and the output of the 74LS30 must be at logic zero. K0 will be low when address lines A10–A15 are low. This is handled by the KIM-1 circuitry. You can see from Fig. 14-10 that the output of the 74LS30 is low when A4–A7 are at logic one and A3, A8, and A9 are at logic zero. The compilation of this information as the requirements to select the 74LS138 is shown in Example 8.

The 74LS138 decodes the lowest three address lines to produce active low *device select pulses* whenever addresses $00F0–$00F7 are on the address lines. Each of the eight outputs of the 74LS138 corresponds to one of the eight addresses $00F0–$00F7, which in turn include the address of the locations where the various registers are stored.

The device select pulse from the 74LS138 is inverted and ANDed with the inverted RAM-R/$\overline{W}$ signal from the KIM-1. This produces a positive pulse from the 74LS02, which occurs only on a WRITE cycle and when the correct address is placed on the address bus. For example, an STA $00F1 instruction will produce such a pulse in the circuit of Fig. 14-10. This pulse is applied to the gate inputs of the 74LS75 Bistable Latches.

As long as the positive pulse is applied to the 75LS75 gates, the Q outputs follow the D inputs, and the $\overline{Q}$ outputs are the D inputs inverted. At the trailing edge of the positive pulse, which occurs when the ϕ_2 clock signal on the KIM-1 changes from logic one to logic zero, the data at the D inputs is latched into the Q outputs. So, when a WRITE occurs to $00F1, the data will appear at the Q outputs and it will be stored there, at least until another WRITE to $00F1 occurs.

The 81LS97 is a data bus buffer. It is activated only on a WRITE command when the R/$\overline{W}$ is low. If only one output port is desired and the data bus lines are kept short, then the 81LS97 may be omitted since the 6502 microprocessor can drive the 74LS75s directly. However, if you want to locate your lights on a front panel, or if you want to add sets of eight lights for several registers, then the bus driver becomes essential.

The LEDs are connected through current-limiting resistors to the $\overline{Q}$ outputs of the 74LS75s. They will glow when $\overline{Q}$ is low and Q is high. Thus, a glowing LED corresponds to a logic one for the bit it represents while an LED in the off state corresponds to a logic zero.

An added feature of the Bug-Light circuit is its ability to be used as an output port as well as a debugging tool. The Q outputs of the

74LS75s are not used for display purposes; they contain the data that was written to them. Thus, they can be used as zero-page memory-mapped output ports.

An application program can make use of these ports to write a 7-bit ASCII word to some external device, such as a video card, an IBM Selectric, or some other device. A/D or D/A converters can be driven from these ports as easily as the PAD and PBD ports on the KIM-1 application connector. The only time the memory locations $00F0-F8 are used by the computer is in an NMI or IRQ jump to the monitor; that is, in debugging. So you have your Bug-Lights and output ports as well.

Table 14-5. Power Connections for Bug-Light Integrated Circuits

Integrated Circuit	+5 V	Ground
74LS138	16	8
74LS30	14	7
74LS02	14	7
74LS04	14	7
74LS75	5	12
81LS97	20	10

Table 14-5 shows the power connections for each of the chips in the logic diagram. All the other connections are shown in the figures. My version was built on a UNICARD I, which contains two breadboard strips and an edge connector pad that matches the KIM-1 expansion pad. I soldered an edge connector to the UNICARD so I could plug the KIM-1 expansion pad into it. All the connections of the Bug-Light circuit except one are to the expansion pad on the KIM-1. All the connections are found on the pad symbols in Fig. 14-10. The $\overline{K0}$ select comes from the application pad on the KIM-1. Its pin number, AB, is also given.

Layout is not critical, and approaches other than the one I used will work. A wire-wrap approach might be more permanent and less expensive, although I have found that the circuits on the breadboards last indefinitely. Fig. 14-13 shows my version. Power was stolen from the KIM-1 power supply, since +5 V and ground are available at the expansion pad.

When you get your circuit built, say a one-port version, select the location you want to view with the DIP switch or by the appropriate connection. With the KIM-1 running in the monitor, address the location and store $FF in it, using the keypad on the KIM-1. All the LEDs should light. Change the contents of the port until you are sure that each LED is responding to the correct bit value. Stepping through the sequence $00, $01, $02, $04, $08, $10, $20, $40, $80 of data values will test each light in turn.

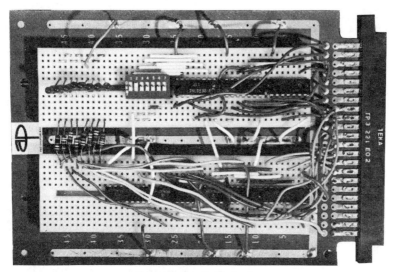

Fig. 14-13. Bug-Lights circuit.

Next, load any program, set the KIM-1 up for the SST mode, and step through the program. The lights should reflect the current contents of the register you have selected to view. I had no trouble. For once my design worked the very first time I tried it. I hope you have the same kind of success. If you don't, recheck all your wiring, check the polarity on your LEDs, make sure they all work, and finally make sure you haven't made a mistake on numbering the pins on the ICs.

If some bits work and some do not, then exchange signal paths for the two bits. For example, if one bit is working, then the 74LS75 latch for this bit will also be working. Use the same latch for a nonworking bit to see if the problem is in the latch. The circuit is simple enough so that it should not take too long to figure out any problems.

Beginning programmers have a lot more trouble visualizing what is happening as a result of a certain instruction than veteran programmers imagine. One application of Bug-Lights is to illustrate the results of various instructions. For example, set up Bug-Lights to show the contents of the accumulator ($00F3). Then write a short program (shown in Example 9) in which the accumulator is loaded with 01 followed by an ASL A in an infinite loop.

Now single-step through the program and watch the "1" move from right to left on the LEDs. Replace the ASL A with an ROL A and note the difference. Other instructions can be illustrated in the same way, giving students, who have difficulty visualizing zeros and ones among bits and bytes, an excellent visual aid.

Example 8: Address Decoding for Bug-Lights Circuit

A15	A14	A13	A12	A11	A10	A9	A8	A7	A6	A5	A4	A3	A2	A1	A0	— Address Line
0	0	0	0	0	0	0	0	1	1	1	1	0	X	X	X	— Logic Value
	0				0				F				0-7			— Hex Number

(X means "don't care.")

Example 9: Program to Demonstrate ASL Instruction With Bug-Lights Circuit

```
BEGIN   LDA $01
THERE   ASL A
        JMP THERE
```

LUNAR OCCULTATION OF A STAR*

The program described here is designed to measure the light intensity from a star as it passes behind the dark face of the moon, a so-called lunar occultation. A photometer and amplifier attached to a telescope provide a signal proportional to the light intensity, and this intensity drops rapidly (in a few milliseconds) as the moon passes in front of the star. This signal voltage is measured periodically, and the data is stored in 256 memory locations in the KIM-1. When the star is occulted and the level drops below a predetermined value, the measurement is stopped, and the previous 256 measurements, representing about 1 second of data, are displayed on an oscilloscope.

Fig. 14-14 shows the support circuitry for the program which is given in Example 10. When a logic one appears on PB2 (from, say, a radio time signal), the timer is set, the measurements START, and a zero mark is placed in the data every ¼ second to allow accurate measurements of the time of the event. The arming switch SW can be set on position "B" which ensures a logic zero on PB3 to keep the program from inadvertently stopping before the event takes place. Near the predicted time of the occultation, it can be switched to "A," at which time it is armed to stop when the light level falls below the cut-off point determined by the 100K potentiometer.

The time constants RC and R'C' can be selected to integrate the incoming signal as desired. We use RC = 5 msec and R'C' = 20 msec. This delays the cut-off point slightly after the actual occultation. The sampling time can be selected by changing the number stored in location $003E (we sample about every 4 msec), and the number stored in locations $002F and $009D can be used as a fine adjustment to make the timing marks appear at exactly ¼ sec intervals. The data is stored in locations $0200 through $02FF but may appear folded over on display. For example, if the cut-off time occurs

---

*Courtesy of Dr. Thomas D. Strickler, John Drake, and Jesse Maupin, Berea College, Berea, Ky.

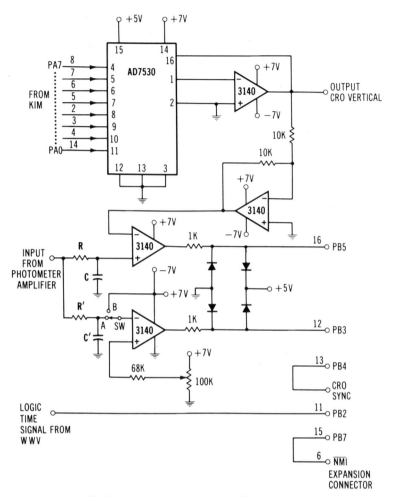

Fig. 14-14. Support circuitry for Occultation program.

while data is being stored in memory location $0280, then the most recent measurements are in locations $027F, $027E, . . . , while the earliest measurements are in locations $0281, $0232, . . . , etc. Every ¼ second, the number in location $00CB is incremented, and every 256 (FF_{hex}) ¼ seconds, the number in location $00CC is incremented, so that the total time since the START signal can be determined.

Photoelectric measurements of bright stars as they are occulted often show a diffraction pattern typical of that observed in the laboratory by a point source diffracted from a straight edge. They can be used to measure angular diameters of stars and can often resolve very close double and triple stars. For further information on lunar occultations, the reader is referred to the articles "Photoelectric Observing of Occultations," by David S. Evans, in *Sky and Telescope*, Vol. 54, Nos. 3 and 4 (1977).

Example 10: Occultation Program

$002F and $009D = Additional count to make timer equal ¼ second
$003E = Convert time count (40 = 4 msec)
$0096 = Comparator Delay Count (02)
$00C9 = BIT2 (04) Test BIT2 to start timer from WWV
$00CA = REM   Remainder in timer after last ¼ sec count
$00CB = QSEC No. of ¼ sec counts since start (or since last MIN)
$00CC = MIN   No. of minutes (actually 64 secs) since start
$00CD = KEY
$00CE = SP
$00CF = BIT5 (20) Test BIT5 to test comparator

0004	A9	04		LDA	$04	Initialize and set port directions.
0006	85	C9		STA	BIT2	
0008	A9	9C		LDA	$9C	
000A	8D	FA	17	STA	17FA	
000D	A9	00		LDA	$00	
000F	8D	FB	17	STA	17FB	
0012	A9	00		LDA	$00	
0014	85	CB		STA	QSEC	
0016	A9	00		LDA	$00	
0018	85	CC		STA	MIN	
001A	A9	10		LDA	$10	
001C	8D	03	17	STA	BPD	
001F	0A			ASL		
0020	85	CF		STA	BIT5	
0022	A9	FF		LDA	$FF	
0024	8D	01	17	STA	PAD	
0027	AD	02	17	WAIT	LDA	PB	Wait until logic one appears on PB2.
002A	24	C9		BIT	BIT2	
002C	F0	F9		BEQ	WAIT	
002E	A9	D0		LDA	$D0	Extra count to make timing
0030	8D	04	17	STA	TIME4	marks = ¼ second.
0033	2C	07	17	TMI	BIT	TIME7	
0036	10	FB		BPL	TMI	
0038	A9	F4		LDA	$F4	Set timer to count 244 × 1024 =
003A	8D	0F	17	STA	TIMEF	249,856 microseconds.
003D	A9	40		RTIME	LDA	$40	Set convert time using
003F	8D	46	17	STA	1746	"other counter."
0042	A9	80		CONV	LDA	$80	Initialize conversion.
0044	85	CD		STA	KEY	
0046	0A			ASL		
0047	85	CE		STA	SP	
0049	A5	CD		LOOP	LDA	KEY	OR KEY into result and output.
004B	05	CE		ORA	SP	
004D	8D	00	17	STA	PA	
0050	20	95	00	JSR	CDLY	Wait for comparator delay.
0053	AD	02	17	LDA	PB	Check comparator, jump if

0056	24	CF			BIT	BIT5	too large.
0058	F0	05			BEQ	LARGE	
005A	AD	00	17		LDA	PA	If too small, store result
005D	85	CE			STA	SP	in SP.
005F	46	CD		LARGE	LSR	KEY	Shift KEY right and repeat
0061	D0	E6			BNE	LOOP	eight times.
0063	A5	CE			LDA	SP	Store result in TABLE, starting
0065	9D	00	02		STA	TABLE,X	with $0200.
0068	AD	47	17	DT	LDA	TIMER	Wait until timer stops.
006B	F0	FB			BEQ	DT	
006D	E8				INX		Increment X.
006E	EA	EA			NOP NOP		
0070	AD	02	17		LDA	PB	Look for logic one on PB3.
0073	29	08			AND	$08	
0075	F0	C6			BEQ	RTIME	If no, repeat conversion
0077	EA	EA			NOP NOP		measurement.
0079	AD	06	17		LDA	TIMER	If yes, read remaining time,
007C	85	CA			STA	REM	store and jump to SYNC.
007E	EA				NOP		
007F	A9	10		SYNC	LDA	$10	Generate SYNC pulse for CRO.
0081	8D	02	17		STA	PB	
0084	A9	00			LDA	$00	
0086	8D	02	17		STA	PB	
0089	BD	00	02	OUT	LDA	TABLE,X	Display spectrum on CRO.
008C	8D	00	17		STA	PA	
008F	E8				INX		
0090	D0	F7			BNE	OUT	
0092	4C	7F	00		JMP	SYNC	
0095	A9	02		CDLY	LDA	$02	Delay for comparator.
0097	A8				TAY		
0098	88			DELAY	DEY		
0099	D0	FD			BNE	DELAY	
009B	60				RTS		

INTERRUPT ROUTINE

009C	A9	D0			LDA	$D0	Reset 1/4 second timer.
009E	8D	04	17		STA	TIME4	
00A1	2C	07	17	TM2	BIT	TIME7	
00A4	10	FB			BPL	TM2	
00A6	A9	F4			LDA	$F4	
00A8	8D	0F	17		STA	TIMEF	
00AB	E6	CB			INC	QSEC	Increment 1/4 second counter.
00AD	A9	00			LDA	$00	Check 1/4 second counter for
00AF	C5	CB			CMP	QSEC	overflow (00).
00B1	D0	02			BNE	CONT	If no, continue.
00B3	E6	CC			INC	MIN	If yes, increment MIN counter.
00B5	A9	00		CONT	LDA	$00	Put zero in TABLE X at 1/4 second
00B7	9D	00	02		STA	TABLE,X	intervals.
00BA	E8				INX		
00BB	40				RTI		Return from interrupt.

Decimal, Binary, and Hexadecimal Number Systems

OBJECTIVES

At the completion of this appendix you should be able to:

- Understand and define the terms number, face value, place value, base, bit, byte, and nibble.
- Understand that numbers are used to indicate quantity, to indicate order, or to indicate codes for various operations.
- Convert binary numbers to decimal numbers and decimal numbers to binary numbers.
- Convert hexadecimal numbers to binary numbers and binary numbers to hexadecimal numbers.

INTRODUCTION

Microprocessors use binary numbers to control internal operations, to communicate with other components in the microcomputer system, and to exchange information with peripheral devices. On the other hand, devices that humans use to input information to a microcomputer and devices that display information output by the microcomputer frequently use hexadecimal numbers. Hexadecimal numbers are representations of binary numbers that provide human beings with readily recognized symbols that aid in handling binary numbers. These facts justify competency in dealing with binary and hexadecimal numbers.

NUMBERS

Numbers are used in the following ways:

- Numbers are used to indicate *quantity*. This is the use with which we are most familiar.
- Numbers are used to indicate *order*. For example, the order in which a mechanical device is assembled is specified by numbers.
- Numbers are used as *names* or *codes*. Your social security number is a code which identifies you.

Sometimes numbers are used in several of these ways. The page numbers of a book *order* the pages, *name* the pages, and indicate the *quantity* of pages.

You will see that a microcomputer uses numbers in each of these three ways.

- A "smart" blood pressure monitor measures a signal and displays a number representing the blood pressure of a patient.
- A microcomputer program is executed one step at a time, and the order is determined by a number stored in the *program counter*.
- All microprocessor instructions have *code numbers*. The number 69 sent to the 6502 microprocessor will cause it to execute an addition operation.
- The memory locations in a microcomputer are ordered and named by a number called the *address* of the location.

A *number* is a sequence of digits. In the familiar decimal (base-10) system, the ten *decimal digits* are 0, 1, 2, . . . , 9. The binary number system (base-two) uses only two *binary digits*, namely 0 and 1. The words *binary digit* are frequently contracted to form the word *bit*. (If the same thing were done with decimal digits we would have *dits*, while hexadecimal digits would be *hits*.) The hexadecimal system (base-16) requires 16 different hexadecimal digits. They are 0, 1, 2, . . . , 9, A, B, C, D, E, and F. Perhaps a better choice could have been made for the last six digits, but these are the ones commonly used.

DECIMAL NUMBERS

In order to understand binary and hexadecimal numbers it will be helpful to dissect a familiar decimal number. Taking the number 1939 as an example, we obtain the following diagram.

```
         ┌──────Digit Number 3
         │ ┌────Digit Number 2
         │ │ ┌──Digit Number 1
         │ │ │ ┌Digit Number 0
         │ │ │ │
         1 9 3 9 = 1000 + 900 + 30 + 9
```

$$= (1 \times 1000) + (9 \times 100) + (3 \times 10) + (9 \times 1)$$

with labels: FACE VALUES and PLACE VALUES

$$= (1 \times 10^3) + (9 \times 10^2) + (3 \times 10^1) + (9 \times 10^0)$$

with labels: DIGIT NUMBERS and BASE = 10

Referring to the preceding diagram, each decimal digit has a *face value*, the meaning of which is acquired from experience and memorization at an early age. There are 10 different face values in a base-10 system. Each decimal digit has a *digit number* or *place* in the decimal number which determines its *place value*. The place value of digit number 0 is $10^0 = 1$; the place value of digit number 1 is $10^1 = 10$. Place values of successive digits are $10^2 = 100$, $10^3 = 1000$, and so on. The place value is equal to the *base* raised to a power equal to the digit number.

BINARY NUMBERS

Binary numbers are constructed the same way as decimal numbers except the base is two and only two face values, 0 and 1, are required. Each binary digit is called a bit. The place values are $2^0 = 1$, $2^1 = 2$, $2^2 = 4$, $2^3 = 8$, and $2^4 = 16$, corresponding to bit numbers 0, 1, 2, 3, and 4, respectively. Table A-1 lists powers of two

To illustrate these ideas and to show you how a binary number may be converted to a decimal number, the binary number 1101 is expanded in a way similar to the decimal number expansion above.

Table A-1. A Table of Powers of Two

		$2^0 = 1$	
$2^1 = 2$	$2^5 = 32$	$2^9 = 512$	$2^{13} = 8192$
$2^2 = 4$	$2^6 = 64$	$2^{10} = 1024$	$2^{14} = 16384$
$2^3 = 8$	$2^7 = 128$	$2^{11} = 2048$	$2^{15} = 32768$
$2^4 = 16$	$2^8 = 256$	$2^{12} = 4096$	$2^{16} = 65536$

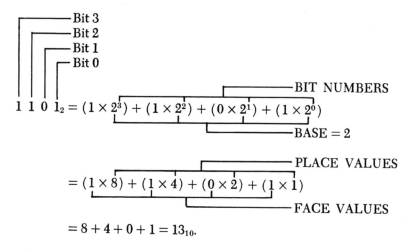

$$1\ 1\ 0\ 1_2 = (1 \times 2^3) + (1 \times 2^2) + (0 \times 2^1) + (1 \times 2^0)$$

$$= (1 \times 8) + (1 \times 4) + (0 \times 2) + (1 \times 1)$$

$$= 8 + 4 + 0 + 1 = 13_{10}.$$

The subscripts "2" and "10" are used to indicate the base of the number unless the base is obvious from the context of the discussion. The expansion diagram for the number 1101_2 also suggests how binary numbers may be converted to decimal numbers. Multiply the face value (either 1 or 0, so the multiplication is easy) by the place value of each bit and add the results. The place values are 2^n, where n is the bit number. The place value for bits numbered 0-16 may be obtained from Table A-1. Example 1 gives another base two to base ten conversion.

Example 1: Conversion of 10100010_2 to Base 10

$$10100010_2 = (1 \times 2^7) + (0 \times 2^6) + (1 \times 2^5) + (0 \times 2^4)$$
$$+ (0 \times 2^3) + (0 \times 2^2) + (1 \times 2^1) + (0 \times 2^0)$$
$$= 128 + 32 + 2$$
$$= 162_{10}$$

Sometimes it is simpler to organize your work from the smallest place value, or *least significant bit* (the bit on the extreme right), to the largest place value, or *most significant bit* (the bit on the extreme left). Thus,

$$1100_2 = (0 \times 1) + (0 \times 2) + (1 \times 4) + (1 \times 8) = 4 + 8 = 12_{10}.$$

There are several techniques to convert a decimal number to a binary number. Here is a simple one; Example 2 illustrates it.

- To find the highest place value that has a face value of one (that is, the most significant nonzero bit), find the largest power of two which will divide the number. Place a one in this bit position and note the remainder of the division.

- The remainder of the first result is then divided by the next largest power of two. If it will not divide the first remainder, then a zero is put in the next lower bit position. Otherwise, a one is placed in this bit position, and the remainder is noted.
- Repeat step two until you finish by dividing by one.

Example 2: Conversion of 233_{10} to Base 2

Clearly the largest power of two which will divide 233 is $2^7 = 128$. The process now proceeds as follows:

$$
\begin{array}{cccccccc}
1 & 1 & 1 & 0 & 1 & 0 & 0 & 1 \\
128\overline{)233} & 64\overline{)105} & 32\overline{)41} & 16\overline{)9} & 8\overline{)9} & 4\overline{)1} & 2\overline{)1} & 1\overline{)1} = 11101001_2 \\
\underline{128} & \underline{64} & \underline{32} & & \underline{8} & & & \underline{1} \\
105 & 41 & 9 & & 1 & & & 0
\end{array}
$$

Although this looks complicated, it proceeds rather quickly because most of the steps can be done mentally. In any case, it will be easier to handle binary numbers in terms of their hexadecimal representations as you shall see in a subsequent section.

BITS, BYTES, AND NIBBLES

Numbers used to express quantity are usually of *variable* length; they have no leading zeros to take up "unused" places. Numbers used as codes, zip codes for example, are usually *fixed* in length and often have leading zeros. All numbers used by a microprocessor are fixed in length regardless of whether they are used to express quantity, determine order, or represent a code. If a binary number represents quantity, the leading zeros are disregarded.

The fixed length of the numbers which the 6502 microprocessor regards as *data* is eight bits. An 8-bit number is called a *byte*. The number 7_{10} is represented as shown in Example 3.

Example 3: How the Number 7_{10} is Represented by a Byte of Data

Data Byte	0	0	0	0	0	1	1	1	$= 7_{10}$
Data Bit Designations	D7	D6	D5	D4	D3	D2	D1	D0	

The 6502 microprocessor also *names* and *orders* 65536 different locations in memory with a 16-bit fixed length binary number called an *address*. The number 1020_{10} representing location 1020_{10} in memory is represented as an address as shown in Example 4.

The 16-bit address number is frequently referred to in terms of two bytes. The low-order byte, or *address low* (ADL) as it is sometimes called, is the eight bits on the top while the high-order byte, or *address high* (ADH) as it is sometimes called, is the eight bits on the bottom.

Example 4: How the Address 1020_{10} is Represented by a 16-Bit Binary Address

ADH

Address (Two Bytes)	0	0	0	0	0	0	1	1
Address Bit Designations	A15	A14	A13	A12	A11	A10	A9	A8

ADL

	1	1	1	1	1	1	0	0
	A7	A6	A5	A4	A3	A2	A1	A0

A 4-bit binary number is sometimes called a *nibble*. This is a useful idea when representing binary numbers by means of hexadecimal digits. A byte consists of a high-order nibble and a low-order nibble.

HEXADECIMAL NUMBERS

The sixteen hexadecimal digits and their decimal and binary equivalents are given in Table A-2. The subscripts 16, 10, and 2 are omitted.

Table A-2. Decimal, Binary, and Hexadecimal Equivalents

Decimal Number	Binary Number	Hexadecimal Number
0	0000	0
1	0001	1
2	0010	2
3	0011	3
4	0100	4
5	0101	5
6	0110	6
7	0111	7
8	1000	8
9	1001	9
10	1010	A
11	1011	B
12	1100	C
13	1101	D
14	1110	E
15	1111	F
16	10000	10

Notice that one hexadecimal digit represents four binary digits or one nibble. This fact provides the most convenient way to convert from binary numbers to hexadecimal numbers and vice versa.

Once the table has been committed to memory, the conversion process is as follows:

- Divide the binary number into groups of nibbles, starting from the least significant bit.
- Mentally convert each nibble to a hexadecimal number and write it down. (This process sometimes calls for a mental translation of the binary number to decimal and a translation of the decimal number to hexadecimal.)

Examples 5 and 6 illustrate how binary numbers are converted into hexadecimal numbers.

Example 5: Conversion of Binary Numbers 01010101_2, 00000101_2, 10101111_2, and 11111110_2 Into Hexadecimal Numbers.

$$01010101_2 = 0101\ 0101 = 55_{16} \qquad 00000101_2 = 0000\ 0101 = 05_{16}$$
$$10101111_2 = 1010\ 1111 = AF_{16} \qquad 11111110_2 = 1111\ 1110 = FE_{16}$$

Example 6: Conversion of Binary Numbers 1001111100011100_2 and 0100010111011011_2 Into Hexadecimal Numbers.

$$1001111100011100_2 = 1001\ 1111\ 0001\ 1100 = 9F1C_{16}$$
$$0100010111011011_2 = 0100\ 0101\ 1101\ 1011 = 45DB_{16}$$

The reverse process, converting from hexadecimal to binary, is done in a similar way.

- Divide the hexadecimal number into separate digits.
- Mentally convert each hexadecimal digit into a binary nibble.

Example 7 illustrates the process.

Example 7: Conversion of $3D_{16}$ and $FC83_{16}$ Into Binary Numbers

$$3D_{16} = 0011\ 1101 = 00111101_2$$
$$FC83_{16} = 1111\ 1100\ 1000\ 0011 = 1111110010000011_2$$

By now it should be easy for the reader to understand that hexadecimal numbers represent 8-bit and 16-bit binary numbers more efficiently than decimal numbers. Practice will produce the familiarity required for rapid calculations. A table of binary to hexadecimal to decimal conversions is provided in Table A-3.

It might be added that hexadecimal numbers are frequently called "hex" numbers, and sometimes the suffix "H" is attached to indicate the hexadecimal representation. The notation used in this book to indicate hexadecimal numbers is a "$" prefix. That is, $36_{16} = \$36$ and $7FFC_{16} = \$7FFC$. This is the most common practice among 6502 users, perhaps to make them feel wealthy. Readers who were not previously familiar with hexadecimal and binary numbers are urged to try the exercises at the end of this appendix.

Table A-3. Binary to Hexadecimal to Decimal Conversions

Binary Number		Hexadecimal Number	Decimal Number
0001	NIBBLE	01	1
0010	"	02	2
0011	"	03	3
0100	"	04	4
0101	"	05	5
0110	"	06	6
0111	"	07	7
1000	"	08	8
0001 0000	BYTE	10	16
0010 0000	"	20	32
0100 0000	"	40	64
1000 0000	"	80	128
1000 1000	"	88	136
1000 1100	"	8C	140
1100 1100	"	CC	208
1111 1111	"	FF	255
0001 0000 0000	3 NIBBLES	0100	256
0010 0000 0000	"	0200	512
0011 0000 0000	"	0300	768
0011 1111 1111	"	03FF	1023
0100 0000 0000	"	0400	1024
1000 0000 0000	"	0800	2048
0001 0000 0000 0000	2 BYTES	1000	4096
0001 1111 1111 1111	"	1FFF	8191
0010 0000 0000 0000	"	2000	8192
0011 1111 1111 1111	"	3FFF	16383
0100 0000 0000 0000	"	4000	16384
0101 1111 1111 1111	"	5FFF	24575
0110 0000 0000 0000	"	6000	24576
0111 1111 1111 1111	"	7FFF	32767
1000 0000 0000 0000	"	8000	32768
1001 1111 1111 1111	"	9FFF	40959
1010 0000 0000 0000	"	A000	40960
1011 1111 1111 1111	"	BFFF	49151
1100 0000 0000 0000	"	C000	49152
1101 1111 1111 1111	"	DFFF	57343
1110 0000 0000 0000	"	E000	57344
1111 1111 1111 1111	"	FFFF	65535

EXERCISES

1. Identify the digit number of the digit 5 in the number 25033. If this is a base 10 number what is the place value of the 5? Would the face value be changed if this were a base 16 number? Would the place value be changed if this were a base 16 number?

2. What is the place value of a digit in the nth place of a number written in base b?

3. Give examples of how numbers are used to indicate quantity, to indicate order, and as codes or names.

4. Convert the following decimal numbers to binary numbers: 17, 31, 64, 65, 127, 255, and 365.

5. Convert the following binary numbers to decimal numbers:

10110110	11110000
00010010	11111111
01000000	01010101
10000001	00110011

6. Convert the decimal numbers in problem 4 to hexadecimal numbers. Use the binary results you obtained by doing problem 4. Also convert the binary numbers in problem 5 to hexadecimal numbers.

7. How many different 4-bit numbers or nibbles are there? 8-bit numbers? 16-bit numbers?

8. Define number, bit, byte, and nibble.

EXERCISE ANSWERS

1. The digit number of 5 is 3. (Digit numbers start with 0 on the right and increase to the left.) Its place value is $10^3 = 1000$ if the base is 10. Face values are the same in numbers of any base, provided that face value exists. For example, there is no face value of 5 in the binary number system. If the base of the number were 16 then the place value of the digit 5 would be $16^3 = 4096_{10}$.
2. The general formula for the place value of a digit in the nth place of a number written in base b is b^n.
3. The number of words on this page is a quantity. If the Kansas City Royals are in 2nd place, the 2 is used as an indication of order. The ASCII for the letter A is 41_{16}. Thus, A is represented by the code number 41_{16}.
4. $17 = 10001_2$, $31 = 11111_2$, $64 = 1000000_2$, $65 = 1000001_2$, $127 = 1111111_2$, $255 = 11111111_2$, $365 = 101101101_2$.
5. $10110110 = 182_{10} = B6_{16}$ $11110000 = 240_{10} = F0_{16}$
   $00010010 = 34_{10} = 12_{16}$ $11111111 = 255_{10} = FF_{16}$

$01000000 = 64_{10}\ = 40_{16}$ $01010101 = 85_{10}\ = 55_{16}$
$10000001 = 129_{10} = 81_{16}$ $00110011 = 51_{10}\ = 33_{16}$

6. Some of the answers are given in problem 5. The conversions from
   problem 4 are $10001 = 11_{16}$, $11111 = 1F_{16}$, $1000000 = 40_{16}$,
   $1000001 = 41_{16}$, $1111111 = 7F_{16}$, $11111111 = FF_{16}$, and
   $101101101 = 16D_{16}$.
7. Notice that there are 2 different 1-bit numbers, 4 different 2-bit
   numbers, 8 different 3-bit numbers and 16 different 4-bit numbers.
   Thus, there are 16 different nibbles. Using induction, if the number of bits in a number is n, then the number of different n-bit
   numbers is 2^n. Thus, there are $2^8 = 256$ different bytes or 8-bit
   numbers and $2^{16} = 65536$ different 16-bit numbers. These answers
   may be verified with the table.
8. A number is a sequence of digits. A bit is a binary digit. A byte is
   an 8-bit binary number, and a nibble is a 4-bit binary number.
   Leading zeros are permitted.

Instruction Set Summary

The following instruction set summary is made available through the courtesy of Synertek Systems Corp. Copyright © 1978 by Synertek Systems Corp. All rights reserved.

6502 INSTRUCTION SUMMARY

Each addressing-mode cell lists: OP (opcode, hex), n (cycles), # (bytes).
Condition codes column lists flags affected (N Z C I D V).

MNEMONIC	OPERATION	IMMEDIATE	ABSOLUTE	ZERO PAGE	ACCUM.	IMPLIED	(IND,X)	(IND),Y	Z.PAGE,X	ABS,X	ABS,Y	RELATIVE	INDIRECT	COND CODES
ADC	A+M+C → A [1]	69 2 2	6D 4 3	65 3 2			61 6 2	71 5 2	75 4 2	7D 4 3	79 4 3			N Z C V
AND	A∧M → A [1]	29 2 2	2D 4 3	25 3 2			21 6 2	31 5 2	35 4 2	3D 4 3	39 4 3			N Z
ASL	C ← [7...0] ← 0		0E 6 3	06 5 2	0A 2 1				16 6 2	1E 7 3				N Z C
BCC	BRANCH ON C=0 [2]											90 2 2		
BCS	BRANCH ON C=1 [2]											B0 2 2		
BEQ	BRANCH ON Z=1 [2]											F0 2 2		
BIT	A∧M		2C 4 3	24 3 2										M_7 Z M_6
BMI	BRANCH ON N=1 [2]											30 2 2		
BNE	BRANCH ON Z=0 [2]											D0 2 2		
BPL	BRANCH ON N=0 [2]											10 2 2		
BRK	BREAK					00 7 1								I
BVC	BRANCH ON V=0 [2]											50 2 2		
BVS	BRANCH ON V=1 [2]											70 2 2		
CLC	0 → C					18 2 1								C
CLD	0 → D					D8 2 1								D
CLI	0 → I					58 2 1								I
CLV	0 → V					B8 2 1								V
CMP	A−M [1]	C9 2 2	CD 4 3	C5 3 2			C1 6 2	D1 5 2	D5 4 2	DD 4 3	D9 4 3			N Z C
CPX	X−M	E0 2 2	EC 4 3	E4 3 2										N Z C
CPY	Y−M	C0 2 2	CC 4 3	C4 3 2										N Z C
DEC	M−1 → M		CE 6 3	C6 5 2					D6 6 2	DE 7 3				N Z
DEX	X−1 → X					CA 2 1								N Z
DEY	Y−1 → Y					88 2 1								N Z
EOR	A∀M → A [1]	49 2 2	4D 4 3	45 3 2			41 6 2	51 5 2	55 4 2	5D 4 3	59 4 3			N Z
INC	M+1 → M		EE 6 3	E6 5 2					F6 6 2	FE 7 3				N Z
INX	X+1 → X					E8 2 1								N Z
INY	Y+1 → Y					C8 2 1								N Z
JMP	JUMP TO NEW LOCATION		4C 3 3										6C 5 3	
JSR	JUMP SUBROUTINE		20 6 3											
LDA	M → A [1]	A9 2 2	AD 4 3	A5 3 2			A1 6 2	B1 5 2	B5 4 2	BD 4 3	B9 4 3			N Z

6502 Instruction Set — Addressing Modes and Condition Codes

MNEMONIC	OPERATION	IMMEDIATE OP	n	#	ABSOLUTE OP	n	#	ZERO PAGE OP	n	#	ACCUM OP	n	#	IMPLIED OP	n	#	(IND,X) OP	n	#	(IND),Y OP	n	#	Z.PAGE,X OP	n	#	ABS,X OP	n	#	ABS,Y OP	n	#	RELATIVE OP	n	#	INDIRECT OP	n	#	Z.PAGE,Y OP	n	#	N	Z	C	I	D	V
LDX	M → X [1]	A2	2	2	AE	4	3	A6	3	2																BE	4	3							B6	4	2	√	√	—	—	—	—
LDY	M → Y [1]	A0	2	2	AC	4	3	A4	3	2													B4	4	2	BC	4	3										√	√	—	—	—	—
LSR	(0→[7...0]→C)				4E	6	3	46	5	2	4A	2	1										56	6	2	5E	7	3										0	√	√	—	—	—
NOP	NO OPERATION													EA	2	1																						—	—	—	—	—	—
ORA	A∨M → A	09	2	2	0D	4	3	05	3	2							01	6	2	11	5	2	15	4	2	1D	4	3	19	4	3										√	√	—	—	—	—
PHA	A → Ms S-1 → S													48	3	1																						—	—	—	—	—	—
PHP	P → Ms S-1 → S													08	3	1																						—	—	—	—	—	—
PLA	S-1 → S Ms → A													68	4	1																						√	√	—	—	—	—
PLP	S-1 → S Ms → P													28	4	1																						(RESTORED)					
ROL	(C←[7...0]←C)				2E	6	3	26	5	2	2A	2	1										36	6	2	3E	7	3										√	√	√	—	—	—
ROR	(C→[7...0]→C)				6E	6	3	66	5	2	6A	2	1										76	6	2	7E	7	3										√	√	√	—	—	—
RTI	RETURN FROM INTERRUPT													40	6	1																						(RESTORED)					
RTS	RETURN FROM SUBROUTINE													60	6	1																						—	—	—	—	—	—
SBC	A-M-C̄ → A [1]	E9	2	2	ED	4	3	E5	3	2							E1	6	2	F1	5	2	F5	4	2	FD	4	3	F9	4	3										√	√	[3]	—	—	√
SEC	1 → C													38	2	1																						—	—	1	—	—	—
SED	1 → D													F8	2	1																						—	—	—	—	1	—
SEI	1 → I													78	2	1																						—	—	—	1	—	—
STA	A → M				8D	4	3	85	3	2							81	6	2	91	6	2	95	4	2	9D	5	3	99	5	3										—	—	—	—	—	—
STX	X → M				8E	4	3	86	3	2																												96	4	2	—	—	—	—	—	—
STY	Y → M				8C	4	3	84	3	2													94	4	2																—	—	—	—	—	—
TAX	A → X													AA	2	1																						√	√	—	—	—	—
TAY	A → Y													A8	2	1																						√	√	—	—	—	—
TSX	S → X													BA	2	1																						√	√	—	—	—	—
TXA	X → A													8A	2	1																						√	√	—	—	—	—
TXS	X → S													9A	2	1																						—	—	—	—	—	—
TYA	Y → A													98	2	1																						√	√	—	—	—	—

[1] ADD 1 TO "N" IF PAGE BOUNDARY IS CROSSED
[2] ADD 1 TO "N" IF BRANCH OCCURS TO SAME PAGE
    ADD 2 TO "N" IF BRANCH OCCURS TO DIFFERENT PAGE
[3] CARRY NOT = BORROW

X   INDEX X
Y   INDEX Y
A   ACCUMULATOR
M   MEMORY PER EFFECTIVE ADDRESS
Ms MEMORY PER STACK POINTER

+   ADD
-   SUBTRACT
∧   AND
∨   OR
⩒   EXCLUSIVE OR
√   MODIFIED

—   NOT MODIFIED
M7 MEMORY BIT 7
M6 MEMORY BIT 6
n   NO. CYCLES
NO. BYTES

PROCESSOR STATUS REG. "P"

7							0
N	V		B	D	I	Z	C

CARRY   1 = TRUE
ZERO   1 = RESULT ZERO
IRQ DISABLE 1 = DISABLE
DECIMAL MODE 1 = TRUE
BRK COMMAND
OVERFLOW   1 = TRUE
NEGATIVE   1 = NEG.

Microcomputer
Technical Data

The following pages contain some technical information pertaining to the 6500-series microprocessor devices. The specification sheets reprinted here are made available through the courtesy of Rockwell International Corporation. Copyright © 1978 Rockwell International Corporation. All rights reserved.

The SY2114 specification sheet is made available through the courtesy of Synertek Systems Corp. Copyright © 1978 Synertek Systems Corp. All rights reserved.

R6500 Microcomputer System

DATA SHEET

R6500 MICROPROCESSORS (CPU's)

SYSTEM ABSTRACT

The 8-bit R6500 microcomputer system is produced with N-Channel, Silicon Gate technology. Its performance speeds are enhanced by advanced system architecture. This innovative architecture results in smaller chips — the semiconductor threshold to cost-effectivity. System cost-effectivity is further enhanced by providing a family of 10 software-compatible microprocessor (CPU) devices, described in this document. Rockwell also provides memory and microcomputer system ... as well as low-cost design aids and documentation.

R6500 MICROPROCESSOR (CPU) CONCEPT

Ten CPU devices are available. All are software-compatible. They provide options of addressable memory, interrupt input, on-chip clock oscillators and drivers. All are bus-compatible with earlier generation microprocessors like the M6800 devices.

The family includes six microprocessors with on-board clock oscillators and drivers and four microprocessors driven by external clocks. The on-chip clock versions are aimed at high performance, low cost applications where single phase inputs, crystal or RC inputs provide the time base. The external clock versions are geared for multiprocessor system applications where maximum timing control is mandatory. All R6500 microprocessors are also available in a variety of packaging (ceramic and plastic), operating frequency (1 MHz and 2 MHz) and temperature (commercial, industrial and military) versions.

FEATURES

- Single +5V supply
- N channel, silicon gate, depletion load technology
- Eight bit parallel processing
- 56 Instructions
- Decimal and binary arithmetic
- Thirteen addressing modes
- True indexing capability
- Programmable stack pointer
- Variable length stack
- Interrupt capability
- Non-maskable interrupt
- Use with any type of speed memory
- 8-bit Bidirectional Data Bus
- Addressable memory range of up to 65K bytes
- "Ready" input
- Direct Memory Access capability
- Bus compatible with M6800
- 1 MHz and 2 MHz operation
- Choice of external or on-chip clocks
- On-the-chip clock options
  - External single clock input
  - RC time base input
  - Crystal time base input
- Commercial, industrial and military temperature versions
- Pipeline architecture

MEMBERS OF THE R6500 MICROPROCESSOR (CPU) FAMILY

Microprocessors with On-Chip Clock Oscillator

Model	Addressable Memory
R6502	65K Bytes
R6503	4K Bytes
R6504	8K Bytes
R6505	4K Bytes
R6506	4K Bytes
R6507	8K Bytes

Microprocessors with External Two Phase Clock Output

Model	Addressable Memory
R6512	65K Bytes
R6513	4K Bytes
R6514	8K Bytes
R6515	4K Bytes

Ordering Information

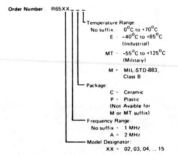

Order Number   R65XX _ _ _

Temperature Range:
No suffix = $0^{\circ}C$ to $+70^{\circ}C$
E = $-40^{\circ}C$ to $+85^{\circ}C$ (Industrial)
MT = $-55^{\circ}C$ to $+125^{\circ}C$ (Military)
M = MIL-STD-883, Class B

Package:
C = Ceramic
P = Plastic (Not Avaible for M or MT suffix)

Frequency Range:
No suffix = 1 MHz
A = 2 MHz

Model Designator:
XX = 02, 03, 04, ... 15

R6500 Signal Description

Clocks (ϕ_1, ϕ_2)

The R651X requires a two phase non-overlapping clock that runs at the V_{CC} voltage level.

The R650X clocks are supplied with an internal clock generator. The frequency of these clocks is externally controlled.

Address Bus (A0-A15)

These outputs are TTL compatible, capable of driving one standard TTL load and 130 pF.

Data Bus (D0-D7)

Eight pins are used for the data bus. This is a bidirectional bus, transferring data to and from the device and peripherals. The outputs are tri-state buffers capable of driving one standard TTL load and 130 pF.

Data Bus Enable (DBE)

This TTL compatible input allows external control of the tri-state data output buffers and will enable the microprocessor bus driver when in the high state. In normal operation DBE would be driven by the phase two (ϕ_2) clock, thus allowing data output from microprocessor only during ϕ_2. During the read cycle, the data bus drivers are internally disabled, becoming essentially an open circuit. To disable data bus drivers externally, DBE should be held low.

Ready (RDY)

This input signal allows the user to halt or single cycle the microprocessor on all cycles except write cycles. A negative transition to the low state during or coincident with phase one (ϕ_1) will halt the microprocessor with the output address lines reflecting the current address being fetched. If Ready is low during a write cycle, it is ignored until the following read operation. This condition will remain through a subsequent phase two (ϕ_2) in which the Ready signal is low. This feature allows microprocessor interfacing with the low speed PROMS as well as fast (max. 2 cycle) Direct Memory Access (DMA).

Interrupt Request (IRQ)

This TTL level input requests that an interrupt sequence begin within the microprocessor. The microprocessor will complete the current instruction being executed before recognizing the request. At that time, the interrupt mask bit in the Status Code Register will be examined. If the interrupt mask flag is not set, the microprocessor will begin an interrupt sequence. The Program Counter and Processor Status Register are stored in the stack. The microprocessor will then set the interrupt mask flag high so that no further interrupts may occur. At the end of this cycle, the program counter low will be loaded from address FFFE, and program counter high from location FFFF, therefore transferring program control to the memory vector located at these addresses. The RDY signal must be in the high state for any interrupt to be recognized. A 3KΩ external resistor should be used for proper wire-OR operation.

Non-Maskable Interrupt (NMI)

A negative going edge on this input requests that a non-maskable interrupt sequence be generated within the microprocessor.

NMI is an unconditional interrupt. Following completion of the current instruction, the sequence of operations defined for IRQ will be performed, regardless of the state interrupt mask flag. The vector address loaded into the program counter, low and high, are locations FFFA and FFFB respectively, thereby transferring program control to the memory vector located at these addresses. The instructions loaded at these locations cause the microprocessor to branch to a non-maskable interrupt routine in memory.

NMI also requires an external 3K Ω register to V_{CC} for proper wire-OR operations.

Inputs IRQ and NMI are hardware interrupts lines that are sampled during ϕ_2 (phase 2) and will begin the appropriate interrupt routine on the ϕ_1 (phase 1) following the completion of the current instruction.

Set Overflow Flag (S.O.)

A negative going edge on this input sets the overflow bit in the Status Code Register. This signal is sampled on the trailing edge of ϕ_1 and must be externally synchronized.

SYNC

This output line is provided to identify those cycles in which the microprocessor is doing an OP CODE fetch. The SYNC line goes high during ϕ_1 of an OP CODE fetch and stays high for the remainder of that cycle. If the RDY line is pulled low during the ϕ_1 clock pulse in which SYNC went high, the processor will stop in its current state and will remain in the state until the RDY line goes high. In this manner, the SYNC signal can be used to control RDY to cause single instruction execution.

Reset

This input is used to reset or start the microprocessor from a power down condition. During the time that this line is held low, writing to or from the microprocessor is inhibited. When a positive edge is detected on the input, the microprocessor will immediately begin the reset sequence.

After a system initialization time of six clock cycles, the mask interrupt flag will be set and the microprocessor will load the program counter from the memory vector locations FFFC and FFFD. This is the start location for program control.

After V_{CC} reaches 4.75 volts in a power up routine, reset must be held low for at least two clock cycles. At this time the R/W and (SYNC) signal will become valid.

When the reset signal goes high following these two clock cycles, the microprocessor will proceed with the normal reset procedure detailed above.

Clock Timing – R6502, 03, 04, 05, 06, 07

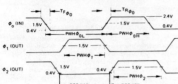

Timing for Reading Data from Memory or Peripherals

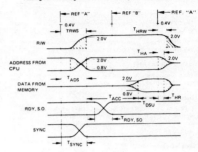

Clock Timing – R6512, 13, 14, 15

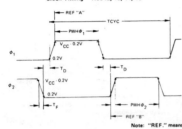

Timing for Writing Data to Memory or Peripherals

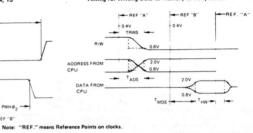

Note: "REF." means Reference Points on clocks.

PROGRAMMING MODEL

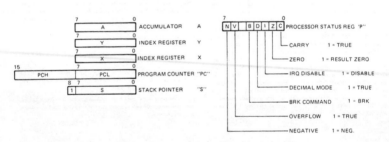

A	ACCUMULATOR	A
Y	INDEX REGISTER	Y
X	INDEX REGISTER	X
PCH PCL	PROGRAM COUNTER "PC"	
1 S	STACK POINTER	"S"

N V   B D I Z C   PROCESSOR STATUS REG "P"

- CARRY   1 = TRUE
- ZERO   1 = RESULT ZERO
- IRQ DISABLE   1 = DISABLE
- DECIMAL MODE   1 = TRUE
- BRK COMMAND   1 = BRK
- OVERFLOW   1 = TRUE
- NEGATIVE   1 = NEG.

1 MHz Timing

Clock Timing — R6502, 03, 04, 05, 06, 07

Characteristic	Symbol	Min	Typ	Max	Units
Cycle Time	T_{CYC}*	1000			ns
$\phi_{o(IN)}$ Pulse Width (measured at 1.5V)	PWHϕ_0	460		520	ns
$\phi_{o(IN)}$ Rise, Fall Time	TRϕ_0, TFϕ_0			10	ns
Delay Time Between Clocks (measured at 1.5V)	T_D	5			ns
$\phi_{1(OUT)}$ Pulse Width (measured at 1.5V)	PWHϕ_1	PWHϕ_{0L} 70		PWHϕ_{0L}	ns
$\phi_{2(OUT)}$ Pulse Width (measured at 1.5V)	PWHϕ_2	PWHϕ_{0H} 40		PWHϕ_{0H} 10	ns
$\phi_{1(OUT)}$, $\phi_{2(OUT)}$ Rise, Fall Time (measured at 0.8V to 2.0V) (Load 30 pf (1 TTL))	T_R, T_F			25	ns

2 MHz Timing

Clock Timing — R6502, 03, 04, 05, 06, 07

Characteristic	Symbol	Min	Typ	Max	Units
Cycle Time	T_{CYC}*	500			ns
$\phi_{o(IN)}$ Pulse Width (measured at 1.5V)	PWHϕ_0	240		260	ns
$\phi_{o(IN)}$ Rise, Fall Time	TRϕ_0, TFϕ_0			10	ns
Delay Time Between Clocks (measured at 1.5V)	T_D	5			ns
$\phi_{1(OUT)}$ Pulse Width (measured at 1.5V)	PWHϕ_1	PWHϕ_{0L} 70		PWHϕ_{0L}	ns
$\phi_{2(OUT)}$ Pulse Width (measured at 1.5V)	PWHϕ_2	PWHϕ_{0H} 40		PWHϕ_{0H} 10	ns
$\phi_{1(OUT)}$, $\phi_{2(OUT)}$ Rise, Fall Time (measured at 0.8V to 2.0V) (Load 30 pf (1 TTL))	T_R, T_F			25	ns

* The lowest operating frequency for the commercial temperature range CPU's is 100 KHz, which corresponds to a maximum cycle time (T_{CYC}) of 10 μs. The lowest operating frequency for the industrial and military temperature range CPU's is 250 KHz, which corresponds to a maximum cycle time (T_{CYC}) of 4 μs.

Clock Timing — R6512, 13, 14, 15

Characteristic	Symbol	Min	Typ	Max	Units
Cycle Time	T_{CYC}*	1000			ns
Clock Pulse Width φ1 (Measured at Vcc 0.2V) φ2	PWH φ1 / PWH φ2	430 / 470			ns
Fall Time (Measured from 0.2V to Vcc 0.2V)	t_F			25	ns
Delay Time between Clocks (Measured at 0.2V)	t_D	0			ns

Clock Timing — R6512, 13, 14, 15

Characteristic	Symbol	Min	Typ	Max	Units
Cycle Time	T_{CYC}*	500			ns
Clock Pulse Width φ1 (Measured at Vcc 0.2V) φ2	PWH φ1 / PWH φ2	215 / 215			ns
Fall Time (Measured from 0.2V to Vcc 0.2V)	t_F			12	ns
Delay Time between Clocks (Measured at 0.2V)	t_D	0			ns

Read/Write Timing **

Characteristic	Symbol	Min	Typ	Max	Units
Read/Write Setup Time from R6500	T_{RWS}		100	225	ns
Address Setup Time from R6500	T_{ADS}		100	225	ns
Memory Read Access Time	T_{ACC}			650	ns
Data Stability Time Period	T_{DSU}	100			ns
Data Hold Time – Read	T_{HR}	10			ns
Data Hold Time – Write	T_{HW}	60	90		ns
Data Setup Time from R6500	T_{MDS}		150	175	ns
RDY, S.O Setup Time	T_{RDY}	100			ns
SYNC Setup Time from R6500	T_{SYNC}			225	ns
Address Hold Time	T_{HA}	30	60		ns
R/W Hold Time	T_{HRW}	30	60		ns

Read/Write Timing **

Characteristic	Symbol	Min	Typ	Max	Units
Read/Write Setup Time from R6500A	T_{RWS}		75	140	ns
Address Setup Time from R6500A	T_{ADS}		75	140	ns
Memory Read Access Time	T_{ACC}			310	ns
Data Stability Time Period	T_{DSU}	50			ns
Data Hold Time – Read	T_{HR}	10			ns
Data Hold Time – Write	T_{HW}	60	90		ns
Data Setup Time from R6500A	T_{MDS}		75	100	ns
RDY, S.O Setup Time	T_{RDY}	50			ns
SYNC Setup Time from R6500A	T_{SYNC}			150	ns
Address Hold Time	T_{HA}	30	60		ns
R/W Hold Time	T_{HRW}	30	60		ns

** Load Conditions = 1 TTL Load + 130 pf

RECOMMENDED TIME BASE GENERATION

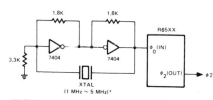

*CRYSTAL: CTS KNIGHTS MP SERIES, OR EQUIVALENT

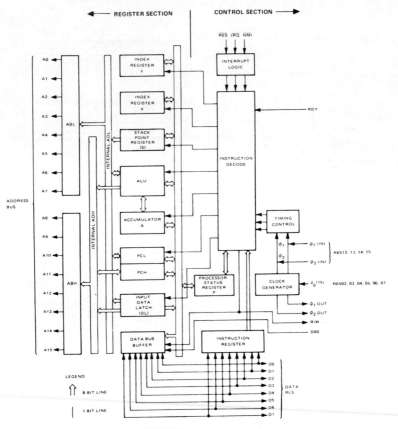

R6500 Internal Architecture

Note   1. Clock Generator is not included on R6512, 13, 14, 15
        2. Addressing Capability and control options vary with each
            of the R6500 Products.

SPECIFICATIONS

Maximum Ratings

Rating	Symbol	Value	Unit
Supply Voltage	V_{CC}	-0.3 to +7.0	Vdc
Input Voltage	V_{in}	-0.3 to +7.0	Vdc
Operating Temperature	T		°C
Commercial		0 to +70	
Industrial		-40 to +85	
Military		-55 to +125	
Storage Temperature	T_{STG}	-55 to +150	°C

This device contains input protection against damage due to high static voltages or electric fields; however, precautions should be taken to avoid application of voltages higher than the maximum rating.

Electrical Characteristics

(V_{CC} = 5.0 ±5%, V_{SS} = 0)

ϕ_1, ϕ_2 applies to R6512, 13, 14, 15, $\phi_{o(in)}$ applies to R6502, 03, 04, 05, 06 and 07.

Characteristic	Symbol	Min	Typ	Max	Unit
Input High Voltage	V_{IH}				Vdc
Logic, $\phi_{o(in)}$		V_{SS} + 2.4	–	V_{CC}	
ϕ_1, ϕ_2		V_{CC} - 0.2	–	V_{CC} + 0.25	
Input Low Voltage	V_{IL}				Vdc
Logic, $\phi_{o(in)}$		V_{SS} - 0.3	–	V_{SS} + 0.4	
ϕ_1, ϕ_2		V_{SS} - 0.3	–	V_{SS} + 0.2	
Input High Threshold Voltage	V_{IHT}				Vdc
$\overline{RES}$, $\overline{NMI}$, RDY, $\overline{IRQ}$, Data, S.O.		V_{SS} + 2.0	–	–	
Input Low Threshold Voltage	V_{ILT}				Vdc
$\overline{RES}$, $\overline{NMI}$, RDY, $\overline{IRQ}$, Data, S.O.		–	–	V_{SS} + 0.8	
Input Leakage Current	I_{in}				μA
(V_{in} = 0 to 5.25V, V_{CC} = 0)					
Logic (Excl. RDY, S.O.)		–	–	2.5	
ϕ_1, ϕ_2		–	–	100	
$\phi_{o(in)}$		–	–	10.0	
Three-State (Off State) Input Current	I_{TSI}				μA
(V_{in} = 0.4 to 2.4V, V_{CC} = 5.25V)					
Data Lines		–		10	
Output High Voltage	V_{OH}				Vdc
(I_{LOAD} = -100 μAdc, V_{CC} = 4.75V)					
SYNC, Data, A0-A15, R/W, ϕ_1, ϕ_2		V_{SS} + 2.4	–	–	
Output Low Voltage	V_{OL}				Vdc
(I_{LOAD} = 1.6 mAdc, V_{CC} = 4.75V)					
SYNC, Data, A0-A15, R/W, ϕ_1, ϕ_2		–	–	V_{SS} + 0.4	
Power Dissipation	P_D				W
Commercial temp. versions			0.25	0.575	
Industrial and military temp. versions			0.25	0.700	
Capacitance at 25°C	C				pF
(V_{in} = 0, f = 1 MHz)					
Logic	C_{in}	–	–	10	
Data		–	–	15	
A0-A15, R/W, SYNC	C_{out}	–	–	12	
$\phi_{o(in)}$	$C_{\phi_{o(in)}}$	–	–	15	
ϕ_1	C_{ϕ_1}	–	30	50	
ϕ_2	C_{ϕ_2}	–	50	80	

Note: $\overline{IRQ}$ and $\overline{NMI}$ require 3K pull-up resistors.

R6500 Microcomputer System

DATA SHEET

VERSATILE INTERFACE ADAPTER (VIA)

R6522 VERSATILE INTERFACE ADAPTER (VIA)

SYSTEM ABSTRACT

The 8-bit R6500 microcomputer system is produced with N-channel, silicon-gate, depletion-load technology. Its performance speeds are enhanced by advanced system architecture. Its innovative architecture results in smaller chips — the semiconductor threshold to cost-effectivity. System cost-effectivity is further enhanced by providing a family of 10 software-compatible microprocessor (CPU) devices, memory and I/O devices . . . as well as low-cost design aids and documentation.

DESCRIPTION

The R6522 VIA adds two powerful, flexible Interval Timers, a serial-to-parallel/parallel-to-serial shift register and input latching on the peripheral ports to the capabilities of the R6520 Peripheral Interface Adapter (PIA) device. Handshaking capability is expanded to allow control of bidirectional data transfers between VIAs in multiple processor systems and between peripherals.

Control of peripherals is primarily through two 8-bit bidirectional ports. Each of these ports can be programmed to act as an input or an output. Peripheral I/O lines can be selectively controlled by the Interval Timers to generate programmable-frequency square waves and/or to count externally generated pulses. Positive control of VIA functions is gained through its internal register organization: Interrupt Flag Register, Interrupt Enable Register, and two Function Control Registers.

FEATURES

- Organized for simplified software control of many functions
- Compatible with the R650X and R651X family of microprocessors (CPUs)
- Bi-directional, 8-bit data bus for communication with microprocessor
- Two Bi-directional, 8-bit input/output ports for interface with peripheral devices
- CMOS and TTL compatible input/output peripheral ports
- Data Direction Registers allow each peripheral pin to act as either an input or an output
- Interrupt Flag Register allows the microprocessor to readily determine the source of an interrupt and provides convenient control of the interrupts within the chip
- Handshake control logic for input/output peripheral data transfer operations
- Data latching on peripheral input/output ports
- Two fully-programmable interval timers/counters
- Eight-bit Shift Register for serial interface
- Forty-pin plastic or ceramic DIP package.

Ordering Information

Order Number	Package Type	Frequency	Temperature Range
R6522P	Plastic	1 MHz	0°C to $+70^{\circ}$C
R6522AP	Plastic	2 MHz	0°C to $+70^{\circ}$C
R6522C	Ceramic	1 MHz	0°C to $+70^{\circ}$C
R6522AC	Ceramic	2 MHz	0°C to $+70^{\circ}$C
R6522PE	Plastic	1 MHz	-40°C to $+85^{\circ}$C
R6522APE	Plastic	2 MHz	-40°C to $+85^{\circ}$C
R6522CE	Ceramic	1 MHz	-40°C to $+85^{\circ}$C
R6522ACE	Ceramic	2 MHz	-40°C to $+85^{\circ}$C
R6522CMT	Ceramic	1 MHz	-55°C to $+125^{\circ}$C

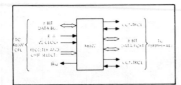

Basic R6522 Interface Diagram

Pin Configuration

OPERATION SUMMARY

Register Select Lines (RS0, RS1, RS2, RS3)

The four Register select lines are normally connected to the processor address bus lines to allow the processor to select the internal R6522 register which is to be accessed. The sixteen possible combinations access the registers as follows:

RS3	RS2	RS1	RS0	Register	Remarks	RS3	RS2	RS1	RS0	Register	Remarks
L	L	L	L	ORB		H	L	L	L	T2L-L	Write Latch
L	L	L	H	ORA	Controls Handshake					T2C-L	Read Counter
L	L	H	L	DDRB		H	L	L	H	T2C-H	Triggers T2L-L/T2C-L Transfer
L	L	H	H	DDRA							
L	H	L	L	T1L-L T1C-L	Write Latch Read Counter	H	L	H		SR	
L	H	L	H	T1C-H	Trigger T1L-L/T1C-L Transfer	H	L	H	H	ACR	
						H	H	L	L	PCR	
L	H	H	L	T1L-L		H	H	L	H	IFR	
L	H	H	H	T1L-H		H	H	H	L	IER	
						H	H	H	H	ORA	No Effect on Handshake

Note: L = 0.4V DC, H = 2.4V DC.

Timer 2 Control

RS3	RS2	RS1	RS0	R/W = L	R/W = H
H	L	L	L	Write T2L-L	Read T2C-L Clear Interrupt flag
H	L	L	H	Write T2C-H Transfer T2L-L to T2C-L Clear Interrupt flag	Read T2C-H

Writing the Timer 1 Register

The operations which take place when writing to each of the four T1 addresses are as follows:

RS3	RS2	RS1	RS0	Operation (R/W = L)
L	H	L	L	Write into low order latch
L	H	L	H	Write into high order latch Write into high order counter Transfer low order latch into low order counter Reset T1 interrupt flag
L	H	H	L	Write low order latch
X	H	H	H	Write high order latch Reset T1 interrupt flag

Reading the Timer 1 Registers

For reading the Timer 1 registers, the four addresses relate directly to the four registers as follows:

RS3	RS2	RS1	RS0	Operation (R/W = H)
L	H	L	L	Read T1 low order counter Reset T1 interrupt flag
L	H	L	H	Read T1 high order counter
L	H	H	L	Read T1 low order latch
L	H	H	H	Read T1 high order latch

Timer 1 Operating Modes

Two bits are provided in the Auxiliary Control Register to allow selection of the T1 operating modes. These bits and the four possible modes are as follows:

ACR7 Output Enable	ACR6 "Free-Run" Enable	Mode
0	0	Generate a single time-out interrupt each time T1 is loaded
0	1	Generate continuous interrupts
1	0	Generate a single interrupt and an output pulse on PB7 for each T1 load operation
1	1	Generate continuous interrupts and a square wave output on PB7

FUNCTION CONTROL

Control of the various functions and operating modes within the R6522 is accomplished primarily through two registers, the Peripheral Control Register (PCR), and the Auxiliary Control Register (ACR). The PCR is used primarily to select the operating mode for the four peripheral control pins. The Auxiliary Control Register selects the operating mode for the Interval Timers (T1, T2), and the Serial Port (SR).

Peripheral Control Register

The Peripheral Control Register is organized as follows:

Bit #	7	6	5	4	3	2	1	0
Function		CB2 Control		CB1 Control		CA2 Control		CA1 Control

Typical functions are shown below:

PCR3	PCR2	PCR1	Mode
0	0	0	Input mode — Set CA2 interrupt flag (IFR0) on a negative transition of the input signal. Clear IFR0 on a read or write of the Peripheral A Output Register.
0	0	1	Independent interrupt input mode — Set IFR0 on a negative transition of the CA2 input signal. Reading or writing ORA does not clear the CA2 interrupt flag.
0	1	0	Input mode — Set CA2 interrupt flag on a positive transition of the CA2 input signal. Clear IFR0 with a read or write of the Peripheral A Output Register.
0	1	1	Independent interrupt input mode — Set IFR0 on a positive transition of the CA2 input signal. Reading or writing ORA does not clear the CA2 interrupt flag.
1	0	0	Handshake output mode — Set CA2 output low on a read or write of the Peripheral A Output Register. Reset CA2 high with an active transition on CA1.
1	0	1	Pulse output mode — CA2 goes low for one cycle following a read or write of the Peripheral A Output Register.
1	1	0	Manual output mode — The CA2 output is held low in this mode.
1	1	1	Manual output mode — The CA2 output is held high in this mode.

Auxiliary Control Register

Many of the functions in the Auxiliary Control Register have been discussed previously. However, a summary of this register is presented here as a convenient reference for the R6522 user. The Auxiliary Control Register is organized as follows:

Bit #	7	6	5	4	3	2	1	0
Function	T1 Control		T2 Control	Shift Register Control			PB Latch Enable	PA Latch Enable

Shift Register Control

The Shift Register operating mode is selected as follows:

ACR4	ACR3	ACR2	Mode
0	0	0	Shift Register Disabled.
0	0	1	Shift in under control of Timer 2.
0	1	0	Shift in under control of system clock.
0	1	1	Shift in under control of external clock pulses.
1	0	0	Free-running output at rate determined by Timer 2.
1	0	1	Shift out under control of Timer 2.
1	1	0	Shift out under control of the system clock.
1	1	1	Shift out under control of external clock pulses.

T2 Control

Timer 2 operates in two modes. If ACR5 = 0, T2 acts as an interval timer in the one-shot mode. If ACR5 = 1, Timer 2 acts to count a predetermined number of pulses on pin PB6.

TIMING CHARACTERISTICS

Read Timing Characteristics (loading 130 pF and one TTL load)

Parameter	Symbol	Min	Typ	Max	Unit
Delay time, address valid to clock positive transition	T_{ACR}	180	–	–	nS
Delay time, clock positive transition to data valid on bus	T_{CDR}	–	–	395	nS
Peripheral data setup time	T_{PCR}	300	–	–	nS
Data bus hold time	T_{HR}	10	–	–	nS
Rise and fall time for clock input	T_{RC} T_{RF}	–	–	25	nS

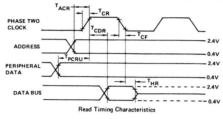

Read Timing Characteristics

Write Timing Characteristics

Parameter	Symbol	Min	Typ	Max	Unit
Enable pulse width	T_C	0.47	–	25	μS
Delay time, address valid to clock positive transition	T_{ACW}	180	–	–	nS
Delay time, data valid to clock negative transition	T_{DCW}	300	–	–	nS
Delay time, read/write negative transition to clock positive transition	T_{WCW}	180	–	–	nS
Data bus hold time	T_{HW}	10	–	–	nS
Delay time, Enable negative transition to peripheral data valid	T_{CPW}	–	–	1.0	μS
Delay time, clock negative transition to peripheral data valid CMOS (VCC - 30%)	T_{CMOS}	–	–	2.0	μS

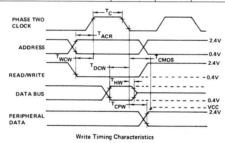

Write Timing Characteristics

I/O Timing Characteristics

Characteristic	Symbol	Min	Typ	Max	Unit
Rise and fall time for CA1, CB1, CA2 and CB2 input signals	T_{RF}	–	–	1.0	μs
Delay time, clock negative transition to CA2 negative transition (read handshake or pulse mode)	T_{CA2}	–	–	1.0	μs
Delay time, clock negative transition to CA2 positive transition (pulse mode)	T_{RS1}	–	–	1.0	μs
Delay time, CA1 active transition to CA2 positive transition (handshake mode)	T_{RS2}	–	–	2.0	μs
Delay time, clock positive transition to CA2 or CB2 negative transition (write handshake)	T_{WHS}	–	–	1.0	μs
Delay time, peripheral data valid to CB2 negative transition	T_{DC}	0	–	1.5	μs
Delay time, clock positive transition to CA2 or CB2 positive transition (pulse mode)	T_{RS3}	–	–	1.0	μs
Delay time, CB1 active transition to CA2 or CB2 positive transition (handshake mode)	T_{RS4}		–	2.0	μs
Delay time, peripheral data valid to CA1 or CB1 active transition (input latching)	T_{IL}	300	–		ns
Delay time CB1 negative transition to CB2 data valid (internal SR clock, shift out)	T_{SR1}		–	300	ns
Delay time, negative transition of CB1 input clock to CB2 data valid (external clock, shift out)	T_{SR2}			300	ns
Delay time, CB2 data valid to positive transition of CB1 clock (shift in, internal or external clock)	T_{SR3}	–		300	ns
Pulse Width – PB6 Input Pulse	T_{IPW}	2			μs
Pulse Width – CB1 Input Clock	T_{ICW}	2			μs
Pulse Spacing – PB6 Input Pulse	I_{IPS}	2	–		μs
Pulse Spacing – CB1 Input Pulse	I_{ICS}	2			μs

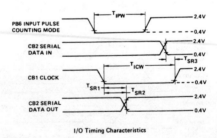

I/O Timing Characteristics

SPECIFICATIONS

Maximum Ratings

Rating	Symbol	Value	Unit
Supply Voltage	V_{CC}	-0.3 to +7.0	Vdc
Input Voltage	V_{IN}	-0.3 to +7.0	Vdc
Operating Temperature Range	T		^{o}C
Commercial		0 to +70	
Industrial		-40 to +85	
Military		-55 to +125	
Storage Temperature Range	T_{STG}	-55 to +150	^{o}C

This device contains circuitry to protect the inputs against damage due to high static voltages. However, it is advised that normal precautions be taken to avoid application of any voltage higher than maximum rated voltages.

Electrical Characteristics

(VCC - 5.0V ±5%, VSS = 0)

Characteristic	Symbol	Min	Max	Unit
Input high voltage (normal operation)	V_{IH}	+2.4	VCC	Vdc
Input low voltage (normal operation)	V_{IL}	-0.3	+0.8	Vdc
Input leakage current — V_{in} = 0 to 5 Vdc R/W, RES, RS0, RS1, RS2, RS3, CS1, CS2, CA1, Ø2	I_{IN}	—	±2.5	μAdc
Off-state input current — V_{in} - 0.4 to 2.4V VCC = Max, D0 to D7	I_{TSI}	—	±10	μAdc
Input high current — V_{IH} = 2.4V PA0-PA7, CA2, PB0-PB7, CB1, CB2	I_{IH}	-100	—	μAdc
Input low current — V_{IL} - 0.4 Vdc PA0-PA7, CA2, PB0-PB7, CB1, CB2	I_{IL}	—	-1.6	mAdc
Output high voltage VCC = min, I_{load} = -100 μAdc PA0-PA7, CA2, PB0-PB7, CB1, CB2	V_{OH}	2.4	—	Vdc
Output low voltage VCC = min, I_{load} = 1.6 mAdc	V_{OL}	—	+0.4	Vdc
Output high current (sourcing) V_{OH} = 2.4V V_{OH} = 1.5V, PB0-PB7, CB1, CB2	I_{OH}	-100 -1.0	— —	μAdc mAdc
Output low current (sinking) V_{OL} = 0.4 Vdc	I_{OL}	1.6	—	mAdc
Output leakage current (off state) IRQ	I_{off}		10	μAdc
Input Capacitance — T_A = 25°C, f = 1 MHz R/W, RES, RE0, RS1, RS2, RS3, CS1, CS2, D0-D7, PA0-PA7, CA2, PB0-PB7, CB1, CB2 Ø2 input	C_{in}	— — 	7.0 10 20	pF
Output capacitance — T_A - 25°C, f = 1 MHz	C_{out}	—	10	pF
Power dissipation	P_d	—	750	mW

R6500 Microcomputer System
DATA SHEET

ROM-RAM-I/O-INTERVAL TIMER DEVICE (RRIOT)

SYSTEM ABSTRACT

The 8-bit R6500 microcompu... system is produced with N-channel, Silicon-Gate techno'.gy. Its performance speeds are enhanced by advanced system architecture. Its innovative architecture results in smaller chips -- the semiconductor threshold to cost-effectivity. System cost-effectivity is further enhanced by providing a family of 10 software-compatible microprocessor (CPU) devices. Rockwell also provides memory and I/O devices that further enhance the cost-effectivity of the R6500 microcomputer system . . . as well as low-cost design aids and documentation.

FEATURES

- 8 bit bidirectional Data Bus for direct communication with the microprocessor
- 1024 x 8 ROM
- 64 x 8 static RAM
- Two 8 bit bidirectional data ports for interface to peripherals
- Two programmable Data Direction Registers
- Programmable Interval Timer
- Programmable Interval Timer Interrupt
- TTL & CMOS compatible peripheral lines
- Peripheral pins with Direct Transistor Drive Capability
- High Impedance Three-State Data Bus
- Allows up to 7K contiguous bytes of ROM with no external decoding

DESCRIPTION

The R6530 is designed to operate in conjunction with the R6500 Microprocessor Family. It is comprised of a mask programmable 1024 x 8 ROM, a 64 x 8 static RAM, two software controlled 8 bit bidirectional data ports allowing direct interfacing between the microprocessor unit and peripheral devices, and a software programmable interval timer with interrupt, capable of timing in various intervals from 1 to 262,144 clock periods.

Ordering Information

Order Number	Package Type	Temperature Range
R6530P	Plastic	0°C to +70°C
R6530C	Ceramic	0°C to +70°C

A custom number will be assigned by Rockwell.

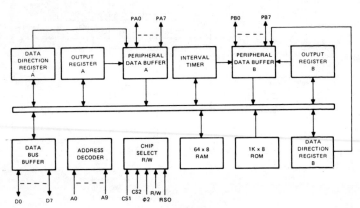

R6530 Block Diagram

INTERFACE SIGNAL DESCRIPTION

Reset (RES)

During system initialization a Logic "0" on the RES input will cause a zeroing of all four I/O registers. This in turn will cause all I/O buses to act as inputs thus protecting external components from possible damage and erroneous data while the system is being configured under software control. The Data Bus Buffers are put into an off state during Reset. Interrupt capability is disabled with the RES signal. The RES signal must be held low for at least one clock period when reset is required.

Read/Write (R/W)

The R/W signal is supplied by the microprocessor and is used to control the transfer of data to and from the microprocessor and the R6530. A high on the R/W pin allows the processor to read (with proper addressing) the data supplied by the R6530. A low on the R/W pin allows a write (with proper addressing) to the R6530.

Interrupt Request (IRQ)

The IRQ pin is an interrupt pin from the interval timer. This same pin, if not used as an interrupt, can be used as a peripheral I/O pin (PB7). When used as an interrupt, the pin should be set up as an input by the Data Direction Register. The pin will be normally high with a low indicating an interrupt from the R6530. An external pull-up device is not required; however, if collector-OR'd with other devices, the internal pullup may be omitted with a mask option.

Data Bus (D0-D7)

The R6530 has eight bidirectional data pins (D0-D7). These pins connect to the system's data lines and allow transfer of data to and from the microprocessor. The output buffers remain in the off state except when selected for a Read operation.

Peripheral Data Ports

The R6530 has 16 pins available for peripheral I/O operations. Each pin is individually software programmable to act as either an input or an output. The 16 pins are divided into two 8-bit ports, PA0-PA7 and PB0-PB7. PB5, PB6 and PB7 also have other uses which are discussed in later sections. The pins are set up as an input by writing a "0" into the corresponding bit of the Data Direction Register. A "1" into the Data Direction Register will cause its corresponding bit to be an output. In the input mode, the Peripheral Data Buffers are in the "1" state and the internal pull-up device acts as less than one TTL load to the peripheral data lines. On a Read operation, the microprocessor unit reads the peripheral pin. When the peripheral device gets information from the R6530 it receives data stored in the Output Register. The microprocessor will read correct information if the peripheral lines are greater than 2.0 volts (for a "1") or less than 0.8 volts (for a "0") as the peripheral pins are all TTL compatible.

Address Lines (A0-A9)

There are 10 address pins (A0-A9). In addition, there is the ROM Select pin (RS0). Further, pins PB5 and PB6 are mask programmable, and can be used either individually or together as chip selects. When used as peripheral data pins they cannot be used as chip selects.

INTERNAL ORGANIZATION

The R6530 is divided into four basic sections: RAM, ROM, I/O and Timer. The RAM and ROM interface directly with the microprocessor through the system data bus and address lines. The I/O section consists of two 8-bit halves. Each half contains a Data Direction Register (DDR) and an Output Register.

ROM 1K Byte (8K Bits)

The 8K ROM is in a 1024 x 8 configuration. Address lines A0-A9, as well as RS0 are needed to address the entire ROM. With the addition of CS1 and CS2, seven R6530's may be addressed, giving 7168 x 8 bits of contiguous ROM.

RAM — 64 Bytes (512 Bits)

A 64 x 8 static RAM is contained on the R6530. It is addressed by A0-A5 (Byte Select), RS0, A6, A7, A8, A9 and, depending on the number of chips in the system, CS1 and CS2.

Internal Peripheral Registers

There are four internal registers, two data direction registers and two output registers. The two data direction registers (A side and B side) control the direction of the data into and out of the peripheral pins. A "1" written into the Data Direction Register sets up the corresponding peripheral buffer pin as an output. Therefore, anything then written into the Output Register will appear on that corresponding peripheral pin. A "0" written into the DDR inhibits the output buffer from transmitting data from the Output Register. For example, a "1" loaded into Data Direction Register A, position 3, sets up peripheral pin PA3 as an output. If a "0" had been loaded, PA3 would be configured as an input and remain in the high state. The two Data Output Registers are used to latch data from the Data Bus during a Write operation until the peripheral device can read the data supplied by the microprocessor.

During a Read operation the microprocessor is reading the peripheral data pins. For the peripheral data pins which are programmed as outputs the microprocessor will read the corresponding data bits of the Output Register. The only way the Output Register data can be changed is by a microprocessor Write operation. The Output Register is not affected by a Read of the data on the peripheral pins.

Interval Timer

The Timer section of the R6530 contains three basic parts: pre-scale divide down register, programmable 8-bit register and interrupt logic.

The interval timer can be programmed to count up to 256 time intervals. Each time interval can be either 1T, 8T, 64T or 1024T increments, where T is the system clock period. When a full count is reached, an interrupt flag is set to a logic "1". After the interrupt flag is set the internal clock begins counting down to a maximum of -255T. Thus, after the interrupt flag is set, a Read of the timer will tell how long since the flag was set up to a maximum of 255T.

The 8 bit system Data Bus is used to transfer data to and from the Interval Timer. If a count of 52 time intervals were to be counted, the pattern 0 0 1 1 0 1 0 0 would be put on the Data Bus and written into the Interval Timer Register.

At the same time that data is being written to the Interval Timer, the counting interval (1, 8, 64 or 1024T) is decoded from address lines A0 and A1. During a Read or Write operation address line A3 controls the interrupt capability of PB7, i.e., $A_3 = 1$ enables IRQ on PB7, $A_3 = 0$ disables IRQ on PB7. When PB7 is to be used as an interrupt flag with the interval timer it should be programmed as an input. If PB7 is enabled by A3 and an interrupt occurs PB7 will go low. When the timer is read prior to the interrupt flag being set, the number of time intervals remaining will be read, i.e., 51, 50, 49, etc.

When the timer has counted down to 0 0 0 0 0 0 0 0 on the next count time an interrupt will occur and the counter will read 1 1 1 1 1 1 1 1. After interrupt, the Timer Register decrements at a divide by "1" rate of the system clock. If after interrupt, the timer is read and a value of 1 1 1 0 0 1 0 0 is read, the time since interrupt is 27T. The value read is in one's complement.

$$\text{Value read} = 1\ 1\ 1\ 0\ 0\ 1\ 0\ 0$$
$$\text{Complement} = 0\ 0\ 0\ 1\ 1\ 0\ 1\ 1 = 27$$

Thus, to arrive at the total elapsed time, merely do a one's complement and add to the original time written into the timer. Again, assume time written as 0 0 1 1 0 1 0 0 (=52). With a divide by 8, total time to interrupt is (52 x 8) + 1 = 417T. Total elapsed time would be 417T + 27T = 444T, assuming the value read after interrupt was 1 1 1 0 0 1 0 0.

After the interrupt, whenever the timer is written or read the interrupt is reset. However, the reading of the timer at the same time the interrupt occurs will not reset the interrupt flag. When the interrupt flag is read on DB7 all other DB outputs (DB0 thru DB6) go to "0".

When reading the timer after an interrupt, A3 should be low so as to disable the $\overline{\text{IRQ}}$ pin. This is done so as to avoid future interrupts until after another Write timer operation.

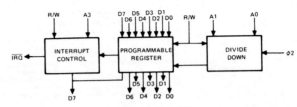

Basic Elements of Interval Timer

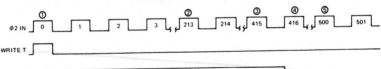

1. Data written into interval timer is 0 0 1 1 0 1 0 0 = 52_{10}

2. Data in Interval timer is 0 0 0 1 1 0 0 1 = 25_{10}
   $$52 \cdot \frac{213}{8} \cdot 1 = 52\cdot26\cdot1 = 25$$

3. Data in Interval timer is 0 0 0 0 0 0 0 0 = 0_{10}
   $$52 \cdot \frac{415}{8} \cdot 1 = 52\cdot51\cdot1 = 0$$

4. Interrupt has occurred at Ø2 pulse #416
   Data in Interval timer = 1 1 1 1 1 1 1 1

5. Data in Interval timer is 1 0 1 0 1 1 0 0
   two's complement is 0 1 0 1 0 0 1 1 = 83_{10}
   $$83 + (52 \times 8) + 1 = 500_{10}$$

ADDRESSING

Addressing of the R6530 offers many variations to the user for greater flexibility. The user may configure his system with RAM in lower memory, ROM in higher memory, and I/O registers with interval timers between the extremes. There are 10 address lines (A0-A9). In addition, there is the possibility of 3 additional address lines to be used as chip-selects and to distinguish between ROM, RAM, I/O and interval timer. Two of the additional lines are chip-selects 1 and 2 (CS1 and CS2). The chip-select pins can also be PB5 and PB6. Whether the pins are used as chip-selects or peripheral I/O pins is a mask option and must be specified when ordering the part. Both pins act independently of each other in that either or both pins may be designated as a chip-select. The third additional address line is RS0. The R6502 and R6530 in a 2-chip system would use RS0 to distinguish between ROM and non-ROM sections of the R6530. With the addressing pins available, a total of 7K contiguous ROM may be addressed with no external decode. Below is an example of a 1-chip and a 7-chip R6530 Addressing Scheme.

One-Chip Addressing

A 1-chip system decode for the R6530 is illustrated on the top of the following page.

Seven-Chip Addressing

In the 7-chip system the objective would be to have 7K of contiguous ROM, with RAM in low order memory. The 7K of ROM could be placed between addresses 65,535 and 1024. For this case, assume A13, A14 and A15 are all 1 when addressing ROM, and 0 when addressing RAM or I/O. This would place the 7K ROM between addresses 65,535 and 58,367. The 2 pins designated as chip-select or I/O would be masked programmed as chip-select pins. Pin RS0 would be connected to address line A10. Pins CS1 and CS2 would be connected to address lines A11 and A12 respectively. See illustration below.

The two examples shown would allow addressing of the ROM and RAM; however, once the I/O or timer has been addressed, further decoding is necessary to select which of the I/O registers are desired, as well as the coding of the interval timer.

I/O Register — Timer Addressing

Addressing Decode for I/O Register and Timer illustrates the address decoding for the internal elements and timer programming. Address lines A2 distinguishes I/O registers from the timer. When A2 is high and I/O timer select is high, the I/O registers are addressed. Once the I/O registers are addressed, address lines A1 and A0 decode the desired register.

When the timer is selected A1 and A0 decode the divide by matrix. In addition, Address A3 is used to enable the interrupt flag to PB7.

R6530 Seven Chip Addressing Scheme

The addressing of the ROM select, RAM select and I/O Timer select lines would be as follows:

		CS2 A12	CS1 A11	RS0 A10	A9	A8	A7	A6
R6530 #1,	ROM SELECT	0	0	1	X	X	X	X
	RAM SELECT	0	0	0	0	0	0	0
	I/O TIMER	0	0	0	1	0	0	0
R6530 #2,	ROM SELECT	0	1	0	X	X	X	X
	RAM SELECT	0	0	0	0	0	0	1
	I/O TIMER	0	0	0	1	0	0	1
R6530 #3,	ROM SELECT	0	1	1	X	X	X	X
	RAM SELECT	0	0	0	0	0	1	0
	I/O TIMER	0	0	0	1	0	1	0
R6530 #4,	ROM SELECT	1	0	0	X	X	X	X
	RAM SELECT	0	0	0	0	0	1	1
	I/O TIMER	0	0	0	1	0	1	1
R6530 #5,	ROM SELECT	1	0	1	X	X	X	X
	RAM SELECT	0	0	0	0	1	0	0
	I/O TIMER	0	0	0	1	1	0	0
R6530 #6,	ROM SELECT	1	1	0	X	X	X	X
	RAM SELECT	0	0	0	0	1	0	1
	I/O TIMER	0	0	0	1	1	0	1
R6530 #7,	ROM SELECT	1	1	1	X	X	X	X
	RAM SELECT	0	0	0	0	1	1	0
	I/O TIMER	0	0	0	1	1	1	0

*RAM select for R6530 #5 would read $= \overline{A12} \bullet \overline{A11} \bullet \overline{A10} \bullet \overline{A9} \bullet A8 \bullet \overline{A7} \bullet \overline{A6}$

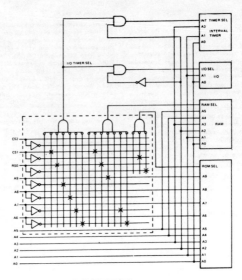

A X indicates mask programming
   i.e. ROM select = $\overline{CS1} \bullet RS0$
       RAM select = $\overline{CS1} \bullet RS0 \bullet A9 \bullet A7 \bullet A6$
       I/O TIMER SELECT = $\overline{CS1} \bullet RS0 \bullet A9 \bullet A8 \bullet A7 \bullet A6$

B Notice that A8 is a don't care for RAM select

C CS2 can be used as PB5 in this example

R6530 One Chip Address Encoding Diagram

Addressing Decode for I/O Register and Timer

Addressing Decode

	ROM Select	RAM Select	I/O Timer Select	R/W	A3	A2	A1	A0
Read ROM	1	0	0	1	X	X	X	X
Write RAM	0	1	0	0	X	X	X	X
Read RAM	0	1	0	1	X	X	X	X
Write DDRA	0	0	1	0	X	0	0	1
Read DDRA	0	0	1	1	X	0	0	1
Write DDRB	0	0	1	0	X	0	1	1
Read DDRB	0	0	1	1	X	0	1	1
Write Per. Reg. A	0	0	1	0	X	0	0	0
Read Per. Reg. A	0	0	1	1	X	0	0	0
Write Per. Reg. B	0	0	1	0	X	0	1	0
Read Per. Reg. B	0	0	1	1	X	0	1	0
Write Timer								
÷1T	0	0	1	0	*	1	0	0
÷8T	0	0	1	0	*	1	0	1
÷64T	0	0	1	0	*	1	1	0
÷1024T	0	0	1	0	*	1	1	1
Read Timer	0	0	1	1	*	1	X	0
Read Interrupt Flag	0	0	1	1	X	1	X	1

*A_3 = 1 Enables IRQ to PB7
A_3 = 0 Disables IRQ to PB7

Write Timing Characteristics

Characteristic	Symbol	Min	Typ	Max	Unit
Clock Period	T_{CYC}	1		10	μS
Rise & Fall Times	T_R, T_F			25	ns
Clock Pulse Width	T_C	470			ns
R/W valid before positive transition of clock	T_{WCW}	180			ns
Address valid before positive transition of clock	T_{ACW}	180			ns
Data Bus valid before negative transition of clock	T_{DCW}	300			ns
Data Bus Hold Time	T_{HW}	10			ns
Peripheral data valid after negative transition of clock	T_{CPW}			1	μS
Peripheral data valid after negative transition of clock driving CMOS (Level = VCC - 30%)	T_{CMOS}			2	μS

Read Timing Characteristics

Characteristic	Symbol	Min	Typ	Max	Unit
R/W valid before positive transition of clock	T_{WCR}	180			ns
Address valid before positive transition of clock	T_{ACR}	190			ns
Peripheral data valid before positive transition of clock	T_{PCR}	300			ns
Data Bus valid after positive transition of clock	T_{CDR}			395	ns
Data Bus Hold Time	T_{HR}	10			ns
IRQ (Interval Timer Interrupt) valid before positive transition of clock	T_{IC}	200			ns

Loading = 30 pF + 1 TTL load for PA0-PA7, PB0-PB7
= 130 pF + 1 TTL load for D0-D7

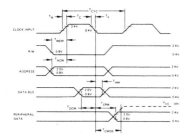

Write Timing Characteristics

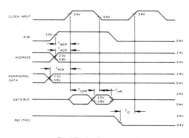

Read Timing Characteristics

R6500 Microcomputer System
DATA SHEET

RAM, I/O, INTERVAL TIMER DEVICE (RIOT)

SYSTEM ABSTRACT

The 8-bit R6500 microcomputer system is produced with N-Channel, Silicon-Gate technology. Its performance speeds are enhanced by advanced system architecture which enables multiple addressing. Its innovative architecture results in smaller chips — the semiconductor threshold to cost-effectivity. System cost-effectivity is further enhanced by providing a family of 10 software-compatible microprocessor (CPU) devices. Rockwell also provides memory and I/O devices that further enhance the cost-effectivity of the R6500 microcomputer system . . . as well as low-cost design aids and documentation.

DESCRIPTION

The R6532 is designed to operate in conjunction with the R6500 Microprocessor Family. It is comprised of a 128 x 8 static RAM, two software controlled 8 bit bidirectional data ports allowing direct interfacing between the microcomputer and peripheral devices, a software programmable interval timer with interrupt, capable of timing in various intervals from 1 to 262,144 clock periods, and a programmable edge detect circuit.

FEATURES

- 8 bit bidirectional Data Bus for direct communication with the microprocessor
- 128 x 8 static RAM
- Two 8 bit bidirectional data ports for interface to peripherals
- Two programmable Data Direction Registers
- Programmable Interval Timer Interrupt
- TTL & CMOS compatible peripheral lines
- Peripheral pins with Direct Transistor Drive Capability
- High Impedance Three-State Data Bus
- Programmable edge-sensitive interrupt

Ordering Information

Order Number	Package Type	Temperature Range
R6532P	Plastic	$0^{\circ}C$ to $+70^{\circ}C$
R6532C	Ceramic	$0^{\circ}C$ to $+70^{\circ}C$

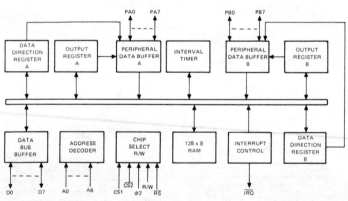

R6532 Block Diagram

R6532 RAM, I/O, INTERVAL TIMER DEVICE (RIOT)

INTERFACE SIGNAL DESCRIPTION

Reset (RES)

During system initialization a logic "0" on the RES input will cause a zeroing of all four I/O registers. This in turn will cause all I/O buses to act as inputs thus protecting external components from possible damage and erroneous data while the system is being configured under software control. The Data Bus Buffers are put into an OFF-STATE during Reset. Interrupt capability is disabled with the RES signal. The RES signal must be held low for at least two clock periods when reset is required.

Read/Write (R/W)

The R/W signal is supplied by the microprocessor and is used to control the transfer of data to and from the microprocessor and the R6532. A high on the R/W pin allows the processor to read (with proper addressing) the data supplied by the R6532. A low on the R/W pin allows a write (with proper addressing) to the R6532.

Interrupt Request (IRQ)

The IRQ pin is an interrupt pin from the interrupt control logic. The pin will be normally high with a low indicating an interrupt from the R6532. An external 3K pull-up resistor is required. The IRQ pin may be activated by a transition on PA7 or timeout of the interval timer.

Data Bus (D0-D7)

The R6532 has eight bidirectional data pins (D0-D7). These pins connect to the system's data lines and allow transfer of data to and from the microprocessor array. The output buffers remain in the off state except when the R6532 is selected for a Read operation.

Peripheral Data Ports (PA0-PA7, PB0-PB7)

The R6532 has 16 pins available for peripheral I/O operations. Each pin is individually software programmable to act as either an input or an output. The 16 pins are divided into 2 8-bit ports, PA0-PA7 and PB0-PB7. PA7 also has other uses which are discussed in later sections. The pins are set up as an input by writing a "0" into the corresponding bit of the data direction register. A "1" into the data direction register will cause its corresponding bit to be an output. When in the input mode, the peripheral output buffers are in the "1" state and the internal pull-up device acts as less than one TTL load to the peripheral data lines. On a Read operation, the microprocessor unit reads the peripheral pin. When the peripheral device gets information from the R6532 it receives data stored in the output register. The microprocessor will read correct information if the peripheral lines are greater than 2.0 volts for a "1" and less than 0.8 volt for a "0" as the peripheral pins are all TTL compatible. Pins PB0-PB7 are also capable of sourcing 3 ma at 1.5V, thus making them capable of Darlington drive.

Address Lines (A0-A6)

There are 7 address pins. In addition to these 7, there is the RAM SELECT (RS) pin. The pins A0-A6 and RAM SELECT are always used as addressing pins. There are two additional pins which are used as CHIP SELECTS. They are pins CS1 and CS2.

INTERNAL ORGANIZATION

The R6532 is divided into four basic sections, RAM, I/O, TIMER, and Interrupt Control. The RAM interfaces directly with the microprocessor through the system data bus and address lines. The I/O section consists of two 8-bit halves. Each half contains a Data Direction Register (DDR) and an Output Register.

RAM — 128 Bytes (1024 Bits)

The 128 x 8 Read/Write memory acts as a conventional static RAM. Data can be written into the RAM from the microprocessor by selecting the chip (CS1=1, CS2 = 0) and by setting RS to a logic 0 (0.4V). Address lines A0 through A6 are then used to select the desired byte of storage.

Internal Peripheral Registers

The Peripheral A I/O port consists of eight lines which can be individually programmed to act as either an input or an output. A logic zero in a bit of the Data Direction Register (DDRA) causes the corresponding bit of the PA port to act as an input. A logic one causes the corresponding PA line to act as an output. The voltage on any line programmed to be an output is determined by the corresponding bit in the Output Register (ORA).

Data is read directly from the PA pins during any read operation. For any output pin, the data transferred into the processor will be the same as that contained in the Output Register if the voltage on the pin is allowed to go to 2.4V for a logic one. Note that for input lines, the processor can write into the corresponding bit of the Output Register. This will not affect the polarity on the pin until the corresponding bit of DDRA is set to a logic one to allow the peripheral pin to act as an output.

In addition to acting as a peripheral I/O line, the PA7 line can be used as an edge-detecting input. In this mode, an active transition will set the internal interrupt flag (bit 6 of the Interrupt Flag register). Setting the interrupt flag will cause IRQ output to go low if the PA7 interrupt has been enabled.

Control of the PA7 edge detecting mode is accomplished by writing to one of four addresses. In this operation, A0 controls the polarity of the active transition and A1 acts to enable or disable interrupting of the processor. The data which is placed on the Data Bus during this operation is discarded and has no effect on the control of PA7.

Setting the PA7 interrupt flag will occur on an active transition even if the pin is being used as a normal input or as a peripheral control output. The flag will also be set by an active transition if interrupting from PA7 is disabled. The reset signal (RES) will disable the PA7 interrupt and will set the active transition to negative (high to low). During the system initialization routine, it is possible to set the interrupt flag by a negative transition. It may also be set by changing the polarity of the active interrupt. It is therefore recommended that the interrupt flag be cleared before enabling interrupting from PA7.

Clearing of the PA7 Interrupt Flag occurs when the microprocessor reads the Interrupt Flag Register.

The operation of the Peripheral B Input/Output port is exactly the same as the normal I/O operation of the Peripheral A port. The eight lines can each be programmed to act as either an input or as an output by placing a 0 or a 1 into the Data Direction register (DDRB). In the output mode, the voltage on a peripheral pin is controlled by the Output Register (ORB).

The primary difference between the PA and the PB ports is in the operation of the output buffers which drive these pins. The PB output buffers are push-pull devices which are capable of sourcing 3 ma at 1.5V. This allows these pins to directly drive transistor switches. To assure that the microprocessor will read proper data on a "Read PB" operation, sufficient logic is provided in the chip to allow the microprocessor to read the Output Register instead of reading the peripheral pin as on the PA port.

Interval Timer

The Timer section of the R6532 contains three basic parts: preliminary divide down register, programmable 8-bit register and interrupt logic.

The interval timer can be programmed to count up to 255 time intervals. Each time interval can be either 1T, 8T, 64T or 1024T increments, where T is the system clock period. When a full count is reached, an interrupt flag is set to a logic "1". After the interrupt flag is set the internal clock begins counting down to a maximum of -255T. Thus, after the interrupt flag is set, a Read of the timer will tell how long since the flag was set up to a maximum of 255T.

The 8-bit system Data Bus is used to transfer data to and from the Interval Timer. If a count of 52 time intervals were to be counted, the pattern 0 0 1 1 0 1 0 0 would be put on the Data Bus and written into the Interval Time register.

At the same time that data is being written to the Interval Timer, the counting intervals of 1, 8, 64, 1024T are decoded from address lines A0 and A1. During a Read or Write operation address line A3 controls the interrupt capability of PB7, i.e., A3 = 1 enables $\overline{IRQ}$, A3 = 0 disables $\overline{IRQ}$. When the timer is read prior to the interrupt flag being set, the number of time intervals remaining will be read, i.e., 51, 50, 49, etc.

When the timer has counted thru 0 0 0 0 0 0 0 0 on the next count time an interrupt will occur and the counter will read 1 1 1 1 1 1 1 1. After interrupt, the timer register decrements at a divide by "1" rate of the system clock. If after interrupt, the timer is read and a value of 1 1 1 0 0 1 0 0 is read, the time since interrupt is 27T. The value read is in two's complement, but remember that interrupt occurred on count number one. Therefore, we must subtract 1.

Value read	=	1 1 1 0 0 1 0 0
Complement	=	0 0 0 1 1 0 1 1
ADD 1	=	0 0 0 1 1 1 0 0 = 28 Equals two's complement of register
SUB 1	=	0 0 0 1 1 0 1 1 = 27

Thus, to arrive at the total elapsed time, merely do a two's complement add to the original time written into the timer. Again, assume time written as 0 0 1 1 0 1 0 0 (=52). With a divide by 8, total time to interrupt is (52 x 8) + 1 = 417T. Total elapsed time would be 416T + 27T = 443T, assuming the value read after interrupt was 1 1 1 0 0 1 0 0.

After the interrupt, whenever the timer is written or read the interrupt is reset. However, the reading of the timer at the same time the interrupt occurs will not reset the interrupt flag. When the interrupt flags are read (D7 for the timer, D6 for the edge detect) data bus lines D0-D5 go to 0.

When reading the timer after an interrupt, A3 should be low so as to disable the $\overline{IRQ}$ pin. This is done so as to avoid future interrupts until after another Write timer operation.

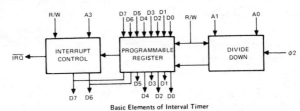

Basic Elements of Interval Timer

ASSUME 52 LOADED INTO TIMER WITH A DIVIDE BY 8.
THE COUNTER CONTENTS AND THE CLOCK PULSE NUMBERS WILL COINCIDE.
Prescale, P - 8
Cycle Time, Tc - 1 μsec (for 1 MHz)
Count, N - 52

Write Timing Characteristics

Characteristic	Symbol	Min	Typ	Max	Unit
Clock Period	T_{CYC}	1		10	μS
Rise & Fall Times	T_R, T_F			25	ns
Clock Pulse Width	T_C	470			ns
R/W valid before positive transition of clock	T_{WCW}	180			ns
Address valid before positive transition of clock	T_{ACW}	180			ns
Data Bus valid before negative transition of clock	T_{DCW}	300			ns
Data Bus Hold Time	T_{HW}	10			ns
Peripheral data valid after negative transition of clock	T_{CPW}			1	μS
Peripheral data valid after negative transition of clock driving CMOS (Level = VCC - 30%)	T_{CMOS}			2	μS

Read Timing Characteristics

Characteristic	Symbol	Min	Typ	Max	Unit
R/W valid before positive transition of clock	T_{WCR}	180			ns
Address valid before positive transition of clock	T_{ACR}	180			ns
Peripheral data valid before positive transition of clock	T_{PCR}	300			ns
Data Bus valid after positive transition of clock	T_{CDR}			395	ns
Data Bus Hold Time	T_{HR}	10			ns
IRQ (Interval Timer Interrupt) valid before positive transition of clock	T_{IC}	200			ns

Loading = 30 pF + 1 TTL load for PA0-PA7, PB0-PB7
= 130 pF + 1 TTL load for D0-D7

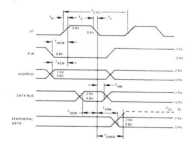

Write Timing Characteristics

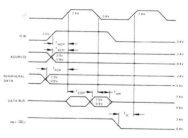

Read Timing Characteristics

RAM Addressing

$\overline{RS}$ = 0
A0-A6 select RAM address

I/O Addressing

$\overline{RS}$ = 1 A2 = 0
R/W = 1 to read, 0 to write

	A1	A0
PA data	0	0
PA data direction	0	1
PB data	1	0
PB data direction	1	1

Write Edge Detect Control

$\overline{RS}$, A2 = 1 R/W, A4 = 0

A1 = 1, enable interrupt from PA7
A1 = 0, disable interrupt from PA7
A0 = 1, positive edge detect (PA7)
A0 = 0, negative edge detect (PA7)

Read and Clear Interrupt Flag

$\overline{RS}$, R/W, A2, A0 = 1
  Bit 7 = Timer Flag
  Bit 6 = PA7 Flag

Read Interval Timer
$\overline{RS}$, A4, A2, R/W, A0 = 1

Read Interval Timer Overflow
$\overline{RS}$, A4, A2, R/W = 1, A0 = 0

Write Count to Interval Timer
$\overline{RS}$, A4, A2 = 1, R/W = 0

	A1	A0
÷1	0	0
÷8	0	1
÷64	1	0
÷1024	1	1

A3 = 1, enable timer interrupt
A3 = 0, disable timer interrupt

NOTE: For all operations CS1 = 1, $\overline{CS2}$ = 0.

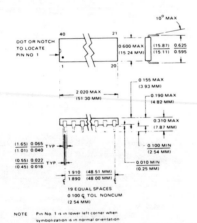

Packaging Diagram

Pin Configuration

SPECIFICATIONS

Maximum Ratings

Rating	Symbol	Voltage	Unit
Supply Voltage	VCC	-0.3 to +7.0	V
Input/Output Voltage	V_{IN}	-0.3 to +7.0	V
Operating Temperature Range	T_{OP}	0 to 70	°C
Storage Temperature Range	T_{STG}	-55 to +150	°C

All inputs contain protection circuitry to prevent damage due to high static charges. Care should be exercised to prevent unnecessary application of voltage outside the specification range.

Electrical Characteristics

(VCC=5.0%, VSS=0V, T_A=25°C)

Characteristic	Symbol	Min	Typ	Max	Unit
Input High Voltage	V_{IH}	V_{SS} + 2.4		VCC	V
Input Low Voltage	V_{IL}	V_{SS} - 0.3		V_{SS} + 0.4	V
Input Leakage Current; V_{IN} = V_{SS} + 5V A0-A6, RS, R/W, $\overline{RES}$, φ2, CS1, $\overline{CS2}$	I_{IN}		1.0	2.5	μA
Input Leakage Current for High Impedance State (Three State); V_{IN} = 0.4V to 2.4V; D0-D7	I_{TSI}		±1.0	±10.0	μA
Input High Current; V_{IN} = 2.4V PA0-PA7, PB0-PB7	I_{IH}	-100.	-300.		μA
Input Low Current; V_{IN} = 0.4V PA0-PA7, PB0-PB7	I_{IL}		-1.0	-1.6	MA
Output High Voltage VCC = MIN, I_{LOAD} ≤ -100 μA (PA0-PA7, PB0-PB7, D0-D7) I_{LOAD} ≤ -3 MA (PB0-PB7)	V_{OH}	VSS + 2.4 VSS + 1.5			V
Output Low Voltage VCC = MIN, I_{LOAD} ≤ 1.6 MA (D0-D7)	V_{OL}			VSS + 0.4	V
Output High Current (Sourcing); VOH ≥ 2.4V (PA0-PA7, PB0-PB7, D0-D7) ≥ 1.5V Available for other than TTL (Darlingtons) (PB0-PB7)	I_{OH}	-100 -3.0	-1000 -5.0		μA MA
Output Low Current (Sinking); VOL ≤ 0.4V (PA0-PA7) (PB0-PB7)	I_{OL}	1.6			MA
Clock Input Capacitance	C_{Clk}			30	pF
Input Capacitance	C_{IN}			10	pF
Output Capacitance	C_{OUT}			10	pF
Power Dissipation	P_D		500	1000	mW

All values are D.C. readings

1024x4 Static Random Access Memory

SY2114

- 300 ns Maximum Access
- Low Operating Power Dissipation 0.1 mW/Bit
- No Clocks or Strobes Required
- Identical Cycle and Access Times
- Single +5V Supply

- Totally TTL Compatible: All Inputs, Outputs, and Power Supply
- Common Data I/O
- 400 mv Noise Immunity
- High Density 18 Pin Package

The SY2114 is a 4096-Bit static Random Access Memory organized 1024 words by 4-bits and is fabricated using Synertek's N-channel Silicon-Gate MOS technology. It is designed using fully DC stable (static) circuitry in both the memory array and the decoding and therefore requires no clock or refreshing to operate. Address setup times are not required and the data is read out nondestructively with the same polarity as the input data. Common Input/Output pins are provided to simplify design of the bus oriented systems, and can drive 2 TTL loads.

The SY2114 is designed for memory applications where high performance, low cost, large bit storage, and simple interfacing are important design objectives. It is totally TTL compatible in all respects: inputs, outputs, and the single +5V supply. A separate Chip Select (CS) input allows easy selection of an individual device when outputs are or-tied.

The SY2114 is packaged in an 18-pin DIP for the highest possible density and is fabricated with N-channel, Ion Implanted, Silicon-Gate technology — a technology providing excellent performance characteristics as well as protection against contamination allowing the use of low cost packaging techniques.

PIN CONFIGURATION

```
A6  ┃1      18┃ Vcc
A5  ┃2      17┃ A7
A4  ┃3      16┃ A8
A3  ┃4      15┃ A9
A0  ┃5 2114 14┃ I/O1
A1  ┃6      13┃ I/O2
A2  ┃7      12┃ I/O3
CS  ┃8      11┃ I/O4
GND ┃9      10┃ WE
```

ORDERING INFORMATION

Order Number	Package Type	Access Time	Supply Current (Max)	Temperature Range
SYC2114	Ceramic	450nsec	100mamp	0°C to 70°C
SYP2114	Molded	450nsec	100mamp	0°C to 70°C
SYC2114-3	Ceramic	300nsec	100mamp	0°C to 70°C
SYP2114-3	Molded	300nsec	100mamp	0°C to 70°C
SYC2114L	Ceramic	450nsec	70mamp	0°C to 70°C
SYP2114L	Molded	450nsec	70mamp	0°C to 70°C
SYC2114L-3	Ceramic	300nsec	70mamp	0°C to 70°C
SYP2114L-3	Molded	300nsec	70mamp	0°C to 70°C

BLOCK DIAGRAM

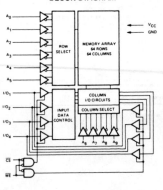

ABSOLUTE MAXIMUM RATINGS

Temperature Under Bias	$-10°C$ to $80°C$
Storage Temperature	$-65°C$ to $150°C$
Voltage on Any Pin with	
Respect to Ground	$-0.5V$ to $+7V$
Power Dissipation	1.0W

COMMENT

Stresses above those listed under "Absolute Maximum Ratings" may cause permanent damage to the device. This is a stress rating only and functional operation of the device at these or any other conditions above those indicated in the operational sections of this specification is not implied.

D.C. CHARACTERISTICS $T_A = 0°C$ to $+70°C$, $V_{CC} = 5V \pm 5\%$ (Unless Otherwise Specified)

Symbol	Parameter	2114-3, 2114 Min	2114-3, 2114 Max	2114L, 2114L-3 Min	2114L, 2114L-3 Max	Unit	Conditions
I_{LI}	Input Load Current (All input pins)		10		10	μA	$V_{IN} = 0$ to 5.25V
I_{LO}	I/O Leakage Current		10		10	μA	$\overline{CS} = 2.0V$, $V_{I/O} = 0.4V$ to V_{CC}
I_{CC1}	Power Supply Current		95		65	mA	$V_{CC} = 5.25V$, $I_{I/O} = 0$ mA, $T_A = 25°C$
I_{CC2}	Power Supply Current		100		70	mA	$V_{CC} = 5.25V$, $I_{I/O} = 0$ mA, $T_A = 0°C$
V_{IL}	Input Low Voltage	-0.5	0.8	-0.5	0.8	V	
V_{IH}	Input High Voltage	2.0	V_{CC}	2.0	V_{CC}	V	
V_{OL}	Output Low Voltage		0.4		0.4	V	$I_{OL} = 3.2$ mA
V_{OH}	Output High Voltage	2.4	V_{CC}	2.4	V_{CC}	V	$I_{OH} = -1.0$ mA

CAPACITANCE $T_A = 25°C$, $f = 1.0$ MHz

Symbol	Test	Typ	Max	Units
$C_{I/O}$	Input/Output Capacitance		5	pF
C_{IN}	Input Capacitance		5	pF

NOTE: This parameter is periodically sampled and not 100% tested.

A.C. CHARACTERISTICS $T_A = 0°C$ to $70°C$, $V_{CC} = 5V \pm 5\%$ (Unless Otherwise Specified)

SYMBOL	PARAMETER	2114-3,2114L-3 MIN	2114-3,2114L-3 MAX	2114, 2114L MIN	2114, 2114L MAX	UNIT
READ CYCLE						
t_{RC}	Read Cycle Time	300		450		nsec
t_A	Access Time		300		450	nsec
t_{CO}	Chip Select to Output Valid		100		120	nsec
t_{CX}	Chip Select to Output Enabled	20		20		nsec
t_{OTD}	Chip Deselect to Output Off	0	80	0	100	nsec
t_{OHA}	Output Hold From Address Change	50		50		nsec
WRITE CYCLE						
t_{WC}	Write Cycle Time	300		450		nsec
t_{AW}	Address to Write Setup Time	0		0		nsec
t_W	Write Pulse Width	150		200		nsec
t_{WR}	Write Release Time	0		0		nsec
t_{OTW}	Write to Output Off	0	80	0	100	nsec
t_{DW}	Data to Write Overlap	150		200		nsec
t_{DH}	Data Hold	0		0		nsec

A.C. Test Conditions

Input Pulse Levels . . . . .0.8V to 2.0V
Input Rise and Fall Time . . . . 10 n sec
Timing Measurement Levels: Input 1.5V
Output . . . . 0.8 and 2.0V
Output Load . . . . 1TTL Gate and 100pF

TIMING DIAGRAMS

Read Cycle [1]

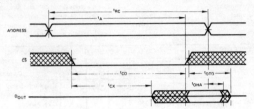

Write Cycle

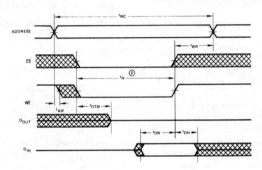

NOTES:

① $\overline{WE}$ is high for a Read Cycle

② t_W is measured from the latter of $\overline{CS}$ or $\overline{WE}$ going low to the earlier of $\overline{CS}$ or $\overline{WE}$ going high.

DATA STORAGE

When $\overline{WE}$ is high, the data input buffers are inhibited to prevent erroneous data from being written into the array. As long as $\overline{WE}$ remains high, the data stored cannot be affected by the Address, Chip Select, or Data I/O logic levels or timing transitions.

Data storage also cannot be affected by $\overline{WE}$, Addresses, or the I/O ports as long as $\overline{CS}$ is high. Either $\overline{CS}$ or $\overline{WE}$ or both can prevent extraneous writing due to signal transitions.

Data within the array can only be changed during Write time — defined as the overlap of $\overline{CS}$ low and

$\overline{WE}$ low. The addresses must be properly established during the entire Write time plus t_{WR}.

Internal delays are such that address decoding propagates ahead of data inputs and therefore no address setup time is required. If the Write time precedes the addresses, the data in previously addressed locations, or some other location, may be changed. Addresses must remain stable for the entire Write cycle but the Data Inputs may change. The data which is stable for t_{DW} at the end of the Write time will be written into the addressed location.

TYPICAL CHARACTERISTICS

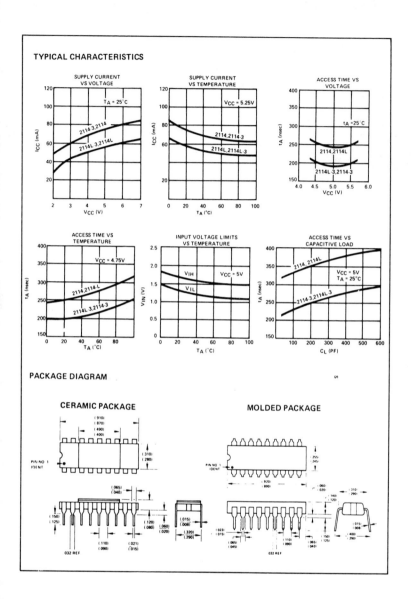

PACKAGE DIAGRAM

Pin Configurations of Frequently Used SN7400-Series Chips

The following pages contain pin configurations reprinted from the TTL Data Book published by Texas Instruments, Inc. and are made available through the courtesy of Texas Instruments, Inc. Copyright © 1976 by Texas Instruments, Inc. All rights reserved.

Pin assignments for the following integrated circuits have been reproduced: 7400, 7402, 7404, 7405, 7430, 7474, 7475, 74100, 74121, 74138, 74139, 74154, and 74367.

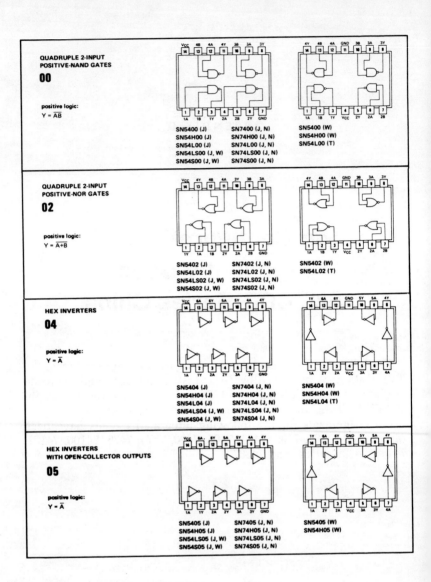

QUADRUPLE 2-INPUT POSITIVE-NAND GATES

00

positive logic:
$Y = \overline{AB}$

SN5400 (J)   SN7400 (J, N)   SN5400 (W)
SN54H00 (J)   SN74H00 (J, N)   SN54H00 (W)
SN54L00 (J)   SN74L00 (J, N)   SN54L00 (T)
SN54LS00 (J, W)   SN74LS00 (J, N)
SN54S00 (J, W)   SN74S00 (J, N)

QUADRUPLE 2-INPUT POSITIVE-NOR GATES

02

positive logic:
$Y = \overline{A+B}$

SN5402 (J)   SN7402 (J, N)   SN5402 (W)
SN54L02 (J)   SN74L02 (J, N)   SN54L02 (T)
SN54LS02 (J, W)   SN74LS02 (J, N)
SN54S02 (J, W)   SN74S02 (J, N)

HEX INVERTERS

04

positive logic:
$Y = \overline{A}$

SN5404 (J)   SN7404 (J, N)   SN5404 (W)
SN54H04 (J)   SN74H04 (J, N)   SN54H04 (W)
SN54L04 (J)   SN74L04 (J, N)   SN54L04 (T)
SN54LS04 (J, W)   SN74LS04 (J, N)
SN54S04 (J, W)   SN74S04 (J, N)

HEX INVERTERS WITH OPEN-COLLECTOR OUTPUTS

05

positive logic:
$Y = \overline{A}$

SN5405 (J)   SN7405 (J, N)   SN5405 (W)
SN54H05 (J)   SN74H05 (J, N)   SN54H05 (W)
SN54LS05 (J, W)   SN74LS05 (J, N)
SN54S05 (J, W)   SN74S05 (J, N)

8-INPUT POSITIVE-NAND GATES

30

positive logic:

$$Y = \overline{ABCDEFGH}$$

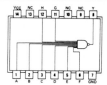

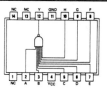

SN5430 (J) SN7430 (J, N) SN5430 (W)
SN54H30 (J) SN74H30 (J, N) SN54H30 (W)
SN54L30 (J) SN74L30 (J, N) SN54L30 (T)
SN54LS30 (J, W) SN74LS30 (J, N)
SN54S30 (J, W) SN74S30 (J, N)

NC—No internal connection

DUAL D-TYPE POSITIVE-EDGE-TRIGGERED FLIP-FLOPS WITH PRESET AND CLEAR

74

FUNCTION TABLE

INPUTS				OUTPUTS	
PRESET	CLEAR	CLOCK	D	Q	$\overline{Q}$
L	H	X	X	H	L
H	L	X	X	L	H
L	L	X	X	H*	H*
H	H	↑	H	H	L
H	H	↑	L	L	H
H	H	L	X	Q_0	$\overline{Q}_0$

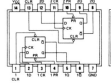

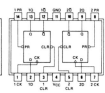

SN5474 (J) SN7474 (J, N) SN5474 (W)
SN54H74 (J) SN74H74 (J, N) SN54H74 (W)
SN54L74 (J) SN74L74 (J, N) SN54L74 (T)
SN54LS74A (J, W) SN74LS74A (J, N)
SN54S74 (J, W) SN74S74 (J, N)

4-BIT BISTABLE LATCHES

75

FUNCTION TABLE
(Each Latch)

INPUTS		OUTPUTS	
D	G	Q	$\overline{Q}$
L	H	L	H
H	H	H	L
X	L	Q_0	$\overline{Q}_0$

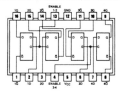

SN5475 (J, W) SN7475 (J, N)
SN54L75 (J) SN74L75 (J, N)
SN54LS75 (J, W) SN74LS75 (J, N)

H = high level, L = low level, X = irrelevant
Q_0 = the level of Q before the high-to-low transistion of G

8-BIT BISTABLE LATCHES

100

FUNCTION TABLE
(Each Latch)

INPUTS		OUTPUTS	
D	G	Q	$\overline{Q}$
L	H	L	H
H	H	H	L
X	L	Q_0	$\overline{Q}_0$

H = high level, X = irrelevant
Q_0 = the level of Q before the high-to-low transistion of G

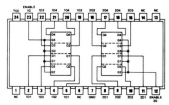

SN54100 (J, W) SN74100 (J, N)

NC — No internal connection

MONOSTABLE MULTIVIBRATORS

121

FUNCTION TABLE

INPUTS			OUTPUTS	
A1	A2	B	Q	$\overline{Q}$
L	X	H	L	H
X	L	H	L	H
X	X	L	L	H
H	H	X	L	H
H	↓	H	$\sqcap$	$\sqcup$
↓	H	H	$\sqcap$	$\sqcup$
↓	↓	H	$\sqcap$	$\sqcup$
L	X	↑	$\sqcap$	$\sqcup$
X	L	↑	$\sqcap$	$\sqcup$

NOTES: 1. An external capacitor may be connected between C_{ext} (positive) and R_{ext}/C_{ext}.

2. To use the internal timing resistor, connect R_{int} to V_{CC}. For improved pulse width accuracy and repeatability, connect an external resistor between R_{ext}/C_{ext} and V_{CC} with R_{int} open-circuited.

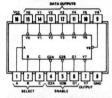

SN54121 (J, W)   SN74121 (J, N)
SN54L121 (J, T)   SN74L121 (J, N)
'121 . . . R_{int} = 2 kΩ NOM
'L121 . . . R_{int} = 4 kΩ NOM

NC—No internal connection

3-TO-8 LINE DECODERS/MULTIPLEXERS

138

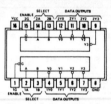

SN54LS138 (J, W)   SN74LS138 (J, N)
SN54S138 (J, W)   SN74S138 (J, N)

DUAL 2-TO-4 LINE DECODERS/MULTIPLEXERS

139

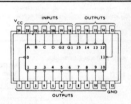

SN54LS139 (J, W)   SN74LS139 (J, N)
SN54S 139 (J, W)   SN74S139 (J, N)

4-LINE TO 16-LINE DECODERS/DEMULTIPLEXERS

154

SN54154 (J, W)   SN74154 (J, N)
SN54L154 (J)   SN74L154 (J, N)

HEX BUS DRIVERS

367 NONINVERTED DATA OUTPUT
4-LINE AND 2-LINE ENABLE INPUTS
3-STATE OUTPUTS

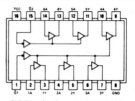

SN54367A (J, W)   SN74367A (J, N)
SN54LS367 (J, W)   SN74LS367 (J, N)

Pin Configuration
of 81LS97

The following pin configuration for the 81LS97 integrated circuit is made available through the courtesy of National Semiconductor Corporation. Copyright © 1976 by National Semiconductor Corporation. All rights reserved.

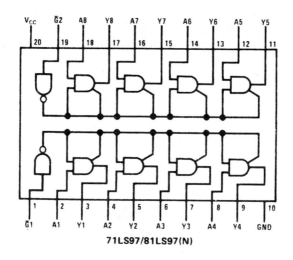

71LS97/81LS97(N)

LS97

INPUTS		OUTPUT
$\overline{G}$	A	Y
H	X	Z
L	H	H
L	L	L

Index

410

TO THE READER

This book is one of an expanding series of books that will cover the field of basic electronics and digital electronics from basic gates and flip-flops through microcomputers and digital telecommunications. We are attempting to develop a mailing list of individuals who would like to receive information on the series. We would be delighted to add your name to it if you would fill in the information below and mail this sheet to us. Thanks.

1. I have the following books:

_____

_____

_____

_____

_____

_____

_____

_____

_____

_____

_____

_____

_____

2. My occupation is: ☐ student   ☐ teacher, instructor   ☐ hobbyist

     ☐ housewife   ☐ scientist, engineer, doctor, etc.   ☐ businessman

     ☐ Other: _____

Name (print): _____

Address _____

City _____ State _____

Zip Code _____

Mail to:

         Books
         P.O. Box 715
         Blacksburg, Virginia 24060